AF510573

Skills for NextGen
Client Scenarios in Torts

EDITORIAL ADVISORS

Rachel E. Barkow
Charles Seligson Professor of Law
Faculty Director, Peter L. Zimroth Center on the Administration of Criminal Law
New York University School of Law

Erwin Chemerinsky
Dean and Jesse H. Choper Distinguished Professor of Law
University of California, Berkeley School of Law

Richard A. Epstein
Laurence A. Tisch Professor of Law
Director, Classical Liberal Institute
New York University School of Law
Peter and Kirsten Bedford Senior Fellow
The Hoover Institution
James Parker Hall Distinguished Service Professor of Law, Emeritus
Senior Lecturer in Law
The University of Chicago

Ronald J. Gilson
Charles J. Meyers Professor of Law and Business, Emeritus
Stanford University
Marc and Eva Stern Professor Emeritus of Law and Business
Columbia Law School

Tracey L. Meares
Walton Hale Hamilton Professor of Law
Founding Director, The Justice Collaboratory
Yale Law School

Marc L. Miller
Ralph W. Bilby Professor of Law
Dean Emeritus
James E. Rogers College of Law, University of Arizona

Richard K. Neumann, Jr.
Alexander M. Bickel Distinguished Professor of Law
Maurice A. Deane School of Law at Hofstra University

Robert H. Sitkoff
Austin Wakeman Scott Professor of Law
John L. Gray Professor of Law
Harvard Law School

David Alan Sklansky
Stanley Morrison Professor of Law
Faculty Co-Director, Stanford Criminal Justice Center
Stanford Law School

EMERITUS EDITORIAL ADVISOR

James E. Krier
Earl Warren DeLano Professor of Law Emeritus
The University of Michigan Law School

Skills for NextGen
Client Scenarios in Torts

Shannon W. Conway
Assistant Professor of Law
UNT Dallas College of Law

Meijken Westenskow
Senior Professor of Practice
UNT Dallas College of Law

ASPEN PUBLISHING

Copyright © 2026 Aspen Publishing. All Rights Reserved.

Thank you for complying with copyright laws by not reproducing or distributing any part of this book in any form without permission. Aspen Publishing supports copyright because it encourages creativity and the sharing of knowledge and fosters a climate of fairness, progress, and innovation.

No part of this publication may be reproduced or transmitted in any form or by any means, electronic or mechanical, including photocopy, recording, or utilized by any information storage or retrieval system, without written permission from the publisher. Under no circumstances may any part of this publication be used in content generation software, systems, or tools such as those that utilize artificial intelligence processes or algorithms. For information about permissions or to request permissions online, visit us at www.AspenPublishing.com.

To contact Customer Service, e-mail customer.service@aspenpublishing.com, call 1-800-950-5259, or mail correspondence to:

Aspen Publishing
Attn: Order Department
1 Wall Street
Burlington, MA 01803

1 2 3 4 5 6 7 8 9 0

ISBN 979-8-8941-0136-1

Library of Congress Cataloging-in-Publication Data

Names: Conway, Shannon, 1968- author | Westenskow, Meijken, 1979- author
Title: Skills for NextGen : client scenarios in torts / Meijken Westenskow, Senior Professor of Practice, UNT Dallas College of Law; Shannon Conway, Assistant Professor of Law, UNT Dallas College of Law.
Description: Burlington, MA : Aspen Publishing, 2025. | Summary: "Skills and exercise book for the torts sections of the NextGen Bar exam"—Provided by publisher.
Identifiers: LCCN 2025037008 (print) | LCCN 2025037009 (ebook) | ISBN 9798894101361 paperback | ISBN 9798894101385 epub | ISBN 9798894101378 epub
Subjects: LCSH: Bar examinations—United States—Study guides | Torts—United States—Examinations, questions, etc. | Law—United States—Examinations, questions, etc. | LCGFT: Study guides
Classification: LCC KF303 .W49 2025 (print) | LCC KF303 (ebook) | DDC 340.076/073—dc23/eng/20250808

LC record available at https://lccn.loc.gov/2025037008
LC ebook record available at https://lccn.loc.gov/2025037009

This book is intended as a general review of a legal subject. It is not intended as a source for advice for the solution of legal matters or problems. For advice on legal matters, the reader should consult an attorney.

Emanuel, the judge logo, Law in a Flash and design, CrunchTime and design, Strategies & Tactics and design, are registered trademarks of Aspen Publishing.

ABOUT ASPEN PUBLISHING

Aspen Publishing is a leading provider of legal education content and digital learning solutions in the United States and globally. Our innovative products and platforms—designed based on best practices in learning science—engage students and enhance outcomes. From textbooks and audiobooks authored by renowned experts to digital platforms and products like LEAF, Connected eBooks, Connected Quizzing, PracticePerfect, and JD-Next, we empower the next generation of legal professionals with innovative, trusted, and accessible resources.

The Aspen Casebook Series, affectionately known as the "red and black" casebooks among law faculty and students, includes hundreds of highly regarded textbooks across more than 80 disciplines. These range from foundational courses like Torts and Contracts to emerging electives such as Sustainability and the Law of Policing. Our study aids, including the popular *Examples & Explanations* series, help law students master complex topics with clarity and confidence.

Aspen's expertise extends to undergraduate education with our Paralegal, Criminal Justice, and Business Law series, offering the same hallmark quality to a broader audience. JD-Next, our groundbreaking online law school prep course and admissions test, provides a realistic preview of law school, equips students with essential skills for academic success, and evaluates their readiness for legal studies.

Aspen Publishing Is Proud to Be a UWorld Company

Since 2003, UWorld has been a global leader in developing high-quality learning tools for students preparing for high-stakes exams. With a commitment to excellence, UWorld has helped millions of students in undergraduate, graduate, and professional programs in fields such as medicine, nursing, finance, and law achieve their academic and career goals.

Founded by Chandra S. Pemmasani, M.D., during his medical residency, UWorld began focusing on medical education and has since expanded into various academic fields, including law. In 2020, UWorld launched its Legal vertical, starting with its comprehensive Multistate Bar Exam (MBE®) Question Bank, followed by the acquisition of Themis Bar Review, which integrated resources to provide a complete bar exam preparation experience. In 2024, UWorld expanded its offerings by acquiring Aspen Publishing, enhancing its suite of legal education products.

Today, UWorld offers an unparalleled range of study materials that blend active learning methods with expert content, ensuring students and educators can access the most effective resources. From bar preparation to law school success, UWorld is committed to supporting the next generation of legal professionals. Learn more at uworld.com.

Summary of Contents

Contents

Introduction

Background

Law students often find that the *study* of law is disconnected from the *practice* of law. 1L students spend several months struggling to understand abstract concepts from their doctrinal courses but have few opportunities to consider how to apply those concepts in "real-world" scenarios. Consequently, while many 1L students finish the year with a new approach to thinking and writing, many feel unprepared to work with clients during internships or in clinical practice. And while many employers appreciate the training students receive in law school, particularly the emphasis on problem-solving, many bemoan the lack of practical training.

Within the last few decades, there has been some shift in the way law schools prepare students for the practice of law. Clinical programs abound, as do opportunities to take courses that emphasize skills such as negotiation, client interviewing, client counseling, etc. Yet those courses often present skills in isolation, as a distinct discipline separate from students' doctrinal studies.

The authors of this textbook believe that skill practice and doctrinal learning should overlap. After all, lawyers do not separate doctrine and skill when they represent clients; lawyers utilize both knowledge and practical skills as they assess the strength of a client's case, counsel a client, negotiate a deal, write an email, or draft pleadings. Therefore, to effectively prepare for the *practice* of law, students should *practice* legal skills. Students should be offered more opportunities to study legal principles in the context of representing clients.

The integration of client-based scenarios into legal education is especially urgent as jurisdictions adopt the NextGen bar exam. The National Conference of Bar Examiners (NCBE) adopted the NextGen bar exam to ensure that the exam reflects the practical demands of contemporary legal practice. The NextGen bar emphasizes essential lawyering skills over rote memorization and aims to assess competencies such as legal research, writing, client counseling, and negotiation. Many NextGen questions will appear within integrated question sets that include the factual background about a case as well as legal authority related to the tested issues. Examinees will be instructed to complete various lawyering tasks utilizing information provided by the examiners as well as memorized knowledge examinees bring with them to the exam.

Goals

Based on our professional experiences, your authors believe that legal education should be rigorous but also practical. Both authors came to academia after several years of practice, Professor Conway in Big Law and Professor Westenskow in Public Interest. Both authors trained new lawyers and interns struggling to transition from law school to practice. Both authors began their academic careers in the field of Academic Success and Bar Readiness and worked with students trying to adapt to the method of legal education and later to the practice of law. While Professor Westenskow retains that focus, Professor Conway now teaches Torts, Advanced Torts, and Insurance Law with a heavy focus on practice readiness.

The exercises in this book are designed to teach students about legal principles in the context of a client's problem. Each client scenario relates to a major legal principle covered in a typical torts casebook. Each scenario offers students information about a potential client, presents relevant legal authority, and asks students to complete exercises that hone various lawyering skills, including the "Foundational Skills" outlined in the NextGen Content Scope Outlines.

This book is useful for several potential audiences:

- **Students**. Students can use the exercises in this book to develop their legal skills, contextualize the law, and ensure a deeper understanding of challenging legal concepts. The book offers multiple opportunities for formative assessment as it includes sample answers that enable students to evaluate their responses. Students can also use the book to prepare for the bar exam as the exercises develop skills tested on the NextGen bar exam.

- **Doctrinal Professors**. Doctrinal professors are pressured to cover sufficient content and have little time to integrate practice in the classroom. Professors might encourage students to utilize this book or even assign exercises from the book to supplement skill development while reserving class time for more guided instruction. The exercises are not tied to a particular textbook or set of cases and can be integrated into any doctrinal course. Professors can offer feedback or ask students to self-reflect on written responses using the book's sample answers.

- **Academic Success and Bar Readiness Professors**. Exercises from the book can be utilized in a skills-based course to supplement doctrinal learning. Academic success faculty can use the exercises to emphasize legal skills, and bar readiness faculty can refer to the exercises to introduce and reinforce NextGen skills. The exercises might also be used as assessment tools to help faculty diagnose and target students' strengths and weaknesses.

Skills Tested

The skills tested in this book focus both on the skills needed by new lawyers and also on the foundation skills tested on the NextGen bar exam. Some exercises only require brief answers, while others ask students to prepare complete arguments or client documents.

Each exercise should look and feel like a task a new lawyer would complete. Law students may have some experience completing formal lawyering tasks—drafting a memo or persuasive brief—but there are fewer opportunities to practice the informal, day-to-day tasks lawyers need to complete in practice: counseling a client, preparing interview notes, speaking with opposing counsel, drafting emails, strategizing about a case, etc. This book focuses on many of those informal tasks and encourages students to be holistic in their approach to client problems. The book also offers materials and documents that lawyers use in representing clients.

This book also encourages students to be comfortable with ambiguity. While many of the client scenarios have answers in precedent, not every client problem has a clear answer. This book encourages students to consider both sides of the argument and produce thoughtful, thorough responses. Students are encouraged to apply established legal rules but also look for counterarguments and alternate perspectives.

Finally, these exercises are designed to be challenging. Law school is hard, which is why it works. Lawyers frequently emphasize that law school is fundamentally a training program in how to think, but that transition requires practice and reflection. Often, we learn more when we make a mistake, face it honestly, and make thoughtful adjustments. We encourage you to approach these exercises with that desire to learn and adapt. We believe that will help you be a better student and lawyer.

Many of the tasks included in this book mirror the "Tasks to Measure Foundational Skills" identified in the NextGen Content Scope Outline (https://www.ncbex.org/exams/nextgen/content-scope):

- **Issue Spotting and Analysis, Investigation and Evaluation**
  - Identify which legal principles are likely to affect the outcome of a matter.
  - Identify which facts are likely to be relevant to or dispositive of a legal issue in a matter.
  - Identify the strengths and weaknesses of a client's position or an opposing party's position based on the relevant legal rules and standards.
  - In a matter that requires additional factual development, identify which facts need to be investigated, or the best strategy for investigating or eliciting those facts, in order to be able to evaluate the strengths and weaknesses of a client's position or an opposing party's position based on the relevant legal rules and standards.
  - Assess the probable outcome of a claim, motion, discovery matter, or objection based on the relevant legal rules and standards.
  - Identify the applicable or dispositive language, standards, elements, or factors of a provided resource (such as a statute, contract, or judicial opinion).
- **Client Counseling and Advising, Negotiation and Dispute Resolution, Client Relationship and Management**
  - Identify which claims to recommend bringing, which remedies to recommend seeking, which evidence to present, which arguments or defenses to raise, or how to respond to arguments or defenses, based on the relevant legal rules and standards and consistent with a client's objectives, interests, and constraints.
  - In a matter requiring review of a provided transcript of an interview, deposition, or examination of a client or fact witness, identify gaps in information obtained, suggestions for improvement, and/or grounds for objection (if applicable).
  - Identify factors that favor a client's position or factors that favor an opposing party's position in a matter.
  - Identify benefits or drawbacks of a proposed resolution of a dispute, consistent with a client's objectives, interests, and constraints.
  - Identify potential terms of an agreement that could lead to a negotiated resolution of a dispute.
  - In a matter in which a client has multiple stated objectives, explain why a legal rule or principle, as applied to the client's situation, may make one of those stated objectives unattainable.
  - Determine the best strategy for identifying a client's needs and interests underlying the client's stated objectives, in order to aid the client in setting goals in a matter.

- **Legal Research**
  - □ In a matter that requires legal research, identify the research questions that need to be answered.
  - □ Given one or more judicial opinions, identify the facts in a matter that are analogous to and/or distinct from the dispositive facts in the opinions.
  - □ Draft or edit correspondence to a client explaining the legal implications of a course of action, updating the client on the status of the client's matter, and/or providing advice on the next steps to be taken in the matter.
  - □ Given a collection of legal sources, draft specified section(s) of a document, demonstrating skill at formulating an original legal analysis.

The book does not include multiple-choice questions (MCQs), even though the NextGen bar exam will. Students typically have access to a variety of MCQ resources through other commercial supplements, and this book is focused on the development of legal research and writing skills.

Structure

This book is organized around the major topics in a Torts course:

- Part I: Intentional Torts
- Part II: Negligence
- Part III: Other Torts (Defamation, Invasion of Privacy, Misrepresentation, Products Liability, Strict Liability, and Nuisance)

Each part contains several chapters that cover specific torts or legal issues. For example, Part I includes chapters covering: Battery and Assault, False Imprisonment, Intentional Infliction of Emotional Distress, Trespass to Land, Trespass to Chattels/Conversion, and Defenses to Intentional Torts. Each chapter includes 1-2 client scenarios that present distinct legal issues, and each chapter includes several exercises that test legal skills such as issue-spotting, drafting, advocacy, negotiation, etc.

Exercises are presented in a comparable format to the "Integrated Question Sets" on the NextGen bar exam. Each exercise is based on a common fact scenario. After completing initial exercises, the book offers additional resources, including case information or legal authority. Each exercise includes a written component asking the student to analyze a question(s) related to the case.

A NOTE ON LEGAL AUTHORITY. While all scenarios are set in the fictitious jurisdiction of Sunport, the book includes several actual cases. We know this presents complicated questions about whether those precedential cases from another jurisdiction are binding in Sunport. For the purposes of this book, you may assume they are binding legal authority. This book does not ask students to evaluate the authoritative weight of each legal authority—if the legal authority is in the book, then students should assume that it is binding and reflects the law in Sunport.

A NOTE ON NEGLIGENCE. A reader might skim the Table of Contents and wonder why Part II: Negligence does not include sections on damages/remedies or defenses. Given the complexity of negligence claims, those issues are integrated into different client scenarios. For example, *In re Drop or Do* presents issues related to duty (attractive nuisance and landowner liability) and also introduces comparative fault.

Readers can find issues related to defenses in the following client files:

- *In re Drop or Do* (comparative fault)
- *Redfearn v. Starr Resorts* (assumption of the risk)
- *Hamilton v. Everest Heights, Inc.* (assumption of the risk)
- *In re Ethan Carter* (comparative fault; assumption of the risk)
- *Baker v. Neon Palms* (comparative fault)
- *Vankirk v. Safe Haven Security Co.* (comparative fault)
- *Parrill v. Mapleton Realty Corp.* (comparative fault)

Readers can find issues related to damages/remedies in the following client files:

- *Redfearn v. Starr Resorts*
- *Norland v. Adobe Animal Clinic*
- *Vankirk v. Safe Haven Security Co.*

Conclusion

Our goal is simple: to help you build the habits and skills of a practicing attorney so you are ready not just for exams, but also ready to represent your future clients. We hope these exercises help you bridge the gap between learning the law and practicing it.

Part I
Intentional Torts

Battery and Assault

1

Battery: *Hainsley v. Patterson*

Douglas Patterson is a close friend from high school who is now a security officer working in a large office building in downtown Sunport. Doug knows you are a new attorney specializing in tort claims, and he called you one afternoon to discuss a potential case.

1.1 Interview Notes

Your notes from the conversation follow:

> **Call with Doug Patterson (Oct. 15)**
>
> Doug began smoking in college and has been trying to quit ever since. He switched to vaping (nicotine only) a year or so ago with the goal of eventually quitting altogether. When at work, Doug steps outside and moves around the corner to vape. The building has a small courtyard in the back for employees who want to take smoke breaks, but Doug avoids the area because he can no longer stand the smell of cigarette smoke, especially the way it lingers on his uniform.
>
> Approximately six months ago, Doug was vaping in his "usual spot." Maggie Hainsley, who is a bank executive in the building where Doug works as a security officer, was walking to her favorite food truck for her morning latte. She walked directly in front of Doug just as he was exhaling the vapor from his vape pen. Ms. Hainsley coughed loudly, rolled her eyes, and said, "You know there is a courtyard out back where people like you can pollute the air." Ms. Hainsley shook her head in disgust and walked away. Doug thought she was overreacting because it was vapor, not smoke, but he ignored Ms. Hainsley and went back inside. A few days later, Doug noticed Ms. Hainsley in the lobby and said, "Good morning," but Ms. Hainsley ignored him.
>
> Nearly two weeks later, a similar incident occurred. Doug was in his usual spot and exhaled vapor exactly as Ms. Hainsley walked past. It was so coincidental that Doug laughed out loud. Ms. Hainsley did not share his humor; Ms. Hainsley rolled her eyes and stormed off toward the food truck. Over the next few months, a similar incident occurred several times. Doug thought it was hilarious, and he started to believe Ms. Hainsley purposely timed her coffee breaks during the times Doug was outside vaping.

One morning last week, Doug was at his security desk when a casually dressed man approached. The man asked if he was Doug Patterson. When Doug answered yes, the man shoved an envelope into his hands and announced, "You've been served."[1] The envelope included a complaint[2] and summons. Ms. Hainsley is suing Doug for battery.

1.2 Legal Authority—Battery

In Sunport, the elements of battery are as follows:

A defendant is subject to liability for battery if:

1. The defendant acts with intent to cause a harmful or offensive contact to the person of another; and
2. A harmful or offensive contact to that person directly or indirectly results.

Exercise 1

1. **Based on the facts you learned during your call with Mr. Patterson and the elements of battery set forth above, do you believe Mr. Patterson may be liable to Ms. Hainsley for battery? (Are both elements satisfied? If not, then which element is lacking?)**

___

___

___

1. **What is Service?** After a plaintiff initiates a civil lawsuit, the plaintiff must notify the defendant by serving the defendant with a copy of the complaint (see Footnote 2 below). Service is a critical component of due process, which guarantees a defendant notice and an opportunity to be heard. Service is also required to establish a court's authority over the defendant, and the plaintiff must strictly comply with the service rules applicable to the court hearing the case.

2. **What is a Complaint?** When a plaintiff initiates a civil lawsuit, the plaintiff files a complaint. The complaint identifies the defendant(s), the plaintiff's cause(s) of action, and the factual background of the case. The complaint must identify:

   1. The grounds for the court's jurisdiction.
   2. A short and plain statement of the claim. This requires the plaintiff to identify the cause of action and briefly identify how each element is satisfied. This also requires the plaintiff to offer enough factual detail to explain why the claim is plausible and give the defendant an opportunity to prepare a defense.
   3. A demand for the relief that identifies what the plaintiff wants to recover.

2. **Which facts, if any, suggest Mr. Patterson acted with intent to cause a harmful or offensive contact to Ms. Hainsley?**

3. **Which facts, if any, suggest Mr. Patterson's conduct caused a harmful or offensive contact to Ms. Hainsley?**

4. **Identify any additional information that might be helpful to assess the strength of Ms. Hainsley's claim.**

1.3 Complaint

Doug provided you with a copy of the complaint:

In The Circuit Court
for Eastvale County, Sunport

CAUSE NO. 0030-89150001

MARGARET HAINSLEY,

Plaintiff,

vs. 51st JUDICIAL DISTRICT

DOUGLAS PATTERSON,

Defendant.

PLAINTIFF'S ORIGINAL COMPLAINT

COMES NOW, Margaret Hainsley ("Plaintiff") and files this, her Original Complaint against Douglas Patterson ("Defendant"). In support thereof, Plaintiff respectfully shows the Court as follows:

PARTIES, VENUE & JURISDICTION

1. Plaintiff Margaret Hainsley is a single individual residing at 5500 Winnipeg Lane, Eastvale, Sunport 22505.
2. Upon information and belief, Defendant Douglas Patterson is an individual residing within the city limits of Eastvale, and located in Eastvale County, in the state of Sunport.
3. Venue is proper in Eastvale County as the county in which all or a substantial part of the events or omissions giving rise to Plaintiff's claims occurred.
4. Jurisdiction is proper in this Court because Plaintiff seeks monetary relief of less than $250,000.

BACKGROUND FACTS

5. On the morning of September 20, Plaintiff left her workplace to walk to a nearby coffee shop.
6. As Plaintiff was walking away from the building where she works, she saw Defendant standing on the sidewalk smoking a vape pen. The building where Plaintiff and Defendant work has a designated courtyard for smoking, but Defendant was nevertheless vaping on the sidewalk, forcing passersby to walk directly in front of him.

7. As Plaintiff passed Defendant on the sidewalk, Defendant intentionally exhaled, blowing smoke into Plaintiff's path. Defendant's smoke caused Plaintiff to cough, and she explained to Defendant that the courtyard designated for smokers was the only area where smoking was authorized.
8. Less than two weeks later, on October 2, Plaintiff was again walking from her workplace to the same coffee shop. Once again, Defendant was smoking a vape pen outside the designated smoking area. As Plaintiff walked in front of Defendant, Defendant again exhaled, causing smoke to come into contact with Plaintiff and causing her to cough.
9. From October 2 to December 16, the same incident occurred approximately 10-12 times. During each incident, Plaintiff coughed and expressed concern about Defendant's conduct, but the Defendant continued to vape outside the designated smoking area.

Count I—Battery

10. Plaintiff incorporates paragraphs 1 through 9 above by reference, as though fully set forth at length herein.
11. Defendant's attack was entirely unjustified and constitutes an intentional battery upon Plaintiff.

WHEREFORE, Plaintiff demands judgment against Defendant for:

a) Compensatory damages in an amount in excess of $10,000;
b) Punitive damages; and
c) Attorneys' fees and such other relief as the court finds appropriate.

Plaintiff demands a trial by jury.

Exercise 2

1. **How do the facts set forth in Ms. Hainsley's complaint differ from the facts Mr. Patterson relayed to you during your phone call with him on October 15?**

____

____

____

2. **Which facts from the complaint, if any, suggest Mr. Patterson acted with intent to cause a harmful or offensive contact to Ms. Hainsley?**

____

____

____

3. **Which facts from the complaint, if any, suggest Mr. Patterson's conduct caused a harmful or offensive contact to Ms. Hainsley?**

4. **Do the facts set forth in the complaint influence your conclusion about whether Mr. Patterson may be liable to Ms. Hainsley for battery?**

1.4 Legal Authority[3]—Harmful or Offensive Conduct

As part of your research, you find the following precedential case that may influence your assessment of Ms. Hainsley's claim:

Leichtman v. WLW Jacor Communications, Inc. et al.
92 Ohio App.3d 232 (1994)

The plaintiff-appellant, Ahron Leichtman, appeals from the trial court's order dismissing his complaint against the defendants-appellees, WLW Jacor Communications ("WLW"), William Cunningham, and Andy Furman, for battery, invasion of privacy, and a violation of Cincinnati Bd. of Health Reg. No. 00083. . . .

3. **A note on legal authority.** While all scenarios are set in the fictitious jurisdiction of Sunport, the book includes several actual cases. We know this presents complicated questions about whether those precedential cases are binding in Sunport. For the purposes of this book, you may assume they are binding legal authority. This book does not ask students to evaluate the authoritative weight of each legal authority—if the legal authority is in the book, then students should assume that it is binding and reflects the law in Sunport.

In his complaint, Leichtman claims to be "a nationally known" antismoking advocate. Leichtman alleges that, on the date of the Great American Smokeout, he was invited to appear on the WLW Bill Cunningham radio talk show to discuss the harmful effects of smoking and breathing secondary smoke. He also alleges that, while he was in the studio, Furman, another WLW talk-show host, lit a cigar and repeatedly blew smoke in Leichtman's face "for the purpose of causing physical discomfort, humiliation, and distress."

***

In determining if a person is liable for a battery, the Supreme Court has adopted the rule that "[c]ontact which is offensive to a reasonable sense of personal dignity is offensive contact." *Love v. Port Clinton* (1988), 37 Ohio St.3d 98, 99, 524 N.E.2d 166, 167. It has defined "offensive" to mean "disagreeable or nauseating or painful because of outrage to taste and sensibilities or affronting insultingness." *State v. Phipps* (1979), 58 Ohio St.2d 271, 274, 12 O.O.3d 273, 275, 389 N.E.2d 1128, 1131. Furthermore, tobacco smoke, as "particulate matter," has the physical properties capable of making contact. R.C. 3704.01(B) and 5709.20(A); Ohio Adm. Code 3745–17.

As alleged in Leichtman's complaint, when Furman intentionally blew cigar smoke in Leichtman's face, under Ohio common law, he committed a battery. No matter how trivial the incident, a battery is actionable, even if damages are only one dollar. *Lacey v. Laird* (1956), 166 Ohio St. 12, 1 O.O.2d 158, 139 N.E.2d 25, paragraph two of the syllabus. The rationale is explained by Roscoe Pound in his essay "Liability": "[I]n civilized society men must be able to assume that others will do them no intentional injury—that others will commit no intentioned aggressions upon them." Pound, An Introduction to the Philosophy of Law (1922) 169.

***

. . . Accordingly, Leichtman's claim for battery with the allegations against the three defendants in the second count of the complaint is sufficient to withstand a motion to dismiss under Civ.R. 12(B)(6) . . .

***

This cause is remanded for further proceedings consistent with law on that claim only.

Judgment accordingly.

Exercise 3

1. **How are the facts in *Leichtman* similar to the facts in Mr. Patterson's case?**

___

___

___

2. **How are the facts in *Leichtman* dissimilar from the facts in Mr. Patterson's case?**

3. **How does the court's reasoning in *Leichtman* influence your assessment of whether Mr. Patterson may be liable to Ms. Hainsley for battery?**

Exercise 4

1. **Review the interview notes, complaint, and legal authority. Applying the facts to the elements, do you believe Ms. Hainsley can establish the elements of battery?**

Assault: *George v. The Haunted Inn*

You are an associate in a small law firm. Your supervising attorney recently met with Taylor George, a potential client who wants to explore whether he has any viable claims based on an incident that happened at the Haunted Inn.

2.1 Client Interview

With Mr. George's permission, your supervising attorney recorded their conversation. The transcript is as follows:

Supervising Attorney	I'm happy to meet you. Our mutual friend, Jefferson Smith, told me a bit about your experience over at the Haunted Inn. I'd love to figure out a way our firm might help you. Why don't you tell me what happened? Just start from the beginning.
George	Well, I don't know if you've ever been to that "SCARE" event that's hosted by the Haunted Inn over in Busby Park every year around Halloween, but that's where it all started. A group of my friends were going to this thing. I had never heard of SCARE before, but of course I've been to a few other haunted houses and "Fright Night" events around the area over the years, so I was definitely game.
Supervising Attorney	Now tell me when this was. Do you recall the exact date and time?
George	I believe it was October 14th. I met up with my friends after dinner right outside the SCARE trail around 8:30 or 9:00.
Supervising Attorney	How many of you would you say there were?
George	Probably between 10 and 15 of us by the time we got to the trail. So this SCARE event takes place along a trail throughout Busby Park. And then there's even this maze thing within the trail. It's crazy! But the SCARE trail basically follows a 1-mile loop through the Park. We all walk along the trail and there's a bunch of scary settings—each of them kind of telling a different, really gruesome story.

	And along the way, these crazy people dressed as different creeps and killers jump out at us from dark spaces or spring out from around corners and they're holding bloody knives, axes, even body parts. It is the craziest, scariest thing I've ever seen! After maybe 20 minutes of walking along and being completely scared, I started hearing chainsaws, and they were getting closer. And then I was shocked to see two or three guys holding chainsaws—and those things were turned on! But I wasn't all that scared because I knew they were just actors, and they were mostly at a bit of a distance from me and behind ropes and they were holding the chainsaws up over their heads. So, it's not like I was scared about being cut up in a chainsaw massacre or anything.
Supervising Attorney	Of course not. And all of this happened inside the Park?
George	Yes, just normal haunted house stuff. But then we got to this gate, which I knew must be the exit, and so I knew the haunted stuff was over. And me and some of my friends were just standing there waiting for the rest of our group to come through. And this guy started his chainsaw and came right up to me—like right into my space—and he was yelling at me and waving that stupid chainsaw at me. And this was OUTSIDE the official event! I kept telling him to stop and get out of my face but he just kept messing with me. I felt like if I didn't leave, this guy was going to hurt me because he got so close to me with that stupid chainsaw—like DANGEROUSLY close. I have no idea what he was thinking but I was definitely fearing for my life at this point. So, I ran away to escape this guy, and this guy would not leave me alone—he chased me! And he chased me for a while, until I fell. And when I fell, my wrists got all cut up on the gravel.
Supervising Attorney	What did the guy with the chainsaw do when he saw you fall? Did he help you up or at least ask if you were okay?
George	No! After I fell, he must have just turned around and went back because he was gone by the time I managed to get myself up again.
Supervising Attorney	And did you go back to the event to report this?
George	Not that night. Look, I was embarrassed and also just really shook up. I just wanted to go home. And so that's what I did.
Supervising Attorney	I completely understand. How are you feeling now?

George	Honestly, I'm really angry. It really hurt my hands, and I couldn't even work for a few weeks after it happened. I did call later to complain about what happened. I learned that the guy who chased me is named Scott Pearce. I looked him up on Facebook, and he wants to be an actor. I think he took his job way too seriously.
Supervising Attorney	OK. Let's stop here. We're going to do some research, and we'll get back to you after we have a better idea about your options.

2.2 Legal Authority—Assault

In Sunport, to establish a cause of action for assault, the plaintiff must prove the following elements:

1. The defendant acted with intent to cause:
   a. a harmful or offensive contact to the plaintiff's person; or
   b. apprehension of an imminent harmful or offensive contact to the plaintiff's person; and
2. The defendant created in the plaintiff a reasonable apprehension of imminent harmful or offensive contact to the plaintiff's person.

Exercise 1

Your supervising attorney is going to draft a complaint alleging the Haunted Inn is liable for assault based on the conduct of Scott Pearce.[4] Your supervising attorney asked you to identify which facts support each of the following assertions:

4. **Vicarious Liability.** You may be asking why your supervising attorney intends to sue Haunted Inn when Scott Pearce is the one who engaged in the allegedly tortious conduct. Your firm is suing based on a theory of *vicarious liability*. Vicarious liability applies when one person or entity is legally liable for the wrongful conduct of another.

Vicarious liability arises most often in the context of an employer-employee relationship, also known as *respondeat superior* ("let the master answer"). Under this doctrine, an employer may be vicariously liable for the tortious conduct of an employee if the employee was acting within the scope of employment at the time of the wrongful act. We explore this doctrine further in Part II: Negligence, Chapter 10.

1. **Scott Pearce acted with the requisite intent to commit a battery.**

2. **Scott Pearce's conduct caused Mr. George to experience reasonable apprehension of an imminent harmful or offensive contact.**

2.3 Legal Authority—Reasonable Apprehension

As you continue your research, you find the following case, with facts similar to Mr. George's. The case evaluates the element of "reasonable apprehension."

Bouton v. Allstate Ins. Co.
491 So.2d 56 (La. Ct. App. 1986)

Shortess, Judge.

This suit arose from the unfortunate events of Halloween night in 1981. Jeffrey Scott Trammel, aged 15, Robert Martin Landry Jr., aged 13, and Daniel Breaux, aged 13, went trick-or-treating that evening. About 6:30 p.m., Trammel and Beaux rang Robert Bouton's (plaintiff) front door bell while Landry waited at the sidewalk. Plaintiff opened the door and saw Beaux standing before him. Breaux was dressed in military fatigues and was holding a plastic model submachine gun. Plaintiff shut the door immediately and locked it, then armed himself with a .357 magnum pistol. He returned to the door, opened it, and saw a flash of light, caused, he alleges, by Trammel's triggering a photographic flash. Plaintiff's pistol then discharged, the bullet striking and killing Breaux.

. . . [Plaintiff] alleged that the three boys' actions were tortious and caused him to be indicted and tried for second-degree murder, incur substantial attorney fees, lose his job, and suffer unfavorable publicity . . . [Plaintiff was ultimately acquitted in the criminal case. After filing his complaint in this civil case, defendants moved for summary judgment, arguing that Plaintiff had no cause of action for assault. The trial court granted their motion.] From that action, plaintiff brings this appeal. . . .

Plaintiff claims that the boys committed an assault, causing him to become frightened and triggering the tragic series of events which ensued. Plaintiff must prove an intentional act by the defendant which would have put a person in reasonable apprehension of receiving a battery. *See Castiglione v. Galpin*, 325 So. 2d 725 (La. App. 4th Cir. 1976); *F. Stone, Tort Doctrine,* §§ 159 and 160 in 12 *Louisiana Civil Law Treatise* 206-207 (1977). We find that the pleadings and evidence fail to establish any right to relief because, under the facts as set out by the plaintiff, he could not have had a *reasonable* apprehension of an impending battery or physical harm. Although it is *possible* for one who opens his door to trick-or-treaters on Halloween to become so frightened that he believes a battery is imminent, under the circumstances here, such an apprehension is not reasonable. Any reasonable person expects to see an endless array of ghouls, beasts, and characters on this evening, especially when he is, as was plaintiff, passing out candy on his doorstep.

Plaintiff contends that "the sole determining issue in this case" is whether we judge the boys' actions from their point of view or from his. We do neither. Instead, "we place the average reasonable [man] in the very situation which confronted the plaintiff and ask of him oracularly" if an apprehension of a battery could be reasonably expected to follow from such a situation. *Stone*, at 209 § 165. We do not believe that a reasonable person acting reasonably would have been apprehensive of a battery when confronted with this situation on Halloween. Therefore, we hold that plaintiff was not the victim of an assault.

***

[The court ruled that it need not address the issue of the boys' intent because the element of reasonable apprehension was lacking.]

For the foregoing reasons, the judgment of the trial court is affirmed at plaintiff's cost.

Exercise 2

1. **Review the interview transcript and legal authority. Applying the facts to the relevant law, do you believe Mr. George can establish the elements of a *prima facie* case for assault based on the conduct of Scott Pearce?**

2.4 Defendant's Response

Your supervising attorney decides to pursue the case. Your firm filed Mr. George's complaint against the Haunted Inn, and the Haunted Inn filed an Answer[5] denying liability and asserting the affirmative defense of consent.[6] The Defendant's answer included the following language:

> The plaintiff's claim is barred because, by voluntarily entering a haunted house attraction, Mr. George impliedly and expressly consented to "scares" and the physical proximity of actors, which are typical features of a haunted house.

In response to the Defendant's answer, your firm served Haunted Inn with Requests for Production.[7] Among other requests, your firm requested the following from Haunted Inn:

> Copies of any and all documents or other evidence, whether in written, electronic, or other format, that support Your contention that Mr. George consented to the assault alleged to have been committed by You.

In response to this discovery request, the Haunted Inn produced a copy of a ticket for entry into the SCARE event. The back of the ticket contains the following language:

> HAUNTED INN, LLC / SCARE
>
> RELEASE, LIABILITY WAIVER, and HOLD HARMLESS AGREEMENT
>
> 
>
> By redeeming this ticket, I acknowledge that the attractions inside Haunted Inn present high impact scares. The event is a theatrical experience which contains graphic scenes of simulated extreme horrors, tight spaces, exposure to darkness, fog, strobe light effects, and forced separation from my path or party at any time during the attraction, including in the areas immediately outside the entrances and exits. I acknowledge and understand that my participation in and use of the premises contain inherent risks and hazards, including but not limited to physical contact by actors, property damage, and personal injury. I understand that if I do not want to take risks or cannot afford to risk any injury, then I should NOT enter the attraction or participate in any use of the premises.

---

5. **What is an Answer?** After the plaintiff files a complaint, the defendant may file an Answer responding to the plaintiff's allegations. The defendant may admit what is true (i.e., facts about the defendant's residence or facts not in dispute) or deny any factual allegations the defendant believes are incorrect. The defendant may also challenge the plaintiff's legal assertions and raises any affirmative defenses.

6. **What is an Affirmative Defense?** An affirmative defense is a legal argument that may allow the defendant to avoid or reduce their liability. Essentially, the defendant argues that, even if the plaintiff's legal assertions are correct, the defendant should not be liable because the defendant's conduct was privileged or justified. In this context, the defendant is alleging that, even if Mr. George can establish the *prima facie* elements of assault, Haunted Inn is not liable because Mr. George consented to interactions like the one he had with Scott Pearce.

7. **What is a Request for Production?** After a lawsuit is filed, the parties engage in *discovery* to gather information and evidence from the opposing party and (sometimes) third parties. This enables them to learn about the other party's legal theories, identify the facts of the case, and review important documentation so each party can prepare their arguments and avoid surprises in court. Discovery tools include written interrogatories, requests for production of documents or physical evidence, depositions, and requests for admission. A Request for Production asks another party to produce specific documents or tangible items that are relevant to the case.

2.5 Legal Authority—Consent

Sunport defines consent as follows:

1) Consent is a complete defense to an intentional tort, and one who consents to the conduct of another cannot recover in an action of tort.
2) Consent may be express or implied.
   a. Consent is express when the willingness is clearly communicated, usually verbally or in writing.
   b. If words or conduct are reasonably understood by another to be intended as consent, they constitute implied (apparent) consent and are as effective as express consent.
3) If the actor exceeds scope of the consent, then it is not effective for the excess.

Exercise 3

1. **Draft an email to Mr. George advising him of the potential implications of the language on the ticket produced by the Haunted Inn. Address the following issues in your email: 1) whether Mr. George's claim for relief is barred because he *expressly* or *impliedly* consented to interactions like the one experienced with Scott Pearce; and 2) whether Scott Pearce *exceeded the scope of consent* by approaching Mr. George outside the park exit (and therefore Mr. George's claim is not barred).**

2.6 Settlement Offer

You spoke by phone with the attorney representing Haunted Inn. Opposing Counsel offered to settle the case to avoid the expense of litigation and any negative publicity. Opposing Counsel indicated the Haunted Inn would be willing to:

1. Pay Mr. George's medical expenses.
2. Offer Mr. George free admission to the Haunted Inn for the next 10 years.

Exercise 4

1. **Based on your assessment of Mr. George's claim, would you advise him to accept the Haunted Inn's offer? Why or why not?**

____

____

____

____

False Imprisonment

2

Finnegan v. Western Airlines

After working for a little over a year in a midsize law firm where you built up experience in civil litigation, you decided to hang your own shingle and open a law office. Having quickly established yourself as a formidable lawyer who gets good results for your clients, a prospective client has requested an appointment to discuss a potential case against her employer.

1.1 Investigation Report

You meet with the prospective client, Marcie Finnegan. She wants to know whether she has any valid claims against employer, her supervisor, and two security officers who were involved in a purported workplace prank. The events are summarized in an investigation report prepared by Ms. Finnegan's employer, Western Airlines Corp. The internal investigation is still pending.

Western Airlines Corp.

INTERNAL INVESTIGATION REPORT

Matter No. 16-65498

Date: August 26

Business location: Sunport

Investigator: Jaclyn Wilson

Employee: Marcela Finnegan, Customer Service Representative

Length of Employment: 11 months

Date of incident: August 3

SUMMARY

Western requires customer-facing employees to complete a probationary period of employment to assess whether they have the requisite skills and capacity to work with airline customers. Employees must serve under the supervision of a manager or senior employee for eight months. At the conclusion of the probationary period, employees are promoted to "Senior Customer Service Representative," which entitles them to higher pay, extended benefits, and travel credits.

On August 1, Finnegan had completed her probationary period and was approved for promotion. Finnegan's supervisor, Tina Tapia, was aware of the pending promotion, but Finnegan had not been notified.

On August 3, Finnegan was serving customers at a ticket counter near Gate A9 of the Sunport airport. Approximately six service representatives from Western and other airlines were in the area. The area was heavily crowded with customers.

Western Security Officer Ron Franks approached Finnegan and instructed her to accompany him to answer some questions. Officer Franks escorted Finnegan to the end of Western's ticket counter. Camilla Hernandez, another security officer, told Finnegan that, during the course of her airport background check, the City Aviation Department found an outstanding warrant for her arrest. Finnegan asserted that she did not have any warrants for her arrest, but Officer Hernandez told her that she needed to confiscate Finnegan's airport badge, her Western employee badge, and her keys. Officers advised Finnegan that they would escort her outside the airport to meet Sunport police officers, who would execute the warrant for her arrest. Finnegan became visibly upset, and she began crying.

Officer Hernandez asked to speak with Finnegan's supervisor. Finnegan directed them to Tapia, who took Finnegan's belongings. Finnegan, still upset and crying, repeatedly asked Tapia if the arrest was a joke. Tapia refused to answer. Finnegan asked for a tissue, and Tapia provided one.

Officer Franks then forcibly handcuffed Finnegan, and she reported that the action caused her "a lot of pain." Finnegan told the officers she was humiliated and embarrassed, so Officer Franks told her they would remove her from the airport via a terminal elevator, which was a more private exit.

The officers escorted Finnegan away from the crowded Western ticket counter, past the busy Allagash Airlines ticket counter, and toward the elevator.

Near the elevator, several Western employees had gathered to watch the incident. One employee yelled, "Congratulations, Marcie, you're off probation!" The other Western employees began clapping and congratulating Finnegan. Tapia then pinned Finnegan's new wings on her lapel and gave her a hug. They explained that they orchestrated the incident as a prank to congratulate Finnegan on her promotion.

The officers unhandcuffed Finnegan, but she continued to cry uncontrollably. Tapia told Finnegan to take a break. Finnegan visited the Western breakroom, where she allegedly took Ibuprofen and Tums. When Finnegan continued to experience emotional distress, Tapia instructed her to go home and rest.

Finnegan filed this incident report, arguing that the actions of her coworkers caused her to feel embarrassed, degraded, and humiliated.

Exercise 1

1. **List any intentional torts that may have been committed by Western's employees.**

____

____

____

1.2 Legal Authority—False Imprisonment

You plan to file suit on behalf of Ms. Finnegan, and you believe she has several potential claims, including employment-related claims such as harassment (which you are not asked to address in this exercise). For now, you are only considering whether Ms. Finnegan might file a claim against Western[1] based on a theory that Western employees committed the intentional tort of false imprisonment.

Under Sunport law, a defendant may be liable for false imprisonment if:

> 1) The defendant intends to confine the plaintiff within a confined area;
> 2) The defendant's conduct causes the plaintiff to be so confined; and
>   a. Confinement may be by physical restraint that restricts movement;
>   b. Confinement may also occur through threats of force or assertion of legal authority;
> 3) The plaintiff is either conscious of the confinement or harmed by it.

1.3 Investigation Report—Findings

While you continue to investigate potential causes of action, Western concludes its internal investigation and sends Ms. Finnegan a copy of its findings. One section concludes:

> **FINDINGS AND RECOMMENDATIONS**
>
> It is essential to consider the events in the light in which they were intended: Ms. Finnegan's coworkers wished to celebrate her promotion and acted in a spirit of good-natured

1. Western may be liable for the conduct of its employees under the doctrine of vicarious liability. See Chapter 1, footnote 4, for a discussion of vicarious liability.

camaraderie. This workplace prank had been perpetuated against many Western employees, and all understood and appreciated the joke. The prank involved security personnel, not law enforcement officers, coincided with a promotion date, and called for the involvement of a supervisor and coworkers. Other employees who experienced the prank winked and played along, and none expressed a similar level of distress.

We find no fault on the part of participating parties, who did not intend to harm Ms. Finnegan, emotionally or physically. In fact, when interviewed by this investigator, Officer Hernandez reported: "I could tell she was upset, but I thought that made the joke better. I assumed she would find it as funny as we did once she realized it was just fun hazing. I didn't even think of it as a 'real' arrest because I'm not authorized to arrest anyone. I'm really sorry it upset her because we thought she would see it as a playful welcome to our family."

No further action is recommended at this time.

1.4 Legal Authority—Intent

Ms. Finnegan asks for your advice about the findings. She is concerned that a jury will reject her claims because, despite her distress, her coworkers did not mean to harm or upset her.

You remember one of the first cases you read during law school, *Garratt v. Dailey*, 270 P.2d 1091 (Wash. 1955). In that case, a five-year-old boy removed a chair from under an elderly woman while she was sitting down. The woman fell to the ground and broke her hip. The court held that, even if the boy did not act with *purpose* to harm the woman, he could still be liable for battery if he *knew with substantial certainty* that by pulling the chair, the woman would fall and hit the ground.

You also find the following case evaluating what it means to act with intent:

Wagner v. Cook County Sheriff's Office
453 F.Supp.3d 1101 (N.D.Ill. 2020)

Plaintiff Paul Wagner was working as a bartender at the Tin Roof Bar in Joliet, Illinois when defendant Michael Doyle, a bar patron and off-duty Cook County Deputy Sheriff, walked behind the bar, pushed plaintiff against the wall, and brandished a knife in his face.***

Plaintiff later filed this action claiming that . . . Officer Doyle is liable for the torts of assault, battery, and intentional infliction of emotional distress as a result of his conduct. Plaintiff now seeks summary judgment of his assault and battery claims. Doyle responds that summary judgment is not appropriate because his conduct was intended as a "prank" or a "joke." But because Doyle's actions satisfy the element of assault and battery under Illinois law regardless of whether he actually intended to scare or harm plaintiff, summary judgment is warranted.***

. . . Doyle does not claim that he unintentionally approached plaintiff, or that he inadvertently pushed him against the wall while pointing a knife in his direction. Instead, Doyle insists that he did not take these actions with the intent to scare or harm plaintiff and suggests that his contact with plaintiff did not rise to the level of "offensive conduct." Neither argument is sufficient to withstand summary judgment.

There is no dispute—and the video footage confirms—that Doyle placed one hand on the upper portion of plaintiff's body and pushed him against the wall while pointing a knife at plaintiff with his other hand. Doyle disputes grabbing plaintiff by the "neck" or "throat," but these details are immaterial. The undisputed and observable facts objectively establish an offensive touching to which plaintiff did not consent. That is a battery. Similarly, Doyle's conduct was sufficiently threatening to place plaintiff in imminent apprehension of a battery regardless of whether he held the knife at plaintiff's "eye level." *See Jones v. Cross*, 637 F.3d 841, 848 (7th Cir. 2011) . . .

Doyle's insistence that his conduct was a "joke" or a "prank" does not change the analysis. As the Restatement (Second) of Torts explains, where an act itself is taken intentionally,

> it is immaterial that the actor is not inspired by any personal hostility to the other. Thus the fact that the defendant who intentionally inflicts bodily harm upon another does so as a practical joke, does not render him immune from liability so long as the other has not consented. This is true although the actor erroneously believes that the other will regard it as a joke, or that the other has, in fact, consented to it. One who plays dangerous practical jokes on others takes the risk that his victims may not appreciate the humor of his conduct and may not take it in good part.

Restatement (Second) of Torts § 13, cmt. c. Accordingly, Doyle's contact with plaintiff was no less a battery—nor was his apparent threat of making some type contact with plaintiff with a knife any less an assault—for his claim that these actions were part of a "prank."

For the foregoing reasons, plaintiff's motion for summary judgment on his assault and battery claims is granted.

***

Exercise 2

1. **What did the court in *Wagner v. Cook County Sheriff's Office* decide about whether an actor can avoid liability for an intentional tort if the actor subjectively believed the action was a "joke" or "prank"?**

____

____

____

____

2. **How does the holding in *Wagner v. Cook County Sheriff's Office* and the holding from *Garratt v. Dailey* influence any advice you offer Ms. Finnegan about the findings from Western's internal investigation?**

3. **Do you believe Ms. Finnegan has a viable claim for false imprisonment against Western for the conduct of its employees? Are all of the elements of a false imprisonment claim satisfied, and, if so, by which facts? If not, which element(s) is lacking and why?**

   Do not address issues of vicarious liability. Assume the employees were acting within the scope of their employment; if their conduct was tortious, then Western may be vicariously liable for their conduct.

Intentional Infliction of Emotional Distress

3

Glover v. BIZ Networks, Inc.

Thanks to your supervising attorney's relationship with an assistant general counsel at BIZ Networks, Inc. ("BIZ"), your firm has been engaged to defend BIZ in a lawsuit alleging a claim for intentional infliction of emotional distress.

The claim relates to an episode of the show "What's Really Happening." The episode exposed a local plastic surgeon, Dr. Fritz Hillard, who was performing cosmetic surgeries despite having his medical license revoked. Without prior consent, the reporter confronted and filmed a patient of the surgeon who was experiencing side effects from Dr. Hillard's treatments.

1.1 Episode Synopsis and Transcript

EPISODE SYNOPSIS

WHAT'S REALLY HAPPENING EPISODE 3.07

Fritz Hillard is one of the most popular surgeons in Sunport. Yet Hillard is hiding a dark secret: Hillard's medical license was revoked because he performed multiple collagen injections using a filler that was specifically rejected for use on humans by the Food and Drug Administration (FDA). Dr. Hillard's patients suffered from severe adverse side effects, including acute swelling at the injection site.

Watch as reporters enter the clinic to confront Dr. Hillard and speak with clinic patients. During a dramatic encounter, reporters stop Janiece Glover as she exits a treatment room immediately after receiving multiple injections in her face and neck. Ms. Glover was unaware that she was already experiencing severe swelling. Watch as Ms. Glover discovers the horrific injuries she sustained due to the dishonesty of Hillard and his cost-saving techniques.

EPISODE TRANSCRIPT

Reporter:	Excuse me, ma'am. We're with BIZ Network's "What's Really Happening" series. Are you a patient of Dr. Hillard's?
J. Glover [attempting to push reporter aside]:	What? Get out of my face! I don't have time for this. Where is the front desk staff? Hello! Yoo hoo!! Where is that woman?
Reporter:	Did you know that Dr. Hillard lost his license because he uses fillers that the FDA said aren't safe for use on humans? Did you know the filler he uses causes extreme swelling and apparently costs just a fraction of FDA-approved collagen fillers? Is he charging you full price for these injections? Has Dr. Hillard ever told you the injections he used aren't FDA-approved?
J. Glover:	What did you say? What? WHAT DID THIS FREAK JUST INJECT IN ME? HELLOOO? Why is no one coming up here to check me out? Never mind, I'm not paying for this anyway! And who are you again? Stop filming me!! [Covers her face.] Turn off that camera!
Reporter:	Before you leave, you might want to know that the treatment you just received seems to have taken effect, and I don't think you're going to like the results. [Pointing at a nearby mirror.] Take a look.
J. Glover [Noticing her reflection and shrieking.]:	OH MY GOSH! LOOK AT MY FACE!! LOOK AT IT! WHAT HAS HE DONE TO ME? [Cries and storms out of the clinic.]
Reporter [Looking into camera.]:	Yet another botched treatment from Dr. Hillard. I hope she will be okay. . . .

Exercise 1

1. **Identify any intentional torts for which BIZ Networks might be liable to Janiece Glover based on the conduct of its reporters and camera crew.**[1]

____

____

1. Biz Networks may be liable for the conduct of its employees under the doctrine of vicarious liability. See Chapter 1, footnote 4, for a discussion of vicarious liability.

1.2 Legal Authority—Intentional Infliction of Emotional Distress

Your supervising attorney spoke with Ms. Glover's attorney, who indicated Ms. Glover plans to file a complaint for Intentional Infliction of Emotional Distress (IIED). In researching the claim of IIED, you came across the following case, which sets forth the elements of the tort:

Zalnis v. Thoroughbred Datsun Car Co.
645 P.2d 292 (Colo. Ct. App. 1982)

KELLY, Judge.

. . . In January 1978, Zalnis contracted with defendant Thoroughbred Datsun for the purchase of a 1978 Datsun automobile. She took possession of the car on that day, and paid the balance of the purchase price two days later. Zalnis dealt directly with Linnie Cade, a salesperson employed by Thoroughbred Datsun. Defendant Trosper, President of Thoroughbred Datsun, approved the transaction based on representations by Cade which were later determined to be based upon erroneous calculations. When Trosper discovered several days later that Cade had sold the car at a loss of approximately $1,000, he instructed Cade and the sales manager to make good the loss by either demanding more money from Zalnis, retrieving the car, or repaying the difference out of Cade's salary.

Cade refused to follow any of Trosper's alternative instructions, but another sales employee, defendant Anthony, telephoned Zalnis and told her to return her car to the dealership because it was being recalled. When Zalnis arrived at Thoroughbred Datsun, she refused to give up possession of her car without a work order explaining the need for the recall. Nevertheless, her car was taken from her. During the next few hours, Zalnis alleges that Anthony called her a "French whore," followed her throughout the showroom, told her they were keeping her automobile, yelled, screamed, used abusive language, grabbed her by the arm in a threatening manner, and continually threatened and intimidated her when she attempted to secure the return of her automobile by telling her to "shut up."

During this period, Zalnis telephoned her attorney, who then telephoned Trosper and eventually obtained the return of her car. During their conversation, Trosper told the attorney that Zalnis had "been sleeping with that *** salesman and that's the only reason she got the deal she got." Trosper had known Zalnis for many years, and had told Cade and the sales manager that she was crazy and she had watched her husband kill himself.

In her complaint, Zalnis made separate claims for outrageous conduct and for slander per se. Thoroughbred Datsun and Trosper moved for partial summary judgment on the outrageous conduct claim. The trial court granted the motion, determining that, although the conduct was "almost shocking to the conscience and person of anyone observing that behavior," it did not amount to outrageous conduct under Colorado precedent.

In *Rugg v. McCarty*, 173 Colo. 170, 476 P.2d 753 (1970), the Supreme Court recognized the tort of outrageous conduct and adopted the definition set forth in the Restatement (Second) of Torts s 46: "One who by extreme and outrageous conduct intentionally or recklessly causes severe emotional distress to another is subject to liability for such emotional distress, and if bodily harm to the other results from it, for such bodily harm." Although the question whether conduct is sufficiently outrageous is ordinarily a question for the jury, the court must determine in the first instance whether reasonable persons could differ on the outrageousness issue. *Meiter v. Cavanaugh*, 40 Colo.App. 454, 580 P.2d 399 (1978); Restatement (Second) of Torts s 46, Comment h . . .

The defendants argue that their actions here were no more than "mere insults, indignities, threats, annoyances, petty oppressions, and other trivialities." Restatement (Second) of Torts s 46, Comment d. However, the defendants did not merely threaten and insult Zalnis; they took away her car and repeatedly harassed her. Conduct, otherwise permissible, may become extreme and outrageous if it is an abuse by the actor of a position in which he has actual or apparent authority over the other, or the power to affect the other's interests. Restatement (Second) of Torts s 46, Comment e; see, e.g., *Rugg v. McCarty, supra*.

***

Defendants assert that their actions must be judged by the impact they would have on an ordinary person with ordinary sensibilities. We disagree. The outrageous character of the conduct may arise from the actor's knowledge that the other is peculiarly susceptible to emotional distress by reason of some physical or mental condition or peculiarity. Restatement (Second) of Torts s 46, Comment f. In *Enright [v. Groves*, 39 Colo.App. 39, 560 P.2d 851 (1977)], . . . outrageous conduct was found where a police officer effecting an illegal arrest grabbed and twisted the plaintiff's arm even after she told him her arm was easily dislocated. In the instant case, plaintiff was peculiarly susceptible to emotional distress because she had witnessed her husband's suicide, and Trosper and Anthony knew about her susceptibility. Here, as in *Enright*, the defendants' knowledge exacerbated the conduct.

There is outrageous conduct where the actor desires to inflict severe emotional distress or knows that such distress is certain or substantially certain. Restatement (Second) of Torts s 46, Comment i; *Hansen v. Hansen*, 43 Colo.App. 525, 608 P.2d 364 (1980). Here, Zalnis has sufficiently alleged that Trosper and Anthony acted with the intent to bully her into giving up her car. In view of their knowledge of her emotional susceptibility, they could be considered to have acted intentionally or recklessly in causing her severe emotional distress.

The defendants argue that we should observe a distinction between a single outrageous occurrence and an outrageous course of conduct. While it is true that "the courts are more likely to find outrageous conduct in a series of incidents or a 'course of conduct' than in a single incident," it is the totality of conduct that must be evaluated to determine whether outrageous conduct has occurred. *See* Colo.J.I. 23:2 at 195 (2d ed. 1980). Our evaluation of the totality of the conduct leads to the conclusion that reasonable persons could differ on the question whether there was outrageous conduct, and thus, summary judgment was improper.

The trial court's alternative basis for granting defendants' motion was erroneous. *Meiter, supra*.

The judgment is reversed and the cause is remanded for further proceedings.

Exercise 2

1. **Using the language and reasoning from *Zalnis*, identify the elements Ms. Glover will need to prove to establish a *prima facie* case of intentional infliction of emotional distress (IIED).**

2. **Applying the facts from the Episode Transcript to each element identified above, discuss whether you believe Ms. Glover can establish a *prima facie* claim of IIED against BIZ Networks.**

3. **Is there any additional information that might help you assess whether Ms. Glover can establish the *prima facie* elements of an IIED claim?**

1.3 Medical Records

During discovery,[2] Ms. Glover's attorney disclosed a report from an expert witness. The report noted:

Mental Health Associates of Eastvale, Sunport

EXPERT REPORT IN RELATION TO JANIECE GLOVER

Firm: Hind LLC

Client: Janiece Glover

Date: April 16

Prepared by: Ruth Carver

This report summarizes relevant findings from my consultation with Janiece Glover regarding an incident that occurred when she was filmed inside a treatment clinic after experiencing negative side effects from a collagen treatment. The relevant background is summarized below.

[REDACTED]

FINDINGS

Ms. Glover's physical symptoms subsided quickly, and she experienced no long-term physical effects from the treatments. Yet the mental toll of the experience lingers.

Ms. Glover experienced extreme distress when reporters confronted her in the clinic. Ms. Glover expected the clinic to be a private and safe location, and reporters intruded on her privacy without warning. Ms. Glover never gave permission to film her reactions, and she repeatedly asked reporters to leave her alone. Despite that, reporters continued to harass her, likely because they noticed her physical symptoms and wanted to capture the moment of her discovery. When Ms. Glover did observe her swollen face, she was especially humiliated because she realized she was on camera and had been speaking to reporters in her "grotesque state."

Despite her distress, Ms. Glover intended to "leave well enough alone" until she began experiencing social ostracism. Two months after the incident, Ms. Glover was with her weekly book club, which Ms. Glover notes is "not really about discussing books but more about watching 'The Real Fiancées of Eastvale.'" During the gathering, the group

2. For a brief discussion of discovery, see Chapter 1, footnote 7.

watched a commercial about the upcoming episode of "What's Really Happening." The clip showed an image of Ms. Glover's swollen face with the caption, "An Injection Too Far: The Price of Vanity."

Ms. Glover was humiliated when members of the book club began whispering about her appearance. Ms. Glover had not told others she was receiving cosmetic treatments and had not gone out in public while her face was swollen. Ms. Glover asserts she has since received fewer invitations to social events.

Ms. Glover's ongoing distress has affected her appetite and interest in social activities. Ms. Glover asserts that she is often "unable to leave the house," and she has stopped engaging in her usual activities.

Exercise 3

1. **Does the Expert Report change your assessment of whether BIZ Networks may be liable for IIED based on the conduct of the BIZ Networks reporters and camera crew?**

2. **BIZ Networks has asked whether they should settle the claim to avoid any negative publicity. Which factors would you consider in evaluating whether BIZ Networks should try to settle the claim or proceed to trial?**

Trespass to Land

4

Wesley v. BlackRidge Energy Production

You receive a referral from a former law school colleague. The colleague believes the potential client, Sarah Wesley, has a cause of action for trespass to land based on fracking operations that have intruded on her property.

1.1 Consultants' Report

Your colleague forwards you the following summary of a report prepared by energy consultants Ms. Wesley hired to evaluate her options:

EASTVALE ENERGY CONSULTANTS

Case No. 05-7843

Wesley Property / Woodford Shale

On November 15, Sarah Wesley ("Owner") signed a Consulting Agreement with Eastvale Energy Consultants ("EEC"). EEC agreed to investigate and assess damage to Owner's property caused by fracking operations performed by BlackRidge Energy Production ("BEP"). The following report summarizes EEC's findings:

In 2019, BEP began extracting natural gas from a well located on property owned by BEP. BEP used hydraulic fracturing ("fracking") to extract natural gas. Fracking is a process that involves drilling a well into the earth and pumping a mixture of water, sand and chemicals ("proppants") into the well at high pressure. The proppant mixture cracks the shale under the ground, releasing natural gas.

Owner's property is directly adjacent to the parcel on which BEP began extracting natural gas. During drilling operations, BEP injected proppants into Owner's land, resulting in subsurface fractures under Owner's property, which BEP used to extract natural gas. The proppants injected by BEP keep the subsurface fractures open, and BEP continues to actively extract natural gas from Owner's property.

The well has remained in use since BEP began extraction operations in 2019. EEC is unable to estimate when the natural gas will be depleted from the well. BEP has declined to indicate how long it intends to use the well to extract natural gas or when it intends to conclude its operations.

***

RECOMMENDATIONS

At this time and without additional evidence, we are unable to assess the level of economic damage, including lost profits and damage to Ms. Wesley's property.

EEC encourages Owner to consult with counsel regarding potential legal remedies.

***

1.2 Legal Authority—Trespass to Land

You find the following information about the tort of trespass to land in *Gregory & Harrow's Civil Practice in Sunport*:

In Sunport, a trespass to land occurs when the defendant acts with intent to cause a physical invasion of another's property.

NOTE: The defendant need only intend to *enter* the land, even if the defendant does not have the intent to commit a wrongful trespass. For example, a defendant may commit a trespass by entering the property of another even under the mistaken belief the defendant was entering her own property.

The defendant may commit a trespass without personally intruding on the property. For example, a defendant may commit a trespass by placing objects on the property or by emitting particulates that enter the property.

Exercise 1

1. **Briefly analyze whether Ms. Wesley can establish the elements of trespass to land.**

____

____

1.3 Legal Authority—Continuing Trespass

As you begin your research into the viability of a claim for trespass to land, you find the following statute:

> **6 Sunport Stat § 84 (2021)**
>
> An action for trespass to land can only be brought within two (2) years after the cause of action accrued.

Because BEP began drilling on Ms. Wesley's property more than two years ago, you realize the potential claim for trespass is barred under Sunport's statute of limitations.[1] This means Ms. Wesley will be unable to bring a cause of action against BEP for trespass.

Yet your research suggests Ms. Wesley may have a claim for "continuing trespass." You find the following definition of the tort in *Civil Practice in Sunport*:

> A continuing trespass to land occurs if an actor fails to remove a thing the actor intentionally placed on the property of another, resulting in an ongoing invasion of land for as long as the thing wrongfully remains on the land. In such a case, the landowner may treat the continuance of the thing on the land as a continuation of the original trespass.

Exercise 2

As described in the EEC report, BEP injected proppants (particles used in fracking to keep fractures open) into Ms. Wesley's property during fracking operations. BEP continues to extract natural gas from the fractures.

1. **Discuss whether the BEP proppants constitute a continuing trespass to land.**

____

____

---

1. **What is a Statute of Limitations?** A statute of limitations is a law that sets a time limit for filing a lawsuit. If a plaintiff fails to file a case within the period established by the statute of limitations, then the court may dismiss the plaintiff's complaint because the deadline has passed.

   Statutes of limitations promote fairness, finality, and judicial efficiency. They acknowledge that evidence may become stale or degrade over time, and they encourage plaintiffs to bring claims while evidence is fresh and reliable. They also ensure that defendants are not subject to a perpetual threat of litigation for alleged misconduct.

1.4 Legal Authority—Injunctive Relief

Ms. Wesley wants payment for the gas extracted from her property, but she also wants the operations to stop. You intend to sue BEP for damages (economic compensation), and you intend to seek injunctive relief (asking the court to enjoin BEP from extracting additional resources from Ms. Wesley's property).[2] *Civil Practice in Sunport* notes that a plaintiff may seek an injunction to prevent an ongoing trespass to land if:

> The plaintiff demonstrates:
>
> 1) the plaintiff will suffer irreparable injury if the injunction is not granted;
> 2) the potential injury outweighs any harm the defendant might incur if the injunction is granted; and
> 3) the public interest will not be adversely affected by granting the injunction.

Exercise 3

1. **Draft an argument in support of injunctive relief:**

   a. **Identify the "irreparable" injury Ms. Wesley will experience if BEP is permitted to continue operations.**

   ____

   ____

   ____

   b. **Identify the harm BEP might experience if the injunction is granted.**

   ____

   ____

   ____

---

2. **What is Injunctive Relief?** Injunctive relief is a court order that tells a party to stop doing something or to do something specific. Instead of or in addition to seeking monetary damages, the plaintiff may ask the court to intervene to prevent future harm or stop an ongoing harm.

c. Evaluate whether Ms. Wesley's potential injury outweighs the harm to BEP.

____

____

____

d. Identify any public interest in BEP's operations.

____

____

____

Trespass to Chattels

5

Lupina v. Ross

You work as an associate in a boutique firm that provides support to small and medium-sized corporate clients. Your supervising attorney asked you to research a client matter.

Booker Ross is a long-standing client of the firm who needs legal counsel regarding a personal matter. The nature of the claim is beyond the scope of services typically provided by the firm, so your supervising attorney is asking you to research whether Mr. Ross might be liable for damages based on the incident.

1.1 Internal Memorandum

The relevant facts are described in a firm memorandum prepared by your supervising attorney:

> **MEMORANDUM**
>
> **TO: The File (Booker Ross, client no. 0029.106)**
>
> **FROM: Supervising Attorney**
>
> **RE:** *In re Booker Ross*
>
> Booker Ross, a long-term client of the firm, was involved in an unfortunate incident six months ago. Mr. Ross responded to an online advertisement placed by the potential plaintiff, Edgar Lupina, offering to sell a small, rare coin collection for $8,200. Mr. Ross has been an avid coin collector for some time and doubted Mr. Lupina's coin collection was genuine, especially because it was offered at such a low price. Mr. Ross nevertheless responded to the ad and asked to see the coins.
>
> Mr. Lupina instructed Ross to meet him in the parking lot of The Parks Shopping Mall at 6:30pm the next evening. Mr. Lupina told Mr. Ross to bring the purchase price of $8,200, payable in cash, to the meeting.

Mr. Ross visited The Parks as instructed, although he did not bring the cash because he was skeptical about the authenticity of the coins. When he arrived, he was surprised to learn Mr. Lupina's coin collection was exactly as advertised—the collection was both genuine and rare. Mr. Ross could not believe his luck as a particular coin in Mr. Lupina's collection was one for which Mr. Ross had been searching for several months. Unfortunately, because Mr. Ross did not have the $8,200 purchase price in cash, Mr. Lupina refused to transfer the coins or hold the coins until Mr. Ross returned with the cash.

In a moment of uncharacteristic impetuousness, Mr. Ross snatched the coin collection from Mr. Lupina and began running to his car, which was parked across the street from The Parks. Mr. Lupina ran after Mr. Ross and tackled him to the ground. Although this caused a laceration to his knee and a sprained ankle, Mr. Ross was able to get free, run to his car, and drive away with the coin collection.

Mr. Ross drove to an emergency clinic to get stitches in his knee and a brace for his severely sprained ankle. He walked with crutches for three days and with a walking boot for two weeks.

While Mr. Ross was waiting for care at the clinic, he transferred the $8,200 purchase price to Mr. Lupina via a banking app. Mr. Lupina accepted the payment. From the moment Mr. Ross snatched the coin collection from Mr. Lupina to the time Mr. Lupina finally accepted payment from Ross via the banking app, approximately two hours had passed.

Mr. Ross had the coin collection appraised. The certified written appraisal values the coin collection at $20,700.

1.2 Legal Authority—Trespass to Chattels and Conversion

You are concerned that Mr. Ross may be liable to Mr. Lupina for two torts: trespass to chattels and conversion. In Sunport, these torts are defined by statute:

Sunport Stat. § 77 (2021)

TRESPASS TO CHATTELS

An actor commits a trespass to chattels if the actor intentionally interferes with another's right of possession by either:

1. dispossessing the owner of his chattel; or
2. using or intermeddling with the chattel.

For purposes of this § 77, the following definitions apply:

A. *Dispossession of chattel*: dispossession requires the actor to treat the chattel as an owner would. Dispossession can occur even if it does not deprive the owner of the chattel for a substantial length of time.
B. *Use of chattel*: use of the owner's chattel occurs when the actor does not assume ownership of the chattel but only uses it.
C. *Intermeddling with chattel*: intermeddling with an owner's chattel requires the actor to make physical contact, direct or indirect, with the chattel.

Sunport Stat. Sunport Stat. § 78 (2021)

CONVERSION

An actor commits conversion if the actor intentionally deprives an owner of possession of his chattel or interferes with the chattel in a manner so serious as to exercise dominion or control and deprive the owner of the use of the chattel.

In distinguishing conversion from a trespass to chattels under § 77, the following factors must be considered: i) the *duration and extent* of the interference; ii) the actor's *intent to assert a right inconsistent* with the owner of the chattel; iii) the actor's *good faith*; iv) the *expense or inconvenience* to the chattel's owner; and v) the *extent of the harm* to the chattel.

Exercise 1

1. **Do you believe that, according to the facts set forth in the Memorandum, Mr. Lupina can successfully establish a *prima facie* case for trespass to chattels? (Are all elements satisfied and, if so, by which facts? If not, which element(s) is lacking?)**

2. **Do you believe that, according to the facts set forth in the Memorandum, Mr. Lupina can successfully establish a *prima facie* case for conversion? Why or why not?**

1.3 Legal Authority—Defense of Property

Mr. Ross wants to sue Mr. Lupina for damages he sustained when Mr. Lupina tackled him. Yet your senior partner believes Mr. Lupina's conduct might be privileged[1] as a defense of property. In Sunport, the defense is defined as follows:

> A defendant is privileged to use force to prevent an intrusion on the defendant's personal property if:
>
> 1. The defendant reasonably believes that the force is necessary to prevent or terminate the plaintiff's intrusion;
> 2. The means used are reasonably proportionate to the value of the interest the actor is protecting; and
> 3. The defendant, prior to the use of force, demands that the plaintiff desist and: 1) the demand is ignored; or 2) it reasonably appears that it would be futile or further endanger the defendant's property to make a demand.

Exercise 2

1. **Do you believe Mr. Lupina can prove that his conduct was justified as a "defense of property"? Why or why not?**

    a. **Did Mr. Lupina reasonably believe that force was necessary to terminate Mr. Ross's intrusion?**

    ____

    ____

    b. **Considering the value of the coin collection, were Mr. Lupina's actions reasonably proportionate? In other words, was Mr. Lupina's $8,200 coin collection worth tackling Mr. Ross?**

    ____

    ____

    ____

1. **What is Privileged Conduct?** In the context of intentional torts, conduct that might otherwise be wrongful (conduct that might constitute a tort) may be "privileged" or legally justified under the circumstances. The term applies if one's actions were authorized by law, done in self-defense, or performed with consent.

c. **Did Mr. Lupina reasonably believe that asking Mr. Ross to stop would be useless or that Mr. Ross would cause substantial harm before Mr. Lupina could make a request?**

Defenses to Intentional Torts

6

Self-Defense: *Finley v. Merchant*

You work for a firm that specializes in sports and entertainment law, and your firm sometimes represents athletes in personal matters. Your firm is approached by Karl Merchant, a college basketball player. Mr. Merchant was recently involved in a fight during a pickup basketball game, and after reading the newspaper article below, he is concerned that the other player may file suit.

1.1 Newspaper Article

EASTVALE CHRONICLE
OCTOBER 23

U of S Forward Punches Teenager During Neighborhood Game

Kelly McIntosh

On October 19, officers responded to a complaint that Trey Finley, age 16, had been assaulted by Karl Merchant, forward for the University of Sunport basketball team. Officers took a report but have not pursued further action.

The alleged assault happened when Merchant and Finley were playing a pickup game with college and high-school athletes near the University of Sunport. During the game, Merchant and Finley began fighting about a play because Finley believed Merchant fouled him. Finley alleges that he attempted to pass the ball to one of his teammates, but Merchant was distracted, and the ball hit Merchant in the face. Merchant then punched Finley, breaking his nose and bruising his face.

Finley's parents assert that, if the county refuses to charge Merchant with battery, then they will pursue a civil claim.

1.2 Client Email

Merchant explained his perspective in an email:

From: **Merchant, Karl**

Sent: **Tuesday, September 2 11:52 A.M.**

To: **Attorney**

Subject: **Ridiculous Claim**

You asked me to explain why I hit that kid. I only did it because I really thought he was going to attack me. He was mad because he thought I fouled him, which I didn't. He just couldn't handle an aggressive game, and he was mad because he kept losing the ball. I turned around because I didn't want to listen to him complain any more, and he took a cheap shot and threw the ball at my head. I didn't even see it coming. But he must have thrown it hard because it really hurt when it hit me.

When I turned around to yell at him, he was standing there like he was going to swing at me and start a fight. I reacted without thinking and hit him, but I only did it because I was sure he was going to hit me if I didn't.

1.3 Legal Authority—Self-Defense

While researching the question of whether Mr. Merchant lawfully used force to defend himself, you find the following excerpt from Monroe & Patel, *Pretrial Strategy and Settlement in Sunport.*

> A person may use physical force upon another person when and to the extent he or she reasonably believes such to be necessary to defend himself or herself from what he or she reasonably believes to be the use or imminent use of unlawful physical force.
>
> ***
>
> In determining whether a belief of harm is "reasonable," courts may consider factors such as the relative physical characteristics of the parties. For example, it may be "unreasonable" for a professional weightlifter to believe that he is in danger of being harmed by an untrained and smaller aggressor.

Exercise 1

1. **Based on the legal authority above, what does Mr. Merchant have to establish for his claim of self-defense?**

____

____

____

2. **What additional information would help you assess whether Mr. Merchant can establish that he acted in self-defense?**

____

____

____

1.4 Investigation Report

You ask the firm's investigator to gather additional information about the incident.

Griner, Wintle & Rice, LLC
INVESTIGATION REPORT

CASE NO. 16-5986

This investigative report was prepared by Melinda Griner, a licensed private investigator, at the request and under the direction of legal counsel for Karl Merchant. The information contained herein was compiled in anticipation of litigation and for the purpose of assisting counsel in providing legal advice. This report and all related materials are confidential and intended to be protected from disclosure as attorney work product.

Karl Merchant is a 21-year-old male. Merchant is 6′3″ and weighs 205 pounds. Merchant has been playing for the University of Sunport for the last two seasons. Merchant also played for his high-school varsity basketball team. Merchant was one of his high school team's most popular players, and he received an athletic scholarship to the University of Sunport.

Trey Finley is a 16-year-old male. Finley is 5′10″ and weighs 160 pounds. Finley recently joined his high school's JV basketball team, but he has not played during any games.

The incident in question occurred during a regular pickup game at Ironground Gym near the University of Sunport. Games regularly include players from the University of Sunport basketball team and occasionally include amateur players from the community. On October 19, nine individuals began playing a game around 6:30pm. All but three players were from the university team. The remaining players included Finley and two friends.

One university player, Rob Turner, reported that the games are "usually pretty rough," and he typically discourages other players from participating if they do not have enough experience. Turner reported, "Those high-school kids weren't up for it. They kept complaining about how we played, and we just told them it is just how 'grown-up' athletes play."

After about 45 minutes of play, Turner noted that Finley got angry because he thought Merchant fouled him. Turner asserted, "I could tell he was really mad. He kind of hurled the ball at Karl [Merchant], and it seemed like he was aiming for Karl's head. Karl wasn't really watching, and the ball hit him pretty hard in the face."

One of Trey Finley's friends reported, "Trey told us that he wanted to be aggressive because he was playing against 'real' players, and he wanted to show them that he could handle college basketball." The friend noted, "Trey was frustrated because he wasn't playing as well as he wanted, and he definitely threw the ball at Merchant harder than he should have. But I know he didn't mean to actually hit him in the face. Karl just wasn't paying attention."

Witness accounts of the punch vary. Turner reported that after the ball struck Merchant, Merchant looked stunned, turned toward Finley, and punched him with "a quick, hard hit—like a reflex." Another university player, Jordan Lane, reported that Merchant appeared "angry but not out of control" and said the punch "looked like it was instinctive, not like he was trying to hurt the kid." In contrast, Finley's friend described the punch as "super aggressive." He said Merchant turned, took a few steps towards Finley and "blasted" him. He indicated Finley "wasn't ready for it at all and didn't do anything to defend himself."

Neither Finley nor his parents were willing to discuss the incident. Finley's friend indicated that Finley sustained visible injuries, including a broken nose and significant bruising around his face.

Exercise 2

1. **Does the information in the investigation report change your assessment of whether Mr. Merchant acted in self-defense? Identify at least three facts that weaken Mr. Merchant's defense and three facts that strengthen Mr. Merchant's defense.**

   a. **Facts that strengthen Mr. Merchant's defense:**

   ____

   ____

b. Facts that weaken Mr. Merchant's defense:

____

____

1.5 Legal Authority — Reasonable Belief

During your research, you find the following order that may bolster Mr. Merchant's claims:

IN THE CIRCUIT COURT OF THE
17TH JUDICIAL CIRCUIT IN AND FOR
BROWARD COUNTY, FLORIDA
CASE NO: CACE-21-013763(18)

JUSTIN BALBOA,

Plaintiff

vs.

BRO MANAGEMENT-LAS OLAS, LLC, d/b/a B SQUARE BURGERS, and

JOE SCHILLING,

Defendants

ORDER ON DEFENDANT JOE SCHILLING'S MOTION FOR STATUTORY IMMUNITY

THIS CAUSE came before the Court on the Defendant Joe Schilling's Motion for Statutory Immunity filed on December 21, 2021. The Court reviewed the pleadings in support thereto, and considered argument of counsel, the credibility of the witnesses and the evidence presented. The Court finds as follows:

I. RELEVANT BACKGROUND AND FINDINGS

On June 27, 2021 Defendant Joe Schilling ("Defendant" or "Schilling"), a former professional fighter, struck Plaintiff Justin Balboa ("Plaintiff" or "Balboa"). The altercation was a result of a brief interaction between the two at a Fort Lauderdale restaurant. Schilling was at the restaurant dining with a friend and colleague, Jamie Gall. Ms. Gall noticed when Balboa entered the restaurant. He was boisterous and calling attention to himself. Balboa, who was celebrating a recent promotion, was admittedly drinking, singing, dancing and walking around the restaurant. He had a few beers, as well as a "good" or "decent" number of shots.

At one point during the night, Balboa went up to Schilling and Gall's table. Balboa, a recreational boxer, testified that he did not know who Schilling was before that night. Ms. Gall, however, testified that she hear [sic] Balboa say something about fighting to Schilling. After a brief exchange they asked Balboa to leave, and he complied.

Later that evening, Schilling stepped outside to smoke. When he was returning to his table, Balboa, who was admittedly intoxicated, stumbled into Schilling. The video taken by Ms. Gall shows that Balboa apologized without looking at Schilling, and Schilling acknowledged the apology while continuing to walk back to his table. For some undetermined reason, Balboa calls out to Schilling. Schilling turns around and looks at Balboa in an unaggressive stance. Schilling's feet were shoulder width apart and his hands were at his side. Balboa makes a feinting gesture towards Schilling. Schilling, who testified that he learned to anticipate punches as part of his training, instantly responded with two quick punches. Balboa fell to the floor unconscious.

II. ANALYSIS

***

The Court must evaluate not whether Schilling's actions were necessary to prevent imminent death or great bodily harm to himself, but rather, whether Schilling ***reasonably believed*** that using such force was necessary to prevent imminent death or great bodily harm.

Based upon a totality of circumstances and the facts presented at the evidentiary hearing, the Court finds that Schilling reasonably believed that Balboa posed a threat of great bodily harm to himself. The Court further finds that Schilling used only such force necessary to neutralize the threat and is therefore entitled to immunity pursuant to [Florida's self-defense statute.]

It is hereby ORDERED AND ADJUDGED that:

The Motion to Dismiss is **GRANTED**.

Exercise 3

1. **How are the facts of Mr. Merchant's case similar to *Balboa v. Schilling*? How are they dissimilar?**

____

____

____

____

2. **Based on the article, interview, and legal authority, prepare a brief legal argument analyzing whether Mr. Merchant is protected from liability for battery because he acted in self-defense.**

____

____

____

Consent: *In re Rhys Clarkson*

Rhys Clarkson came to your office today to discuss two potential battery claims that arose out of a recent incident at Eastvale College. Ms. Clarkson was a star recruit for the Eastvale women's basketball team. She just completed her freshman season as the starting point guard and has ambitions for an early draft to the WNBA (and the talent to make those ambitions a reality).

2.1 Client Interview

Your notes from the meeting with Ms. Clarkson are below.

MTG. w/ RHYS CLARKSON (May 4 10:00 A.M.)

- Clarkson (5′ 6″, 130 lb)—playing for Eastvale College in semifinal game of division championship series against Southland A&M.
- Scrambled for rebound against Southland player—both players ended on floor fighting for ball and ref called jump ball.
- Clarkson got to her feet first and tried to lean down to help the other player up. Other Southland team members misunderstood and thought Clarkson was going to hit the Southland player. Jen Mandel (6′7″, 210 lb center for Southland) shoved Clarkson, knocked her to the floor, and then kicked her. Mandel was ejected from the game by the refs.
- Clarkson's left wrist was sprained—team trainer took her to Eastvale Memorial to have wrist x-rayed and set.

2.2 Legal Authority—Battery

In Sunport, the elements of battery are as follows:

A defendant is subject to liability for battery if:

1) The defendant acts with intent to cause a harmful or offensive contact to the person of another; and
2) A harmful or offensive contact to that person directly or indirectly results.

Exercise 1

1. **Advise Ms. Clarkson about whether she can establish the *prima facie* elements of battery because Ms. Mandel shoved and kicked Ms. Clarkson during the basketball game.**

____

____

____

2.3 Legal Authority—Consent

You assume that, if Ms. Clarkson sues Jen Mandel for battery, then Ms. Mandel will argue that by participating in a basketball game—especially in a high-stakes game such as the division championship semi-final game—Ms. Clarkson consented to the contact that occurred during that competitive play.

During the course of your research, you found . . . the following decisions relevant to the defense of consent. Relevant excerpts of the courts' decisions are set forth below:

Hackbart v. Cincinnati Bengals, Inc.
601 F.2d 516 (10th Cir. 1979)

William E. Doyle, Circuit Judge.

The question in this case is whether in a regular season professional football game an injury which is inflicted by one professional football player on an opposing player can give rise to liability in tort where the injury was inflicted by the intentional striking of a blow during the game.

The injury occurred in the course of a game between the Denver Broncos and the Cincinnati Bengals, which game was being played in Denver in 1973. The Broncos' defensive back, Dale Hackbart, was the recipient of the injury and the Bengals' offensive back, Charles "Booby" Clark, inflicted the blow which produced it.

* * *

The trial court's finding was that Charles Clark, "acting out of anger and frustration, but without a specific intent to injure * * * stepped forward and struck a blow with his right forearm to the back of the kneeling plaintiff's head and neck with sufficient force to cause both players to fall forward to the ground." Both players, without complaining to the officials or to one another, returned to their respective sidelines since the ball had changed hands and the offensive and defensive teams of each had been substituted. Clark testified at trial that his frustration was brought about by the fact that his team was losing the game.

* * *

Despite the fact that the defendant Charles Clark admitted that the blow which had been struck was not accidental, that it was intentionally administered, the trial court ruled as a matter of law that the game of professional football is basically a business which is violent in nature, and that the available sanctions are imposition of penalties and expulsion from the game. Notice was taken of the fact that many fouls are overlooked; that the game is played in an emotional and noisy environment; and that incidents such as that here complained of are not unusual.

* * *

But it is highly questionable whether a professional football player consents or submits to injuries caused by conduct not within the rules, and there is no evidence which we have seen which shows this.

* * *

The general customs of football do not approve the intentional punching or striking of others. That this is prohibited was supported by the testimony of all of the witnesses. They testified that the intentional striking of a player in the face or from the rear is prohibited by the playing rules as well as the general customs of the game. Punching or hitting with the arms is prohibited. Undoubtedly these restraints are intended to establish reasonable boundaries so that one football player cannot intentionally inflict a serious injury on another. Therefore, the notion is not correct that all reason has been abandoned, whereby the only possible remedy for the person who has been the victim of an unlawful blow is retaliation.

* * *

In sum, having concluded that the trial court did not limit the case to a trial of the evidence bearing on defendant's liability but rather determined that as a matter of social policy the game was so violent and unlawful that valid lines could not be drawn, we take the view that this was not a proper issue for determination and that plaintiff was entitled to have the case tried on an assessment of his rights and whether they had been violated.

* * *

The cause is reversed and remanded for a new trial in accordance with the foregoing views.

Koffman v. Garnett

574 S.E.2d 258 (Va. 2003)

In this case, we consider whether the trial court properly dismissed the plaintiffs' [claims for] assault and battery.

***

In the fall of 2000, Andrew W. Koffman, a 13-year-old middle school student at a public school in Botetourt County, began participating on the school's football team. It was Andy's first season playing organized football, and he was positioned as a third-string defensive player. James Garnett was employed by the Botetourt County School Board as an assistant coach for the football team and was responsible for the supervision, training, and instruction of the team's defensive players.

The team lost its first game of the season. Garnett was upset by the defensive players' inadequate tackling in that game and became further displeased by what he perceived as inadequate tackling during the first practice following the loss.

Garnett ordered Andy to hold a football and "stand upright and motionless" so that Garnett could explain the proper tackling technique to the defensive players. Then Garnett, without further warning, thrust his arms around Andy's body, lifted him "off his feet by two feet or more," and "slammed" him to the ground. Andy weighed 144 pounds, while Garnett weighed approximately 260 pounds. The force of the tackle broke the humerus bone in Andy's left arm. During prior practices, no coach had used physical force to instruct players on rules or techniques of playing football.

[The Koffmans] alleged that Andy was injured as a result of Garnett's . . . intentional acts of assault and battery . . . The trial court dismissed the action, finding that . . . the facts alleged were insufficient to state causes of action for . . . assault or battery because the instruction and playing of football are "inherently dangerous and always potentially violent."

In this appeal, the Koffmans . . . assert that they pled sufficient facts . . . to sustain their claims of . . . assault and battery.

***

[The court upheld the dismissal of the Koffman's claim for civil assault because the pleading did not include an allegation that Andy had any apprehension of an immediate battery.]

The [Koffmans' pleading] is sufficient, however, to establish a cause of action for the tort of battery. The Koffmans pled that Andy consented to physical contact with players "of like age and experience" and that neither Andy nor his parents expected or consented to his "participation in aggressive contact tackling by the adult coaches." Further, the Koffmans pled that, in the past, coaches had not tackled players as a method of instruction. Garnett asserts that, by consenting to play football, Andy consented to be tackled, by either other football players or by the coaches.

Whether Andy consented to be tackled by Garnett in the manner alleged was a matter of fact. Based on the [Koffmans' allegations], reasonable persons could disagree on whether Andy gave such consent. Thus, we find that the trial court erred in holding that the Koffmans' [pleading] was insufficient as a matter of law to establish a claim for battery.

***

Reversed and remanded.

[After the case was remanded to the trial court, the parties reached a settlement.]

Exercise 2

Based on your research, you formulate two possible arguments in response to Ms. Mandel's potential assertion that Ms. Clarkson consented to physical contact when she participated in a competitive game of basketball.

1. **Prepare an argument in support of the following assertion: Like the conduct at issue in *Hackbart*, Ms. Mandel's actions violated the rules of the game or the "general customs" of competitive basketball.**

2. **Prepare an argument in support of the following assertion: Like the defendant in *Koffman*, Ms. Mandel exceeded the scope of Ms. Clarkson's consent to contact.**

3. **How might Ms. Mandel respond to the arguments above?**

Exercise 3

Clarkson is worried about her reputation and does not want to appear litigious. She is afraid that getting involved in lawsuits could dissuade WNBA teams from drafting her, so if there is a significant chance that she could lose her claims, then she does not want to file suit.

1. **How would you advise Ms. Clarkson based on those concerns? Identify the factors you might consider.**

____

____

____

____

____

____

____

2.4 Client Interview Continued

During your interview with Ms. Clarkson, she described the treatment she received after she was injured during the game with Ms. Mandel. Based on her description, you believe she may also have a claim against the treating physician. Notes from the interview are excerpted below:

MTG. w/ RHYS CLARKSON
MAY 4 10:00 A.M.

Dr. Issie Newton, the doctor on duty, noticed that Ms. Clarkson seemed bothered by her right leg. Dr. Newton found an abscess on the back of Ms. Clarkson's upper thigh and lanced it to drain the abscess and prevent it from swelling.

Ms. Clarkson didn't know what was going on—in one moment, Dr. Newton was looking at Ms. Clarkson's wrist; the next moment she took a knife and sliced Ms. Clarkson's leg. Ms. Clarkson didn't complain to anyone that day, other than telling the team trainer she didn't want Dr. Newton ever touching her again.

Ms. Clarkson had to go back to her primary physician to have the abscess examined and treated to prevent any infection from the opening left by Dr. Newton.

Exercise 4

1. **Can Ms. Clarkson establish a *prima facie* case of battery against Dr. Newton?**

2.5 Legal Authority—Informed Consent

Because you believe Ms. Clarkson's damages were relatively nominal, you hope to secure an informal resolution of any claim against Dr. Newton. You call Dr. Newton, who angrily asserts:

> I can't believe Rhys is complaining about what happened. Frankly, she should be thanking me. She was in the middle of an important season, and that abscess was going to interfere with her performance. These players are looking for *any* advantage they can get, and it did not occur to me that she would object to a simple procedure that resolved what might have been a restriction on her play.
>
> From my perspective, if someone asks for treatment during a game, then they are asking me to quickly and efficiently resolve *any* medical issue that affects their performance. Rhys sought me out for my expertise in sports medicine, and I provided good treatment. Did I specifically ask, "May I take care of this irritating condition by performing a safe and recognized procedure that is essentially without risk?" No, I did not. The nature of sports medicine calls for me to act quickly and in situations where there isn't time for dialogue, so I don't have the luxury of a prolonged deep dive into someone's feelings.
>
> In any case, what harm did she experience? Aside from hurt feelings about not being asked, I doubt she can point to any physical injuries. In fact, I prevented a problem before it got worse.
>
> I won't give her a dime. In fact, she should pay me for wasting my time during this phone call.

Your research uncovered the following decision relevant to Ms. Clarkson's claim against Dr. Newton:

Mohr v. Williams
95 Minn. 261, 104 N.W. 12 (1905)

Syllabus by the Court

***

Plaintiff consulted defendant concerning a difficulty with her right ear. Defendant examined the organ and advised an operation, to which plaintiff consented. After being placed under the influence of anaesthetics [sic], and when plaintiff was unconscious therefrom, defendant examined her left ear, and found it in a more serious condition than her right, and in greater need of an operation. He called the attention of plaintiff's family physician to the conditions he had discovered, who attended the operation at plaintiff's request, and finally concluded that the operation should be performed upon the left instead of the right ear, to which the family physician made no objection. Plaintiff had not previously experienced any difficulty with her left ear, and was not informed prior to the time she was placed under the influence of anaesthetics [sic] that any difficulty existed with reference to it, and she did not consent to an operation thereon.

***

. . . It cannot be doubted that ordinarily the patient must be consulted, and his consent given, before a physician may operate upon him.* * *

. . . The physician impliedly contracts that he possesses, and will exercise in the treatment of patients, skill and learning, and that he will exercise reasonable care and exert his best judgment to bring about favorable results. The methods of treatment are committed almost exclusively to his judgment, but we are aware of no rule or principle of law which would extend to him free license respecting surgical operations. Reasonable latitude must, however, be allowed the physician in a particular case; and we would not lay down any rule which would unreasonably interfere with the exercise of his discretion, or prevent him from taking such measures as his judgment dictated for the welfare of the patient in a case of emergency. If a person should be injured to the extent of rendering him unconscious, and his injuries were of such a nature as to require prompt surgical attention, a physician called to attend him would be justified in applying such medical or surgical treatment as might reasonably be necessary for the preservation of his life or limb, and consent on the part of the injured person would be implied. And again, if, in the course of an operation to which the patient consented, the physician should discover conditions not anticipated before the operation was commenced, and which, if not removed, would endanger the life or health of the patient, he would, though no express consent was obtained or given, be justified in extending the operation to remove and overcome them. But such is not the case at bar. The diseased condition of plaintiff's left ear was not discovered in the course of an operation on the right, which was authorized, but upon an independent examination of that organ, made after the authorized operation was found unnecessary. Nor is the evidence such as to justify the court in holding, as a matter of law, that it was such an affection as would result immediately in the serious injury of plaintiff, or such an emergency as to justify proceeding without her consent. She had experienced no particular difficulty with that ear, and the questions as to when its diseased condition would become alarming or fatal, and whether there was an immediate necessity for an operation, were, under the evidence, questions of fact for the jury.

***

The last contention of defendant is that the act complained of did not amount to an assault and battery. This is based upon the theory that, as plaintiff's left ear was in fact diseased, in a condition dangerous and threatening to her health, the operation was necessary, and having been skillfully performed at a time when plaintiff had requested a like operation on the other ear, the charge of assault and battery cannot be sustained; that, in view of these conditions, and the claim that there was no negligence on the part of defendant, and an entire absence of any evidence tending to show an evil intent, the court should say, as a matter of law, that no assault and battery was committed, even though she did not consent to the operation. In other words, that the absence of a showing that defendant was actuated by a wrongful intent, or guilty of negligence, relieves the act of defendant from the charge of an unlawful assault and battery. We are unable to reach that conclusion, though the contention is not without merit. It would seem to follow from what has been said on the other features of the case that the act of defendant amounted at least to a technical assault and battery. If the operation was performed without plaintiff's consent, and the circumstances were not such as to justify its performance without, it was wrongful; and, if it was wrongful, it was unlawful. As remarked in 1 Jaggard on Torts, 437, every person has a right to complete immunity of his person from physical interference of others, except in so far as contact may be necessary under the general doctrine of privilege; and any unlawful or unauthorized touching of the person of another, except it be in the spirit of pleasantry, constitutes an assault and battery. In the case at bar, as we have already seen, the question whether defendant's act in performing the operation upon plaintiff was authorized was a question for the jury to determine. If it was unauthorized, then it was, within what we have said, unlawful. It was a violent assault, not a mere pleasantry; and, even though no negligence is shown, it was wrongful and unlawful. The case is unlike a criminal prosecution for assault and battery, for there an unlawful intent must be shown. But that rule does not apply to a civil action, to maintain which it is sufficient to show that the assault complained of was wrongful and unlawful or the result of negligence. [Citation omitted.]

The amount of plaintiff's recovery, if she is entitled to recover at all, must depend upon the character and extent of the injury inflicted upon her, in determining which the nature of the malady intended to be healed and the beneficial nature of the operation should be taken into consideration, as well as the good faith of the defendant.

Order affirmed.

Exercise 5

1. **Briefly summarize the rules articulated in the case above. Specifically, summarize what the court held about the nature of consent in a medical context.**

2. **If Ms. Clarkson asserts a claim of battery against Dr. Newton, is Dr. Newton likely to succeed in asserting the defense of consent? Why or why not?**

Part II
Negligence

Duty of Care

7

Attractive Nuisance Doctrine: *In re Drop or Do Laundromat*

Danny Martinelli, the owner of Drop or Do Laundromat, is a long-standing client and friend. Mr. Martinelli took you to lunch today to discuss an incident that occurred at the laundromat. He is sure that a lawsuit is coming soon and he asked for your advice about how best to protect his business.

1.1 Interview Notes

Your client file for Drop or Do includes the following notes:

Drop or Do, LLC

- Business
  - □ Drop or Do is Eastvale's largest self-serve washateria/laundromat, and it occupies nearly the entire block.
  - □ The business includes 200 coin-operated washers and dryers.
  - □ Services also include a drop-off laundry service, where customers can leave clothing for employees to wash and fold.
- Client
  - □ Martinelli is an aggressive business owner who expanded the operation after taking over from his father.
  - □ Two years ago, Martinelli installed a "Game Zone," where patrons can play classic arcade games while waiting on the machines. There is also an area for kids, which includes toys, books, and crafts.
- Legal services
  - □ Previous services: incorporation, vendor agreements, revise HR policies, update employee handbooks.
  - □ On retainers for routine legal needs—workers' comp, HR issues, licenses, tax compliance, insurance, customer complaints, etc.

Your notes from the meeting with Mr. Martinelli are below.

MTG. w/ Danny Martinelli (June 6 noon)

- On April 28, a customer visited Drop or Do with her children, 11-year-old old Sam and 8-year-old Kobe Malone. The customer was using the washers and dryers inside, and Sam and Kobe were just outside the entrance. The children snuck around the corner to the employees' entrance and found a maintenance cart that had been left outside by an employee. Sam dared Kobe to drive the cart, and Kobe drove it over Sam's leg, causing him injuries.

- The customer insists the keys to the cart were left in the ignition, but the employee swears they were left in a cubby hole in the cart.

- Immediately after the incident, Martinelli's employee called him, and Martinelli arrived at the laundromat. The boys' mother approached Martinelli, and the confrontation was caught on the laundromat's security cameras. The mother screamed, "What did you think would happen when you left a motorized cart with the keys in the ignition right here? You KNOW we have to bring our kids to the laundromat with us—that's why you have your stupid arcade games and toys. Why in the world would anyone leave the keys here . . . BEGGING my kids to hop in and take a ride? How could you be so stupid?"

- The customer took Sam to the Urgent Care clinic. His leg was broken and he had bruises, scrapes, and cuts across his leg.

- Martinelli is confident the customer is on the brink of suing him. He saw her looking at the bulletin board in the laundromat pulling the business cards of any lawyer who posted there. He knows he has insurance that should cover him in the event of a lawsuit, but he is worried about his exposure to liability. He is also worried about the publicity because a lot of families use Drop or Do, given its reputation as a family-friendly location.

- Martinelli talked to his younger sister, who is about to graduate from law school. She suggested Martinelli consider three issues:

    1) Is Drop or Do liable for Sam's injuries under the "attractive nuisance" doctrine?

    2) Even if the doctrine of attractive nuisance does not apply, is Drop or Do liable for Sam's injuries based on Drop or Do's negligence in leaving the maintenance cart unattended?

    3) Is the customer's claim barred because Sam was contributorily negligent?

1.2 Legal Authority—Attractive Nuisance Doctrine

To address the client's questions, you refer to one of your favorite research tools, the Sunport Civil Pattern Jury Charges.[1]

The Sunport Civil Pattern Jury Charge includes the following information about the attractive nuisance doctrine:

> Ladies and gentlemen of the jury, you are instructed as follows regarding the issue of negligence:
>
> To determine whether the defendant is liable for negligence, you must first determine whether the defendant owed a duty to the plaintiff and whether the defendant breached that duty by failing to comport their conduct to the applicable standard of care.
>
> In most cases, the applicable standard of care is that of reasonableness: The defendant has a duty to act as ordinary, prudent and reasonable person and avoid creating an unreasonable risk of injury to others.
>
> In other cases, the defendant may have a duty to conform their conduct to a *particular* standard of care. For example, landowners owe particular duties to entrants on their property depending on the status of the entrant. While landowners do not owe a duty of care to unknown trespassers, landowners do owe a duty of care to *known* trespassers: A landowner has a duty to warn or protect discovered or anticipated trespassers from concealed, dangerous and artificial conditions on the land.
>
> A category of "known trespassers" includes children. Under the "attractive nuisance" doctrine, a landowner may be liable for a child's injuries, even if the child is trespassing on the property, if the landowner fails to exercise reasonable care to protect the child from harm caused by an artificial condition upon his land.
>
> A defendant is liable for physical harm to children trespassing upon his land if:
>
> 1) An artificial condition existed on the defendant's property where the defendant knows or has reason to know that children are likely to trespass;
> 2) The condition is one of which the defendant knows or has reason to know will involve an unreasonable risk of death or serious injury to such children;
> 3) The children, because of their youth, do not discover the condition or realize the risk involved;

1. **What is a Pattern Jury Charge?** A pattern jury charge is a standardized set of instructions that a judge may give to a jury before the jury begins deliberations and renders a verdict. The instructions define the legal issues the jury must consider and advise the jury about what they must find for the relevant doctrine(s) to apply. Charges are often drafted by judicial committees or bar associations and reflect settled legal principles in clear, neutral, and legally accurate terms. Attorneys often review pattern charges to anticipate how a jury might be instructed at trial, which helps an attorney assess the strength of a client's case, prepare discovery requests, develop themes for trial, and structure closing arguments.

4) It was reasonably practicable for the defendant to either prevent the children's access or render the artificial condition safe without obstructing its purpose; and
5) The defendant failed to exercise reasonable care to eliminate the danger or otherwise to protect the children.

You should deliberate carefully and apply these instructions fairly and impartially to the facts as you determine them to be.

Exercise 1

1. **Assess whether the customer can establish each element of the attractive nuisance doctrine.**

2. **Prepare a list of questions for your next meeting with Mr. Martinelli. What additional information would you like to know to assess whether Drop or Do might be liable for Sam's injuries under the attractive nuisance doctrine?**

____

____

____

____

____

1.3 Legal Authority—Attractive Nuisance Continued

While you continue your research, you find the following case with facts similar to the potential case against Drop or Do:

Morningstar v. Maynard
798 N.E.2d 920 (Ind.App. 2003)

MATHIAS, Judge.

Jayla Morningstar ("Jayla") and Robert Mendez, individually and as next friends of Corbin Mendez ("Corbin"), filed a tort claim against Brian and Elizabeth Maynard in Adams Circuit Court. The trial court granted summary judgment in favor of the Maynards. The Plaintiffs appeal, raising the issue of whether the doctrine of attractive nuisance may be asserted in this case. Concluding as a matter of law that the plaintiffs cannot prevail on the theory of attractive nuisance, we affirm.

FACTS AND PROCEDURAL HISTORY

In the spring of 2000, the Maynards bought a fourteen-foot circular trampoline and installed it at their home. On October 4, 2001, Jayla, and her seven-year-old son Corbin, went to visit her father, who lived near the Maynards. While there, Corbin asked and received permission from his step-grandmother, Jenny Morningstar ("Jenny"), to go outside with his uncle, ten-year-old Perry Morningstar ("Perry"), to play on the Maynards' trampoline. Because Brian was away—due to his sister's death—and Elizabeth was in Ohio on work-related matters, the Maynards were not home while Corbin and Perry were using their trampoline.

Jenny could see Corbin and Perry, as well as two other neighbor children, jumping and playing on the trampoline. Appellee's App. p. 4. Shortly thereafter, Jenny heard Corbin crying, looked out her window, and saw him on the ground near the trampoline. Allegedly, all four children simultaneously were jumping on the trampoline; as a result, Corbin was catapulted from the trampoline and fell to the ground, causing injury.

Through the trampoline's owner's manual and expert deposition testimony, the Plaintiffs submitted evidence indicating that it is not safe for more than one person to jump on the trampoline at the same time and that many backyard trampoline-related injuries occur when there are multiple users bouncing at the same time. The Plaintiffs further allege that the Maynards had constructive knowledge of this danger, knew or should have known that neighborhood children might use their trampoline without permission, and did not take reasonable steps to prevent injury.

The Maynards moved to dismiss the Plaintiffs' claims by way of summary judgment. The trial court granted the Maynards' motion, and the Plaintiffs now appeal.

DISCUSSION AND DECISION

***

The attractive nuisance doctrine recognizes that a child may be incapable of understanding and appreciating all of the possible dangers that may be encountered in trespassing. [*Kelly v. Ladywood Apartments,* 622 N.E.2d 1044, 1048 (Ind.Ct.App.1993)] (citing 62 Am.Jur.2d Premises Liability §§ 270, 273 (1990)).

***

The policy reasons behind the attractive nuisance doctrine include the consideration that children may not be mature enough to understand the dangers associated with trespassing and the latent dangers associated with the objects in question. *See Kelly*, 622 N.E.2d at 1049. *Kelly* stated:

> [The child] was brought to the hill by his father and supervised by his father. Under the attractive nuisance doctrine, the trespassing child must have failed, because of his youth, to discover the condition or realize the danger involved in going on to the defendant's property. 62 Am.Jur.2d Premises Liability § 326 (1990). As an adult, [the child's] father, not [the landowner], is charged with the care of his son and with understanding and appreciating the possible danger . . . As a matter of law, the presence of Kelly's father precludes the application of the attractive nuisance doctrine.
>
> *Id.*

In the case at bar, Jenny, as Corbin's supervising step-grandmother, assumed the responsibility of understanding the dangers involved when she gave Corbin permission to use the Maynards' trampoline and witnessed Corbin and the other children jumping on the trampoline before Corbin's injury. Thus, as with Kelly, the permission of Corbin's supervising adult—who is deemed capable of and responsible for understanding the dangers of trespassing and latent conditions—precludes the applicability of the doctrine of attractive nuisance.

CONCLUSION

The doctrine of attractive nuisance is inapplicable to the case at bar.

Affirmed.

Exercise 2

1. **How are the facts of *Morningstar v. Maynard* similar to the facts of your current case? How are they different?**

2. **How does the court's reasoning in *Morningstar v. Maynard* influence your assessment of whether Drop or Do might be liable for Sam's injuries under the attractive nuisance doctrine?**

3. **The parties disagree about whether the keys for the maintenance cart were in the ignition of the cart or in a cubby hole near the ignition. Is your assessment of the claim impacted by where the keys were stored?**

4. **What is the significance of the fact that Drop or Do has an area for kids inside the laundromat?**

5. **Does your assessment change if Drop or Do posted signs throughout the laundromat warning parents to watch their children? What if the signs warn parents to keep their children inside at all times?**

6. **Does your assessment change if children routinely play outside Drop or Do? If Drop or Do installed a play structure immediately outside the laundromat?**

7. **Does your assessment change if the maintenance cart had visible notices that the cart was "For Employees Only?" What if the sign included warnings that the cart was dangerous?**

____

____

____

1.4 Legal Authority—Duty to Invitees

Even if the customer cannot establish that the attractive nuisance doctrine applies, you expect the customer to argue that Drop or Do is liable for Sam's injuries under a different legal theory.[2] Specifically, you expect the customer to argue that Drop or Do owed a heightened duty of care to customers as invitees upon the property, and it breached that duty when it left the maintenance cart outside the store where any customer could access it.

The Sunport Pattern Jury Instructions define the duty of care owed by a business owner to an invitee as follows:

> "Invitees" include business visitors, who are persons invited to enter or remain on the land for a purpose connected to business dealings of the owner.
>
> The duty of care owed to an invitee includes a duty to maintain safe premises. This includes a duty to regularly inspect the property for hazards and to repair or eliminate dangerous conditions.
>
> To establish that the defendant breached the duty of care to invitees, the plaintiff must prove the following by a preponderance of the evidence:
>
> 1) That the defendant owned, occupied, or controlled the premises;
> 2) That the plaintiff was an invitee at the time of the incident;
> 3) That there was a concealed condition on the land that presented an unreasonable risk of harm to invitees;
> 4) That the defendant knew or, through reasonable inspection, should have known about the dangerous condition; and
> 5) That the defendant failed to use ordinary care to maintain the premises in a safe condition or failed to adequately warn the plaintiff of the danger.

2. **Pleading in the Alternative.** Pleading in the alternative is a legal strategy that allows a party to present multiple legal theories or claims in a single complaint, even if those claims are logically inconsistent with each other. Courts generally permit this practice (*See* Federal Rule of Civil Procedure 8(d)(2)) because it allows parties to assert all possible claims and preserves a party's options when the facts and evidence are not yet developed. The practice also promotes judicial efficiency because it allows courts to consider which legal theory, if any, is supported by the evidence.

Exercise 3

1. **How might Ms. Malone argue that Drop or Do breached a duty of care to her and her sons?**

2. **How would you respond to Malone's arguments?**

1.5 Legal Authority—Comparative Fault

Even if you believe you have a strong case and Malone will be unable to establish the *prima facie* elements of negligence, you want to prepare the best possible arguments in case the jury disagrees with you. Therefore, you research whether Drop or Do has any defenses[3] if Malone establishes her *prima facie* case. One possible defense is comparative fault.

The Sunport Civil Pattern Jury Charge on comparative fault is as follows:

> Under the principle of comparative fault, if a plaintiff's own negligence played a role in causing their harm, then the amount of damages they recover should be reduced in proportion to their degree of fault.
>
> To establish that the plaintiff was comparatively at fault, the defendant must prove:
>
> 1) The plaintiff had a duty to use reasonable care for their own safety;
> 2) The plaintiff failed to exercise that reasonable care; and
> 3) The plaintiff's failure to use reasonable care contributed to their injury.
>
> If you determine that both the defendant and the plaintiff were negligent, then you must decide the percentage of fault attributable to each party. If the plaintiff was partially at fault, then you must reduce any damages awarded in proportion to their percentage of fault.

The jury instruction about the standard of care applicable to children is as follows:

> A child is not held to the same standard of care as an adult. Instead, a child is required to exercise the degree of care that would ordinarily be exercised by a child of the same age, intelligence, and experience under similar circumstances. A child is not expected to possess the same judgment, knowledge, or experience as an adult.
>
> However, if you find that the child was engaged in an activity that is normally undertaken only by adults and requires adult skill, judgment, or experience, then the child is held to the same standard of care as an adult engaged in that activity.

3. See Chapter 1, footnote 6, for the definition of an affirmative defense. In this context, you might argue that, even if Ms. Malone can establish the *prima facie* elements of negligence, Drop or Do should not be liable for the full extent of Sam's injuries because Sam was also negligent, which caused or contributed to his injuries.

Exercise 4

1. **What standard of care applies to determine whether Sam acted negligently under the circumstances?**

2. **If Sam is held to the standard of care of a child of the same age, intelligence, and experience under similar circumstances, then did he breach that duty of care?**

Exercise 5

1. **Prepare a memorandum for Martinelli. Summarize your legal conclusions and assessments about his potential liability. Make a recommendation based on your findings and the client's goals.**

Common Carriers and Innkeepers: *Redfearn v. Starr Resorts*

You are in-house counsel for Starr Resorts, a hotel chain that operates luxury hotels and resorts around the country. One of Starr's properties is located just outside the city of Eastvale in the mountainous area of Bear Creek. Bear Creek Lodge is a luxury ski resort that caters to an exclusive clientele.

During the Christmas season, Bear Creek hosts "Winter Wonderland," an attraction featuring ice sculptures, toboggan rides, and an arts and crafts fair where world-renowned artists sell their work. There is also a food hall with food, drinks, and alcohol available for purchase. Guests from around the world visit Bear Creek Lodge during Winter Wonderland because there are activities suited for every guest.

Yesterday, the hotel manager sent you a copy of a complaint that had recently been filed against Bear Creek Lodge. Relevant excerpts from the complaint are set forth below.

2.1 Complaint

IN THE DISTRICT COURT FOR EASTVALE COUNTY

Jacqueline Redfearn, **Plaintiff,**	))	**COUNTY COURT AT LAW No. 4**
	)	
v.	)	
	)	
Bear Creek Lodge, **Defendant.**	))	

PLAINTIFF'S ORIGINAL PETITION

COMES NOW, Plaintiff Jacqueline Redfearn ("Ms. Redfearn" or "Plaintiff") and files this, her Original Petition against Defendant Bear Creek Lodge ("Bear Creek" or "Defendant"). In support, thereof Plaintiff respectfully shows the Court as follows:

1. On or about December 2, Plaintiff was a guest at Defendant's property. Plaintiff and her boyfriend rode the Winter Wonderland toboggan ride. Lodge represented that the ride was safe for any guest aged "10 & older."
2. As Plaintiff and her boyfriend were tobogganing down the Winter Wonderland hill, their toboggan suddenly and without warning lurched off the path, hit a large,

unexpected bump, and landed with a startling thump. Plaintiff was thrown several inches off the toboggan and fell to the ground.

3. The shock caused Plaintiff to suffer cardiac arrest. Fortunately, Plaintiff's boyfriend, Dr. Eric Greene, is a pulmonary specialist, and he immediately began to perform CPR.
4. Defendant's employee notified security and the medical team of the emergency. Security personnel and an on-duty nurse, Janice Williams, responded to the incident. Nurse Williams brought a medical kit containing basic first aid supplies.
5. When Nurse Williams arrived, Dr. Greene asked her for an intubation kit. Nurse Williams indicated that, while the Lodge had a kit in its medical tent, Lodge policy prohibited medical personnel from using intubation kits unless qualified to use them. Nurse Williams had not been trained to use intubation kits, so she had left it in the medical tent.
6. Dr. Greene continued to perform CPR while waiting for the ambulance to arrive. After several minutes, an ambulance and EMT unit arrived at the scene. With the help of Dr. Green, an EMT technician intubated Plaintiff, who immediately regained a pulse.

COUNT I—NEGLIGENCE

7. As a resort hotel, Defendant Lodge qualifies as an "innkeeper" under Sunport statutes, and Defendant owes a duty to provide medical care to its patrons.
8. Defendant Lodge breached this duty when it failed to provide the equipment and skilled personnel necessary to intubate Plaintiff.
9. Defendant Lodge also breached a voluntarily assumed duty to provide reasonable medical care by failing to provide Dr. Greene the intubation kit he requested. The kit was on site and available to Nurse Williams, but she refused to bring it to the scene.
10. As an actual and proximate result of Defendant Lodge's negligence, Plaintiff suffered damages in an amount to be determined at trial. Plaintiff would not have sustained injuries but for the Lodge's failure to provide proper medical equipment, and the failure to provide such equipment foreseeably led to Ms. Redfearn's injuries.

***

2.2 Incident Report

With a property as large as Bear Creek Lodge, it is nearly impossible for you to be informed of every incident that occurs involving the Lodge's guests. Therefore, you implemented an elaborate reporting and record-keeping system. If an incident escalates to litigation, then you are confident there will be sufficient records to enable you to quickly understand and evaluate the Lodge's potential exposure to liability.

You checked the Lodge's internal system and found the following incident report describing the events described in Ms. Redfearn's petition:

Bear Creek Lodge

INCIDENT REPORT

INCIDENT NO. **01-642** **Date: December 2**

Resort Location: **Winter Wonderland Toboggan Ride**

Reporting Employee(s): **Hugh Dennis, ride operator**
Darian Knox, security officer
Janice Williams, on-duty nurse

SUMMARY

(by Hugh Dennis): Jackie Redfearn, approx. 60 years old, approached the Winter Wonderland toboggan ride with her boyfriend, Eric Greene. Both guests were visibly intoxicated, and I suggested they wait to ride the toboggan until they were in better shape to stomach its twists and turns. Ms. Redfearn became belligerent and screamed at me, "Your sign says it's safe for people 10 and older. If a 10-year-old can ride this silly thing, then there is no reason we can't. We're 60 for God's sake!"

The guests paid for the tickets and signed the electronic waiver. As soon as they sat on the toboggan, Ms. Redfearn began bouncing up and down saying, "Let's make this silly kid's ride exciting. It's making me feel like a kid again!" I warned Ms. Redfearn not to bounce once they started down the hill because it would make it difficult to stay on the toboggan. Dr. Greene urged her to calm down so they could "get down this hill in one piece." As soon as I pushed the toboggan to start their downhill descent, Ms. Redfearn began bouncing up and down again.

As they reached the hairpin curve, I shouted, "Now sit still for this turn!" Ms. Redfearn either didn't hear me or just ignored me because she kept bouncing. As they rounded the curve, I saw Ms. Redfearn bounce pretty high into the air and slam back down. The next thing I knew, Dr. Greene was shouting, "Help! She's having a heart attack. Call an ambulance!"

I immediately pushed the emergency call button at the ride station. Dr. Greene was already performing CPR on Ms. Redfearn. Someone from the Security Command Post called an ambulance and contacted the medical station. The station is located just around the corner from the Winter Wonderland toboggan ride, and immediately inside the main resort building. It only took Nurse Williams a minute or two to get to us.

(by Janice Williams): On December 2, at about 4:30pm, I received a radio call from the Security Command Post indicating that a guest was in medical need and might be having a heart attack at the Winter Wonderland toboggan ride station. I immediately grabbed my Ambu-bag, oxygen and an airway kit and took a snowmobile to the scene. About 90 seconds passed from the moment I received the call to the moment I arrived to Ms. Redfearn.

At that point, the patient's boyfriend saw me. He said he was a pulmonary specialist, and he yelled at me to give him the intubation kit. I told him I didn't have one with me because I wasn't qualified to use one. But I connected the Ambu-bag to oxygen and placed it over Ms. Redfearn's face while Dr. Greene was doing chest compressions. Dr. Greene and I both noted that air was entering Ms. Redfearn's respiratory system, and she was being adequately oxygenated. Dr. Greene said, "This will keep her in decent shape until the EMTs can get here."

The EMT technician who arrived on the scene was immediately able to intubate Ms. Redfearn. After the intubation, Ms. Redfearn regained a pulse and her color improved. The EMTs then loaded her into the ambulance and headed to the hospital.

I called the hospital later that afternoon and received a call back from Dr. Greene. He thanked me for my quick help and said Ms. Redfearn was going to be "just fine."

Exercise 1

1. What are the primary differences between the Plaintiff's account of the incident as set forth in the Complaint, and the employees' account of the incident as set forth in the Incident Report?

2. How will those differences impact Bear Creek Lodge's potential liability?

2.3 Legal Authority—Innkeepers & Duty to Act

Your initial theory of the case is that Ms. Redfearn will be unable to establish a *prima facie* case for negligence because Bear Creek Lodge was not responsible for Ms. Redfearn's medical emergency. Although there are risks associated with tobogganing, they do not typically include cardiac arrest, which was more likely caused by Ms. Redfearn's personal circumstances and own actions.

During your next team meeting, you confidently discuss the case with your colleagues. One colleague expresses concern that, as alleged in the complaint, innkeepers owe a heightened duty of care to guests. Your colleague notes that this heightened duty may even include a duty to render first aid to injured guests. Thus, even if a court finds that Bear Creek Lodge was not negligent in maintaining or operating the ride (i.e., the Lodge did not cause Ms. Redfearn's injuries), the Lodge might nevertheless be liable because it breached its duty to render aid after it learned a guest was injured.

Another colleague suggests the Lodge might be liable because, once Lodge employees rendered aid, the Lodge assumed a duty to render *capable* care. Your colleague argues that the Lodge may have assumed a duty to render aid because it employed a nurse and stocked a medical station with supplies. Your colleague is concerned that, because the medical station had an intubation kit, the Lodge might have assumed a duty to use it or allow a qualified professional to access the kit if necessary to render first aid. Moreover, because the Lodge employed a medical professional, the Lodge may have assumed a duty to render capable and thorough care.

You refer to a practice manual, *Tort Remedies and Risks in Sunport*, to evaluate your colleagues' concerns.

INNKEEPER LIABILITY

Under the law, an innkeeper owes a heightened duty of care to its guests due to the special relationship between the parties. An innkeeper must exercise reasonable care to protect guests from foreseeable dangers, including by addressing dangerous conditions that may cause injury to guests. An innkeeper is generally not liable for injuries caused by open and obvious dangers.

***

By nature of their "special relationship" with guests, common carriers and innkeepers have a duty to render first aid to a guest if the entity knows or has reason to know a guest is injured. In such cases, the entity should render first aid to the patron until the patron can receive care from medical professionals.

DUTY TO RENDER AID

Generally, a bystander has no duty to provide affirmative aid to an injured person, even if the bystander has the capacity and resources to help. Yet Sunport courts have long held that, even if an actor does not have a duty to render aid to an injured party, the actor may be subject to liability if the actor *voluntarily* renders assistance and exacerbates the injured party's harm. Specifically, if one voluntarily renders aid, then the actor may be liable for injuries caused by the actor's failure to exercise reasonable care in securing the safety of the injured party. An actor may also be liable if the actor discontinues aid and by so doing he leaves the injured party in a worse position than when the actor began to render aid.

***

While you concede that Bear Creek Lodge likely had a duty to render aid, you do not believe Bear Creek Lodge has a duty to provide all medical equipment that might be needed by a guest during a medical emergency. Nor do you believe that Bear Creek Lodge must provide trained personnel in every foreseeable medical intervention. After all, there is limited space at the Winter Wonderland venue, and the medical tent is relatively small. Bear Creek Lodge has a limited medical budget for the event and does not employ physicians or EMTs.

You research the issue further and find the following excerpt from a precedential case:

[T]he duty "to take reasonable action . . . to give . . . first aid" in times of emergency requires only that carriers, innkeepers and landowners procure appropriate medical care as soon as the need for such care becomes apparent and provide such first aid prior to the arrival of qualified assistance as the carrier's, innkeeper's or landowner's employees are reasonably capable of giving. Clearly, the duty . . . does not extend to providing all medical care that the carrier or innkeeper could reasonably foresee might be needed by a patron. . . . The defendant . . . will seldom be required to do more than give such first aid as he reasonably can, and take reasonable steps to turn the sick man over to a physician, or to those who will look after him and see that medical assistance is obtained." *Lundy v. Adamar of New Jersey, Inc.*, 34 F.3d 1173 (C.A.3 (N.J.), 1994).

Exercise 2

Using the above sources of law, prepare an argument for Bear Creek Lodge and for Ms. Redfearn to support their respective positions on whether Bear Creek Lodge breached a duty of care owed to Ms. Redfearn.

1. Bear Creek Lodge's argument that it did not breach a duty of care:

____

____

2. Ms. Redfearn's argument that Bear Creek Lodge breached a duty of care:

2.4 Legal Authority—Good Samaritan Statute

Another colleague argues that Sunport's Good Samaritan statute may protect the Lodge.

Sunport Revised Statutes
Title 2A:15A-1. Civil immunity for emergency care

An individual, including a person licensed to practice any method of treatment of human ailments, disease, injury, deformity, mental or physical condition, or licensed to render services ancillary thereto, who in good faith renders emergency care at the scene of an accident or emergency to the victim or victims therefor, shall not be liable for any civil damages as a result of any acts or omissions by such person in rendering the emergency care.

***

Comment: The public policy goals advanced by this provision, sometimes referred to as the "Good Samaritan Statute," are to promote societal welfare, encourage altruism, and mitigate potential barriers to offering aid in emergency situations. The provision recognizes that actors may hesitate to render aid during an emergency for fear their good-faith actions might subject them to civil liability, and immunity encourages more individuals to provide critical help until emergency personnel can respond. Timely intervention is often critical, and protecting individuals who render aid advances positive health outcomes.

The provisions above do not apply to persons or entities with a preexisting duty to provide aid given their special relationship with the injured party.

Exercise 3

1. **Do you believe the provisions above minimize the risk of liability for the Lodge? Why or why not?**

____

____

____

2.5 Legal Authority—Express Assumption of the Risk

While you continue your research about the case, you reread the Incident Report and notice the following sentence: "The guests paid for the tickets and signed the electronic waiver." You excitedly look through your record-keeping system and find the waiver signed by Ms. Redfearn:

Winter Wonderland Toboggan Ride

RULES AND RELEASE

Welcome to the Winter Wonderland Toboggan Ride! Experience the thrill of our toboggan rides—it's snow joke! Don't get left out in the cold; join us for a sled-tacular adventure that will sleigh your expectations. Whether you're a seasoned pro or a first-time slider, we guarantee you'll have snow much fun. So, bundle up and let's make every moment extraordinary!

To ensure a fun and accident-free experience, please remember the following rules:

- √ Avoid areas with obstacles like trees, rocks, or fences.
- √ Ensure the path doesn't lead toward roads, parking lots, or bodies of water.
- √ Wear appropriate winter gear, including gloves and sturdy boots with good traction.
- √ Wear a helmet for safety.
- √ Always ride feet-first; never go down head-first.
- √ Keep all body parts inside the toboggan during the ride.
- √ Do not bounce or jostle the sled.
- √ Maintain a safe distance between your toboggan and others to prevent collisions.
- √ After completing your ride, promptly clear the track to make way for others.
- √ Warn inattentive pedestrians by calling out or using the bell.
- √ Avoid alcohol or drugs before and during tobogganing as they impair judgment and reaction times.
- √ Ensure children are accompanied by adults and can understand and follow the rules.

By following these guidelines, you can enjoy a safe and thrilling tobogganing experience:

I have read and reviewed the Winter Wonderland Rules and agree to comply with all recommendations.

Date: December 2

Full Name: Jacqueline Redfearn

Jacqueline Redfearn

SIGN HERE

In consideration of being permitted to participate in the toboggan ride, I hereby release, waive, discharge, and covenant not to sue Starr Resorts, its officers, employees, agents, and affiliates (collectively referred to as "the Releasees") from any and all liability, claims, demands, actions, or causes of action arising out of or related to any loss, damage, injury, or death that may be sustained by me, or to any property belonging to me, whether caused by the negligence of the Releasees or otherwise, while participating in the toboggan ride or any activities related thereto.

You are encouraged that Ms. Redfearn signed a waiver. Yet you are surprised to see the language releasing the Lodge from liability is in small font and placed after the rules and guest signature. You know this does not comport with Starr Resorts principles regarding waivers and releases. You find an internal memorandum regarding releases:

MEMORANDUM

To: Starr Resorts Legal Department

From: General Counsel

Re: Drafting Waivers and Releases of Liability

Date: September 5, 2018

The following principles ensure that waivers and releases are fully enforceable and protect the corporation from frivolous claims. Although contractual exculpatory clauses are not prohibited by law, they are strictly construed against the drafter, so the provisions must be carefully and thoughtfully drafted before they are presented to guests.

Guests should sign a release of liability for any activity that involves a risk of injury. To ensure enforceability, the form must include the following sections:

- **Acknowledgment of Risk**: The release must include an acknowledgment of risks that: 1) identifies the primary risks of the particular activity*; and 2) expressly notes that the guest agrees to voluntarily participate in and assume identified risks.

  Some courts have refused to enforce provisions that do not expressly name the "inherent risks" of an activity; therefore, Legal Department personnel should be over- rather than under-inclusive when identifying possible risks.

- **Release of Liability**: The release must include the following language:

  I hereby release, waive, discharge, and covenant not to sue Starr Resorts, its officers, employees, agents, and affiliates (collectively referred to as "the Releasees") from any and all liability, claims, demands, actions, or causes of action arising out of or related to any loss, damage, injury, or death that may be sustained by me, or to any property belonging to me, whether caused by the negligence of the Releasees or otherwise, while participating in [the activity] or any activities related thereto.

  Courts may invalidate a waiver if it is not clear, unambiguous, unmistakable, and conspicuous. The exculpatory language must effectively notify a party that he or she is releasing the other party from claims arising from the other party's own negligence.

- **Consent for Medical Treatment**: The guest must consent to receive medical treatment deemed necessary if the guest is injured or requires medical attention, and the guest must consent to pay related expenses and waive any claim for injuries related to the medical treatment.

These policies promote the enforceability of contractual waivers and minimize Starr Resort's exposure to legal liability. It is critical to ensure that the documents comply with these policies. Courts are suspicious of waivers and releases, especially if the plaintiff was a guest in a hospitality context, as it might appear that the Starr Resort is avoiding its legal obligation to protect guests. It must be clear that guests knowingly and voluntarily participated in the designated activity despite warnings about dangers and potential legal implications.

Exercise 4

1. **Does the Winter Wonderland waiver comply with the Starr Resorts' principles set forth in the memorandum above? Why or why not?**

2. If you answered "no" to Question 1 above, then how do any of the deficiencies you identified impact the potential enforceability of the waiver in the event of litigation?

3. If you answered "no" to Question 1 above, then how would you revise the waiver to ensure it complies with Starr Resorts' internal policies and is enforceable?

4. Considering all the evidence in the case, what advice will you offer your client with respect to Ms. Redfearn's claims? Evaluate the strength of Ms. Redfearn's claims and any other considerations that might influence the Lodge's response.

2.6 Settlement Offer

You receive the following letter from Ms. Redfearn's attorney:

Greene & Blackstone Attorneys at Law

BEAR CREEK, SUNPORT
GPLAW.COM

February 12

VIA EMAIL AND CERTIFIED MAIL

General Counsel
Starr Resorts, LLC
d/b/a Bear Creek Lodge

Re: Injury to Jackie Redfearn at Bear Creek Lodge—Settlement Demand

Dear Counsel:

I represent Ms. Jackie Redfearn, who sustained serious injuries while participating in the Winter Wonderland Toboggan Ride at your Bear Creek Lodge property. Ms. Redfearn previously filed a complaint outlining her legal arguments. This letter proposes a resolution of the matter.

As a direct result of the Lodge's negligence, Ms. Redfearn incurred substantial medical expenses, experienced profound pain and trauma, and continues to suffer emotional distress. To resolve this matter before trial, we demand payment in the amount of **$145,000**, which accounts for:

- Past and anticipated medical expenses,
- Pain and suffering,
- Emotional distress,
- Missed employment, and
- Costs and related financial consequences, including attorneys' fees.

The proposed settlement is reasonable given the extent of Ms. Redfearn's injuries. We are prepared to provide supporting documentation during settlement discussions.

We are confident that, given Bear Creek Lodge's stated commitment to guest safety, your client is eager to resolve the case without the consequences of the public trial. Therefore, if the terms are acceptable, then Ms. Redfearn is willing to execute a settlement agreement and release, including standard confidentiality and no-fault provisions.

Please respond to this demand no later than February 26. If we do not receive a response by that date, we will proceed with discovery.

Sincerely,

Nadia Greene

Nadia Greene, Attorney at Law
Greene & Blackstone
Attorney for Jackie Redfearn

Exercise 5

1. **Do you believe Starr Resorts should accept the settlement offer? Explain.**

Rescuers/Firefighters Rule: *Gilmore v. J.S. Bar & Grill*

You are a member of City Women Network, a professional women's networking group that convenes monthly over coffee to network, share experiences, and explore opportunities to work together across members' respective careers. At last week's meeting, you met Shari Gilmore, who asked you for advice about an incident that occurred a few weeks ago. You set up a meeting to discuss her concerns.

3.1 Background

Officer Gilmore mentioned that the incident made the news. Before the meeting with the potential client, you find and review the related news coverage, including the following article:

Eastvale Gazette

EASTVALE POLICE OFFICER INVOLVED IN DUST-UP AT J.S. BAR & GRILL

On May 16, friendly soccer rivalries turned violent as intoxicated patrons began to brawl over a contentious call. On many a weekend morning, patrons of J.S. Bar & Grill gather to watch soccer matches broadcast from Europe. On most occasions, patrons watch the matches in good spirits, with competitive banter rarely going beyond an occasional tossed beer, aggressive jab in the ribs, or overly enthusiastic pat on the back.

On May 16, however, a heated argument broke out after a controversial call during a game. Several patrons who had already been at the bar for several hours became aggressive, and the situation escalated into what one patron called an "all-out brawl." Several patrons sustained minor injuries. Also injured was Eastvale Police Officer Shari Gilmore. When Officer Gilmore arrived at the scene, one or more people attacked her. Officer Gilmore was repeatedly struck, and she sustained head and neck injuries.

Officers arrested several patrons. The bar owner, Martin Melman, was not available for comment.

During your meeting with Officer Gilmore, you asked how she wanted to respond. She indicated:

Part of me wants to let it go because I'm so embarrassed that I got stuck in the middle of such a crazy situation. But I'm also pretty shaken and frankly, I'm furious. This wasn't the first time I had to go to that bar to stop crazed patrons. Each time, I told Marty [the

> owner of J.S. Bar & Grill] that he was bringing this on himself. I mean, what does he expect when he opens the bar at 8 A.M. and starts serving beer? Patrons drink all day long while they get more and more upset about their precious teams, and you can imagine the scene when the games end in the late afternoon. I told him that he was going to get himself in trouble and someone was going to get seriously hurt. I just didn't expect it to be me.
>
> Also, the women in blue need to protect each other. I want to send a message that bar owners can't keep putting law enforcement at risk because they want to make some extra money.

3.2 Legal Authority—Rescuer Doctrine

Officer Gilmore told you that she did receive compensation under Sunport's workers' compensation system because she was injured on the job, but you know that does not necessarily bar her from pursuing a claim against J.S. Bar & Grill.[4]

You believe the "Rescuer Doctrine" might allow Officer Gilmore to sue the bar directly.

You find the following case that applies the doctrine:

> **Garcia v. Colorado Cab Company LLC**
> 467 P.3d 302 (Colo. 2020)
>
> ***
>
> **I. FACTS AND PROCEDURAL HISTORY**
>
> A driver for Colorado Cab Company LLC ("Colorado Cab") picked up an intoxicated Curt Glinton and one of Glinton's friends. After stopping at their destination, the driver told Glinton the total fare. Glinton became upset, started yelling at the driver, and eventually grabbed and punched the driver from behind.

---

4. **What is Workers' Compensation?** Employers create a workers' compensation system to compensate employees who are injured on the job or suffer work-related illnesses. It ensures workers receive prompt and certain relief if they sustain an injury in the course and scope of employment.

While workers' compensation is generally an employee's exclusive remedy against her employer (here, the police department or city), it does not bar recovery against third parties who are responsible for causing an injury to the employee (here, J.S. Bar & Grill). Yet Ms. Gilmore cannot receive "double compensation" for the same losses. For example, if Ms. Gilmore already received compensation for medical expenses, then she cannot seek those damages against the bar. Moreover, depending on the terms of Officer Gilmore's benefits, the entity or insurer that paid the benefits may seek reimbursement if Ms. Gilmore receives damages from the bar.

. . .[Jose Garcia] heard the driver screaming for help. Garcia ran to the cab and, through the cab's open driver's-side door, told Glinton to stop. Glinton shifted his aggression to Garcia, telling him to "mind his own business." This gave the driver the chance to exit the vehicle. Glinton also exited the vehicle, escalated his aggression toward Garcia, and began to throw punches at Garcia. Garcia was then hit over the head in the melee, causing him to fall to the ground.

Glinton then entered the driver's seat of the still-running cab and started driving. He hit the still-down Garcia once with the cab, then backed up and again ran Garcia over. As a result, Garcia suffered several severe injuries.

Garcia filed a negligence action against Colorado Cab, arguing that Colorado Cab had knowledge of forty-four passenger attacks on its drivers in the previous three years but had failed to install partitions or security cameras in its cabs. In asserting his claim, Garcia relied on the rescue doctrine. He argued that he was injured while rescuing the driver, who was owed a duty by Colorado Cab, meaning it also owed a duty to him . . .

***

B. The Rescue Doctrine

The rescue doctrine traces back to then-Judge Cardozo's opinion in [*Wagner v. Int'l Ry. Co.*, 232 N.Y. 176, 133 N.E. 437, 437 (1921)]. In *Wagner*, the plaintiff and his cousin boarded a packed train. Sometime after the train began moving, the cousin was thrown from it after the conductor failed to close the train's doors. *Id.* The plaintiff exited the train to search for his cousin underneath a nearby bridge, and he ultimately fell off the bridge's trestle. *Id.* On the relationship among the law, human instinct, and rescuers, the court recognized that people act instinctively to help another in peril:

> Danger invites rescue. The cry of distress is the summons to relief. The law does not ignore these reactions of the mind in tracing conduct to consequences. It recognizes them as normal. It places their effects within the range of the natural and probable. The wrong that imperils life is a wrong to the imperiled victim; it is a wrong also to his rescuer . . . . The risk of rescue, if only it be not wanton, is born of the occasion. The emergency begets the man. The wrongdoer may not have foreseen the coming of a deliverer. He is accountable as if he had.

Id. at 437-48.

***

[T]he relevant case law and the rescue doctrine's purpose illustrate that there are three important factors in assessing whether a plaintiff can qualify as a rescuer: (1) the plaintiff's purpose in acting, (2) the plaintiff's reasonable belief that someone was in imminent peril, and (3) the utility of the plaintiff's conduct.

First, a plaintiff's purpose in acting is critical for the rescue doctrine. After all, the rescue doctrine seeks to protect only those who genuinely act on the instinct to help.

This is what courts in cases like *Barnes* have emphasized: A plaintiff who happens to get injured while investigating the scene of an accident cannot sue under the rescue doctrine. [*See Barnes v. Geiger*, 15 Mass. App. Ct. 365, 446 N.E.2d 78, 82 (1983)]. ("[A] claimant's purpose must be more than investigatory.") Instead, a plaintiff must actually intend to aid or rescue.

Second, this intent must be based on a reasonable belief that someone is in imminent peril. The rescue doctrine is not designed to protect those who respond to obviously benign situations. For example, a baby's cry alone is not evidence of imminent peril, *see* [*Connelly v. Redman Development Corp.*, 533 P.2d 53, 55 (Colo. App. 1975)]; neither is a car crash alone evidence that the crash's victim is in imminent peril when that victim is engaging in casual conversation, *see* [*Maloney v. Jussel*, 125 Colo. 125, 241 P.2d 862, 867 (1952)]. But the presence or absence of danger is not always certain; a person may genuinely and reasonably believe that a third party is in imminent peril even when that is not the case. Therefore, we conclude that a plaintiff must have reasonably believed that someone was in imminent peril to qualify as a rescuer.

Third, the plaintiff's action must have some utility; it must stand a chance at substantially helping the person(s) in peril. Intent to rescue alone is not enough because the rescue doctrine was created for those who actually effectuate their intent to help, not for those who claim to want to help but instead do nothing. Thus, a plaintiff's conduct must be reasonably calculated to prevent or alleviate the imminent peril. Accordingly, a mere warning or observation will not suffice because calling attention to incoming danger is vastly different from attempting to thwart or eliminate imminent danger. *See Schwartzman v. Del. Coach Co.*, 264 A.2d 519, 520 (Del. Super. Ct. 1970) (holding that the plaintiff was not a rescuer because he gave "only a verbal warning" that a car crash was about to occur).

Synthesizing these principles, we hold that for a person to qualify as a rescuer under the rescue doctrine, he must satisfy a three-pronged test: He must have (1) intended to aid or rescue a person whom he, (2) reasonably believed was in imminent peril, and (3) acted in such a way that could have reasonably succeeded or did succeed in preventing or alleviating such peril.

***

The record of the case before us evidences that Garcia satisfied this test and thus qualified as a rescuer.

First, Garcia intended to rescue the driver. Garcia testified that when he ran up to the cab, he saw Glinton punching the driver. He could have walked away. Instead, he chose to get involved and, according to his testimony, "went to help" the driver; he stuck his head in the cab and started yelling at Glinton to stop. The only possible explanation for this conduct is that Garcia intended to aid the driver.

Second, it is clear that Garcia reasonably believed that the driver was in imminent peril. Garcia testified that he ran to the cab because he heard the driver yelling, "help me, help me, they're hurting me, they're trying to kill me." And the attack that Garcia saw when he approached the cab confirmed that the driver was, in fact, in imminent peril. As Garcia testified, the driver "could have been murdered" that night.

Last, Garcia succeeded in preventing the driver's imminent peril. He jogged to the cab and, within feet of the violent aggressor, yelled at Glinton to stop. This was not a mere warning to the driver that danger was coming; the danger was imminent, and the driver's best chance at escape was for a bystander to intervene. That is exactly what Garcia did. In other words, Garcia's conduct had real utility in helping the driver and was ultimately successful.

Thus, the record establishes that Garcia satisfied the three-pronged test we are announcing today, meaning Colorado Cab owed a duty to Garcia as a rescuer of the driver if it owed a duty to the driver.

IV. CONCLUSION

For the foregoing reasons, we reverse the judgment of the court of appeals and remand for the court of appeals to address Colorado Cab's remaining issues argued on appeal.

Exercise 1

1. **Based on the three-pronged test outlined in *Garcia*, what must Officer Gilmore show to establish that the Rescuer Doctrine applies to her case?**

2. **Do you believe Officer Gilmore can satisfy the three-pronged test outlined in *Garcia*? Why or why not?**

3.3 Demand Letter

You draft a letter to the attorney for J.S. Bar & Grill, and you assert that the Bar is liable for Officer Gilmore's injuries under the Rescuer Doctrine. A few days later, you receive the following letter:

Pinnacle Law Partners

Eastvale | Sunport

June 5

In Re J.S. Bar & Grill

We represent Martin Melman, owner of J.S. Bar & Grill. We received your letter alleging that J.S. Bar & Grill is liable for injuries Officer Gilmore sustained when she responded to an altercation at the J.S. Bar & Grill on May 16. You assert that J.S. Bar & Grill acted negligently by overserving patrons, who became violent.

From the outset, we assert that this claim will fail because our client cannot bear liability for the intentional or criminal acts of bar patrons.

You also allege that our client's actions were a cause of Officer Gilmore's injuries because it was foreseeable that any altercation among drunken patrons would require "rescue," by way of law enforcement intervention. This claim is clearly barred because Officer Gilmore was acting pursuant to her official duties as a law enforcement officer.

Sunport's "Firefighter's Rule" prevents emergency responders from recovering damages for injuries sustained while responding to the very hazards they are employed to address.

> Firemen, whose occupation by its very nature exposes them to particular risks of harm, "cannot complain of negligence in the creation of the very occasion for [their] engagement" . . . While denominated the fireman's rule, the rule is applicable to policemen as well.

Walters v. Sloan, 20 Cal.3d 199 (1977) (barring recovery for a police officer who was attacked and injured after responding to complaints of disorder at a party of nearly 200 minors who had consumed alcohol, marijuana, and dangerous drugs).

When Officer Gilmore responded to the report of an altercation at J.S. Bar & Grill, she assumed risks inherent to her profession, including a risk of injury from brawling patrons.

> In terms of duty, it may be said there is none owed the fireman to exercise care so as not to require the special services for which he is trained and paid. Probably most fires are attributable to negligence, and in the final analysis the policy decision is that it would be too burdensome to charge all who carelessly cause or fail to prevent fires with the injuries suffered by the expert retained with public funds to deal with those inevitable, although negligently created,

> occurrences. Hence, for that risk, the fireman should receive appropriate compensation from the public he serves both in pay which reflects the hazard and in workmen's compensation benefits for the consequences of the inherent risks of the calling. *Krauth v. Geller*, 157 A.2d 129, 130-131.
>
> Therefore, because Officer Gilmore's claim is barred under the Firefighter's Rule, we expect that you will rescind any threat of litigation against our client.

Exercise 2

1. **Does the Firefighter's Rule bar Officer Gilmore's claim for negligence? Why or why not?**

   ____

   ____

   ____

3.4 Legal Authority—Dram Shop Statute

While you consider whether the Firefighter's Rule bars Officer Gilmore's claim, you conduct further research about other possible claims against the bar. You find the following provision of the Sunport Alcoholic Beverages Code:

> **SUNPORT ALCOHOLIC BEVERAGES CODE**
>
> § 13-365-5955
>
> 2.1. A licensed establishment that sells, furnishes, or serves alcoholic beverages to a person who is visibly intoxicated shall be liable for damages caused by the intoxicated person's subsequent actions if those actions result in injury, death, or property damage to another.
>
> 2.2 A party seeking damages under this statute must establish that the licensed establishment served alcoholic beverages to a visibly intoxicated person and that the service of alcohol was a proximate cause of the damages sustained.
>
> 2.3 Nothing in this section shall be construed to preclude a law enforcement officer, firefighter, emergency medical technician, or other emergency responder from seeking damages under this statute for injuries sustained in the course and scope of their employment, provided that all other elements of liability set forth in this section are satisfied.

Exercise 3

1. **Can Officer Gilmore establish that J.S. Bar & Grill is liable for her injuries under the code provisions above?**

2. **You would like to identify a resolution that allows the parties to settle the case without costly litigation. Identify possible terms for a settlement with J.S. Bar & Grill.**

Primary Assumption of the Risk: *Hamilton v. Everest Heights, Inc.*

You are in-house counsel for Everest Heights, a gymnastics facility featuring an in-ground foam pit and trampoline, a full-length rod ("spring") floor, a rock-climbing wall, and a pre-school area and equipment. Everest Heights offers various recreational classes, sponsors gymnastics teams, and hosts parties and events—most often birthday parties where children of all ages jump about either on the spring floor or in the in-ground foam pit.

4.1 Demand Letter

Today, you received the following demand letter:

Via Certified Mail & Email

Everest Heights
1234 Summit Drive
Peakville, SP 55849

Demand for Compensation—Zoey Hamilton v. Everest Heights

Our firm represents Zoey Hamilton and her parents in connection with the injuries Zoey sustained at Everest Heights on February 17th of last year. This letter serves as a formal demand for compensation due to Everest Heights' negligence.

On the above date, 10-year-old Zoey attended a birthday party at Everest Heights. The children initially gathered in the party room adjacent to the main gymnasium, after which an Everest Heights employee opened the door to allow them to enter the gym. Shortly after entering, Zoey jumped on the spring floor, fell, and sustained a serious arm fracture.

Everest Heights, as a business open to the public, owed a duty of care to maintain its premises in a reasonably safe condition and to protect its patrons—especially young children—from foreseeable harm. Everest Heights breached this duty by failing to provide adequate supervision, failing to warn patrons of the risks associated with the spring floor, and failing to ensure a safe environment for children engaging in gym activities.

To resolve this matter without resorting to litigation, our clients demand compensation in the amount of $30,000 for medical expenses, pain and suffering, and other damages.

We request a response within 10 days of receipt of this letter. If we do not receive a satisfactory resolution by that time, then we will proceed by filing a lawsuit against Everest Heights.

You are a bit dumbfounded. After all, Zoey voluntarily jumped on a spring floor, and it performed exactly the way a spring floor is intended to perform. The spring floor is a large, thickly padded floor that is typically used by gymnasts for floor exercises because it offers more lift on jumps. When guests come to Everest Heights, they are actively seeking to experience the spring floor and other attractions. Zoey attended a birthday party at Everest Heights, presumably with her parents' permission and knowledge, for that exact experience.

Exercise 1

1. **What additional information would you like to know to assess whether the Hamiltons have a viable claim against Everest Heights?**

____

____

2. **Are there any legal issues you would like to research to assess whether the Hamiltons have a viable claim against Everest Heights?**

____

____

____

4.2 Legal Authority—Assumption of the Risk

If the Hamiltons file a complaint for negligence, you plan to file a motion to dismiss[5] the complaint on the grounds that Everest Heights did not breach a duty to Zoey or her parents because Zoey assumed the risks associated with jumping on the spring floor when she attended the birthday party at Everest Heights.

The *Compendium of Sunport Civil Jury Instructions* outlines the doctrine of assumption of the risk as follows:

5. **What is a Motion to Dismiss?** Before a case proceeds to trial, either party may file a motion to dismiss, which asks the court to dismiss specific claims or the entire case based on a procedural or legal defect(s). The moving party may allege that the case must be dismissed because the court does not have authority to hear the case (i.e., the court does not have subject matter jurisdiction over the claims or personal jurisdiction over the parties, the court is an improper venue, and/or the parties did not receive proper notice) or because the suit does not include all indispensable parties. The moving party may also allege that the other party failed to state a claim upon which relief can be granted. The moving party may assert that, even if the facts in the other party's pleadings are true, the party is not entitled to legal relief. In this case, you would allege that, even if Zoey's allegations are factually true, she cannot establish the elements of a *prima facie* case for negligence because Everest Heights did have a duty to protect her under the circumstances.

The doctrine of assumption of the risk is a complicated principle given its applicability as a limitation on duty ***and*** as a defense to negligence.

> As every leading tort treatise has explained, the assumption of risk doctrine long has caused confusion both in definition and application, because the phrase "assumption of risk" traditionally has been used in a number of very different factual settings involving analytically distinct legal concepts. [citation omitted]. Indeed, almost a half-century ago, Justice Frankfurter described the term "assumption of risk" as a classic example of a felicitous phrase, "undiscriminatingly used to express different and sometimes contradictory ideas," and whose uncritical use "bedevils the law." (*Tiller v. Atlantic Coast Line R. Co.* (1943) 318 U.S. 54, 68, 63 S.Ct. 444, 452, 87 L.Ed. 610 (conc. opn. of Frankfurter, J.).)

Knight v. Jewett, 3 Cal.4th 296, 303 (Cal., 1992).

Assumption of risk has meaning in two contexts, sometimes distinguished as "primary" and "secondary" assumption of the risk.

- **Primary assumption of the risk**: In some cases, usually involving sports, the plaintiff may participate in an activity that involves certain inherent risks, and a court may find that the defendant does not owe the plaintiff a duty to protect them from those risks. In such cases, "by virtue of the nature of the activity and the parties' relationship to the activity, the defendant *owes no legal duty* to protect the plaintiff from the particular risk of harm that caused the injury." *Knight v. Jewett*, 3 Cal.4th 296, 314-15 (Cal., 1992) (emphasis added). In other words, the plaintiff cannot establish a *prima facie* case for negligence because the plaintiff cannot establish that the defendant had a duty to protect the plaintiff from risks of harm inherent in the activity.

> As a general rule, persons have a duty to use due care to avoid injury to others, and may be held liable if their careless conduct injures another person . . . In the sports setting, however, conditions or conduct that otherwise might be viewed as dangerous often are an integral part of the sport itself. Thus, although moguls on a ski run pose a risk of harm to skiers that might not exist were these configurations removed, the challenge and risks posed by the moguls are part of the sport of skiing, and a ski resort has no duty to eliminate them. (*See generally* Annot. (1987) 55 A.L.R.4th 632.) In this respect, the nature of a sport is highly relevant in defining the duty of care owed by the particular defendant.
>
> Although defendants generally have no legal duty to eliminate (or protect a plaintiff against) risks inherent in the sport itself, it is well established that defendants generally do have a duty to use due care not to increase the risks to a participant over and above those inherent in the sport. Thus, although a ski resort has no duty to remove moguls from a ski run, it clearly does have a duty to use due care to maintain its towropes in a safe, working condition so as not to expose skiers to an increased risk of harm. The cases establish that the latter type of risk, posed by a ski resort's negligence, clearly is not a risk (inherent in the sport) that is assumed by a participant. (*See generally* Annot. (1979) 95 A.L.R.3d 203.)

Knight v. Jewett, 3 Cal.4th 296 (Cal., 1992).

- **Secondary assumption of the risk**: In some cases, assumption of the risk acts as a defense to a claim of negligence because "the defendant does owe a duty of care to the plaintiff but the plaintiff proceeds to encounter a known risk imposed by the defendant's breach of duty." *Knight*, 3 Cal.4th at 315 (citing 2 Harper & James, The Law of Torts (1st ed. 1956) § 21.1, p. 1162, fns. omitted, cited in *Li v. Yellow Cab Co.*, 13 Cal.3d 804, 825 (Cal. 1975)).

  In these cases, "the doctrine is *merged into the comparative fault scheme,* and the trier of fact, in apportioning the loss resulting from the injury, may consider the relative responsibility of the parties." *Knight*, 3 Cal.4th at 315. (emphasis added).

  > "'To simplify greatly, it has been observed . . . that in one kind of situation, to wit, where a plaintiff Unreasonably undertakes to encounter a specific known risk imposed by a defendant's negligence, plaintiff's conduct, although he may encounter that risk in a prudent manner, is in reality a form of contributory negligence . . . .' *Grey v. Fibreboard Paper Products Co.*, 418 P.2d 153, 156, 53 Cal.Rptr. 545, 548, 65 Cal.2d 240, 245 (Cal. 1966)

You believe this case may implicate *primary* assumption of the risk because the dangers encountered by Zoey were inherent in the activities she participated in. The doctrine of primary assumption of the risk was explained by the court in the following case:

Santho v. Boy Scouts of America
857 N.E.2d 1255 (Ohio App. 10th Dist. 2006)

[The suit was brought by Lynn and Rick Santho, on behalf of their 9-year-old son, Jamie Santho. Jamie was a member of the Boy Scouts of American, Cub Scout Pack 210. The troop's Cub Scout Master was Fred Bigney, and Margaret Bennett was a den leader. Bennett was an experienced ice skater and had significant experience teaching and training instructors. At the time of the suit, Bennett was a salaried employee of the Chiller, an ice rink located in Dublin, Ohio.]

. . . On November 13, 1994, Bennett organized a "family fun skate" at the Chiller for the members and parents of Pack 210. She filled out the "Agreement for Ice Rental" and provided information and fliers to the members at their pack meeting.

Jamie Santho, his father, and his siblings attended the fun skate. Jamie was an avid skater, participated in hockey leagues, and took hockey lessons at the Chiller. Jamie's father was a volunteer hockey coach at the Chiller. On the night of the event, Jamie's father permitted Jamie to skate without his hockey helmet. Shortly after arriving, Jamie was racing with his friend, Colin Innes, from board to board. When Jamie looked over his shoulder to see where Colin was, he crashed into the boards and suffered a skull fracture and concussion. Appellants allege that Bennett had organized the relay race against the rules of the Chiller.

[The Santhos filed suit against Boy Scouts of America, the church group licensed to oversee the Pack 210, the Chiller, and Bennett. Among other claims, the Santhos sought recovery for negligence.] The trial court granted summary judgment to all appellees on the claim for negligence, under the doctrine of primary assumption of the risk. [The plaintiffs appealed, alleging the court misapplied the doctrine of primary assumption of the risk.]

***

Under the doctrine of primary assumption of the risk, an individual injured in the course of a recreational activity is presumed to have assumed the ordinary risks of that activity unless it can be shown that another actor acted recklessly or intentionally in causing the injury. *Marchetti v. Kalish* (1990), 53 Ohio St.3d 95, 559 N.E.2d 699; *Gentry v. Craycraft,* 101 Ohio St.3d 141, 2004-Ohio-379, 802 N.E.2d 1116. The doctrine serves to remove liability for negligence under these circumstances. The trial court applied the three-part test for primary assumption of the risk in sporting events set forth in *Gallagher v. Cleveland Browns Football Co., Inc.* (1994), 93 Ohio App.3d 449, 638 N.E.2d 1082, reversed on other grounds, 74 Ohio St.3d 427, 659 N.E.2d 1232. The test requires that (1) the danger is ordinary to the game, (2) it is common knowledge that the danger exists, and (3) the injury occurs as a result of the danger during the course of the game.

It is foreseeable that any time an individual, regardless of skill, steps onto ice, they risk falling or coming into contact with the barriers that set the perimeter of the skating surface. It is foreseeable that any time an individual falls on ice, or strikes the perimeter boards, they risk injury. Therefore, every time Jamie Santho went onto the ice, either to play hockey or to participate in any other activity, he assumed the risk of falling or running into the perimeter boards and injuring himself. There is no question that Jamie was participating in a recreational activity at the time he was injured. Falling is an ordinary danger of ice skating. Colliding with the perimeter boards is an ordinary danger of ice-rink skating. It was during the course of ice skating and participating in the relay race that Jamie was injured. The appellant's age and ability to appreciate the danger involved is immaterial to the doctrine of primary assumption of the risk. Only the conduct of the appellee is relevant to recovery. *Gentry,* 101 Ohio St.3d 141, 2004-Ohio-379, 802 N.E.2d 1116.

. . . [A] recreation provider ordinarily owes no duty to a participant or spectator of an active sport to eliminate the risks inherent in the sport. *Gallagher,* 93 Ohio App.3d 449, 638 N.E.2d 1082. Here, Bennett organized the fun skate for Pack 210, as she had on several previous occasions. That was her main project for the pack. Therefore, Bennett qualifies as a recreation provider. Bennett is relieved of liability under the doctrine of primary assumption of the risk even though she was a nonparticipant in the relay race. Based upon the case law and the facts of this case, we find that the trial court properly applied the doctrine of primary assumption of the risk and properly granted summary judgment in favor of appellees on appellants' negligence claim. Appellants' third assignment of error is not well taken and is overruled.

***

Judgment affirmed.

Exercise 2

1. **Draft an initial argument supporting the claim that Zoey's potential lawsuit is barred under the doctrine of primary assumption of the risk.**

____

____

2. **How do you anticipate the plaintiff will respond to the arguments above?**

____

____

4.3 Maintenance Report

Everest Heights provides you with a copy of a Maintenance Report prepared after Zoey Hamilton was injured at the gym. It provides the following information:

Everest Heights

MAINTENANCE REPORT

Date: February 17

Time of Incident: 3:40 P.M.

Report Filed By: John Doe, Store Manager

Store Location: Eastvale, Sunport

INCIDENT DETAILS:

A birthday party guest fell off the spring floor in the main gym. At the time of the incident, seven party guests were jumping on the spring floor. Zoey Hamilton collided with another guest, fell off the spring floor, and landed on the ground in an area without springs or padding.

INJURIES/IMPACT:

The guest broke her arm when she fell. Employees called 911, and the guest was treated at Eastvale General Hospital. The manager spoke with the family and assured them that the gym would investigate the incident.

WARNINGS:

Everest policies limit the number of guests on the spring floor to five. Guests or their legal guardians sign a waiver agreeing to comply with all gym rules, and rules are visible to guests on entry to the gym. The sign was visible on February 17, and Zoey Hamilton's father signed the waiver on her behalf.

A Guest Relations Coordinator is assigned to oversee each birthday party at the gym. Before releasing birthday guests into the gym, the Guest Relations Coordinator must remind guests of the rules. On February 17, Guest Relations Coordinator Amara Patel spoke with the birthday guests and reminded them to comport with all gym rules. Ms. Patel cannot remember if she specifically mentioned the rule limiting use of the spring floor, but she asserts: "I always do, because the spring floor is one of the most popular apparatuses in the gym, especially among young kids." Ms. Patel also remembers the birthday party on February 17 was especially large, and she had to shout to be heard over the noise in the party room. She does not remember seeing or interacting with Zoey Hamilton.

SUPERVISION:

Whenever any apparatus is in use, an Everest employee monitors the area to ensure guests are using devices appropriately. On February 17, Sofia Reyes was assigned to oversee the spring floor. Ms. Reyes was also monitoring the ball pit, and she cannot recall when the birthday party guests began using the floor. She asserts that she was responding to an incident in the ball pit when she heard Zoey Hamilton scream and saw her on the ground just outside the spring floor area.

RECOMMENDATIONS:

Management met with Ms. Patel and Ms. Reyes to discuss the incident. Because management cannot confirm that either employee failed to follow gym policies, neither employee was officially disciplined.

Management will post signs next to each attraction identifying rules for use of each apparatus. The gym will post an employee at each apparatus to monitor use.

The guest in question was injured because she failed to comply with gym rules. No further action is recommended at this time.

Exercise 3

1. **You know you may have to produce this report as part of discovery. Draft an email to your client advising them of the implications of the report and the Hamiltons' claim.**

___

___

___

Negligent Infliction of Emotional Distress: *In re Denise Franklin*

Denise Franklin, who found your business card on the bulletin board in her local laundromat, the Drop or Do, left a message with your answering service. She asked for a meeting to discuss a potential lawsuit against Jared Graver. You immediately returned her call to explain you were in trial for the next week, but you sent her a client intake form via email. You promised to review the form and schedule a meeting after your trial concludes.

5.1 Client Questionnaire

After your trial (which you won, of course), you found Denise's intake form among your accumulated email from the week:

CLIENT QUESTIONNAIRE

Date: April 3

Name: Denise Franklin

Email: df917@hotmail.net

Telephone: (222) 646-9292

Preferred method of communication: (circle one) **email** (circled) **phone**

SUMMARY OF CONCERN/CLAIM/QUESTION:

In early January, I went shopping with my mother, Carolyn Franklin, at the Bullseye Market on Division Street in Eastvale. We were walking down the sidewalk in front of Bullseye, heading to the next block where the smaller shops are located. Jared Graver, who is apparently some hotshot lawyer, was talking on his phone AND texting while speeding over 50 mph. It is a pedestrian area, and he must have flown right by all the signs that marked the speed limit as 20 mph. My mother and I didn't see the car coming because we were walking with our backs to him and were talking. But I suddenly heard someone scream, "Slow down!!" I started to turn around, but before I realized what was happening, I heard my mother scream, and there was a huge crash. I realized then that Graver had lost control of the car and crashed. He barely missed me, and I couldn't believe I wasn't hurt. But then I saw Mom on the ground, and I could tell she was badly hurt. An ambulance took Mom to the hospital, but she died later that night.

Since it happened, I can't sleep because I keep thinking about how scared and hurt Mom looked after it happened. At first, I could barely work and kept calling in sick because I just cried all day. My boss finally had to let me go because he needed someone who could get stuff done. Even now, I find that my heart starts beating real fast like I'm going to have a heart attack. The hospital nurse told me to expect this kind of thing and said I should get some counseling, but I can't afford it.

I don't know what to do, but one of my friends said I should sue Graver. My dad already has a lawyer and is suing Graver for wrongful death, but his attorney told me Sunport law does not allow adult children to join the suit, especially because I wasn't a dependent. I really just want to stay out of that suit because my dad is already dealing with enough. I don't know what options I have when I wasn't even hurt in the accident, but I want to at least talk to someone about a possible lawsuit.

Exercise 1

1. **Can Ms. Franklin establish the *prima facie* elements of a negligence claim against Mr. Graver? Why or why not?**

5.2 Legal Authority—Negligent Infliction of Emotional Distress (NIED)

You realize that Ms. Franklin's case is complicated because she did not experience any *physical* harm from the accident. You wonder if this precludes her from filing a suit for negligence. You refer to the *Redress in the Redlands: Tort Law in Sunport* and find the following explanations:

Impact Rule

Traditionally, Sunport did not recognize a duty to avoid infliction of *emotional* distress to others; if a plaintiff experienced *only* emotional distress as a result of the defendant's conduct, then the plaintiff could not recover damages under traditional theories of negligence. However, if the defendant's conduct caused the plaintiff *physical* injury, then the plaintiff could seek damages for emotional distress as a "parasitic" consequence of any physical injury. The rule requiring the plaintiff to show that the defendant subjected the plaintiff to actual physical impact is referred to as the "**Impact Rule.**"

The skepticism against awarding damages for emotional distress arises from concerns about fictitious or trivial claims and the difficulty in assessing the nature and extent of emotional injuries.

> We know that, from repeated scares or frights, persons are liable to have their sensibilities easily, and in some cases morbidly excited . . . But the law furnishes no remedy for such sensitive condition. To attempt to furnish a legal remedy in such case, would open the door to the wildest speculation. Without for a moment intimating that simulation existed in this case, yet the nature of such claim would render it easy of simulation; and if not simulated, the temptation would be strong to exaggeration, and the assigning of one cause for another in the production of the morbid state of the nervous sensibilities; and all this, though it might be without real foundation, would be most difficult to disprove by the party sought to be charged.
>
> *Washington & Georgetown R.R. Co. v. Dashiell*, 7 App.D.C. 507, 515 (1896).
>
> The law does not, and doubtless should not, impose a general duty of care to avoid causing mental distress. For the sake of reasonable freedom of action, in our own interest and that of society, we need the privilege of being careless whether we inflict mental distress on our neighbors.
>
> *Clark v. Associated Retail Credit Men of Washington, D.C.*, 105 F.2d 62, 64 (C.A.D.C. 1939)

Negligent Infliction of Emotional Distress—"Zone of Danger" theory

Modern Sunport decisions reject the rigidity of the Impact Rule and allow plaintiffs in the "zone of danger" to recover damages for negligent infliction of emotional distress ("NIED"). A plaintiff may recover for NIED if the defendant's conduct unreasonably endangered the plaintiff's physical safety, placing them at risk of serious bodily injury or death and, as a result of being in this zone of danger, the plaintiff suffered emotional distress. With respect to this tort, Sunport has abandoned the requirement that the plaintiff's emotional distress manifest itself in physical symptoms.

To recover under this theory, the plaintiff must be *aware* of the danger.

> [A] party who was in the zone of danger but unaware of it until after the danger had passed could not state a claim for negligent infliction of emotional distress based on his reaction to his narrow escape . . . [T]he 'reasonable fear of danger' that can occur in the 'zone of danger' must occur *during*, not after, the presence of the danger itself.
> *Gillman v. Burlington Northern R. Co.*, 1988 WL 56921 (N.D.Ill.,1988) (plaintiff denied recovery for emotional distress because he was not aware of risks to his safety from fallen railroad line until he was out of danger).

You also find the following case that outlines the evolution of legal theories related to damages for emotional distress:

Robb v. The Pennsylvania Railroad Co.
210 A.2d 709 (Del. 1965)

HERRMANN, J.:

The question before us for decision is this: May the plaintiff recover for the physical consequences of fright caused by the negligence of the defendant, the plaintiff being within the immediate zone of physical danger created by such negligence, although there was no contemporaneous bodily impact?

Considering the record in the light most favorable to the plaintiff, the facts may be thus summarized:

A private lane leading to the home of the plaintiff, Dixie B. Robb, was intersected by a railroad right-of-way leased to the defendant, The Pennsylvania Railroad Company. On March 11, 1961, the plaintiff was driving an automobile up the lane toward her home when the vehicle stalled at the railroad grade crossing. A rut about a foot deep had been negligently permitted by the defendant to form at the crossing. The rear wheels of the automobile lodged in the rut and, although the plaintiff tried to move the vehicle for several minutes, she was unable to do so. While thus engaged in attempting to move the vehicle, the plaintiff saw the defendant's train bearing down upon her. With only seconds to spare, she jumped from the stalled vehicle and fled for her life. Immediately thereafter, the locomotive collided with the vehicle, hurled it into the air and demolished it. The plaintiff was standing within a few feet of the track when the collision occurred and her face was covered with train soot and dirt. However—and this is the nub of the problem—she was not touched by the train; there was no bodily impact; and she suffered no contemporaneous physical injury. Nevertheless, the plaintiff was greatly frightened and emotionally disturbed by the accident as the result of which she sustained shock to her nervous system. The fright and nervous shock resulted in physical injuries including cessation of lactation which interfered with the plaintiff's ability to nurse and otherwise care for her infant child. Her nervous and general physical condition resulting from the accident also obliged the plaintiff to abandon a horse breeding business and an article which she had been engaged to write for substantial compensation.

The defendant moved for summary judgment taking the position that, assuming the defendant's negligence and its proximate causation of the plaintiff's fright and nervous shock, she may not recover because there was no "impact" and contemporaneous physical injury. The trial judge agreed and granted summary judgment in the defendant's favor, stating: "In spite of a modern trend to the contrary in other jurisdictions, I feel compelled to follow the 'impact theory' in this matter by reason of well established precedents in this State." . . .

* * *

It is the duty of the courts to afford a remedy and redress for every substantial wrong. Part of our basic law is the mandate that 'every man for an injury done him in his * * * person * * * shall have remedy by the due course of law * * *.' Del.Const. Art. 1, § 9, Del.C.Ann. Neither volume of cases, nor danger of fraudulent claims, nor difficulty of proof, will relieve the courts of their obligation in this regard. None of these problems are insuperable. Statistics fail to show that there has been a 'flood' of such cases in those jurisdictions in which recovery is allowed; but if there be increased litigation, the courts must willingly cope with the task. As to the danger of illusory and fictional claims, this is not a new problem; our courts deal constantly with claims for pain and suffering based upon subjective symptoms only; and the courts and the medical profession have been found equal to the danger. Fraudulent claims may be feigned in a slight-impact case as well as in a no-impact case. Likewise, the problems of adequacy of proof, for the avoidance of speculative and conjectural damages, are common to personal injury cases generally and are surmountable, being satisfactorily solved by our courts in case after case.

We are unwilling to accept a rule, or an expediency argument in support thereof, which results in the denial of a logical legal right and remedy in all cases because in some a fictitious injury may be urged or a difficult problem of the proof or disproof of speculative damage may be presented. Justice is not best served, we think, when compensation is denied to one who has suffered injury through the negligence of another merely because of the possibility of encouraging fictitious claims or speculative damages in other cases. Public policy requires the courts, with the aid of the legal and medical professions, to find ways and means to solve satisfactorily the problems thus presented—not expedient ways to avoid them. We recognize that '[e]xpediency may tip the scales when arguments are nicely balanced,' *Woolford Realty Co. v. Rose*, 286 U. S. 319, 330, 52 S.Ct. 568, 570, 76 L.Ed. 1128; but, in our view, such nice balance no longer exists as to the subject matter.

Accordingly, we decline to adopt the impact rule, as urged by the defendant in this cause. The impact rule 'is almost certainly destined for ultimate extinction, although it displays surprising vitality, and the process may not be a rapid one. * * * it seems clear that the courts which deny all remedy in such cases are fighting a rearguard action.' Prosser on Torts (3d Ed.) pp. 351–352.

> We hold, therefore, that where negligence proximately caused fright, in one within the immediate area of physical danger from that negligence . . . such as would be elements of damage if a bodily injury had been suffered, the injured party is entitled to recover under an application of the prevailing principles of law as to negligence and proximate causation . . .
>
> This view has the general approval of the writers on the subject and is now distinctly the majority rule. We are satisfied that it is the better rule, supported by reason, logic and fairness.
>
> We conclude, therefore, that the Superior Court erred in the instant case in holding that the plaintiff's right to recover is barred by the impact rule . . . The summary judgment granted in favor of the defendant must be reversed and the cause remanded for further proceedings.

Exercise 2

1. **Based on the excerpts from *Redress in the Redlands* and the principles discussed in *Robb*, what must Ms. Franklin prove to establish a cause of action for NIED?**

   ___

   ___

   ___

2. **Which facts, if any, suggest Mr. Graver's conduct unreasonably endangered Ms. Franklin's physical safety, placing her at risk of serious bodily injury or death?**

   ___

   ___

   ___

3. **Can Ms. Franklin successfully argue that she suffered emotional distress *because* she was in the zone of danger? Does it matter that she was not aware of Mr. Graver's proximity to her and her mother until after the crash?**

   ___

   ___

   ___

5.3 Legal Authority—Bystander Rule

You learn that the defendant, Jared Graver, is from the nearby state of Solera. Mr. Graver's law office is in Solera, and he was speaking with a client in Solera when he crashed his car.

As you discuss the case with a colleague, she tells you, "You know, Solera has adopted some pretty favorable rules related to bystander liability. You should look it up and consider filing your suit there.[6] Graver will be subject to jurisdiction in Solera[7] because he is from there and was conducting business when he caused the crash. Honestly, I'd love to see that guy go down. He's a real jerk who thinks he can get away with everything."

After consulting *Solera Rules and Practice: A Litigator's Handbook*, you find that Solera has adopted the "Dillon bystander rule," which provides:

> A plaintiff may recover for emotional distress if the plaintiff:
>
> i. Is closely related to the person injured by the defendant;
> ii. Was present at the scene of the injury; and
> iii. Personally and contemporaneously observed or perceived the injury.

The "Dillon Rule" arises from an influential 1968 California case, excerpted below:

> **Dillon v. Legg**
> 411 P.2d 912 (Cal. 1968)
>
> [A car negligently driven by defendant David Luther Legg struck and killed Erin Lee Dillon, a young child, while she was crossing a public street. At the time, Erin's mother (Dillon, Plaintiff) and minor sister Cheryl (Plaintiff) were walking near her. The Plaintiffs brought suit against Legg for wrongful death. Additionally, the Plaintiffs claimed damages for emotional distress suffered because they witnessed Erin's death. At trial, the evidence showed that Dillon was in "close proximity" to Erin at the time of the accident but was outside the "zone of danger" threatened by the defendant's car. The trial court dismissed Dillon's claim for emotional distress because she was not fearful about her own safety. Dillon appealed.]

---

6. **Conflict of Laws.** This case raises a choice-of-law issue because Sunport and Solera follow different approaches to NIED claims, which may influence the likelihood of Ms. Franklin recovering damages. If multiple jurisdictions have authority to hear the case and have different laws that could change the client's outcome, then lawyers must think strategically about where to file the client's claim. While the precise legal issues are beyond the scope of a 1L Torts class (you can look forward to a more painstaking overview if you take Conflict of Laws), this introduces some of the important strategic decisions lawyers make during litigation.

7. **What is Jurisdiction?** If you are enrolled in or took Civil Procedure, then you are likely a jurisdiction expert and should skip this footnote. Otherwise, jurisdiction is the court's authority to hear and decide a case. A court must have *subject matter* jurisdiction to hear the specific legal claims in a case. A court must also have *personal jurisdiction* over the parties in the case. Generally, subject matter jurisdiction is established pursuant to constitutional or statutory authority. A party is subject to personal jurisdiction in a court based on consent, residence, or contacts with/activities in the place where the court sits.

. . . [P]ast American decisions have barred the mother's recovery. Refusing the mother the right to take her case to the jury, these courts ground their position on an alleged absence of a required 'duty' of due care of the tortfeasor to the mother. Duty, in turn, they state, must express public policy; the imposition of duty here would work disaster because it would invite fraudulent claims and it would involve the courts in the hopeless task of defining the extent of the tortfeasor's liability. In substance, they say, definition of liability being impossible, denial of liability is the only realistic alternative.

We have concluded that neither of the feared dangers excuses the frustration of the natural justice upon which the mother's claim rests. We shall point out that in the past we have rejected the argument that we should deny recovery upon a legitimate claim because other fraudulent ones may be urged. We shall further explain that the alleged inability to fix definitions for recovery on the different facts of future cases does not justify the denial of recovery on the specific facts of the instant case; in any event, proper guidelines can indicate the extent of liability for such future cases.

***

In order to limit the otherwise potential infinite liability which would follow every negligent act, the law of torts holds defendant amenable only for injuries to others which to defendant at the time were reasonably foreseeable.

***

Harper and James state the prevailing view [of a defendant's duty to others]. The obligation turns on whether 'the offending conduct foreseeably involved unreasonably great risk of harm to the interests of someone other than the actor. * * * (T)he obligation to refain from * * * particular conduct is owed only to those who are foreseeably endangered by the conduct and only with respect to those risks or hazards whose likelihood made the conduct unreasonably dangerous. Duty, in other words, is measured by the scope of the risk which negligent conduct foreseeably entails.' (2 Harper & James, The Law of Torts, [(1956) s.16.15]. p. 1018; fns. omitted.)

This foreseeable risk may be of two types. The first class involves actual physical impact. A second type of risk applies to the instant situation. 'In other cases, however, plaintiff is outside the zone of physical risk (or there is no risk of physical impact at all), but bodily injury or sickness is brought on by emotional disturbance which in turn is caused by defendant's conduct. Under general principles recovery should be had in such a case if defendant should foresee fright or shock severe enough to cause substantial injury in a person normally constituted. Plaintiff would then be within the zone of risk in very much the same way as are plaintiffs to whom danger is extended by acts of third persons, or forces of nature, or their own responses (where these things are foreseeable).' (2 Harper & James, The Law of Torts, *supra*, at pp. 1035—1036; fns. omitted.)

***

. . . In determining . . . whether defendant should reasonably foresee the injury to plaintiff, or, in other terminology, whether defendant owes plaintiff a duty of due care, the courts will take into account such factors as the following: (1) Whether plaintiff was located near the scene of the accident as contrasted with one who was a distance away from it. (2) Whether the shock resulted from a direct emotional impact upon plaintiff from the sensory and contemporaneous observance of the accident, as contrasted with learning of the accident from others after its occurrence. (3) Whether plaintiff and the victim were closely related, as contrasted with an absence of any relationship or the presence of only a distant relationship.

The evaluation of these factors will indicate the degree of the defendant's foreseeability: obviously defendant is more likely to foresee that a mother who observes an accident affecting her child will suffer harm than to foretell that a stranger witness will do so. Similarly, the degree of foreseeability of the third person's injury is far greater in the case of his contemporaneous observance of the accident than that in which he subsequently learns of it. The defendant is more likely to foresee that shock to the nearby, witnessing mother will cause physical harm than to anticipate that someone distant from the accident will suffer more than a temporary emotional reaction. All these elements, of course, shade into each other; the fixing of obligation, intimately tied into the facts, depends upon each case.

In light of these factors the court will determine whether the accident and harm was Reasonably foreseeable. Such reasonable foreseeability does not turn on whether the particular defendant as an individual would have in actuality foreseen the exact accident and loss; it contemplates that courts, on a case-to-case basis, analyzing all the circumstances, will decide what the ordinary man under such circumstances should reasonably have foreseen. The courts thus mark out the areas of liability, excluding the remote and unexpected.

In the instant case, the presence of all the above factors indicates that plaintiff has alleged a sufficient prima facie case. Surely the negligent driver who causes the death of a young child may reasonably expect that the mother will not be far distant and will upon witnessing the accident suffer emotional trauma. As Dean Prosser has stated: 'when a child is endangered, it is not beyond contemplation that its mother will be somewhere in the vicinity, and will suffer serious shock.' (Prosser, The Law of Torts, supra, at p. 353. See also 2 Harper & James, The Law of Torts, supra, at p. 1039.)

***

Thus we see no good reason why the general rules of tort law, including the concepts of negligence, proximate cause, and foreseeability, long applied to all other types of injury, should not govern the case now before us. Any questions that the cause raises 'will be solved most justly by applying general principles of duty and negligence, and * * * mechanical rules of thumb which are at variance with these principles do more harm than good.' (2 Harper & James, The Law of Torts, *supra*, p. 1039; fn. omitted.) 'The refusal to apply these general rules to actions for this particular kind of physical injury is nothing short of a denial of justice.' (Throckmorton, Damages for Fright (1921) 34 Harv.L.Rev. 260, 277; fn. omitted.)

***

To deny recovery would be to chain this state to an outmoded rule of the 19th century which can claim no current credence. No good reason compels our captivity to an indefensible orthodoxy.

The judgment is reversed.

Exercise 3

Evaluate each of the factors analyzed in *Dillon* against the facts in Ms. Franklin's case. In particular, assess whether each factor makes it more or less foreseeable that Ms. Franklin would suffer extreme emotional disress as a result of Mr. Graver's negligent conduct.

1. **Ms. Franklin's proximity to the accident.**

2. **Whether Ms. Franklin contemporaneously observed the accident or learned of it later.**

3. **The nature of the relationship between Ms. Franklin and her mother.**

Exercise 4

1. **Which approach to NIED offers Ms. Franklin a better likelihood of success: Sunport's "zone of danger" theory or Solera's "bystander rule"?**

Negligent Infliction of Emotional Distress: *Norland v. Adobe Animal Clinic*

A colleague recently contacted you to make a potential referral. Your colleague notes that she does not have the resources to take the case because it is very unusual, but she believes it may have merit. Your colleague forwards notes she took during a brief phone conversation with the potential client.

6.1 Background

September 19

5:14 P.M.

James ("Jimmy" Norland)

46-year-old welder

- Jimmy's dog, a 10-year-old labrador named Pickle, was erroneously diagnosed with cancer last year.
- Jimmy had been visiting Adobe Animal Clinic since Pickle was a puppy. Jimmy is extremely attached to his dog and is rarely seen without him. Jimmy got Pickle when he returned from military service in Iraq, and he stated, "Pickle is the one thing in my life I can always rely on to be consistent and everlastingly loyal." He believes Pickle is critical to his treatment for PTSD and depression, and he credits Pickle with saving his life.
- Last year, Jimmy noticed that Pickle had a strange lump on his leg. It didn't seem to bother Pickle, but Jimmy is always cautious about Pickle's health. He took Pickle to Adobe Animal Clinic, and a veterinarian performed a physical examination. The veterinarian told Jimmy that the location of the lump, its size, and Pickle's behavior suggested it was "almost certainly a malignant tumor."
- The veterinarian spent the rest of the visit discussing Jimmy's options. Jimmy told the veterinarian he would do anything he could to protect Pickle.
- The veterinarian acknowledged that Jimmy was in a difficult situation, but he suggested that Jimmy "remain open to the possibility of euthanasia." The veterinarian told Jimmy that most pet owners who wait for the cancer to progress ultimately regret it. He cautioned Jimmy that it is easier to remember and love your pet when he is at his best, and it is often worse to see the pet suffer. The veterinarian recommended that Jimmy go home and process the news. He told Jimmy that treatment wasn't urgent, but Jimmy would need to return within a month to discuss tests and treatment plans.

- Jimmy was devastated. He became extremely depressed and apathetic, and he couldn't sleep. He experienced a recurrence of PTSD symptoms, which had been under control. He quit his job to spend more time with Pickle and refused to speak to anyone because he "couldn't stand that look of pity when I told them about Pickle." He "basically gave up on being healthy." He began drinking a case of beer every night, "ate everything in sight," and gained 10 pounds.
- Jimmy waited several weeks to pursue additional care because he did not feel prepared to discuss treatment options. Jimmy was also afraid to return to Adobe Animal Clinic because he was afraid they would continue to recommend euthanasia. When he finally visited an oncology clinic, the clinic performed a biopsy. The clinic told Jimmy the mass was benign and did not create any risk to Pickle.

Exercise 1

1. **What are your initial thoughts about Mr. Norland's case? What potential claims might he file, and what barriers do you anticipate?**

____

____

____

____

____

____

____

____

6.2 Legal Authority—Negligent Infliction of Emotional Distress

You find a case that outlines how a misdiagnosis might create a cause of action for negligent infliction of emotional distress, and you wonder if it might provide a legal remedy for Mr. Norland.

The factual and procedural history of the case is best summarized in a decision later overturned on appeal (we provide excerpts from both decisions below).

Hedgepeth v. Whitman Walker Clinic
980 A.2d 1229 (D.C. 2009).

* * * [A]fter learning that his girlfriend was being treated for HIV, appellant [Terry Hedgepeth] went to [Whitman Walker Clinic ("WWC")] and requested an HIV test on December 13, 2000. At WWC, appellant told an intake worker that he "thought [he] had HIV" because he "found out that [his] girlfriend was HIV-positive." Relying at least in part on appellant's self-report, the intake worker made a notation in his file that he was HIV-positive. Appellant then underwent a blood test. Blood was drawn at WWC and sent to American Medical Laboratories, Inc. ("AML") for testing. The test administered by AML, an HIV–1/HIV–2 Antibodies ELISA test, was "non-reactive," meaning that appellant was not HIV-positive. WWC admits that because of an erroneous interpretation of the negative test report, a "Client Lab Results" form showed appellant as testing positive for HIV. The Client Lab Results form showing appellant as HIV-positive and the negative AML test results were made available to Dr. Mary Fanning, M.D. at WWC. When Dr. Fanning met with appellant, however, she misinformed appellant that he was HIV-positive, and noted in his patient file that he was HIV-positive, but asymptomatic and with a "normal" viral load.

***

Appellant continued to believe he was HIV-positive for five years, when another blood test revealed he is not positive for HIV. During that time, appellant suffered severe emotional distress. Appellant became depressed, which in turn affected all aspects of his life, including his relationship with his twelve-year-old daughter. Appellant's depression (as well as a knee injury) also eventually led him to lose his job as a restaurant manager. Following his misdiagnosis for HIV, appellant began to have suicidal thoughts, and he was committed to psychiatric wards on two occasions, first at George Washington University Hospital in January of 2001, and, later, at Sibley Hospital in 2002. He was prescribed medications for his depression, including Zoloft, Ambien, Trazodone, and Wellbutrin. Despair over the misdiagnosis led appellant to "heavy" use of illegal drugs, to suffer from an eating disorder, and to become isolated from his relatives because of the shame he experienced from being HIV-positive. Appellant also began to have sexual intercourse with a woman he knew to be HIV-positive "[b]ecause [he] was diagnosed with HIV and there was no reason for [him] to live."

In mid–2005, appellant visited a different medical clinic, the Abundant Life Clinic, which ran an ELISA test to confirm his HIV status. The test revealed instead that he was not HIV-positive, and appellant was informed that he was HIV-negative.***

[Appellant sued WWC and Dr. Fanning for negligence.] The Superior Court granted summary judgment against appellant and dismissed his complaint, concluding that it was bound by our precedent requiring that a claimant be exposed to a "zone of physical danger" in order to claim negligent infliction of emotional distress. *See Williams v. Baker*, 572 A.2d 1062, 1064 (D.C.1990) (en banc).

[The appellate court affirmed.]

On review, the court evaluated legal standards related to negligent infliction of emotional distress.

Hedgepeth v. Whitman Walker Clinic
22 A.3d 789 (D.C. 2011)

We granted the petition for rehearing *en banc* to decide whether the "zone of physical danger test" should be applied to preclude appellant's claim that his doctor's negligent misdiagnosis caused him serious emotional injury. *Hedgepeth v. Whitman Walker Clinic,* 990 A.2d 455 (D.C.2010). After reviewing the development of the law on this issue and the reason for the *Williams* zone of physical danger test, we conclude that appellant's claim should not be barred simply because he was not put at risk of physical injury. [*Williams v. Baker*, 572 A.2d 1062, 1064 (D.C.1990) (en banc)]. Although the rule in *Williams* continues to be generally applicable to claims of negligent infliction of emotional distress, the zone of physical danger requirement imposes an unnecessary limitation upon, and is not to be applied indiscriminately in all cases to, claims of emotional distress brought against a defendant who has a relationship with the plaintiff, or has undertaken an obligation to the plaintiff, and whose negligence causes serious emotional distress to the plaintiff. We, therefore, adopt a rule—itself a limited one—that supplements the zone of physical danger test. We hold that a duty to avoid negligent infliction of serious emotional distress will be recognized only where the defendant has an obligation to care for the plaintiff's emotional well-being or the plaintiff's emotional well-being is necessarily implicated by the nature of the defendant's undertaking to or relationship with the plaintiff, and serious emotional distress is especially likely to be caused by the defendant's negligence. We conclude this is such a case: the appellees, in the context of a doctor-patient relationship, undertook to test and treat appellant for HIV, an undertaking that would necessarily implicate the patient's emotional well-being and entailed a specially likely risk of serious emotional distress. Appellant has presented evidence supporting his allegations that appellees negligently misdiagnosed him as being HIV positive and that this misdiagnosis caused him to suffer serious emotional distress. We, therefore, reverse the grant of summary judgment for appellees and remand the case for further proceedings consistent with the principles we set out in this opinion.

I. GENERAL PRINCIPLES OF NEGLIGENCE

It is well-established that a claim alleging the tort of negligence must show: (1) that the defendant owed a duty to the plaintiff, (2) breach of that duty, and (3) injury to the plaintiff that was proximately caused by the breach. *See, e.g., District of Columbia v. Cooper,* 483 A.2d 317, 321 (D.C.1984) (citing Prosser, Handbook of the Law of Torts § 30 (4th ed. 1971) (hereinafter "Handbook of the Law of Torts")). The court's threshold determination—namely, the existence of a duty—is "essentially a question of whether the policy of the law will extend the responsibility for the conduct to the consequences which have in fact occurred." *Id.* at 321 (quoting Handbook of the Law of Torts, *supra,* § 42). Stated another way: "The statement that there is or is not a duty begs the essential question—whether the plaintiff's interests are entitled to legal protection against the defendant's conduct." *Id.* (quoting Handbook of the Law of Torts, *supra,* § 53). In this case, we are tasked with determining the scope of the duty to avoid causing emotional distress that results from negligence.

A. Duty and Foreseeability

In general, courts rely on the concept of "foreseeability" to determine whether the defendant owed a duty to the claimant in a negligence action and examine whether the risk to the claimant was "reasonably foreseeable" to the defendant. *See, e.g., District of Columbia v. Shannon,* 696 A.2d 1359, 1366 (D.C.1997); *Haynesworth v. D.H. Stevens Co.,* 645 A.2d 1095, 1098 (D.C.1994). If the injury that befell the plaintiff was "reasonably foreseeable" to the defendant, then courts will usually conclude that the defendant owed the plaintiff a duty to avoid causing that injury; if the injury was not "reasonably foreseeable," then there was no duty. [Citation omitted.] . . .

B. Duty and the Relationship Between the Parties

The relationship between the plaintiff and the defendant is closely related to a court's determination of the foreseeability of the plaintiff's injury and, ultimately, the scope of the defendant's duty . . . Thus, "the scope of the defendant's undertaking determines the scope of its duty," *Haynesworth,* 645 A.2d at 1098, by which we mean that the foreseeable risks associated with the defendant's failure to complete an undertaking provide the basis for the court's assessment of duty. Recently, we have even suggested that "the relationship between the parties is *the key* to determining whether the defendant had a legally enforceable duty to the plaintiff," *Bd. of Trs.*, 974 A.2d at 871 n. 1 (quoting *Workman v. United Methodist Comm*, 355 U.S.App.D.C. 131, 137, 320 F.3d 259, 265 (2003)) (emphasis added) . . .

In general, therefore, there is only a minimal duty—if any—owed to a party who is at arms' length. Once the defendant enters into a relationship with the plaintiff, however, a corresponding duty of care arises. *See, e.g., Tolu v. Ayodeji* 945 A.2d 596, 603 (D.C. 2008) . . . If the applicable standard of care is breached, the person to whom the duty is owed may recover for damages proximately caused by the negligence, including damages for physical injury, monetary loss, and ancillary or "parasitic" damages for related mental distress (sometimes referred to as "pain and suffering"). *See, e.g., Washington & Georgetown R.R. Co. v. Dashiell,* 7 App.D.C. 507, 514 (1896) . . .

***

III. EMOTIONAL DISTRESS DAMAGES IN ESTABLISHED RELATIONSHIPS

[T]he issue presented in this appeal is whether . . . the law should allow courts to conclude that a defendant has assumed a duty to avoid inflicting emotional distress in certain cases where the underlying relationship or undertaking is such that it is not only foreseeable, but especially likely, that the defendant's negligence will cause serious emotional distress to the plaintiff . . .

***

The draft Third Restatement, which has been under consideration since 1996 . . . adds "specified categories of activities, undertakings, or relationships" as additional bases for establishing a defendant's liability for emotional distress. These changes are intended to reflect developments in the law, specifically the "line of cases [that] recognizes an exception to the general no-liability rule when an actor undertakes to perform specified obligations, engages in specified activities, or is in a specified relationship fraught with the risk of emotional disturbance." RESTATEMENT (THIRD) OF TORTS, *supra*, § 46 cmt. b.

***

Indeed, a number of courts around the country have held that a defendant has a duty to avoid causing emotional distress to a plaintiff if the defendant has undertaken an obligation to benefit the plaintiff *and* if that undertaking, by its nature, creates not only a foreseeable, but an especially likely, risk that the defendant's negligent performance of the obligation will cause serious emotional distress. This means that not every existing relationship or undertaking will suffice to create a duty to avoid the negligent infliction of emotional distress. Thus, courts consider the nature of the relationship between the parties and the likelihood that emotional distress will be caused by negligent performance of a recognized obligation before permitting standalone claims for emotional distress. *See, e.g . . . . Corgan v. Muehling*, 143 Ill.2d 296, 158 Ill Dec. 489, 574 N.E.2d 602, 607 (1991) ("[T]he nature of the therapist-patient relationship gives rise to duty on behalf of the therapist to refrain from activity which carries with it a foreseeable, and unreasonable, risk of causing emotional or mental harm to the patient."). . . *Curtis v. MRI Imaging Servs. II*, 327 Or. 9, 956 P.2d 960, 963 (1998) ("Where the standard of care in a particular medical profession recognizes the possibility of adverse psychological reactions or consequences as a medical concern and dictates that certain precautions be taken to avoid or minimize it, the law will not insulate persons in that profession from liability if they fail in those duties.") . . .

***

IV. THE DUTY TO AVOID INFLICTING SERIOUS EMOTIONAL DISTRESS

We hold that a plaintiff may recover for negligent infliction of emotional distress if the plaintiff can show that (1) the defendant has a relationship with the plaintiff, or has undertaken an obligation to the plaintiff, of a nature that necessarily implicates the plaintiffs emotional well-being, (2) there is an especially likely risk that the defendant's negligence would cause serious emotional distress to the plaintiff, and (3) negligent actions or omissions of the defendant in breach of that obligation have, in fact, caused serious emotional distress to the plaintiff . . . The likelihood that the plaintiff would suffer serious emotional distress is measured against an objective standard: what a "reasonable person" in the defendant's position would have foreseen under the circumstances in light of the nature of the relationship or undertaking. In addition, the plaintiff must establish that she actually suffered "serious and verifiable" emotional distress. *Jones*, 589 A.2d at 424 . . .

***

VI. REMAND

[T]here is evidence in the record to support that the nature of appellees' duty to appellant necessarily implicated his emotional well-being and that it was especially likely that a doctor's breach of duty in misdiagnosing a patient with HIV-infection would result in serious emotional harm. Appellant's actions and suffering after the misdiagnosis reveal that when a patient is told that he has a life-altering or life-threatening chronic disease, this information can and does cause serious emotional distress . . .

Applying the rule we enunciate in this opinion, we conclude that on this record appellees are not entitled to summary judgment on appellant's claim of negligent infliction of emotional distress. Accordingly, we reverse and remand the case for further proceedings in the trial court consistent with this opinion.

So ordered.

Exercise 2

1. **What does the court in *Hedgepeth* identify as the elements of negligent infliction of emotional distress in a medical misdiagnosis case?**

____

____

____

2. **Do you believe Mr. Norland can establish the elements identified above? Why or why not?**

____

____

____

3. **How will the Clinic likely respond to Mr. Norland's arguments?**

____

____

____

6.3 Legal Authority—Companion Animals

As you continue to research the possibility of filing a claim for NIED based on a misdiagnosis, you find the following case:

Rabideau v. City of Racine
243 Wis.2d 486 (Wis. 2001)

WILLIAM A. BABLITCH, J.

Dakota was shot by a City of Racine police officer. He subsequently died from the injury. Dakota lived with Julie Rabideau (Rabideau), who witnessed the events leading to his death. Rabideau subsequently filed a claim for damages against the City of Racine (the City) [under a theory of negligent infliction of emotional distress].

The primary question presented in this case is whether Rabideau is entitled to damages for emotional distress. Although the question of whether or not a bystander may recover damages after witnessing an accident is a legal question that this court has previously addressed, this particular case is distinguishable from others: Dakota was a dog, a companion to Rabideau.

At the outset, we note that we are uncomfortable with the law's cold characterization of a dog, such as Dakota, as mere "property." Labeling a dog "property" fails to describe the value human beings place upon the companionship that they enjoy with a dog. A companion dog is not a fungible item, equivalent to other items of personal property. A companion dog is not a living room sofa or dining room furniture. This term inadequately and inaccurately describes the relationship between a human and a dog.

The association of dog and human is longstanding. Dogs have been a part of human domestic life since 6,300 B.C. Debra Squires-Lee, *In Defense of Floyd: Appropriately Valuing Companion Animals in Tort,* 70 N.Y.U. L.Rev. 1059, 1064 (1995). Archaeologists have uncovered a 12,000-year-old burial site in which a human being and a dog lay buried together. "The arm of the person was arranged on the dog's shoulder, as if to emphasize the bonds that existed between these two individuals during life." *Id.* (internal quotation marks and footnote omitted). Dogs are so much a part of the human experience that we need not cite to authority when we note that dogs work in law enforcement, assist the blind and disabled, perform traditional jobs such as herding animals and providing security, and, of course, dogs continue to provide humans with devoted friendship.

Nevertheless, the law categorizes the dog as personal property despite the long relationship between dogs and humans. To the extent this opinion uses the term "property" in describing how humans value the dog they live with, it is done only as a means of applying established legal doctrine to the facts of this case.

. . .[A]s a predicate matter to bringing a claim for damages based upon the tort of negligent infliction of emotional distress the plaintiff must be related to the victim as spouse, parent-child, grandparent-grandchild, or sibling. Because the relationship between Rabideau and Dakota did not fall within one of these categories, we find that she cannot maintain a claim on this basis.

***

Rabideau urges that we extend this category to include companion animals. In her words, "[a]nyone who has owned and loved a pet would agree that in terms of emotional trauma, watching the death of a pet is akin to losing a close relative." Further, she contends that we need not engage in an analysis of whether companion animals are "family," but should instead examine the rationale supporting the limitation to certain family members. Rabideau argues that the limitation of claims to family members is a means of assuring foreseeability as well as a reasonable limitation of the liability of a negligent tortfeasor. According to Rabideau, the bond between companion animals and humans is one that is sufficiently substantial to ensure that these concerns are met.

We agree, as we must, that humans form important emotional connections that fall outside the class of spouse, parent, child, grandparent, grandchild or sibling . . . However, the relationships between a victim and a spouse, parent, child, grandparent, grandchild or sibling are deeply embedded in the organization of our law and society. The emotional loss experienced by a bystander who witnessed the negligent death or injury of one of these categories of individuals is more readily addressed because it is less likely to be fraudulent and is a loss that can be fairly charged to the tortfeasor. The emotional harm occurring from witnessing the death or injury of an individual who falls into one of these relationships is serious, compelling, and warrants special recognition. [Bowen v. Lumbermens Mut. Cas. Co., 183 Wis.2d 627, 657, 517 N.W.2d 432 (1994).].

***

Had Rabideau been a bystander to the negligent killing of her best human friend, our negligence analysis would be complete. However, as we have previously noted the law categorizes dogs as property. We turn, therefore, to consider whether Rabideau can maintain a claim for negligent infliction of emotional distress arising from property loss.

In *Kleinke v. Farmers Cooperative Supply & Shipping,* 202 Wis.2d 138, 145, 549 N.W.2d 714 (1996), we concluded that under Wisconsin's formulation of tort law, "it is unlikely that a plaintiff could ever recover for the emotional distress caused by negligent damage to his or her property." This conclusion was founded upon public policy.

The public policy analysis in *Kleinke* drew upon the reasoning of *Bowen.* In *Bowen* this court listed six public policy factors addressed by courts when considering the authenticity and fairness of an emotional distress claim . . .

> (1) Whether the injury is too remote from the negligence; (2) whether the injury is wholly out of proportion to the culpability of the negligent tortfeasor; (3) whether in retrospect it appears too extraordinary that the negligence should have brought about the harm; (4) whether allowance of recovery would place an unreasonable burden on the negligent tortfeasor; (5) whether allowance of recovery would be too likely to open the way to fraudulent claims; or (6) whether allowance of recovery would enter a field that has no sensible or just stopping point.

Kleinke, 202 Wis.2d at 144-45, 549 N.W.2d 714 (quoting *Bowen,* 183 Wis.2d at 655, 517 N.W.2d 432).

In this case we need only examine one of the *Bowen-Kleinke* factors to conclude that there is no basis for recovery here. This factor concerns whether allowance of recovery would enter a field that has no sensible or just stopping point. Rabideau suggests that limiting liability to the human companion of a companion animal who is killed may satisfy this concern. We find this proposed resolution unsatisfactory. First, it is difficult to define with precision the limit of the class of individuals who fit into the human companion category. Is the particular human companion every family member? the owner of record or primary caretaker? a roommate? Second, it would be difficult to cogently identify the class of companion animals because the human capacity to form an emotional bond extends to an enormous array of living creatures. Our vast ability to form these bonds adds to the richness of life. However, in this case the public policy concerns relating to identifying genuine claims of emotional distress, as well as charging tortfeasors with financial burdens that are fair, compel the conclusion that the definition suggested by Rabideau will not definitively meet public policy concerns.

Based upon all the above, we conclude that Rabideau cannot maintain a claim for the emotional distress caused by negligent damage to her property.

***

Exercise 3

1. **How does the court's analysis in *Rabideau* influence your analysis of whether Mr. Norland has a viable claim for NIED?**

____

____

____

____

6.4 Legal Authority—Veterinary Malpractice

Because you are uncertain whether a court will award Mr. Norland damages for negligent infliction of emotional distress, you also consider whether the clinic is liable for Mr. Norland's injuries under a traditional theory of veterinary malpractice.

Professionals are held to a higher standard of care in Sunport, as outlined in Brenner's *Sunport Trial Handbook*:

> If an actor has superior knowledge about an activity, then the law expects them to apply that knowledge to mitigate risks to others. A professional is held to the standard of care of a reasonably prudent professional with similar training and experience, acting under similar circumstances and in the same or similar community.
>
> The standard is based on customary and accepted practices in the profession and typically requires expert testimony to establish how a competent professional would have responded under the circumstances.

You find the following case that provides an overview of veterinary malpractice:

> **Moreland v. Lowdermilk**
> 709 F.Supp. 722 (W.D. La. 1989)
>
> STAGG, Chief Judge.
>
> This case is about a fine young, female, equine athlete whose untimely demise is sought to be laid at the door of her attending veterinarian. Her owners seek monetary damages based on her potential earnings on the race track and as a brood mare of

a future generation of purse winners. After many years of hearing and deciding cases involving sick people and their doctors, this is this court's first veterinary malpractice case. It is brought by Mike and Jane Moreland, who raised Sandhill Diamond from a colt and, as a two- and three-year-old filly, moved her from track to track on the racing circuit.

Named as defendants are the three veterinarians who allegedly treated Sandhill Diamond, D.M. Lowdermilk, D.M. Cooley and R.A. Baker and their liability insurer, Associated Indemnity Corp . . .

FINDINGS OF FACT

. . . At the time of her untimely death on October 13, 1986, Sandhill Diamond was the leading Nebraska filly and had career race winnings in excess of $100,000.

Late in the afternoon on Sunday, October 5, 1986, Sandhill Diamond ran what was to be her last race at Louisiana Downs in Bossier City, Louisiana. [Later that evening, she stopped eating or drinking.]

***

Dr. D.M. Lowdermilk examined the horse on October 7, 1986, and strongly suspected that Sandhill Diamond suffered from thromboembolic colic. [From October 7 to 11, Dr. Lowdermilk administered several drugs and provided various treatments for the horse. Sandhill Diamond's condition began to decline rapidly on October 11.]

***

Dr. Lowdermilk advised [Sandhill Diamond's trainer, Linda Davidson,] that the horse "was not going to make it," and that she had basically two choices: euthanasia or watch the horse suffer and die. Distraught with these alternatives, Davidson insisted there must be another choice . . .

Both Dr. Lowdermilk and Davidson left the horse at about 10:00 P.M. Davidson returned at 11:00 P.M. She telephoned Dr. Lowdermilk and told him that Sandhill Diamond's legs were cold and that the mare was in pain. Dr. Lowdermilk stated that he would come out to the race track and put the horse to sleep. Dissatisfied with this response, Davidson telephoned [the owners. They] advised her to try to find someone else, whereupon Davidson contacted Dr. R.J. Wolfe.

Dr. Wolfe arrived at the race track at 1:30 A.M. on October 12. [Dr. Wolfe referred the horse to a hospital for abdominal surgery. Dr. Robert D. Lewis performed an exploratory surgery.]

***

The surgery revealed rampant peritonitis which resulted from a classic case of a thromboembolic disease. Dr. Lewis also [removed between 60 and 70 per cent of the large colon because it was gangrenous.]

Sandhill Diamond died about 1:00 P.M. on October 13. Dr. Lewis's opinion was that the horse died due to overwhelming septic shock that resulted in cardiac failure . . . [The surgeon opined that the shock was triggered by a thromboembolic episode caused by artery disease.]

***

ANALYSIS OF LAW AND FACTS

Plaintiffs contend that Dr. Lowdermilk's treatment of Sandhill Diamond, as a specialist in equine veterinary practice, fell below the accepted standard of care . . .

***

[S]tandards governing medical malpractice actions control in veterinary malpractice cases. *Ladnier v. Norwood,* 781 F.2d 490, 492 (5th Cir.1986); *Carter v. Louisiana State University,* 520 So.2d 383, 387 (La.1988). The locality standard of care is inapplicable to a veterinary specialist. *Id.* Under La.Rev.Stat.Ann. § 9:2794 (West Supp.1989), a plaintiff in a malpractice action bears a three-part burden:

1. [W]here the defendant practices in a particular specialty and where the alleged acts of medical negligence raise issues peculiar to the particular medical specialty involved, then the plaintiff has the burden of proving the degree of care ordinarily practiced by [veterinarians] . . . within the involved medical specialty.
2. That the defendant either lacked this degree of knowledge or skill or failed to use reasonable care and diligence, along with his best judgment in the application of that skill, and
3. That as a proximate result of this lack of knowledge or skill or the failure to exercise this degree of care the plaintiff suffered injuries that would not otherwise have been incurred.

Injury alone does not raise a presumption of negligence. *Id.* at § 9:2794.C. As this court held in *Sewell v. United States,* 629 F.Supp. 448, 454-55 (W.D.La.1986):

> In determining whether the plaintiff has met his burden of proof, the court relies upon the testimony and opinion of medical experts. [Citations omitted.] This expert testimony must be tempered by the knowledge that Louisiana law does not hold the physician to a standard of perfection.

See also, Garrett v. United States, 667 F.Supp. 1147, 1150-51 (W.D.La.1987). This court concludes that the plaintiffs have not come forward with sufficient evidence to sustain their burden of proof with respect to any of the elements required by La.Rev.Stat.Ann. § 9:2794.

***

Two conclusions can be drawn from the testimony of [the experts in the case]: (1) experts in equine veterinary medicine disagree on the proper treatment for thromboembolic colic; and (2) the same experts disagree on how Sandhill Diamond should have been treated. The effect of these conclusions is that plaintiffs have failed first to sustain their burden of proving the degree of care ordinarily practiced by equine veterinary specialists and, second, that Dr. Lowdermilk either lacked this degree of knowledge or skill or failed to use reasonable care and diligence.

***

Due to the extent of the infestation of parasites and the resulting disease, Dr. Lewis expressed serious doubt as to whether *any* treatment between October 7 and 11 could have saved Sandhill Diamond.

***

All of the veterinarians who testified . . . stated that the soundest manner to prevent the infestation of parasites and virtually eliminate the possibility of any colic is to have the horse "wormed" every 60 days. Sandhill Diamond had not been wormed in over nine months at the time of her death. Even [the Plaintiffs' expert] admitted that this failure properly to worm the horse would have contributed to the migration of bloodworms that resulted in the thromboembolic colic. According to [another expert], nothing could have saved Sandhill Diamond except a proper worming program.

A worming treatment costs approximately $10. Davidson testified that she doesn't worm a horse while it is on the race track circuit. The reason given by Davidson is that she would have to stop training the horse for a day. Also, she was under the impression that the drugs would remain in the system for approximately a week and would show up in the tests performed after each race, causing "problems." Dr. Lewis testified, however, that good trainers of race horses will worm every 60 days.

Based upon the foregoing, this court concludes that the precipitating cause of Sandhill Diamond's death was overwhelming septic shock that was triggered by a thromboembolic episode. The episode was made possible by severe cranial mesenteric artery disease that resulted from the migration of strongylus vulgaris larvae. The sole cause of the migration of this parasite was failure to maintain a proper worming program—not the actions or inactions of Dr. Lowdermilk.

Accordingly, even if the court were to find—which it clearly does not—that Dr. Lowdermilk breached the accepted professional standard of care, then the court would nonetheless deny plaintiffs recovery because neither the treatment given by Dr. Lowdermilk nor any additional treatment would have prevented the thromboembolic episode and septic shock that resulted in Sandhill Diamond's death.

***

6.5 Expert Reports

Because you believe a veterinary malpractice claim is Mr. Norland's strongest claim, you sign consulting agreements with two experts. You ask them to evaluate whether the Adobe Animal Clinic's veterinarian complied with professional standards of care when he treated and misdiagnosed Pickle.

Expert Report of Dr. Morgan Feldman, DVM, DACVIM (Oncology)

PREPARED FOR POTENTIAL USE IN CIVIL LITIGATION—
NORLAND V. ADOBE ANIMAL CLINIC

I. QUALIFICATIONS

I am a board-certified veterinary oncologist with more than 20 years of clinical experience, currently practicing at the Sierra Veterinary Medical Group in Eastvale, Sunport. I received my Doctor of Veterinary Medicine (DVM) from Sunport State University and completed a residency in medical oncology. I have published extensively on diagnostic standards and ethical treatment planning in veterinary cancer cases and have provided expert consultation in multiple veterinary standard-of-care disputes.

I have reviewed the following materials in forming my opinions:

- Medical records from Adobe Animal Clinic
- Records and biopsy results from Summit Veterinary Oncology Specialists
- Written statements from Jimmy Norland
- Relevant veterinary oncology literature and clinical guidelines
- Standard reference texts, including Withrow & MacEwen's Small Animal Clinical Oncology (6th ed.)

My compensation is not contingent on the outcome of this matter.

II. SUMMARY OF OPINIONS

In my expert opinion, the attending veterinarian at Adobe Animal Clinic deviated from the applicable standard of care in the following ways:

a. Failure to recommend immediate diagnostic testing before reaching a definitive or near-definitive diagnosis.

Veterinary standards require that any mass or lump be evaluated through cytological or histological testing before making a diagnosis of cancer. The standard first step is a fine needle aspirate (FNA), which can often be performed during the initial visit. If inconclusive, a biopsy is warranted. Clinical signs such as lump size, location, or behavior of the animal may inform suspicion, but they are not sufficient to justify a conclusive diagnosis of malignancy.

Here, the veterinarian reportedly told the client that the lump was "almost certainly malignant" based solely on physical palpation. This is a gross deviation from accepted diagnostic practice. In fact, the subsequent oncology workup determined that the lump was benign, indicating that the initial diagnosis was not only speculative but incorrect.

b. Introducing euthanasia as an option based on speculative, unconfirmed clinical impressions.

The veterinarian also introduced the possibility of euthanasia at the initial visit, before any diagnostic testing was conducted. While euthanasia is sometimes an appropriate part of end-of-life veterinary care, ethical practice demands it not be raised as a recommendation absent either (a) diagnostic confirmation of a terminal condition, or (b) overt, observable suffering by the animal. Neither was present in this case.

Presenting euthanasia as an option based on a speculative diagnosis may cause undue psychological distress and emotional harm resulting from professional negligence, especially when dealing with a known vulnerable client.

It is well-established in veterinary practice that clients may have strong emotional or psychological bonds with their animals, particularly when animals serve as emotional support companions. Here, the veterinarian was reportedly aware of the owner's unique attachment to Pickle and the dog's role in managing the client's PTSD. This awareness should have prompted additional care and caution during communication with the client, not increased speculation or premature prognostication.

III. CONCLUSION

Each of these actions falls below the standard of care expected of a reasonably prudent veterinarian practicing in a general small animal clinic in Sunport. Had the veterinarian acted according to standard practice and conducted or referred for a diagnostic test, the correct benign diagnosis would have been made much earlier, averting substantial emotional distress and resulting lifestyle deterioration suffered by the owner.

I reserve the right to amend this opinion upon review of additional evidence.

Respectfully submitted,
Dr. Morgan Feldman, DVM, DACVIM (Oncology)
Board-Certified Veterinary Oncologist

You receive the second report a week later. Relevant excerpts include the following:

Expert Report of Dr. Camille Hawkin, DVM, MS, DACVIM (Oncology)

PREPARED FOR USE IN CIVIL LITIGATION—
NORLAND V. ADOBE ANIMAL CLINIC

I. QUALIFICATIONS

I am a board-certified veterinary oncologist and associate professor at Sierra Mesa Veterinary College in Sunport. I received my Doctor of Veterinary Medicine from the University of Sunport and completed a residency and Master of Science in veterinary oncology at North Sunport University. I am board certified by the American College of Veterinary Internal Medicine (ACVIM) in the specialty of Oncology.

I have authored peer-reviewed articles on clinical decision-making in general practice settings, diagnostic thresholds for oncology referrals, and communication ethics in veterinary care. I regularly teach and consult on best practices for general practitioners faced with presumptive neoplastic diagnoses in small animals.

***

II. SUMMARY OF OPINIONS

It is my expert opinion, held to a reasonable degree of veterinary certainty, that the veterinarian at Adobe Animal Clinic did not deviate from the applicable standard of care in his treatment of Pickle. Specifically:

a. The veterinarian appropriately made a preliminary assessment based on physical examination and clinical judgment;
b. The veterinarian clearly communicated the need for follow-up testing and did not initiate any irreversible course of treatment;
c. Discussions regarding possible outcomes, including the potential for euthanasia, were presented not as directives, but as compassionate disclosures intended to help the client prepare for a difficult range of possibilities; and
d. The owner's delay in seeking further diagnostic care contributed significantly to the emotional distress he later experienced.

III. EVALUATION OF CARE PROVIDED

A. Clinical Assessment of the Mass

In first-opinion general practice settings, it is common and appropriate to offer a differential diagnosis based on the physical characteristics of a mass (e.g., size, fixation, location, and the dog's age). It is not a breach of the standard of care to express a suspicion of malignancy when clinical signs strongly support such a suspicion. Here, the veterinarian explained that the mass appeared "almost certainly malignant," a statement that clearly signals a clinical impression rather than a definitive diagnosis.

There is no indication that the veterinarian claimed absolute certainty or advised the owner to forgo further testing. On the contrary, the record reflects a recommendation for a diagnostic follow-up within a month.

B. Communication and Discussion of Euthanasia

The veterinarian did not recommend euthanasia or schedule any procedure to that effect. Instead, the record and testimony suggest the veterinarian offered a compassionate discussion about potential outcomes, which included euthanasia as one possible option down the line—conditional on confirmation of a serious diagnosis. The veterinarian's tone and language were empathetic and consistent with ethical communication practices outlined by the American Veterinary Medical Association (AVMA).

It is also notable that the veterinarian explicitly stated that treatment was not urgent, encouraging the owner to return in a few weeks. That recommendation reflects a measured and responsible approach, giving the client time to process and decide next steps.

C. Emotional Harm and Causation

Mr. Norland's emotional suffering is tragic and deserving of compassion. However, in assessing whether it arose from veterinary negligence, it is critical to consider that:

- No irreversible treatment was undertaken;
- The owner did not follow up for several weeks, despite knowing that a final diagnosis had not been made; and
- The benign diagnosis ultimately reached by the oncology clinic could have been made earlier if the recommended testing had occurred promptly.

Veterinarians are not trained mental health professionals. It is unreasonable to expect them to anticipate severe psychiatric deterioration in clients following a clinical discussion conducted with reasonable care.

IV. CONCLUSION

It is unfortunate that the client experienced psychological distress, but the available evidence does not support a finding that this distress resulted from veterinary malpractice. Instead, the record shows that the veterinarian provided thoughtful, measured care consistent with accepted veterinary practices in similar contexts.

Respectfully,
Dr. Camille Hawkin, DVM, MS, DACVIM (Oncology)
Sierra Mesa Veterinary College

Exercise 4

Analyze whether Mr. Norland can establish the elements of veterinary malpractice.

1. **What is the standard of care that applies in this case?**

____

____

____

____

____

____

____

____

____

2. If both experts are qualified and offer plausible interpretations of the same facts, how is a factfinder expected to resolve the dispute?

3. Which of the expert reports do you find more influential, and why? How can you undermine the credibility of the other report?

Breach

8

Res Ipsa Loquitur: Charlton v. Lemmon

Claire Lemmon was referred to you by your client, Danny Martinelli. She made a telephone appointment with you, and your notes from the call are below.

1.1 Interview Notes

CALL w/ Jennifer Charlton (July 16 10 A.M.)

- Claire and Fred Lemmon own a farm, which is managed by Jennifer Charlton and her husband, Curtis Charlton. Curtis Charlton was the farm's manager—he and Jennifer lived on the farm to ensure that Curtis was immediately available to handle any issues and perform his responsibilities.
- The property includes a pond, and the Lemmons built a wooden dock across the pond more than 30 years ago. The dock facilitates access to the pond's drainage pipe.
- On April 25, Jennifer walked out onto the dock for the first time since the Charltons moved onto the farm. After a few steps, the boards gave way, and Jennifer's left leg plunged through the dock up to her hip. She broke her leg.
- After the accident, the Lemmons hired a work crew to remove the dock instead of repairing it. They decided not to repair the dock because they had already agreed to sell the farm, and the new owners planned to level the area around the pond to build a school.
- The sale closed in mid-June, and Jennifer and Curtis Charlton moved to another home. They weren't happy about the sale and complained that the Lemmons "yanked the rug out from under them." The Lemmons are concerned that Jennifer will use her injury to retaliate against them, so Claire wants to know whether she might be liable for Jennifer's injuries.
- I told her I needed some time to think through potential claims and would touch base with her again within a week (**by July 23**).

Exercise 1

You expect that if Jennifer Charlton decides to sue the Lemmons, then she will claim that the Lemmons negligently maintained the dock in an unsafe manner.

1. **Identify which facts support each element of a potential cause of action for negligence. Also identify whether there are potential gaps in Ms. Charlton's claim.**

____

____

____

____

____

____

____

____

____

1.2 Legal Authority—*Res Ipsa Loquitur*

In Sunport, landowners are subject to liability for harm caused to their tenants by a condition on the land if the landowner knew or, through reasonable care, should have known that a condition on the property posed an unreasonable risk of harm to their tenants. In this case, Jennifer Charlton must show that the Lemmons breached a duty to her because the condition of the deck created an unreasonably dangerous condition that she would not discover.

You believe Ms. Charlton will have difficulty proving that the condition of the dock was dangerous because the dock was destroyed. In other words, Ms. Charlton will be unable to demonstrate *whether* or *how* the dock was in an unreasonably dangerous condition because there is no way to inspect the dock to determine its condition when Ms. Charlton fell.

Despite that problem, you recall the doctrine of *res ipsa loquitur* that you studied during law school. Back then, you assumed it was one of those doctrines you would study in school and never see in "real life." Now you wonder if you are evaluating a case that might implicate the doctrine.

You do some research and find the following from Monroe & Patel, *Pretrial Strategy and Settlement in Sunport*:

Res ipsa loquitur: "The thing speaks for itself"

The doctrine is implicated in cases when the plaintiff is injured by some negligent act, but the plaintiff is unable to identify the precise circumstances of breach. For example, a surgical instrument is left in a patient's stomach after surgery, but records do not show who was responsible (nurse, surgeon, etc.).

The elements of *res ipsa* are as follows:

1. The injury is the type that does not occur but for negligence on the part of the defendant.

   "[I]f an article calculated to cause damage is put in a wrong place and does mischief, I think that those whose duty it was to put it in the right place are prima facie responsible, and if there is any state of facts to rebut the presumption of negligence, they must prove them." *Byrne v. Boadle,* 59 English Reports 299; 2 Hurlstone & Coltman's Exchequer Reports 722. In *Byrne*, the plaintiff was walking past the defendant's shop when a barrel of flour fell from a window above the shop, striking and seriously injuring the plaintiff. Witnesses were unable to identify what caused the accident, but the court found the accident itself offered *prima facie* evidence of negligence. "A barrel could not roll out of a warehouse without some negligence, and to say that a plaintiff who is injured by it must call witnesses from the warehouse to prove negligence seems to me preposterous." *Id.*

2. The injuries are caused by an instrumentality within the exclusive control of the defendant.

   "If the defendant does not have exclusive control of the instrumentality producing the injury, he cannot offer a complete explanation of the physical cause of an injury which cannot be explained by the plaintiff. Thus, it would work an injustice upon him to presume negligence on his part and thus in practice demand of him an explanation when the facts indicate such is beyond his ability." *Morner v. Union Pac. R.R. Co.*, 31 Wash.2d 282, 196 P.2d 744 (1948).

3. The injury-causing accident or occurrence is not due to any voluntary action or contribution on the part of the plaintiff.

If the plaintiff establishes the applicability of the *res ipsa loquitur* doctrine, then it "permits the inference of negligence on the basis that the evidence of the cause of the injury is practically accessible to the defendant but inaccessible to the injured person." *Pacheco v. Ames*, 69 P.3d 324, 326 (2003).

> "The doctrine of res ipsa loquitur spares the plaintiff the requirement of proving specific acts of negligence in cases where a plaintiff asserts that he or she suffered injury, the cause of which cannot be fully explained, and the injury is of a type that would not ordinarily result if the defendant were not negligent." *Id.*

You also find the following decision that offers additional clarity about how the doctrine applies in Sunport:

Tinder v. Nordstrom, Inc.
84 Wash.App. 787 (Wash.App. Div. Jan. 1, 1997)

[Cheryl Tinder was shopping at Nordstrom and boarded an escalator while holding several packages. Tinder was not holding the handrail when the escalator came to a sudden stop, and she was injured when she reached across with her right hand and grabbed the opposite handrail to stop herself from falling.]

***

Apart from the sudden stop, nothing indicated that something was wrong with the escalator . . . A regular maintenance examination was performed on the escalator six days before the incident. After the incident, a maintenance specialist examined the escalator and did not find any malfunctions.

Warning signs are placed at the top of all the escalators at Nordstrom, including the one Tinder was riding. The signs warn customers to . . . "hold handrails." Tinder does not specifically recall seeing the warning sign at the top of the escalator, however, she knew from experience that escalator riders are warned to hold the handrail . . .

***

. . . Mechanical devices, like escalators and elevators, can wear out or break without negligence . . . Examination of the escalator the day after the sudden stop revealed no evidence of a malfunction, and the stop remains an unexplained event.

The sudden stop of the escalator in this case was not the type of unusual situation which normally does not occur in the absence of negligence. There was no palpably negligent act, common experience does not suggest that escalators only make sudden stops when there has been negligence, and there was no expert testimony offered to establish the inference that negligence caused Tinder's injuries. The evidence presented is insufficient to establish the first element necessary for the application of res ipsa loquitur.

***

To conclude that the sudden, unexplained stop of an escalator is the type of occurrence that does not ordinarily occur in the absence of negligence, and to permit an inference of negligence based on such an event, would in effect make Nordstrom the insurer of all who use the escalator. We decline to adopt such a rule.

We turn now to a discussion of the second and third elements of res ipsa loquitur. In [*Marshall v. Western Air Lines, Inc.*], the court noted that with the advent of comparative fault, the third element, the absence of the plaintiff's contribution in causing the accident, is generally merged into the second element, the defendant's exclusive control over the instrumentality causing the injury. [62 Wash.App. 251, 259, 813 P.2d 1269, *review denied,* 118 Wash.2d 1002, 822 P.2d 287 (1991).] These elements are therefore analyzed together. The inference of negligence gained by res ipsa loquitur must be such that the defendant would be responsible for any negligence connected with it. Exclusive control does not mean actual physical control, but rather refers to the responsibility for the proper and efficient functioning of the instrumentality that caused the injury. However, exclusive control is not established merely by showing that the defendant has a superior ability to investigate and possibly determine causation.

The facts do not justify an inference of negligence against Nordstrom. Nordstrom is not an insurer of the safety of its customers who choose to ride an escalator under circumstances similar to the facts of this case. Tinder is not entitled to the inference of negligence that is provided by the application of res ipsa loquitur.

***

Exercise 2

If Ms. Charlton files a claim for negligence, then you plan to file a motion to dismiss.[1] You have two primary arguments: 1) Ms. Charlton cannot allege specific facts to prove that the Lemmons breached a duty of care because Ms. Charlton is unable to prove whether the dock was in an unreasonably dangerous condition; and 2) Ms. Charlton cannot rely on the doctrine of *res ipsa loquitur* to establish that the Lemmons breached a duty of care.

1. **Using the court's analysis in *Tinder*, draft an argument about whether the doctrine of *res ipsa loquitur* should apply to create an inference of negligence on the part of the Lemmons.**

___

___

___

___

___

___

___

___

___

1. For a discussion of a motion to dismiss, see Chapter 7, footnote 5.

1.3 Email Correspondence

While you continue to research Ms. Charlton's potential claim, Claire Lemmon forwards you an email from Arthur Bennet, one of the Lemmons' employees. The Lemmons employ Arthur to perform routine maintenance on their farm and other properties.

Arthur contacted Ms. Lemmon because Jennifer told Arthur she planned to sue the Lemmons for her injury. Arthur was "disgusted" and believes "Jenn had no business being on that dock in the first place. I can't believe she's trying to sue you when she was hurt from her own recklessness."

Arthur asserts that he had warned Jennifer about the condition of the dock and warned her to stay away from the area. He forwards the following email:

From: **arthurvbennet@gmail.com**

To: **Jennandcurtis4ever@hotmail.com**

Date: **February 16**

Re: **Dock near the pond**

Jenn and Curt-

I just want to let you know that, when I was checking the drainage at the pond today, I noticed that the dock across the pond is in pretty bad shape. It is starting to rot in a few places, and it is very unstable. I ended up walking around the pond to check the drainage system, which is still working properly.

I wanted to let you know so you wouldn't try to use the dock until it can be repaired or torn down. It is pretty old, and I don't trust that it is safe.

-Arthur

Exercise 3

1. **How does the email influence your assessment of whether the *res ipsa loquitur* doctrine applies?**

____

____

____

____

1.4 Legal Authority—Comparative Fault

If the court finds that the Lemmons were negligent in the maintenance of the docks (which Arthur Bennet's email seems to suggest), then Mr. Bennet's email suggests another legal theory; you believe that the Lemmons might defend any lawsuit by arguing that Jennifer Charlton's negligence was the cause of or contributed to her injuries.

Tanner & Breck's Law of Personal Injury in Sunport offers the following summary of the doctrine of comparative fault:

> The doctrine of comparative fault limits the plaintiff's recovery if the plaintiff acted negligently and contributed to the plaintiff's injuries. If the defendant alleges that the plaintiff's negligence caused or contributed to the plaintiff's injuries, then the trier of fact must make a special finding identifying the degree of fault of each party's negligence. The plaintiff's damages are then reduced in proportion to the plaintiff's own contribution to the plaintiff's injuries.
>
> In Sunport, the plaintiff may only recover if the defendant's negligence equals or exceeds that of the plaintiff. If the jury finds that the plaintiff was 50 percent at fault or less, then she may still recover that proportionate amount of her damages. Yet if the plaintiff was 51 percent or more at fault, then the plaintiff cannot recover damages.
>
> EXAMPLE: Plaintiff and Defendant are in a crash. The jury finds Defendant was 75 percent at fault for driving in excess of the speed limit. The jury finds Plaintiff was 25 percent at fault because her view was partially obstructed by an item in her dashboard. The Plaintiff may recover 75 percent of awarded damages.
>
> LIMITATION: Same facts as above, but the jury finds that Plaintiff was 51 percent at fault. Plaintiff may not recover because her negligence exceeded that of Defendant's.

Exercise 4

1. **If Jennifer Charlton files a claim for negligence against the Lemmons and establishes the *prima facie* elements, do you believe the comparative fault doctrine will limit her damages or even preclude her from recovering? Explain.**

___

___

___

___

Informed consent: *Battle v. Twist*

One of your classmates from law school is now working as in-house counsel for Hubbs Insurance Company. She contacted you last week to see if you would be interested in defending some of the professional negligence lawsuits in which Hubbs's insureds are named as defendants. You quickly realize this is a great opportunity for repeat business and eagerly agree.

2.1 Complaint

Yesterday, you received your first case from Hubbs, a malpractice claim filed against Jackson Twist. Dr. Twist is a chiropractor. Relevant excerpts from the Complaint against Dr. Twist are below:

Sunport State Court
Eastvale County

Sharon Battle, Plaintiff,

v.

Jackson Twist, D.C., Defendant.

NO. 25CV0882

Jury Trial Demanded.

COMPLAINT FOR DAMAGES

COMES NOW Sharon Battle, Plaintiff in the above-styled civil action, and files her Complaint against Defendant as follows:

* * *

Statement of Facts

1. On August 27, Plaintiff sought chiropractic treatment from Defendant Dr. Jackson Twist for lower back pain. During that appointment, Dr. Twist made an adjustment of Plaintiff's lower back. Dr. Twist then asked Plaintiff to return for another visit on August 30.
2. When Plaintiff returned to Dr. Twist on August 30, Dr. Twist suddenly and without warning to Plaintiff twisted Plaintiff's head to the side with extreme force. Plaintiff immediately felt severe pain in her neck.

3. Over the next few weeks, Plaintiff's neck pain worsened. After several weeks of attempting without success to treat Plaintiff's neck pain, Dr. Twist finally referred Plaintiff to an orthopedic surgeon, who diagnosed a herniated disc in Plaintiff's neck and ultimately performed neck surgery on Plaintiff.

* * *

COUNT 1 — Professional Negligence

4. Plaintiff realleges and incorporates by reference all preceding paragraphs as if they were fully restated verbatim here.
5. Defendant Dr. Twist was required and obligated to provide professional care to Plaintiff that complied with the standard of care and skill of such persons generally under the same or similar circumstances.
6. While providing care to Plaintiff on August 30, Defendant Dr. Twist violated the standard of care and skill exercised by chiropractors in the provision of medical care to patients with lower back pain.
7. Specifically, Dr. Twist failed to inform Plaintiff that twisting her head to the side with the extreme force applied as part of his treatment of her lower back pain might result in severe pain in her neck that could require surgery. Dr. Twist also failed to inform Plaintiff of any alternative treatments that might effectively treat her lower back pain without causing the severe neck pain Dr. Twist's treatment caused.
8. Plaintiff avers that had Dr. Twist informed her of such risks or alternative treatments, she would not have consented to the treatment applied on August 30.
9. As a direct and proximate result of Dr. Twist's treatment, which was performed without Plaintiff's informed consent, Plaintiff has suffered damages in an amount to be proven at trial.

COUNT 2 — Battery

10. Plaintiff realleges and incorporates by reference all preceding paragraphs as if they were fully restated verbatim here.
11. Defendant intentionally acted to cause a harmful and offensive touching of Plaintiff when he twisted her head to the side with extreme force as part of his purported chiropractic treatment.
12. A harmful and offensive touching of Plaintiff resulted from Defendant's actions in that Plaintiff's neck pain worsened and Plaintiff ultimately was left with a herniated disc in her neck as a result of Defendant's actions.
13. Defendant failed to obtain Plaintiff's valid consent before treating her neck pain in the manner he did. As a licensed chiropractor, Defendant was required to comply with 6 Sunport Rev. Stat. § 114-6, which explicitly requires that a doctor obtain the patient's consent before administering a procedure.
14. As a direct and proximate result of Dr. Twist's failure to comply with the above-referenced statute, Plaintiff has suffered damages in an amount to be proven at trial.

* * *

Exercise 1

1. What legal issues do you plan to research before you advise the client?

2. What questions do you plan to ask your client when you speak with him?

3. What standard of care applies to Dr. Twist's conduct?

____

____

____

____

____

____

____

____

2.2 Client Interview

You had a call with Dr. Twist this morning. Dr. Twist is furious and asserts Ms. Battle is "completely untethered to reality." Dr. Twist made the following arguments:

> It was obvious that tension in Sharon's neck was contributing to her lower back pain. The body operates as a connected system, and tension in one area can lead to compensations and strain in another. I am good at what I do, and I saw during her first consultation that tightness in her neck caused imbalances in her ligaments and fascia that put stress on the lower back. The neck tension was positioning her head forward, which shifted her center of gravity. This caused her lower back to compensate by increasing the lumbar curve. I treated that tension the way any chiropractor would. It's a typical procedure that is usually performed without any problems and with much relief to the patient. Injuries occur only if the patient ignores instructions during the session. I told Sharon that she needed to relax her muscles, and she was only hurt because she resisted the treatment when I tried to readjust her neck.
>
> In any case, I don't think Sharon appreciates that she signed a release and consent form. I am careful to secure these from every patient; they are a routine part of my intake process.

2.3 Expert Opinion

You consult with an expert and ask for an initial assessment about whether Dr. Twist's treatment decisions were within professional norms. You receive the following opinion:

From: malik.rivera@sunporthospitalsystem.org

Date: September 17

Re: Battle v. Twist – PRELIMINARY OPINION

I am a licensed chiropractor with 13 years of experience and a background in musculoskeletal treatments and spinal care. You asked me to provide an initial review of the case filed against Dr. Jackson Twist, No. 25cv0882. Specifically, you asked me to address the reasonableness of Dr. Twist's treatment.

PLEASE NOTE THAT THIS OPINION IS RENDERED WITHOUT A FULL REVIEW OF THE FILE OR RELATED LITERATURE. I reserve the right to amend this opinion upon review of additional evidence.

The chiropractic adjustment performed by Dr. Twist on August 30, wherein he applied force to Plaintiff's neck, was, from a professional standpoint, not unusual. Based on the facts provided and common chiropractic practices, the treatment performed falls within the range of standard procedures employed by chiropractors to address spinal misalignments, particularly when addressing issues related to neck and lower back pain. Chiropractors routinely perform similar adjustments to the cervical spine, and the technique itself is widely accepted within the chiropractic community.

I render no opinion as to whether the procedure was performed safely under the circumstances. I also render no opinion as the cause of the patient's injury.

You did not ask me to review Dr. Twist's consent forms or practices, but my initial review suggests Dr. Twist's apparent failure to secure informed consent was a significant oversight. If Ms. Battle's allegations are correct, then it appears the patient was not fully aware of the nature, risks, and potential outcomes of the proposed treatment. If Dr. Twist did not sufficiently communicate the risks of neck manipulation or obtain explicit consent from Plaintiff prior to the adjustment, then his conduct may constitute a breach of professional standards.

Respectfully submitted,

Dr. Malik Rivera, DC

2.4 Informed Consent Form

You believe the report from Dr. Rivera may resolve the question of whether Dr. Twist's treatment decisions were negligent, yet you are concerned about Dr. Rivera's note about informed consent.

To evaluate whether Dr. Twist breached a duty to secure informed consent, you ask him to send a copy of the release signed by Ms. Battle.

DR. JACKSON TWIST, Doctor of Chiropractor

123 MAIN STREET, EASTVALE, SUNPORT 55002 TEL: (733) 555-5555

INFORMED CONSENT FOR CHIROPRACTIC TREATMENT

Patient Name: Sharon Battle

Chiropractic care focuses on the relationship between the body's structure—primarily the spine—and its function. Chiropractic care involves the diagnosis and treatment of spinal and musculoskeletal conditions through various techniques, which will be reviewed with you based on any diagnosis or treatment plans. This form serves to inform you about the nature of chiropractic treatment and any associated risks.

While chiropractic treatment is generally safe, certain risks exist, including but not limited to temporary soreness or discomfort, mild bruising or stiffness, muscle or ligament strain, and risk of fractures in patients with osteoporosis or bone weakness.

I have been informed about the nature and purpose of chiropractic care, including the benefits, potential risks, and alternative treatment options. I have had an opportunity to ask questions, and my concerns have been addressed.

SB I consent to chiropractic treatment.

___I do not consent to chiropractic treatment.

Patient (or Legal Guardian) Signature: *Sharon Battle*

Printed Name: Sharon Battle

Date: August 27

Exercise 2

1. **What are your initial impressions of Dr. Twist's Informed Consent form? Do you have any concerns about the enforceability of its provisions?**

_____

_____

_____

_____

_____

2.5 Call with Opposing Counsel

You call Ms. Battle's attorney to introduce yourself and assess whether you might settle the case. You explain that Dr. Twist performed a routine procedure, and there is no evidence he acted negligently.

In your opinion, Opposing Counsel is arrogantly confident and seems somewhat unreasonable. Opposing Counsel asserts, "Listen. I know you want to get your client out of this case without paying my client anything, but you need to review the *Northport Urology Clinic* case, and you need to look up the Sunport Informed Consent statute. If you ask me, it's a slam dunk case that will ensure my client gets whatever she wants in the way of damages from Dr. Twist."

2.6 Legal Authority—Informed Consent Statute

Immediately after ending the call, you review Sunport's Informed Consent statute:

6 Sunport Stat. § 114-6. Consent to certain medical or diagnostic procedures; disclosure of information to person from whom consent is required.

(a) A medical professional must obtain informed consent from a patient before performing any treatment or procedure that presents a material risk of harm. The professional must disclose, in clear and understandable language:

a. A diagnosis of the patient's condition;
b. The nature and purpose of the proposed treatment;
c. The known risks and possible complications associated with the treatment;
d. Any reasonable alternatives to the proposed treatment, including risks and benefits of those alternatives; and
e. The likelihood of success of the proposed treatment or diagnostic procedure.

(b) For procedures involving a material risk of harm, the professional must obtain a written informed consent, signed by the patient (or legal guardian if applicable).

(c) A failure to comply with the requirements of this Code section shall not constitute a separate cause of action but may give rise to an action for medical malpractice or other causes of action that exist under common law, upon a showing:

a. That the patient suffered an injury which was proximately caused by the treatment or diagnostic procedure;
b. That information concerning the injury suffered was not disclosed as required by this Code section; and
c. That a reasonably prudent patient would have refused the treatment or diagnostic procedure or would have chosen a practical alternative to such proposed treatment or diagnostic procedure if such information had been disclosed.
d. A failure to comply with the requirements of this Code may give rise to an action for battery. Battery is defined as any unauthorized physical contact with a person. A claim for battery may be brought against the healthcare provider if the treatment or procedure performed was not within the scope of the informed consent provided by the patient.

Exercise 3

1. **Does the consent obtained by Ms. Battle's signature on Dr. Twist's consent form comply with the consent required by § 114-6? Why or why not?**

2. **How would you recommend that Dr. Twist amend the form for future patients?**

2.7 Legal Authority—Informed Consent Precedent

You also read the *Northport Urology Clinic* case, as suggested by opposing counsel:

SUNPORT SUPREME COURT

Northport Dermatology Clinic

v.

Cinci

No. K21N0500 Apr. 4, 2021

Macy, J.

Patient sued dermatologist and clinic that employed him, asserting claims for medical negligence and battery, and alleging that dermatologist failed to disclose the risks of infection and allergic reaction associated with the skin removal procedure she performed, thereby exacerbating patient's medical condition.

We hold that (i) the Sunport informed consent statute imposes a duty upon the physician to disclose the risks of treatment; (ii) because the informed consent statute is in derogation of the common law rule against requiring physicians to disclose medical risks to their patients, it must be strictly construed and cannot be extended beyond its plain and explicit terms; and (iii) the statute does not create an independent cause of action for failure to obtain informed consent but rather a violation of the statute merely supports a professional negligence claim against the physician.

I. Facts and Background

In 2016, James Cinci consulted with dermatologist Caitlyn Markle, M.D., of the Northport Dermatology Clinic, about a discoloration on the shin of his left leg. Markle expressed concern that Cinci might have skin cancer and after Cinci signed an informed consent statement, Markle performed surgery under general anesthesia to remove the discolored skin. Thereafter, Cinci began to experience an acutely painful sensation in his leg and because there was insufficient skin to help the wound heal, Cinci also experienced an infection that turned into sepsis and nearly caused him to lose part of his left leg.

Cinci sued Markle and the Northport Dermatology Clinic where she practiced, claiming that Markle negligently performed unnecessary surgery for non-existent skin cancer, and thereby exacerbated Cinci's medical condition. In his complaint, Cinci alleged that Markle was liable for medical negligence and battery (for failure to obtain informed consent). Cinci's expert testified that Cinci's skin discoloration was not caused by cancer but rather by Vitiligo, which might have been confirmed with proper testing and treated effectively without surgery.

* * *

We granted certiorari to determine whether the violation of Sunport's informed consent statute supports an independent cause of action of negligence or battery based on improperly-obtained consent.

II. Duty to Disclose

Prior to 2004, Sunport physicians were not required to disclose to their patients any of the risks associated with a particular medical treatment or procedure. Although a physician did then and does now have a common law duty to answer truthfully a patient's questions regarding medical or procedural risks, absent such inquiry the common law of this state does not designate the failure to disclose such risks a fraud that may vitiate a patient's consent to medical procedures.

This common law rule was changed in 2004 by the legislature, when the Sunport General Assembly adopted Sunport Stat. Stat. § 114-6, which sets forth five specified categories of information that must be disclosed by medical care providers to their patients before they undergo certain specified surgical or diagnostic procedures. The Sunport informed consent statute does not impose a general requirement of disclosure upon physicians; rather, it requires physicians to disclose only those factors listed in § 114-6.

Any attempt to broaden the statute's reach or impose additional requirements beyond those expressly stated in the law would be inconsistent with the statute's legislative purpose and the common law deference to physicians' judgment. Because the law historically allowed physicians a certain degree of discretion in determining what information was necessary to disclose to a patient, the informed consent statute cannot be extended beyond its plain and explicit terms.

III. Professional Negligence

As noted in § 114-6(c), the informed consent statute does not create an independent cause of action for failure to obtain informed consent. Rather, a violation of the statute supports a professional negligence claim against the physician because a physician who violates the statute is *presumed* to have breached their professional duty of care. The violation of the informed consent statute is not merely *evidence* of negligence; it is *negligence per se*. When a healthcare provider disregards the statutory duty to provide clear and adequate information, the breach itself constitutes a violation of the standard of care. This presumption of negligence shifts the burden to the defendant to show that their actions did not cause harm, or that the patient's consent was, in fact, properly obtained.

Therefore, a plaintiff need only prove that the statutory requirements for informed consent were not met and that the violation of those requirements led to the plaintiff's injury. The plaintiff need not independently establish the provider's negligence or failure to act reasonably under the circumstances; the statutory violation itself is sufficient to prove breach of the standard of care.

IV. Battery

Failure to comply with the informed consent statute may also expose physicians to liability for battery. The statute shapes the parameters of what constitutes consent and makes clear that, if a patient is not properly informed about the risks and alternatives of a certain procedure, then consent is not properly obtained. If a physician performs a procedure without proper consent, then the physician has exceeded the scope of what the patient consented to and has caused unauthorized contact. The lack of informed consent, coupled with the performance of an unauthorized procedure, may transform what would otherwise be a simple negligence claim into an actionable battery, as the physical contact is no longer deemed consensual. ***

Here, we have no issue finding the informed consent statute applicable to the procedure that took place involving Mr. Cinci. The evidence at trial made clear that Dr. Markle did not inform Mr. Cinci of any of the categories of information required by the statute before subjecting him to surgery for skin removal that ultimately not only was proven unnecessary but to which Mr. Cinci would not have consented had he been adequately informed about his prognosis, the procedure, and the risks of infection.

Thus, the consent that Dr. Markle and the Northport Dermatology Clinic obtained from Mr. Cinci was not informed consent, and Mr. Cinci was free to pursue his battery and malpractice claims based on the fact that Dr. Markle performed the surgical procedure without properly obtaining Mr. Cinci's consent.

* * *

Exercise 4

1. **How is your case similar to *Northport Dermatology Clinic*? How is it different?**

___

___

___

2. **Do you agree with Opposing Counsel that the precedent from *Northport* makes Ms. Battle's claim a "slam dunk" case? Why or why not?**

2.8 Legal Authority—Informed Consent Statute Continued

You can't shake the feeling that you are missing something in the case, and you believe that Opposing Counsel's confidence is misplaced. You continue to research the implications of the Informed Consent statute, and you find the following definition in a different section of the statute:

> "Medical professional" means any individual licensed or certified under state law to practice medicine or osteopathy, including physicians (MDs and DOs), physician assistants, advanced practice registered nurses (APRNs), registered nurses (RNs), and other practitioners authorized to diagnose, prescribe, and treat medical conditions under the supervision of a physician.

Exercise 5

1. **How is this definition of a "medical professional" relevant to your defense of Dr. Twist?**

2.9 Call with Opposing Counsel Round Two

You call Opposing Counsel again to outline your findings and opinions about the case. Opposing Counsel asserts, "You can pick apart legal definitions all you want, but the truth is your guy still messed up by not telling my client about the risks of the procedure. At a minimum, he should have warned her what he was about to do so she was prepared for a fairly violent procedure. I know he doesn't want the negative publicity associated with this case, especially because Ms. Battle's sister is a social media influencer. Present us an offer and we'll see if we can make this go away before it starts to damage Twist's practice."

Exercise 6

1. **Prepare a recommendation for your client regarding a proposed settlement.**

Negligence Per Se: *Darby v. Ballgamers*

You received an unsolicited call from Brian Darby. Mr. Darby knows of your expertise in sports law, and he is interested in exploring a lawsuit against Ballgamers, a popular sports bar near the Sunport Pelicans baseball stadium.

3.1 Client Interview

You agree to meet with Mr. Darby and take the following notes during your meeting:

Meeting with B. Darby re: Ballgamers
OCT. 10 (11 A.M.)

- When the Sunport Pelicans play at home, Ballgamers Bar installs a temporary tent in its parking lot (check to see if they have a permit for this). The tent is immediately next to a public sidewalk, which abuts a public street.
- Mr. Darby and his friends often meet at Ballgamers before or after Pelicans games, and they watch the game from the tent if they don't have tickets to attend at the stadium.
- On April 28, the Pelicans had a home game beginning at noon; weather was sunny for most of the game. Mr. Darby went to a game with friends, then they went to Ballgamers after the game to celebrate the Pelicans' win. They knew Ballgamers would have a DJ playing great music and would be conducting team trivia games.
- While Mr. Darby and his friends were at the bar, Mr. Darby saw the TVs occasionally flashing warnings about an approaching storm, with "Seek Shelter" running across the screen. Mr. Darby figured Ballgamers would tell people to move inside if there was a risk, but no one ever said anything, and everyone remained outside.
- Between 3:45 and 3:50 P.M., high winds from the storm came through the Ballgamers parking lot, lifted the tent from its moorings, and caused it to fly—almost swirl—around the parking lot. One of the tent poles hit Mr. Darby in the head, leaving a huge gash. He also broke his ankle and sprained his wrist when the tent wrapped around him and knocked him to the ground.
- Mr. Darby wants to know if he can sue Ballgamers for negligence for not moving people inside, taking down the tent, or at least somehow securing the tent so it could withstand the storm. He wants Ballgamers to pay his medical bills and absorb his losses from missing several days of work.

Exercise 1

1. **What are your initial thoughts about the claim? Can Mr. Darby establish the *prima facie* elements of negligence?**

3.2 Legal Authority—Negligence Per Se

You confirm that Ballgames had a permit to erect the tent. The permit references the following regulatory provision:

Eastvale Municipal Code § 415-23 (2020). Regulation Requiring Business Owners to Secure Outdoor Structures to Prevent Obstruction of Traffic.

Section 1: Purpose

The purpose of this regulation is to ensure that outdoor structures associated with businesses are properly secured to prevent obstruction of public streets, sidewalks, and rights-of-way, thereby ensuring public safety and maintaining accessibility.

Section 2: Securing Outdoor Structures

(a) The following regulations apply to any business owner that operates a business with a permanent or temporary outdoor structure on property adjacent to public streets, sidewalks, or rights-of-way. Outdoor structures include seating areas, tents, canopies, kiosks, signage, fences, barriers, or any other installation placed outside a business establishment.

(b) Owners must ensure that all outdoor structures are properly anchored, weighted, or secured in accordance with local building and safety codes to prevent displacement due to wind, impact, or other environmental factors. Structures should not encroach upon or obstruct pedestrian pathways, bike lanes, or vehicular traffic lanes beyond what is permitted by local zoning or permitting authorities.

You believe this regulation offers an opportunity to argue negligence under the theory of negligence per se. You find the following definition of the principle from *Sunport Practice Guide to Civil Litigation*:

Negligence per se arises when a statute or regulation dictates or defines reasonable conduct under specified circumstances. In such cases, the general standard of care is supplanted or defined by the statutory standard of care. If the plaintiff proves that the defendant violated the statute, then the plaintiff has established a conclusive presumption that the defendant breached the applicable standard of care. When a case based on negligence per se is submitted to the jury, the standard of care is omitted because the statutory violation itself constitutes a breach of the standard of care.

To establish a claim of negligence per se, the plaintiff must plead and prove the following four elements: 1) the defendant violated a statute; 2) the injured plaintiff was a member of the class of persons intended to be protected by the statute; 3) the injury complained of was of the kind the statute was designed to prevent; and 4) the violation of the statute was the proximate cause of the plaintiff's injury.

Exercise 2

Evaluate whether Mr. Darby can establish the elements necessary to prove breach under a theory of negligence per se.

1. **Ballgamers violated Eastvale Municipal Code § 415-23.**

2. **Mr. Darby was a member of the class of persons § 415-23 was designed to protect.**

3. **Mr. Darby's injuries were the kind § 415-23 was designed to prevent.**

4. **The violation of § 415-23 was the proximate cause of Mr. Darby's injuries.**

Exercise 3

1. **If the court concludes that the doctrine of negligence per se is inapplicable, then what other legal theories might apply to establish Ballgamers' liability?**

3.3 Legal Authority—Implied Assumption of the Risk

You are concerned that, because Mr. Darby knew about the oncoming storm, Ballgamers may raise a defense of comparative negligence or assumption of the risk.

Sunport still recognizes the defense of implied assumption of the risk, which is defined as follows:

> Implied or secondary assumption of the risk applies if a plaintiff voluntarily and knowingly exposes themselves to a known risk. It assumes that the defendant breached a duty, but the plaintiff nevertheless chose to encounter the risk created by the defendant's conduct. The doctrine involves a *subjective* inquiry into what the plaintiff knew and appreciated about the risks involved in an activity. If the plaintiff knew or should have known of the specific risks involved in the activity and *voluntarily* accepted them, then the doctrine may reduce or eliminate the defendant's liability in a negligence case. The doctrine does not apply if the defendant acted intentionally, recklessly, or with gross negligence.

Exercise 4

1. **Do you believe the doctrine of implied assumption of the risk will limit or prevent Mr. Darby from recovering damages? Explain.**

Causation

9

Alternative Causation: *In re Ethan Carter*

You are a first-year associate in one of Sunport's largest law firms, with offices in Eastvale, Northaven, and Southlake. One of the senior litigation partners, Evan Carter, called you into his office and started drilling you on the cases covered in your 1L Torts class. "I was in law school back in the mid-1970s, and we talked about some case involving quail hunting. What was that case called?" You think for a minute and then answer, "Ummm . . . was it *Summers v. Tice*?" Evan responds, "Yeah! That's it! *Summers v. Tice*. Well, I think I've got a case for you to handle on your own. And I'm pretty sure if you reread that case and follow its lead, then you'll have yourself a winner with this one." Mr. Carter tells you he will summarize the story and send it to you via email.

1.1 Case Summary

Mr. Carter emails to you the following summary about his 13-year-old grandson, Ethan, and a recent incident involving fireworks.

> Last July, Ethan and his friends, Jake Moreno and Miles Harrington, were in a lot behind one of the boys' houses with several fireworks they purchased from a roadside stand just outside of Eastvale's city limits.
>
> The boys mostly bought small firecrackers, but Miles bought a couple of cherry bombs, and Jake bought at least one larger, more powerful firework. At first, the boys just lit a few sparklers, bottle rockets, and ground spinners. Then Jake and Miles decided to light their more powerful firecrackers.
>
> According to Ethan, he told his friends they needed to be careful, and he was worried when Miles held up a cherry bomb and said, "This one's gonna be loud." Yet Jake and Miles agreed they should "light, run, and watch." Miles flung a smoke bomb at the same

time Jake hurled an M-80. Unfortunately, they both threw their firecrackers in the same direction—directly at Ethan. Before Ethan could respond or move out of the way, they all heard a big bang, and the fireworks exploded. Ethan was knocked to the ground, and his arm was badly burned where a firework hit him. The boys weren't sure which firework hit Ethan, and they both apologized for not warning him or using better aim.

At first, Ethan tried to hide his injury from his parents, but they noticed the burns when he returned home that evening. He admitted what happened, and they took Ethan to an emergency clinic for treatment.

Ethan's father has always believed that Jake and Miles are a bad influence on Ethan, and he was furious. Yet when he confronted Jake and Miles's parents, they brushed off the incident as "boys being boys." Miles's mother also argued that Ethan was an active participant and "was just as much at fault as the other boys." Neither boy was punished, and their parents refused to pay any of Ethan's medical expenses.

Ethan's parents want to know whether they can sue the other boys' families for damages.

Exercise 1

As you assess whether Ethan can establish a *prima facie* case for negligence, you consider the following:

1. **Duty: What standard of care applies to determine whether the boys acted negligently?**

   ____

   ____

   ____

2. **Breach: Did Jake and Miles breach the applicable standard of care? Why or why not?**

   ____

   ____

   ____

3. **Actual cause: Is the conduct of Jake or Miles the actual cause of Ethan's injury?**

   ____

   ____

   ____

4. Proximate cause: Were Ethan's injuries a foreseeable consequence of the boy(s)' negligence?

____

____

____

____

____

1.2 Legal Authority—Alternative Theories of Causation

You begin to prepare a memo for your senior partner outlining your recommendations. You feel confident that Jake and Miles acted negligently when they threw the firecrackers without warning; however, you are unsure how you will prove causation because you don't know which firework struck Ethan. This makes it difficult to establish actual cause under the traditional "but for" test. If you argue that, but for Jake's negligence, Ethan would not have been injured, then Jake will refute your argument by asserting that Miles threw the firework that caused injury. Similarly, if you argue that, but for Miles's negligence, Ethan would not have been injured, then Miles will refute your argument by asserting that Jake threw the firework that caused injury.

You recall your conversation with Mr. Carter and locate the decision in *Summers v. Tice*, excerpted below.

Summers v. Tice
33 Cal.2d 80 (Cal. 1948)

CARTER, Justice.

Each of the two defendants appeals from a judgment against them in an action for personal injuries. Pursuant to stipulation the appeals have been consolidated.

Plaintiff's action was against both defendants for an injury to his right eye and face as the result of being struck by bird shot discharged from a shotgun. The case was tried by the court without a jury and the court found that on November 20, 1945, plaintiff and the two defendants were hunting quail on the open range. Each of the defendants was armed with a 12-gauge shotgun loaded with shells containing 7 1/2 size shot. Prior to going hunting plaintiff discussed the hunting procedure with defendants, indicating that they were to exercise care when shooting and to 'keep in line.' In the course of hunting plaintiff proceeded up a hill, thus placing the hunters at the points of a triangle. The view of defendants with reference to plaintiff was unobstructed and they knew his location. Defendant Tice flushed a quail which rose in flight to a ten foot elevation and flew between plaintiff and defendants. Both defendants shot at the quail, shooting in plaintiff's direction. At that time defendants were 75 yards from plaintiff. One shot struck plaintiff in his eye and another in his upper lip. Finally it was found by the court that as the direct result of the shooting by defendants the shots struck plaintiff as above mentioned and that defendants were negligent in so shooting and plaintiff was not contributorily negligent.

* * *

It has been held that where a group of persons are on a hunting party, or otherwise engaged in the use of firearms, and two of them are negligent in firing in the direction of a third person who is injured thereby, both of those so firing are liable for the injury suffered by the third person, although the negligence of only one of them could have caused the injury. *Moore v. Foster,* Miss., 180 So. 73; *Oliver v. Miles,* Miss., 110 So. 666, 50 A.L.R. 357; *Reyher v. Mayne*, 90 Colo. 856, 10 P.2d 1109; *Benson v. Ross*, 143 Mich. 452, 106 N.W. 1120, 114 Am.St.Rep. 675 . . .

* * *

. . . Dean Wigmore has this to say: 'When two or more persons by their acts are possibly the sole cause of a harm, or when two or more acts of the same person are possibly the sole cause, and the plaintiff has introduced evidence that the one of the two persons, or the one of the same person's two acts, is culpable, then the defendant has the burden of proving that the other person, or his other act, was the sole cause of the harm. (b) * * * The real reason for the rule that each joint tortfeasor is responsible for the whole damage is the practical unfairness of denying the injured person redress simply because he cannot prove how much damage each did, when it is certain that between them they did all; let them be the ones to apportion it among themselves. Since, then, the difficulty of proof is the reason, the rule should apply whenever the harm has plural causes, and not merely when they acted in conscious concert. * * *' (Wigmore, Select Cases on the Law of Torts, sec. 153.) . . .

* * *

When we consider the relative position of the parties and the results that would flow if plaintiff was required to pin the injury on one of the defendants only, a requirement that the burden of proof on that subject be shifted to defendants becomes manifest. They are both wrongdoers, both negligent toward plaintiff. They brought about a situation where the negligence of one of them injured the plaintiff, hence it should rest with them each to absolve himself if he can. The injured party has been placed by defendants in the unfair position of pointing to which defendant caused the harm. If one can escape the other may also and plaintiff is remediless. Ordinarily defendants are in a far better position to offer evidence to determine which one caused the injury. This reasoning has recently found favor in this Court . . .

* * *

. . . We have seen that for the reasons of policy discussed herein, the case is based upon the legal proposition that, under the circumstances here presented, each defendant is liable for the whole damage whether they are deemed to be acting in concert or independently.

The judgment is affirmed.

Exercise 2

1. **Relying on the reasoning from *Summers v. Tice,* prepare an argument that the negligence of Jake and Miles was the actual cause of Ethan's injuries.**

Exercise 3

You meet with your partner, Evan Carter, to review your memorandum and findings. Mr. Carter is confident about the case but hopes the parties can resolve the disagreement without long-term animosity in the neighborhood. Mr. Carter asks you to call Jake and Miles's parents to discuss a possible settlement. You know Jake's mother is a personal injury lawyer, so you want to be prepared for the discussion.

1. **What arguments might the boys present to avoid or minimize liability?**

2. How would you respond to the arguments you identify above?

Proximate Cause: *Baker v. Neon Palms*

You met Lucy Baker in a hotel bar called the Neon Palms. You were there to attend the monthly Sip n' Learn hosted by the Eastvale Bar Association Torts Section. The presentation had just ended when you bumped into Ms. Baker at the bar. Later, over a second cocktail, Ms. Baker recounted her last visit to the Neon Palms a few months ago and asked whether you think she might have a cause of action against Neon Palms.

2.1 Client Consultation

Rather than discussing a possible suit inside the very establishment against which there is a possible claim (and avoiding the risk of dispensing poor legal advice over a second round of drinks), you invite Ms. Baker to your office during business hours the following week.

Your notes from the meeting with Ms. Baker are below:

OFFICE CONSULTATION W/ LUCY BAKER (FEBRUARY 1)

- Ms. Baker and her friends were at Neon Palms celebrating the recent engagement of Ms. Baker's best friend, Tyler Morgan. They met at the bar around 5 P.M. on the Friday after Thanksgiving last year (3 months ago). They arrived via Uber/cabs so that no one had to be a designated driver.
- By around 7 P.M., the group had consumed several rounds of shots and everyone was getting "pretty loopy." They had planned to eat at the hotel restaurant for dinner, but they decided to continue drinking instead.
- At about 7:30 P.M., Ms. Baker became worried about how drunk everyone was. She asked the bartender to help her slow everyone down. She asked the bartender to either stop serving her friends drinks or to at least mix water into the shots. The bartender told her to "lighten up." He said no one was driving so there was no harm. He also noted that Ms. Baker's friends were "tipping big" and he wasn't going to risk those tips by serving diluted shots.
- At around 8 P.M.—memorable to Ms. Baker because the Sunport Storm game began around the same time—Tyler Morgan stepped outside to smoke a cigarette. Ms. Morgan is not typically a smoker but was quite drunk and followed someone outside and bummed a cigarette. Ms. Baker tried to watch Ms. Morgan through the windows and suddenly saw that Ms. Morgan was bent over and heaving. Ms. Baker watched as the man with Ms. Morgan walked away in disgust.
- Ms. Baker raced outside to help Ms. Morgan. She saw that the sidewalk was icy, so she tried to slow down. But when she got near Ms. Morgan, she slipped in Ms. Morgan's vomit.
- Ms. Baker immediately felt pain in her tailbone from the fall. When the pain lingered the next morning, she went to a clinic. The clinic performed x-rays and found she had a broken tailbone (coccyx). The clinic noted the injury is difficult to treat and usually requires a few months of physical therapy and massage until fully healed.

Exercise 1

1. **Based on the facts you learned from your office consultation with Ms. Baker, set forth the allegations that you can use to support each element of a negligence claim against the Neon Palms.**

2. Can you anticipate any arguments Neon Palms might make to avoid or minimize liability?

3. **Are there any other facts you think will provide additional support for the claim? Is there any additional information you would like to know?**

____

____

____

2.2 Legal Authority (Proximate Cause)

You believe there are two possible claims against Neon Palms: 1) Neon Palms acted negligently in overserving Ms. Baker and her friends; and/or 2) Neon Palms acted negligently by failing to address the dangerous conditions on the sidewalk outside the bar.

With respect to the first potential claim, you are primarily concerned about whether you can establish that the bar caused Ms. Baker's injuries. You believe you can establish that "but for" the bartender overserving Ms. Baker and her friends, Ms. Morgan would not have vomited, and Ms. Baker would not have exited the bar and slipped outside. Yet you are concerned about whether you can prove the bar was the *proximate* cause of injuries.

You find the following excerpts from *Trial Tactics in Sunport: A Practitioner's Toolkit*:

> In addition to proving *actual* cause, the plaintiff must prove the defendant's conduct was a *proximate* or *legal* cause of the plaintiff's injuries. Proximate cause serves as a limit on damages when the plaintiff's injuries are an unforeseeable consequence of the defendant's negligent conduct. Stated differently, the plaintiff may only recover damages associated with foreseeable harms that are not too remote and are within the scope of risks created by the defendant's conduct.
>
> Proximate cause is easier to assess if the plaintiff's injury was caused *directly* by the defendant's negligent act. For example, if a speeding driver strikes the plaintiff's car and causes injury to the plaintiff, then the plaintiff's injuries are a direct, foreseeable consequence of the defendant's negligent conduct (speeding).
>
> Yet in some cases, an event may occur *after* the defendant's negligent act that causes or exacerbates the plaintiff's injury. These are *intervening* causes of the plaintiff's injury. For example, if a speeding driver loses control of his car and strikes a telephone pole, then the pole falling onto the plaintiff's car is an "intervening cause" of the plaintiff's injury. The defendant's liability for harm caused by such intervening acts depends on whether such intervening acts are a foreseeable consequence of the defendant's negligent conduct. If the intervening cause is *foreseeable,* then it will not sever the chain of causation to allow the defendant to avoid liability. For example, a driver who violates the speed limit should foresee that his conduct creates a risk of a crash, including a collision with structures that might subsequently fall to cause property damage or injury to others.

> "[A]n intervening cause reasonably foreseeable by the defendant, is not such a new and independent cause as to break the chain of causation between the defendant's negligence and the injury complained of to the extent of relieving the defendant of liability for such injury." *Teer v. J. Weingarten, Inc.*, 426 S.W.2d 610 (Tex.Civ. App.— Houston [14th Dist.] 1968)

If the intervening cause is *unforeseeable*, then it may be considered a *superseding* event that breaks the chain of causation between the defendant's conduct and the plaintiff's injury. For example, if a speeding driver takes his car and passenger onto a highway overpass, which collapses because of an unforeseeable earthquake, then the unforeseeable "Act of God" acts as a superseding event that severs the chain of causation between the defendant's speeding and any injuries sustained by the plaintiff as a result of the bridge collapse.

You also find the below decision that you believe is not only factually similar but also relevant to the issue of proximate cause:

Crankshaw v. Piedmont Driving Club
156 S.E.2d 208 (Ga. Ct. App. 1967)

SYLLABUS BY THE COURT

The trial court correctly sustained a general demurrer to the petition where the defendant's negligence was not the proximate cause of the plaintiff's injury.

Plaintiff Elizabeth Crankshaw seeks damages against Piedmont Driving Club, Inc. alleging that on January 15, 1966, she in company with R. M. Harris and Miss Arlene Harris patronized the dining room of the defendant; that Miss Harris ordered shrimp and began eating same at which time she noticed a peculiar odor emanating from the shrimp dish causing her to feel nauseated; that Miss Harris excused herself and proceeded toward the rest room; shortly thereafter plaintiff proceeded toward the rest room to give aid and comfort to Miss Harris and as plaintiff entered the rest room she saw Miss Harris leaning over one of the bowls; that 'unbeknownest to plaintiff, Miss Harris had vomited just inside the entrance to the rest room' and that as she hurried toward her she 'stepped into the vomit, and her feet flew out from under her,' causing her to fall and break her hip. The petition alleged negligence of the defendant in selling unwholesome, deleterious food and in failing to clean up the floor of the rest room or to warn plaintiff of the condition of the floor . . .

OPINION

JORDAN, Presiding Judge.

Appellant in her brief properly abandons the allegation of negligence due to defendant's failure to clean the regurgitated substance from the floor since under the facts alleged the defendant had no notice, actual or constructive, of its presence on the floor prior to plaintiff's fall. Appellant contends, however, that 'the heart of the legal question presented' is whether or not the negligent serving of unwholesome food to Miss Harris was the proximate cause of her (appellant's) injury. Viewing the case from this posed question we conclude that the trial court was correct in sustaining the general demurrer.

'If the damages are only the imaginary or possible result of the tortious act, or other and contingent circumstances preponderate largely in causing the injurious effect, such damages are too remote to be the basis of recovery against the wrongdoer.' Code, s 105-2008. Damages must flow from the 'legal and natural result of the act done.' Code, s 105-2009. The question of proximate cause is one of a jury except in palpably clear and indisputable cases. We think the facts alleged in this petition bring it within the exception and subject it to be ruled upon as a matter of law. The court must assume this burden where a jury can draw but one reasonable conclusion if the facts alleged are proved, that conclusion being that the acts of the defendant were not the proximate cause of the injury. *Stallings v. Georgia Power Co.*, 67 Ga.App. 435, 20 S.E.2d 776. In our opinion a jury could not reasonably conclude that the plaintiff's injury was proximately caused by the defendant's negligence in serving unwholesome food to another person.

Judgment affirmed.

Exercise 2

1. How are the facts from *Crankshaw* similar to the facts in Ms. Baker's case? How are the facts different?

2. Does the court's reasoning in *Crankshaw* influence your assessment of Ms. Baker's possible claims? Why or why not?

____

____

____

2.3 Answer

You decide to take Ms. Baker's case and file a negligence claim against Neon Palms. You allege both causes of action: 1) Neon Palms breached a duty to prevent risk to bar patrons when it overserved Ms. Baker and her friends, causing the circumstances that led to Baker's fall; and 2) Neon Palms breached a duty to prevent risk to bar patrons when it failed to remedy or warn patrons of the icy conditions outside the bar, causing Ms. Baker to fall and sustain injury.

In its Answer, Neon Palms alleged the following:

> 15. Pursuant to the court's reasoning in *Byrne v. Wal-Mart Stores, Inc.*, this court should find Neon Palms did not have actual or constructive notice of the icy conditions outside the bar. The ice on the sidewalk was caused by a pipe that burst at approximately 6:30 P.M. on the night of the incident and about which no Neon Palms employee or member of management was aware of until later that evening. The weather the night of the incident was cold but clear with no precipitation, and no one notified management of water or ice outside the bar.
>
> ***
>
> 26. Neon Palms' conduct was not the proximate cause of Plaintiff's injuries because the event was unforeseeable and Plaintiff's intervening conduct broke the chain of causation.

2.4 Legal Authority—Landowner Liability

Neon Palms references the following case to support its argument that it did not breach a duty to Ms. Baker because it did not have actual or constructive notice of dangerous conditions on the sidewalk.

Byrne v. Wal-Mart Stores, Inc.
877 So. 2d 462 (Miss. Ct. App. 2004)

***

The undisputed facts in this case are that Byrne was shopping in Wal-Mart on April 8, 1998. While walking through the ladies' apparel department on her way to the front of the store, Byrne stepped on an unidentified substance, thought to be a cookie, causing her to injure her back and knee. Byrne filed suit against Wal-Mart and two employees, Andrew Lightsey, Wal-Mart's manager, and Jane Doe on November 7, 2000. On June 17, 2002, a motion for summary judgment was made by the defendants. The trial court considered arguments from both sides and subsequently granted the defendants' motion for summary judgment. Finding no genuine issue of material fact and that the defendants are entitled to a judgment as a matter of law, we affirm.

***

This cause of action is one of negligence, particularly premises liability. The standard of proof for this type of action was outlined in the case of *Downs v. Choo*, 656 So.2d 84, 86 (Miss. 1995). According to *Downs*, in order to succeed in a premises liability action, the plaintiff must prove one of three things: (1) a negligent act by the defendant caused the plaintiff's injury; or, (2) that defendant had actual knowledge of a dangerous condition, but failed to warn the plaintiff of the danger; or, (3) the dangerous condition remained long enough to impute constructive knowledge to the defendant. *Downs*, 656 So.2d at 86; *see also Drennan v. Kroger*, 672 So.2d 1168, 1170 (Miss. 1996); [*Young v. Wendy's Int'l, Inc.*, 840 So.2d 782, 784 (Miss.Ct.App.2003].

To meet the first prong of *Downs*, Byrne needed to produce evidence that demonstrated the defendants' negligence with regard to the unidentified object that allegedly led to her injuries. The duty of a store owner to its invitees has repeatedly been cited as a duty to exercise ordinary care and to keep the premises reasonably safe while warning invitees of dangerous conditions known to the store owner. *Munford Inc. v. Fleming*, 597 So.2d 1282, 1284 (Miss. 1992). However, the store owner is not an insurer of business invitees' injuries. *Sears, Roebuck Co. v. Tisdale*, 185 So.2d 916, 917 (Miss. 1966). In *Sears, Roebuck*, the court stated, "The basis of liability is negligence and not injury. Proof merely of the occurrence of a fall on a floor within business premises is insufficient to show negligence on the part of the proprietor. Proof that the floor on which the fall occurred had present thereon litter and debris is similarly insufficient." *Id.* at 917. In the case, *sub judice*, Byrne failed to produce evidence that the defendants breached the duty owed to her as a business invitee.

Byrne failed to produce any proof that the object which caused her injury was the result of an affirmative act by Wal-Mart or Andrew Lightsey, as manager. In fact, she stated in her deposition that she did not know how the cookie came to be on the floor. The Wal-Mart employees who were deposed stated that they too did not know how the cookie got on the floor. Byrne did not offer any proof that met her burden under the first prong of Downs. However, she could still survive summary judgment by proving that Wal-Mart or Andrew Lightsey had actual or constructive knowledge of the dangerous condition.

In the case of *Miss. Winn-Dixie Supermarkets, Inc. v. Hughes*, 247 Miss. 575, 584, 156 So.2d 734, 736 (1963), the court stated:

> Where it appears that a floor in a store or similar place of business has been made dangerous by litter or debris present thereon, and that the presence of the

> litter or debris is traceable to persons for whom the proprietor is not responsible, proof that the proprietor was negligent in relation to the floor condition requires a showing that he had actual notice thereof, or that the condition existed for such a length of time that, in the exercise of reasonable care, he should have known of it.

No proof was offered that the defendants had actual knowledge of the cookie's being on the floor. In fact, there was no possible way that Andrew Lightsey had actual knowledge because, according to his deposition, he was not at work on the day of Byrne's injury. Constructive knowledge is imputed to the store by a showing of the length of time the dangerous condition existed prior to the plaintiff's injury. *Waller v. Dixieland Food Stores, Inc.*, 492 So.2d 283, 285 (Miss. 1986). Based on the length of time the condition was present, the store owner exercising reasonable care should have known of its existence. *Id*. There was no proof offered by Byrne on this matter either. She stated in her deposition that she did not know how long the cookie had been on the floor and that she did not take a good look to see what type of object caused her injury. Byrne failed to show that the object was on the floor long enough for the defendants to have notice and remedy the situation.

. . . There is a striking lack of evidence in the present case. The appellate courts of this state have previously reversed summary judgments in premises liability cases. [Citation omitted.] However, those cases presented the court with genuine issues of material fact and summary judgment should have been denied. In the case, *sub judice*, the trial court committed no error by granting the summary judgment motion because Byrne failed to sustain her burden of proof by showing that genuine issues of material fact existed for the court's consideration.

***

Exercise 3

1. **Prepare notes for a call with Ms. Baker advising her of the implications of Neon Palms' assertion that they were unaware of the burst pipe the night Ms. Baker visited the bar.**

Proximate Cause: *Vankirk v. Safe Haven Security Co.*

Hubbs Insurance Company was pleased with your representation of Dr. Twist in the case involving Sharon Battle, and it assigned another matter to you. This time, they asked you to represent Safe Haven Security Company.

Safe Haven received a demand letter from an attorney representing Samantha Vankirk. Safe Haven installed a security system in Ms. Vankirk's home, but the system failed to detect or sound an alarm when a burglar broke into her home in March. The perpetrators took valuables and assaulted Ms. Vankirk during the incident.

Your contact at Hubbs Insurance asked you to evaluate Ms. Vankirk's claims. Specifically, Hubbs would like a recommendation about whether it should pay the demand or attempt to settle for a lower amount.

3.1 Demand Letter

The demand letter reads as follows:

Davidson Law Group

6000 MAIN STREET, STE. 450
Eastvale, Sunport 00440
(222) 555-1234

February 17

Safe Haven Security Co.
2000 Airport Blvd. Unit A
Southlake, Sunport 00550

Re: Demand for Just Compensation—Samantha Vankirk

To whom it may concern:

This firm is counsel to Ms. Samantha Vankirk, who was victim of the substandard installation practices of your company. In reliance on representations that a Safe Haven system would protect her home against potential burglaries and other threats, Ms. Vankirk hired Safe Haven to install a security system at her residence located at 7617 Ivy Lane, Southlake, Sunport 00579.

Unfortunately, less than one month after the installation, Ms. Vankirk was the victim of a burglary. On December 15 of last year, Ms. Vankirk's valuable property—including several luxury jewelry items and high-end electronics—was stolen after intruders entered her home without triggering the alarm system. Ms. Vankirk heard the intruders and attempted to leave her home through the back door in the kitchen, but as she rounded the corner from the hallway into her kitchen, she collided with one of the intruders who was carrying a stack of stereo components. The force of the collision caused Ms. Vankirk to sustain multiple gashes and bruises to her face and torso. Ms. Vankirk fell, resulting in a severe sprain to her ankle. The perpetrators fled when they realized Ms. Vankirk was in the home.

An inspection revealed that Safe Haven's installers failed to properly connect the wires leading from the control panel to the system's visual and audio alarms. Thus, Ms. Vankirk was not alerted to the entry by the burglars, and the system's deterrence features were never triggered.

As a direct result of the incident, Ms. Vankirk suffered not only physical injuries but also severe emotional distress. Ms. Vankirk also sustained significant property losses, including the costs to replace a new security system, and she incurred extensive medical expenses. Finally, Ms. Vankirk missed several weeks of work while she oversaw repairs to her home and received necessary medical care.

This letter serves as a formal demand that Safe Haven Security Company compensate Ms. Vankirk for her damages, including the following:

- **Medical Expenses:** all costs related to the physical injuries sustained by Ms. Vankirk during the burglary (currently approximating $7,500);
- **Property Loss:** compensation for stolen personal property, including the value of several luxury watches and other jewelry ($22,450);
- **Repair Costs:** costs to repair damage caused to Ms. Vankirk's home during the burglary ($6,500);
- **Replacement Costs**: costs to replace Ms. Vankirk's security system ($10,500);
- **Lost Income:** income Ms. Vankirk lost by missing two weeks of work to perform/ supervise home repairs, replace personal property, receive medical treatment, and recuperate from trauma ($30,000).

Accordingly, we hereby demand that Safe Haven Security Company immediately pay Ms. Vankirk the amount of $70,450 in exchange for a full release and settlement of all claims arising from the matters discussed herein.

Please respond to this demand within sixty (60) days. Should Safe Haven Security Company fail to make the demanded payment by that time, we will be left with no choice but to file a lawsuit seeking any and all damages legally available to Ms. Vankirk, including damages to be proven at trial for any pain, suffering, and emotional distress as well as attorneys' fees Ms. Vankirk incurs while prosecuting her claims against you.

We look forward to your prompt response.

Regards,

Ronald Davidson, Esq.

Counsel to Samantha Vankirk

You believe a factfinder will almost certainly find that Safe Haven breached a duty to properly install the system. Moreover, Ms. Vankirk can prove that the break-in caused significant damages.

Yet you believe Ms. Vankirk will have difficulty establishing the element of causation, both actual and proximate cause.

Exercise 1

1. **What are the challenges Ms. Vankirk will experience in establishing causation?**

3.2 Client Interview

You speak with Safe Haven's product manager, John Hartgrove, who oversaw the installation of Samantha Vankirk's security system. You also forward Mr. Hartgrove a copy of the police report from the incident.

Mr. Hartgrove was incensed during your phone interview, repeatedly insisting that Safe Haven shouldn't "pay a dime." He argued that Ms. Vankirk's demand was outrageous and "completely overblown." Mr. Hartgrove asserted the company cannot be legally liable for injuries caused by "law-breaking hooligans. Our company had nothing to do with the burglary. Obviously, we didn't participate, and she is essentially asking us to take responsibility for someone else's criminality. It's absurd." Mr. Hartgrove also believes the monetary demand is excessive, especially Ms. Vankirk's claims for lost wages.

Near the end of your call, Mr. Hartgrove grudgingly noted, "If the deterrence features had worked as intended, then they probably would have prevented the criminals from getting into the house the way they did."

You believe Mr. Hartgrove's assessment establishes actual cause because, but for the failure of the system, the burglary would have been prevented. Yet you wonder if, as Mr. Hartgrove asserted, Safe Haven should bear liability for the criminal acts of others.

3.3 Legal Authority—Intervening Causes

You find the following overview from *Gregory & Harrow's Civil Practice in Sunport*, which reviews whether the criminal conduct of another party is a foreseeable consequence of a defendant's negligence.

"Generally, an intervening intentional or criminal act severs the liability of the original tort-feasor. [*Kush v. City of Buffalo,* 59 N.Y.2d 26, 462 N.Y.S.2d 831, 449 N.E.2d 725, 729 (1983).] But that 'doctrine has no application when the intentional or criminal intervention of a third party or parties is reasonably foreseeable.' *Id.*" *In re September 11 Litigation*, 280 F.Supp.2d 279, 302 (S.D.N.Y., 2003).

For example:

- In *Martinez v. California*, a state parole board released a prisoner who committed a murder five months later. The court found the board was not legally responsible for damages related to the murder because the murder was "too remote a consequence of the parole officers' action to hold them responsible." 444 U.S. 277 (1980).
- In contrast, in *Cotton v. Smith*, a high school employee failed to perform her ministerial duties and check an individual's identification to verify he was authorized to remove a 14-year-old student from school. 310 Ga.App. 428, 428 (Ga. Ct. App. 2011).

The man, who claimed to be the student's uncle, was actually a 52-year-old convicted felon who offered a false name. *Id.* The school released the student to the man, who later molested her. *Id.* The court held that the man's criminal act did not necessarily sever the chain of causation between the school's negligent act and the plaintiff's injury. *Id.* at 441. The court found that a jury could reasonably find that the administrator could have prevented the student from leaving with the perpetrator had she performed her ministerial duties. *Id.* Moreover, "[a] jury would also be authorized to find not only that [the perpetrator's] molestation of N.F. was a reasonably foreseeable consequence of negligently releasing the 14–year–old girl to an unidentified, unrelated, and unauthorized 52–year–old man, but that the school's rules at issue here were *specifically intended,* at least in part, to avoid that very consequence." *Id.*

The court cited *Ontario Sewing Machine Co. v. Smith,* 275 Ga. 683, 686–687(2), 572 S.E.2d 533 (2002) to support its finding:

> [I]f the character of the intervening act claimed to break the connection between the original wrongful act and the subsequent injury was such that its probable or natural consequences could reasonably have been anticipated, apprehended, or foreseen by the original wrong-doer, the causal connection is not broken, and the original wrong-doer is responsible for all of the consequences resulting from the intervening act. The rule that an intervening and independent wrongful act of a third person producing the injury, and without which it would not have occurred, should be treated as the proximate cause, insulating and excluding the negligence of the defendant, would not apply if the defendant had reasonable grounds for apprehending that such wrongful act would be committed.

- In *Century Alarm of Tucson v. Ganem*, an employee overseeing the installation of an ultrasonic security system at a pawn shop negligently left a key where an unauthorized person could obtain access. 116 Ariz. 74, 74-75 (Ct. App. 1977). An unknown third party did so, deactivated the system, and robbed the store. *Id.* at 75. The court held that the negligence was the proximate cause of the owner's injury because the intervening criminal act of thief was within the "ambit of risk" created by alarm company and did not constitute a superseding cause. *Id.* at 77.

Exercise 2

1. **After reviewing your notes above, how do you respond to Mr. Hartgrove's assertion that Safe Haven is not legally liable for injuries caused by "law-breaking hooligans"? What is your opinion about whether Ms. Vankirk can establish that the burglary was a foreseeable intervening cause of her injuries?**

____

____

____

3.4 Recommendation

You meet with your contact at Hubbs to discuss the case. After you present your findings and opinions about the legal issues in the case, your contact asks for your recommendation about a settlement. You note that the client is concerned about the negative publicity of a trial but is willing to contest the claim if they are certain to win.

Exercise 3

1. **What is your recommendation about a settlement with Vankirk? Explain your answer in light of the client's goals.**

3.5 Negotiations

While your Hubbs contact considers your recommendations, she asks you to contact Ms. Vankirk's attorney. Hubbs believes that Ms. Vankirk's claims for damages are not recoverable and wants you to gather more information about the claims. Specifically, Hubbs wants to understand why Ms. Vankirk is claiming $30,000 in lost income when she only missed a few weeks of work.

You speak with Mr. Davidson and ask him to explain Ms. Vankirk's claims. Notes from your conversation are below:

- Ms. Vankirk's medical expenses are documented and have currently reached $8,200. Ms. Vankirk's insurance has a high deductible, and certain cosmetic treatments to minimize scarring to her face were not fully covered by her insurance plan.
- Ms. Vankirk has receipts or appraised values for the items stolen from her home and can demonstrate that the lost items were worth $22,450. Some of the stolen electronic equipment was used, and the suggested values are speculative.
- Ms. Vankirk replaced a window and repaired a door in her home, and there was damage to her walls and floors where the perpetrators removed or dragged items through the house. Ms. Vankirk has an itemized invoice from the contractor who performed repairs totaling $6,500.
- Ms. Vankirk has an invoice demonstrating that she paid a different security system $10,500 to remove the Safe Haven system and install a new security system in her home.
- Ms. Vankirk is a self-employed healthcare consultant and does not have paid leave. Ms. Vankirk declined three speaking engagements immediately after the burglary so she could supervise home repairs, assess lost property, and rest and recuperate from the trauma she experienced. Ms. Vankirk would have earned $30,000 had she accepted the engagements.
- Ms. Vankirk has already incurred around $4,000 in costs and fees related to Mr. Davidson's legal representation.

At the end of the call, Mr. Davidson stated:

> Honestly, her request is very fair considering the circumstances. This could be a publicity nightmare for your client, and there are plenty of people who would take advantage of the situation. My client just wants to move on if you give her what she is due.
>
> But know this: If Safe Haven decides to fight, then I can guarantee it will be expensive. Just imagine the press about a high-end security system that completely failed to protect the person who paid for its installation. If we have to file suit, then we'll ask for punitive damages, attorneys' fees, and damages for emotional distress. A jury will be very sympathetic and will certainly understand that this situation caused a great deal of immediate and long-term suffering. That claim could be ten times what we're asking for now, so I strongly recommend your client accept this reasonable offer.

3.6 Legal Authority—Shabby Millionaire

Before you speak with Hubbs about your recommendations, you evaluate whether Ms. Vankirk's demands for compensation are reasonable/recoverable. You find the following excerpts from a *Gregory & Harrow's Civil Practice in Sunport* outlining the "shabby millionaire" principle:

> On the issue of damages, difficulty arises if, because of some sensitivity of the plaintiff, damages are more severe than might be anticipated were the plaintiff an average person. From such emerges the "eggshell-skull doctrine," which demands that a negligent defendant be liable for *all* the plaintiff's injuries, even if those injuries are more severe than what a typical person might experience. "The defendant must take the victim as he finds him and he is responsible for all natural and probable consequences of his tortious conduct." *Abbasi v. State Farm Ins. Co.*, 875 So.2d 988, 995, 04-44 La.App. 5 Cir. 5/26/04, 10 (La.App. 5 Cir.,2004)
>
> Related to this doctrine is the less familiar "shabby millionaire rule," which applies if the plaintiff's *economic* harm is more severe than a typical person.
>
>> The true value or "shabby millionaire" rule complements the thin skull doctrine. Gary Bahr & Bruce Graham, *The Thin Skull Plaintiff Concept: Evasive or Persuasive?,* 15 Loy.L.A.L.Rev. 409, 410 (1982). The thin skull doctrine declares that foreseeability of plaintiff's injuries is not an issue in determining the *extent of injury* suffered, while the . . . shabby millionaire rule declares that foreseeability is not an issue in determining *the extent of damages* that the injuries cause. *Id.* (citing Rowe, *The Demise of the Thin Skull Rule,* 40 Mod.L.Rev. 377 (1977)).[1]
>
> *Schafer v. Hoffman*, 831 P.2d 897, 902 (1992).
>
> ---
>
> 1. If a person fires across a road when it is dangerous to do so and kills a man who is in receipt of a large income, he will be liable for the whole damage, however great, that may have resulted to his family, and cannot set up that he could not have reasonably expected to have injured any one but a laborer. Gary Bahr & William Graham, The Thin Skull Plaintiff Concept: Evasive or Persuasive?, 15 Loy.L.A.L.Rev. 409, 410-11 (1982) (*citing Smith v. London & S.W. Ry.*, L.R. 6 C.P. 14, 22-23 (1870)); Glanville Williams, The Risk Principle, 77 L.Q.Rev. 179 (1961).

Exercise 4

1. **How does the "shabby millionaire" rule influence your assessment of whether Ms. Vankirk can recover lost income of $30,000?**

____

____

____

3.7 Legal Authority—Damages

To evaluate Vankirk's other claims, you refer to Sunport's Pattern Jury Instructions:

Sunport Pattern Jury Instructions (Civil Cases)
§ 8.6 COMPENSATORY DAMAGES:

If you find that the defendant is liable to the plaintiff, then you must determine an amount that is fair compensation for all of the plaintiff's damages. The purpose of compensatory damages is to make the plaintiff whole—that is, to compensate the plaintiff for the damage that the plaintiff has incurred because of the defendant's conduct.

There are two categories of compensatory damages to which a plaintiff is liable.

1) In the first category are *special damages*, which are *economic* losses caused by the defendant's misconduct. These include but are not limited to lost wages or diminished earning capacity, medical expenses, and property repairs.
2) The second category includes *general damages*, which are designed to compensate the plaintiff for noneconomic harms and for which there is no actual market value. These might include a plaintiff's physical pain and suffering and emotional distress.

In determining the amount(s) of plaintiff's compensatory damages in each of the categories set forth above, you may not refuse to award nor reduce the amount of any such damages because of any physical frailties or financial status of the plaintiff that may have made her more susceptible to injury, disability, or impairment.

§ 8.8 PUNITIVE DAMAGES:

In negligence cases, punitive damages are generally not recoverable. Punitive damages are typically reserved for instances where the defendant's actions are particularly egregious, transcending mere negligence to reach a level of gross negligence, willful misconduct, or malice.

§ 8.9 ATTORNEYS' FEES:

Sunport follows the "American Rule" which requires litigants to pay for their own attorneys' fees. Only when a party can point to a specific statute that permits a prevailing party to recover their attorneys' fees or a governing contract between the litigants that provides for the payment of attorneys' fees may such fees be recovered.

Exercise 5

1. **Based on the rules above, evaluate whether Ms. Vankirk may recover damages for the injuries Opposing Counsel identified in his original demand letter or during your phone call.**

Claim	Category (Special, General, Other)	Likelihood of Recovery
a. Medical expenses $8,200		
b. Stolen property $22,450		
c. Property repair $6,500		
d. Security system replacement $10,500		
e. Lost income $30,000		
f. Pain and suffering *Potentially raised at trial		
g. Punitive damages *Potentially raised at trial		
h. Attorneys' fees *Potentially raised at trial, currently estimated to be $4,000		

Exercise 6

1. **Will you recommend that Hubbs accept Ms. Vankirk's demand to pay $74,450 on behalf of Safe Haven? Why or why not?**

____

____

____

Special Cases

10

Respondeat Superior: Varela Furniture & Appliance Store

Your supervising attorney has asked you to help her prepare a motion for summary judgment[1] to be filed on behalf of the firm's client, Varela Furniture & Appliance Store. The business is owned by Mike Varela.

1.1 Pleadings

You reviewed the pleadings and the evidence gathered in the case and understand the following facts are undisputed:

- Mr. Varela employs drivers to deliver furniture and appliances to its customers. Deliveries are made using Varela Furniture vans painted with the store's logo. Ian Sterling was employed as a Varela delivery driver.
- On the day in question, Mr. Sterling delivered a small dining room set and a flat-screen TV to Valentina Perez, a Varela customer who lived in north Eastvale. Once Mr. Sterling delivered and unloaded the furniture and TV, Ms. Perez asked if Mr. Sterling would take her old television to her sister's home, which was about six blocks from Mr. Sterling's next delivery. The customer offered Mr. Sterling $100 to make this delivery. Mr. Sterling agreed, anticipating this delivery would add no more than 30 minutes to his workday.

1. **What is Summary Judgment?** Either party may file a motion for summary judgment before trial begins. A party may file if the party believes that there are no issues of material fact in dispute so the moving party is entitled to judgment as a matter of law. For example, the plaintiff might file a motion for summary judgment if the plaintiff believes she has established the elements of a *prima facie* case, and the defendant has failed to dispute them or present any defenses. A defendant might file a motion for summary judgment if the defendant believes the plaintiff failed to establish an element(s) of the *prima facie* case or if the defendant believes a defense conclusively bars the plaintiff's claim.

   The judge must review available evidence, including the non-moving party's response, in the light most favorable to the non-moving party. If the judge agrees with the moving party's arguments, then the judge may decide the case without a trial.

- When Mr. Sterling arrived at the home, there was no available parking on the street. Consequently, in violation of a local traffic ordinance, Mr. Sterling double-parked the delivery van in front of the house and unloaded the TV.
- While Mr. Sterling was carrying the TV into the home, a car driven by Nik Varga swerved to avoid Mr. Sterling's delivery van and skidded into oncoming traffic. Mr. Varga's car was struck by a garbage truck, and Mr. Varga was seriously injured. Mr. Varga sued Mr. Varela to recover damages based on his personal injuries and damage to his car.

The defendant sued Mr. Varela under the doctrine of *respondeat superior*. Nik Varga likely sued Mr. Varela instead of Ian Sterling because Mr. Varela has more extensive financial resources and is more likely to pay a large judgment.

1.2 Legal Authority—Vicarious Liability

You find the following excerpt defining the doctrine of *respondeat superior* from *Brenner's Sunport Trial Handbook*:

Generally, there is no vicarious liability (holding one party liable for the actions of another); a person has no duty to control the conduct of another and is not responsible for another party's tortious acts. Yet in some cases, given the nature of the relationship between the parties, the fault of one party may be imputed to another.

The relationship between an employer and employee is one such relationship. This category of vicarious liability is identified as *respondeat superior* ("let the master answer").

To prove vicarious liability under a theory of *respondeat superior*, a plaintiff must show that the negligent actor: 1) was an employee, and 2) was acting in the course and score of employment.

An employee is acting in the course and scope of employment if the employee's acts are done within the scope of the employee's general authority, in furtherance of the employer's business, and for the accomplishment of the object for which the employee was hired.

***

The question is complicated if the employee commits a negligent act while temporarily deviating from employment responsibilities (i.e., an employee commits a tort while stopped for a meal).

> A servant is acting in the course of his employment, when he is engaged in that which he was employed to do, and is at the time about his master's business. He is not acting in the course of his employment if he is engaged in some

pursuit of his own. Not every deviation from the strict execution of his duty is such an interruption of the course of employment as to suspend the master's responsibility, but, if there is a total departure from the course of the master's business, the master is not answerable for the servant's conduct. Tiffany on Agency, p. 270. *Robertson v. Power Co.*, 204 N.C. 359, 168 S.E. 415.

Parrott v. Kantor, 6 S.E.2d 40, 43 (N.C. 1939)

The concepts of "frolic and detour" give some clarity here. If the employee's deviation is minor in time and geographic area—a mere "detour"—then the employer likely remains liable for the tortious acts of the employee. Yet if the employee's deviation is unauthorized and substantial—a "frolic"—then the employer is likely absolved of liability.

Your supervisor believes that, regardless of whether Mr. Sterling was in fact negligent when he double-parked the delivery van, Mr. Varela cannot be liable under the doctrine of *respondeat superior* because Mr. Sterling was not acting within the scope of his employment when he made the delivery. Mr. Varela did not direct him to make the delivery; in fact, Mr. Sterling accepted the "job" from a client and was consequently acting on his own behalf.

1.3 Legal Authority—Frolic and Detour

You also find the following case that discusses the issues implicated in the case.

Chorey, Taylor & Feil, P.C. v. Clark
539 S.E.2d 139 (Ga. 2000)

BENHAM, Chief Justice.

We granted a writ of certiorari to the Court of Appeals in order to address that court's application of the doctrine of respondeat superior to the facts of this case . . .

In April 1996, appellee Dannice Clark was injured when her automobile was struck by a car driven by Wanda Chatham, an employee of a law firm named Vincent, Chorey, Taylor & Feil, P.C. ("Vincent Chorey"). The collision occurred while Ms. Chatham was on her way in her personal vehicle to deliver a check for telephone service for Vincent, Berg, Stalzer & Menendez, P.C. ("Vincent Berg"). Vincent Berg was a new law firm not yet open for business that had been established by some of the Vincent Chorey attorneys, and was the law firm for which Chatham had agreed to begin work in May 1996. Appellant Chorey, Taylor & Feil, P.C. ("Chorey Taylor") is the current configuration (following the departure of the Vincent Berg attorneys) of the law firm that employed Chatham at the time of the collision. Appellee Clark filed a personal injury action against Chatham and, citing the doctrine of respondeat superior, included as defendants Chatham's employer at the time of filing suit (Vincent Berg) and Chorey Taylor . . .

"The clearest case of vicarious liability [that is, liability for the tort of another] is that of a master for harm caused by acts of his servant." Harper, James & Gray, *The Law of Torts,* § 26.6, p. 23 (2nd ed. 1986). Under the principle of respondeat superior, "employers are generally jointly and severally liable along with the tortfeasor employee for the torts of employees committed within the scope of employment." Dobbs, *The Law of Torts,* § 333, p. 905 (2000). . . .

When an employee causes an injury to another, the test to determine if the employer is liable is whether the employee was acting within the scope of the employee's employment and on the business of the employer at the time of the injury. *Allen Kane's Major Dodge v. Barnes,* 243 Ga. 776, 777, 257 S.E.2d 186 (1979). . . . The employer is not liable for the employee's tort if the tort was committed, "not by reason of the employment, but because of matters disconnected therewith. . . ." *Frazier v. Southern R. Co.,* 200 Ga. 590(2), 37 S.E.2d 774 (1946). Stated another way, if the employee was authorized to accomplish the purpose in pursuance of which the tort was committed, the employer is liable.

. . . In the case at bar, Chatham was asked by a fellow employee to deliver a check issued by an entity other than Chatham's employer for initiation of phone service for an entity other than Chatham's employer. There is no evidence that Chatham's attempt to deliver the check was in furtherance of her employer's business. In fact, it appears that the opposite is true inasmuch as the delivery of the check would aid some of Chatham's fellow employees in their effort to open a business in competition with Chatham's employer. The fact that some of her fellow employees might benefit from her delivery of the check is not evidence that Chatham was in the business of her employer when she attempted to deliver the check. Without evidence that Chatham's employer's business was to assist in the set up of new law firms, the fact that the fellow employee who asked the favor of Chatham later described herself as having acted in her capacity as an employee of Chatham's employer when she made the request is not evidence that Chatham was on the business of her employer when she collided with Ms. Clark.

However willing we are to commit to the jury the solution of every question of fact, yet in the very nature of things, when the determination of the issue rests not on direct proof, but on circumstances, there exists a point where the inferences to be drawn can not, as a matter of law, be sufficient to [defeat the grant of summary judgment.] [Cit.]

Allen Kane's Major Dodge v. Barnes, 243 Ga. 776, 779, 257 S.E.2d 186 (1979). Accordingly, we reverse the judgment of the Court of Appeals and order the reinstatement of the trial court's entry of summary judgment in favor of Chorey Taylor.

Judgment reversed.

Exercise 1

1. **Using the legal authority from your research above and the facts you learned from your review of the file, draft an argument to insert into the motion for summary judgment. The heading summarizing your argument is included below.**

   The doctrine of *respondeat superior* is inapplicable because defendant's employee was not acting within the scope of his employment when the incidents described in plaintiff's complaint occurred.

2. How might the plaintiff respond to the argument above?

1.4 Deposition

Before the motion for summary judgment was filed, the plaintiff deposed Ian Sterling. During the deposition, Mr. Sterling testified as follows:

Counsel for Plaintiff:	Did you tell your employer you planned to drop the TV at the home of the customer's sister?
Mr. Sterling:	Yeah. I texted him and said I was going to do another quick delivery, but I was sure I could get my remaining deliveries done.
Counsel for Plaintiff:	How did your employer respond?
Mr. Sterling:	He sent a thumbs up.

Exercise 2

1. **Does this testimony influence your analysis of whether the doctrine of *respondeat superior* is applicable? Why or why not?**

2. **Would it change your opinion if, with Mr. Varela's knowledge, Ian Sterling routinely accepted extra payment to dispose of replaced furniture?**

3. **Would it change your opinion if Ian Sterling customarily gave Mr. Varela a "cut" of his earnings after disposing of used furniture?**

Professional Negligence: *Varela Furniture & Appliance Store*

Before your firm files its motion for summary judgment in its case involving Varela Furniture & Appliance Store, *supra*, the plaintiff (Nik Varga) filed a motion for summary judgment, alleging he was entitled to judgment as a matter of law under theories of negligence per se and *respondeat superior*.

2.1 Background

Your attorney asked you to reconfigure your arguments to respond to the arguments in the plaintiff's motion. You completed a draft Response in Opposition to Plaintiff's Motion for Summary Judgment and sent the draft to your supervising attorney. Your attorney thanked you for your work and said she would review, edit, and file the Response before the deadline. You entered time spent in the firm's billing software, which automatically generated an invoice for the client.

Eight days later, you sent an email to your supervising attorney with the following note: "As a reminder, the Response to Varga's motion for summary judgment is due in two days. Please let me know if you need me to make any further revisions." The next week, you learned your supervising attorney failed to file the Response before the deadline.

You realize this has severe consequences for the client; the judge may make a decision about the plaintiff's motion without considering your arguments or, even worse, deem the failure to respond as a concession to the plaintiff's arguments.[2]

Yesterday, your supervising attorney asked you to take notes while she spoke by phone with Mr. Varela. During that call, you were shocked and dismayed to hear that your supervising attorney did not admit to missing the court's briefing deadline. Instead, she advised Mr. Varela

2. **What are the consequences of failing to respond to a motion for summary judgment?** When a party files a Motion for Summary Judgment, the party outlines the legal arguments that support the motion (why they believe they are entitled to judgment as a matter of law). The moving party may also submit supporting evidence, including affidavits, deposition transcripts, exhibits, etc. The non-moving party typically has between 14-21 days to file a response. The response should outline the non-moving party's arguments and may include supporting evidence.

   If the non-moving party fails to respond before the filing deadline, then there may be serious implications. The non-responding party effectively waives any arguments or defenses they might have had against the motion, and the motion may be granted in their absence. Courts may even draw an adverse inference from the failure to respond, which can be interpreted as evidence that the non-responding party does not object or even agrees with the facts or conclusions set forth in the motion. In some jurisdictions, the court may deem the failure to respond an admission of the arguments presented in the motion. Some courts might also impose sanctions for failing to comply with procedural rules. Finally, a failure to respond limits the non-moving party's objections or arguments on appeal.

that his legal position was "very risky" and that he should "strongly consider" settling with Mr. Varga before trial. You feel confident that your supervising attorney was actually trying to mitigate the damage she caused by missing the deadline. Clearly, she hoped that, if Mr. Varela settled the case before trial, then she could secure a "win" before the court ruled on the plaintiff's motion for summary judgment.

After thinking long and hard about this dilemma, you decide to speak with your firm's managing partner to report the incident. The partner was justifiably concerned about the firm's potential exposure to a potential malpractice/professional negligence claim. The partner asked you to consider whether Mr. Varela might have a claim against the firm based on the conduct of your supervising attorney.

Exercise 1

1. **Are the elements of a professional negligence claim any different from the elements for a general negligence claim? If so, how?**

2. **Do you believe Mr. Varela has a viable claim for negligence? Can he plead all of the elements to establish a *prima facie* claim?**

Part III
Other Torts

Defamation

11

Shakin' Cajun v. Richmond

You received another client referral about a case involving the Shakin' Cajun, a local restaurant with a creole flair. You spoke by phone with the owner, Cher O'Brien, who is livid about an online review that a former patron, Terrence Richmond, left on multiple restaurant review apps. The customer cut and pasted the review to the *Shriek* app, which has been ranked the most-used restaurant review app for the last 10 years.

11.1 Customer Review

Ms. O'Brien emailed you the text of the review, which reads as follows:

> *If I could give the Shakin' Cajun negative stars, I would. This place is an absolute disaster from the moment you walk in. The smell? A little burnt grease mixed with a whole lot of regret. The ambience? Flickering lights, greasy floors, and a wait staff as bitter as its crawfish etouffee.*
>
> *I'm from New Orleans and I know my crawfish. The Shakin' Cajun doesn't use crawfish in its "crawfish" dishes—it uses imitation lobster meat and tries to pass it off as crawfish. I said as much to our server (better titled "Space Cadet"), who swore up and down that it wasn't true, basically calling me a liar in front of my friends.*
>
> *What's more is I saw the bartender pouring cheap-a** vodka into a top shelf vodka bottle, and I know they charged me full top-shelf price for a rail drink. They were cited by the ABC (Alcohol & Beverage Commission) for this type of activity in the past and I guess they haven't learned their lesson yet.*
>
> *Save your money, your taste buds, and your dignity. Don't patronize this culinary criminal.*

Ms. O'Brien tells you this review has no less than three false statements: 1) that the Shakin' Cajun uses imitation lobster that it passes off as crawfish; 2) that it replaces top shelf vodka with cheaper vodka; and 3) that it has been cited for this activity by the ABC.

Ms. O'Brien also provided you a copy of some of the comments left under the defamatory review:

> **[User]:** *Amen, brother. Thanks for this — Shakin' Cajun's never getting my money again.*
>
> **[User]:** *I agree! Food sucks, alcohol is too expensive! No more Shakin' Cajun for me!*
>
> **[User]:** *Wow. I didn't even realize I was getting rail drinks instead of top shelf. This is so disappointing — I used to love Shakin' Cajun but I guess not anymore.*
>
> **[User]:** *Dude — you sure about that? I used to work there and there was no switching alcohol that I ever saw. Management is so conscientious because they know reputation is everything. Only reason I stopped working there is because I finally decided to go to law school, but that place is SHAKIN'! (get it?) Seriously, y'all . . . don't give up on them based on this clown's bogus review.*

Ms. O'Brien also presented you with data about the financial impact of the review. Her notes indicate:

> - For the 6 months prior to Mr. Richmond's review, Shakin' Cajun was at full capacity between the hours of 6 P.M. and 10 P.M. on Thursdays, Fridays, and Saturdays, and at 60 percent capacity on all other nights during those hours.
> - In the 3 months since the review, Shakin' Cajun has never exceeded 80 percent capacity on any given night between the hours of 6 P.M. and 10 P.M.
> - Our accountant's rough estimate of the resulting lost profits for this 3-month period is $13,500. I am concerned about our ability to stay afloat if these losses keep occurring.
> - I want to save our restaurant's reputation by sending a message that the Shakin' Cajun is not afraid to sue those who post baseless and defamatory reviews that do nothing but spread lies.

1.2 Legal Authority — Defamation

You believe the restaurant may have a valid claim for defamation.

You find the following overview of defamation in *Gregory & Harrow's Civil Practice in Sunport*:

> To establish a cause of action for defamation, the plaintiff must demonstrate that there has been:
>
> 1) A publication;
> 2) Of a defamatory statement;

3) Of and concerning the plaintiff; and
4) Damages to the plaintiff's reputation.

***

In order to be actionable as defamation, a statement must comprise language that tends to harm the reputation of a person, business, or organization by exposing them to public hatred, contempt, ridicule, or disgrace, or by lowering them in the estimation of others. A statement may also be defamatory if it affects the subject's ability to engage in business or other activities.

The statement must be false. Truth is an absolute defense to a defamation claim. If the statement is true, then it cannot be defamatory, regardless of how damaging it may be.

Opinions are actionable only if the defendant implies that there is a factual basis for that opinion.

Exercise 1

1. **Use the limited facts available so far to draft allegations that Mr. Richmond: 1) published, 2) an actionable defamatory statement, 3) of and concerning the Shakin' Cajun, and 4) the statement damaged Shakin' Cajun's reputation.**

2. **Are there any additional facts that, if they exist, would strengthen the Shakin' Cajun's defamation claim? Are there any that, if they exist, will weaken the claim?**

____

____

____

1.3 Legal Authority—Defamatory Meaning

As you consider the strength of the potential defamation claim, you realize that you cannot get to a jury trial (of course, you are hoping that a win or favorable settlement will come long before trial) unless the court agrees that Mr. Richmond's review has defamatory meaning. Your research turns up the following case that speaks to this issue:

James v. Gannett Co.
353 N.E.2d 834 (N.Y. 1976)

***

On July 9, 1972, an article entitled "Samantha's Belly Business" appeared in the Sunday supplement, Upstate, of the Rochester Democrat & Chronicle, a newspaper published by the Gannett Co., Inc. The story, prepared by one of the newspaper's reporters based upon an interview with the plaintiff, described the plaintiff as the "undisputed queen of the exotic stages of Upstate New York, Rochester's belly dancer in residence." Without delving into unnecessary detail, it suffices to note that the four-page story discussed the plaintiff 's background, set forth her views on life in general, her approach to her business, and described two of her dancing routines. Accompanying photographs depicted the plaintiff in her dressing room, on the stage, and arriving for work. Quotations from the interview with the plaintiff are sprinkled liberally throughout the article.

***

The plaintiff finds fault with two sentences in the article, denying that she made statements attributed to her. Specifically, she objects to the statement that "she admits to selling her time to lonely old men with money, for as much as $400 an evening in one case, 'just to sit with him and be nice to him.'" In a later paragraph, the plaintiff is quoted as saying: 'Most men can talk to me. They can't talk to their wives because they're blocked by society. Do you understand what I'm saying? They're looking for something they've lost at home. This is my business. Men is my business.' Of this paragraph, the plaintiff objects only to the phrase, "Men is my business." The plaintiff does not deny making any of the other quotations attributed to her in the article.

In her complaint, the plaintiff alleged that, by the two sentences cited, "the defendant meant, and intended to mean, and was understood by the readers of said newspaper as meaning that the plaintiff was acting as a prostitute who was offering her body and her time for sale at a price, was committing the crime of prostitution, was committing adultery, was sleeping and having intercourse with various and sundry male persons for a profit; that plaintiff was a person of low and despicable moral character." The plaintiff claimed that the allegedly false publication discredited her reputation in the community, resulting in damages of $500,000. She also asserted that, as a result of the article, she has not been able to open a planned dancing school, that she has not been able to teach cosmetology and is "in imminent danger" of losing her membership in the American Guild of Variety Artists. Her claims of "special" damage total $135,000. In its answer, the defendant stood by its article, asserting that the plaintiff did make the disputed statements and that her remarks were accurately reported.

We agree with the dissenting Justices at the Appellate Division that the published article, when read in context, was not defamatory. . . . [W]hether the words complained of would constitute a libel . . . it is for the court to decide whether the words are susceptible of the meaning ascribed to them. [Cit.] The court must decide whether there is a reasonable basis for drawing the defamatory conclusion. If the contested statements are reasonably susceptible of a defamatory connotation, then "it becomes the jury's function to say whether that was the sense in which the words were likely to be understood by the ordinary and average reader." (*Mencher v. Chesley*, 297 N.Y. 94, 100, 75 N.E.2d 257, 259.) In analyzing the words in order to ascertain whether a question of fact exists for resolution upon trial, the court will not pick out and isolate particular phrases but will consider the publication as a whole. (*Julian v. American Business Consultants*, 2 N.Y.2d 1, 23, 155 N.Y.S.2d 1, 21, 137 N.E.2d 1, 15.) The publication will be tested by its effect upon the average reader. (*Sydney v. Macfadden Newspaper Pub. Corp.*, 242 N.Y. 208, 214, 151 N.E. 209, 210; *Everett v. Gross*, 22 A.D.2d 257, 258, 254 N.Y.S.2d 561, 562.) The language will be given a fair reading and the court will not strain to place a particular interpretation on the published words. (*See Drug Research Corp. v. Curtis Pub. Co.*, 7 N.Y.2d 435, 440, 199 N.Y.S.2d 33, 36, 166 N.E.2d 319, 321; *Julian v. American Business Consultants, supra.*) . . . "The construction which it behooves a court of justice to put on a publication which is alleged to be libelous is to be derived as well from the expressions used as from the whole scope and apparent object of the writer." (*Cooper v. Greeley*, 1 Denio 347, 358; *More v. Bennett*, 48 N.Y. 472, 475–476.)

In applying these traditional standards to this case, we find there is absolutely no basis from which the ordinary reader could draw an inference of prostitution from the paragraph containing the statement: "Men is my business." The thrust of the paragraph, read as a whole with the entire article, was that the plaintiff believed that men attended her shows in order to obtain a form of entertainment not available in their homes. It cannot be said, as a matter of law, that, so construed, these remarks may impute unchastity or prostitution to the plaintiff. Indeed, it is to be expected that the talents of a female belly dancer would generally hold a greater attraction for men than for women and, since the plaintiff's audience is predominantly male, it is but a truism to suggest that men are her business. From the entire article, it is clear that her "business" consists of displaying her dancing ability and does not involve acts of illegality or promiscuity.

The second alleged libel, that plaintiff sold her time to lonely old men, is a bit more difficult. However, we again conclude that this sentence is not susceptible to a defamatory construction. Although, on its face, this portion of the article states that the plaintiff sold her time to men on occasion, the statement itself negates the possibility that the plaintiff was thereby committing an act of prostitution since her role was to do no more than "sit with him and be nice to him." Whether a publication alleging that a woman sold her time to men charges an act of prostitution depends necessarily upon what services were to be performed in exchange for the money tendered to the woman. (See *Hemmens v. Nelson*, 138 N.Y. 517, 530–531, 34 N.E. 342, 346–347.) For it is plain that many women sell legitimate, professional services, involving an expenditure of personal time, to male customers. Doctors, lawyers, designers, and nurses are but a few examples. Here, the publication does no more than allege that the plaintiff accepted money in return for providing a few hours of companionship to lonely men. There is nothing in the sentence complained of to support an inference that the sale of anything more was involved. Any lingering doubt is resolved by a review of the entire article which establishes that plaintiff is a professional belly dancer who markets her own nightclub act "as an all-but-lost art as much as erotica entertainment." We conclude that the article, read as a whole, is incapable, as a matter of law, of bearing the libelous meaning that plaintiff would ascribe to it. We reject plaintiff's attempt to pick at two sentences from a feature article and impute to them a libelous connotation that the whole article, let alone the specific sentences, will not bear.

***

You also found a case that analyzes the difference between statements of fact and statements of opinion under New York's defamation law, which is similar to Sunport's:

Gross v. New York Times Co.
82 N.Y.2d 146 (1993)

OPINION OF THE COURT

Titone, J.

This dispute has its origin in a series of investigative reports published by defendant New York Times between January of 1985 and February of 1986. The articles in question charged plaintiff, the former Chief Medical Examiner of the City of New York, with having mishandled several high profile cases and having used his authority to protect police officers and other city officials from suspicion after individuals in their custody had died under questionable circumstances. . . . Plaintiff thereafter commenced the present action for libel. The issue . . . is whether plaintiff's pleadings sufficiently allege false, defamatory statements of *fact* rather than mere nonactionable statements of *opinion*. We hold that plaintiff's complaint, which encompasses actionable assertions of fact as well as nonactionable opinions and conclusions, is sufficient to withstand a motion to dismiss under CPLR 3211(a)(7).

I.

Plaintiff's 59-page complaint cites essentially eight "false and defamatory" articles as the basis for his libel action. The first article in the series, which was published on January 27, 1985 under defendant Philip Shenon's byline, was entitled *Chief Medical*

Examiner's Reports in Police-Custody Cases Disputed and had, as a subheadline, *Cover-Ups Charged in Autopsies in Some Deaths — Gross Denies 'Misleading in Any Instance'* . . . The tenor of the other articles cited in plaintiff's complaint was similar, with quotes from documents and individuals describing plaintiff's specific actions, disagreeing with his medical conclusions and drawing conclusions about his motives. The over-all thrust of the series was that plaintiff had issued false or misleading reports about deaths occurring within his jurisdiction in order to protect the police and that his conduct ranged from "highly suspicious" (article published Feb. 5, 1985) to "possibly illegal" (article published Jan. 28, 1985).

Before discovery had begun, defendants moved to dismiss the libel claims in plaintiff's complaint, arguing that the articles on which it was based conveyed only the opinion of its staff and their interviewees and were therefore not actionable. The trial court agreed with defendants' position and on June 10, 1991 granted the requested relief.

***

II.

At the core of the dispute in this case is the much discussed distinction between expressions of opinion, which are not actionable, and assertions of fact, which may form the basis of a viable libel claim. The distinction has been the subject of considerable analysis and legal evolution in recent years. [Cit.] . . . The Supreme Court's decision in *New York Times Co. v Sullivan* (376 US 254) . . . recognized that there are constitutional restrictions on the "permissible scope" of defamation actions and, specifically, that evident "rhetorical hyperbole" is simply not actionable *(see, Milkovich v Lorain Journal Co., supra,* at 16; *see also, Hustler Mag. v Falwell,* 485 US 46, 50; *Letter Carriers v Austin,* 418 US 264, 284-286).

. . . The dispositive inquiry, under either Federal or New York law, is "whether a reasonable [reader] could have concluded that [the articles were] conveying facts about the plaintiff" (*600 W. 115th St. Corp. v Von Gutfeld, supra,* at 139). Since falsity is a necessary element of a defamation cause of action and only "facts" are capable of being proven false, "it follows that only statements alleging facts can properly be the subject of a defamation action" (*id.,* at 139; *accord, Immuno AG. v Moor-Jankowski, supra,* at 254). In our State the inquiry . . . entails an examination of the challenged statements with a view toward (1) whether the specific language in issue has a precise meaning which is readily understood; (2) whether the statements are capable of being proven true or false; and (3) whether either the full context of the communication in which the statement appears or the broader social context and surrounding circumstances are such as to "'signal . . . readers or listeners that what is being read or heard is likely to be opinion, not fact'" (*Steinhilber v Alphonse, supra,* at 292, quoting *Ollman v Evans,* 750 F2d 970, 983, *cert denied* 471 US 1127; *accord, Immuno AG. v Moor-Jankowski, supra).*

***

. . . [I]n determining whether a particular communication is actionable, we continue to recognize and utilize the important distinction between a statement of opinion that implies a basis in facts which are not disclosed to the reader or listener (*see, Hotchner v Castillo-Puche,* 551 F2d 910, 913, *cert denied sub nom. Hotchner v Doubleday &*

Co., 434 US 834; Restatement [Second] of Torts § 566), and a statement of opinion that is accompanied by a recitation of the facts on which it is based or one that does not imply the existence of undisclosed underlying facts (*see, Ollman v Evans, supra,* at 976; *Buckley v Littell,* 539 F2d 882, 893, *cert denied* 429 US 1062; Restatement [Second] of Torts § 566, comment *c*). The former are actionable not because they convey "false opinions" but rather because a reasonable listener or reader would infer that "the speaker [or writer] knows certain facts, unknown to [the] audience, which support [the] opinion and are detrimental to the person [toward] whom [the communication is directed]" *(Steinhilber v Alphonse, supra,* at 290). In contrast, the latter are not actionable because, as was noted by the dissenting opinion in *Milkovich v Lorain Journal Co. (supra,* at 26-27, 28, n 5 [Brennan, J.]), a proffered hypothesis that is offered after a full recitation of the facts on which it is based is readily understood by the audience as conjecture *(see, e.g., Potomac Valve & Fitting v Crawford Fitting Co.,* 829 F2d 1280, 1290) . . .

III.

Applying these principles to plaintiff's cause is not a simple task because plaintiff's pleadings cite the whole series of articles, each in its entirety, as the basis for plaintiff's defamation claim. Obviously, not every word and assertion in the disputed articles is false or defamatory. Some of the actions and words attributed to plaintiff undoubtedly did take place. Furthermore, many of the objective assertions made in this series of many thousand words are uncontroversial and are therefore not the proper subject for a defamation action.

(1) We conclude, however, that the courts below erred in dismissing the complaint, since the articles it cited contain many assertions of objective fact that, if proven false, could form the predicate for a maintainable libel action. Additionally, although the articles contain many assertions that would be understood by the reasonable reader as mere hypotheses premised on stated facts, there are also actionable charges made in the articles—such as the charges that plaintiff engaged in cover-ups, directed the creation of "misleading" autopsy reports and was guilty of "possibly illegal" conduct—that, although couched in the language of hypothesis or conclusion, actually would be understood by the reasonable reader as assertions of fact (*see, Rinaldi v Holt, Rinehart & Winston,* 42 NY2d 369, 382).

***

In this case, the assertion that plaintiff engaged in "corrupt" conduct in his capacity as Chief Medical Examiner cannot be treated as a mere rhetorical flourish or the speculative accusation of an angry but ill-informed citizen made during the course of a heated debate (*see, 600 W. 115th St. Corp. v Von Gutfeld, supra*). Rather, the accusation was made in the course of a lengthy, copiously documented newspaper series that was written only after what purported to be a thorough investigation. Having been offered as a special feature series rather than as coverage of a current news story, the disputed articles were calculated to give the impression they were "the product of some deliberation, not of the heat of [the] moment" (*id.,* at 142). Moreover, since the articles appeared in the news section rather than the editorial or "op ed" sections, the common expectations that apply to those more opinionated journalistic endeavors were inapplicable here (*see, Immuno AG. v Moor-Jankowski, supra*). Thus, the circumstances under which these accusations were published "encourag[ed]

> the reasonable reader to be less skeptical and more willing to conclude that [they] stat[ed] or impl[ied] facts" (*600 W. 115th St. Corp. v Von Gutfeld, supra,* at 142).
>
> . . . In this case, the reputation of a public official with significant professional credentials was allegedly impaired by a series of widely read newspaper articles that portrayed him as unethical and corrupt. Under the circumstances of his case, we conclude that this individual should be permitted to go forward in an effort to establish a right to a libel recovery . . .
>
> ***

Exercise 2

1. **Assuming you move forward with the lawsuit against Mr. Richmond, what arguments do you anticipate he will make about whether his *Shriek* review is capable of defamatory meaning?**

2. **How will you respond to those arguments?**

Invasion of the Right to Privacy/Intrusion upon Seclusion

12

Embry v. Harman Woodworks

Once again, posting your business card on the bulletin board at the Drop or Do Laundromat has paid off. Micky Harman, the founder and CEO of Harman Woodworks happened into the Drop or Do because his washing machine broke down and he needed to wash a load of bed linens. Mr. Harman said he forgot his laptop and had nothing to do except play stupid games on his phone and read all the business cards on the bulletin board. The following week, he was served with a complaint in a lawsuit filed by his former employee, Elton Embry. Mr. Harman recalled your business card and, well, here he is!

1.1 Client Interview

Mr. Harman relayed the following facts to you:

> **Meeting with Mickey Harman, Harman Woodworks re: Elton Embry**
>
> July 6, 8:30 A.M.
>
> - In April of last year, Mr. Harman's employee, Elton Embry, sustained a work injury to his thoracic spine while stacking wood onto a cart as part of his job with Harman Woodworks. Mr. Embry filed a claim with the workers' compensation office and Mr. Harman retained Regions Surveillance (co-Defendant) to adjust the claim and manage Mr. Embry's workers' compensation case.[1]

1. For a discussion of workers' compensation, see Chapter 7, footnote 4. An employee who intends to file a claim for compensation must usually follow a proscribed process to demonstrate their eligibility. Typically, the employer files the employee's claim and the employer's report of injury with the organization processing the claim, and the processor will assign an adjuster to investigate. If eligibility is clear, then any investigation is likely to be cursory. If there is a dispute about eligibility, then the adjuster may conduct a more thorough review. The adjuster may conduct interviews, request records, require an independent medical examination, etc.

- Last November, Regions' investigator, Dan Kennedy, approached Mr. Embry's mobile home and sought entry under the false pretense that he was looking for a missing child. According to Mr. Embry's complaint, the investigator was holding the picture of a young girl when he approached the home. Once inside, Mr. Embry reported that Mr. Kennedy asked him questions about the missing girl.
- The investigator used a hidden camera in a fanny pack to record Mr. Embry's movement and conversation while the investigator was inside Mr. Embry's home. But according to the investigator, the recording device didn't capture the conversation he had with Mr. Embry, only the visual interaction.
- All of the above facts are undisputed.
- Mr. Embry filed and served his complaint, alleging intrusion upon seclusion based on these facts alone. The complaint was served on Mr. Harman last week.

Your first move was to call Mr. Embry's counsel and ask for an extension of time to respond to the complaint.[2] You wanted time to evaluate whether you should file an answer and engage in discovery or file a motion to dismiss to end this lawsuit quickly based on insufficiently pleaded allegations. Mr. Embry's counsel agreed to the extension so you have 60 extra days to figure out your plan of action.[3]

1.2 Legal Authority—Invasion of Privacy

It took no time to find several decisions with cases involving very similar facts, including the following:

McLain v. Boise Cascade Corp.
533 P.2d 343 (Or. 1975)

[The plaintiff alleged a cause of action for invasion of privacy and demanded general and punitive damages. The trial court granted an involuntary nonsuit.] . . . Plaintiff appeals. We affirm.

Plaintiff was employed by Boise Cascade Corporation as a glue mixer. On May 19, 1972 he strained his back when he fell while carrying a 100 pound sack of flour to a glue machine. Plaintiff was taken to the office of Dr. D. H. Searing in Salem. Dr. Searing sent plaintiff to the hospital where he was placed in traction. On June 6, 1972, Dr. Searing wrote to Richard Cyphert, then in charge of the Boise Cascade Workmen's Compen-

2. **Can attorneys really do that?** The short answer is yes; attorneys have some latitude to extend filing deadlines by agreement. This is a common practice in civil cases when both sides agree to extend filing deadlines, discovery deadlines, or hearing dates. In some cases, the attorney may need to file a motion for an extension and/or secure court approval, although courts generally grant unopposed requests, especially early in the litigation process.

3. For an overview of a motion to dismiss, see Chapter 7, Footnote 5.

sation program, advising that plaintiff might be disabled for as much as 12 months. Dr. John D. White was called in as a consultant. He performed a myelogram on plaintiff and reported to Mr. Cyphert that he found no evidence of nerve root or lumbar disc disease and that it was possible that plaintiff was 'consciously malingering.' Cyphert received this letter on June 22, 1972.

On the basis of Dr. White's report Mr. Cyphert notified plaintiff his compensation payments would be terminated. At about that time Mr. Cyphert also was informed that plaintiff was performing part-time work for a mortuary while he was ostensibly disabled. On June 27, 1972 plaintiff received a written release from Dr. White permitting him to return to work with the restriction that he was not to lift more than 50 pounds. Plaintiff returned to work and was assigned an easier job, but was unable to work due to continued pain in his hip.

Plaintiff then consulted an attorney, who filed a request for a hearing with the Workmen's Compensation Board asking that plaintiff's temporary disability payments be reinstated. Mr. Cyphert received a copy of this request on July 5, 1972. On July 12, 1972 Mr. Cyphert hired the defendant United Diversified Services, Inc., to conduct a surveillance of the plaintiff to check the validity of plaintiff's claim of injury. United assigned two of its employees, Rick Oulette and Steve Collette, to conduct a surveillance. The two investigators took 18 rolls of movie film of plaintiff while he was engaged in various activities on his property outside his home. Some of the film showed plaintiff mowing his lawn, rototilling his garden and fishing from a bridge near his home.

***

There was a barbed wire fence a short distance west of the east boundary of plaintiff's tract and west of the row of walnut trees from which some of the film was taken. Collette testified that he stayed east of the fence and did not know that he was on plaintiff's land. He testified, however, that he crossed over a fence under the bridge near the northeast corner of plaintiff's property in order to get to his vantage point near the walnut trees. He probably trespassed on plaintiff's property when he crossed the fence, but that does not appear clearly from the record.

On one occasion while Collette was near the walnut trees he was seen by plaintiff. When Collette realized he had been seen he left the area. He had parked his pickup truck on Ward's property near the southwest corner of plaintiff's tract, but abandoned the pickup when he was spotted by McLain and retrieved his truck later.

McLain did not learn about the film and picture taking until the film was shown at the Workmen's Compensation Hearing.

United's investigators did not question any of plaintiff's neighbors or friends and limited their activities to taking pictures while plaintiff was engaged in various activities outside his home. Plaintiff testified that these activities could have been viewed either by neighbors or passersby on the highway. Plaintiff further testified that he was not embarrassed or upset by anything that appeared in the films. He said:

'Q You did all of the things that were shown in the film? There was no deception in the film?

'A No.

'Q You agree that what you saw there was what you did?

'A Right.

'Q And you weren't embarrassed by it or mad or upset?

'A No, the only thing I was mad about was the fact they snuck around behind my back.

***

The general rule permitting recovery for [invasion of privacy] is stated in Restatement of the Law of Torts 2d, s 652B (Tent. Draft No. 13, 1967) as follows:

> 'One who intentionally intrudes, physically or otherwise, upon the solitude or seclusion of another, or his private affairs or concerns, is subject to liability to the other for invasion of his privacy, if the intrusion would be highly offensive to a reasonable man.'

See, also, Prosser, Torts (4th ed. 1971), 807; Prosser, Privacy, 48 Cal.L.Rev. 383, 389 (1960).

It is also well established that one who seeks to recover damages for alleged injuries must expect that his claim will be investigated and he waives his right of privacy to the extent of a reasonable investigation. *Tucker v. American Employers' Ins. Co.*, 171 So.2d 437, 13 A.L.R.3d 1020 (Fla.App.1965); *Souder v. Pendleton Detectives, Inc.*, 88 So.2d 716 (La.App.1956); *Forster v. Manchester*, 410 Pa. 192, 189 A.2d 147, 150 (1963); *Ellenberg v. Pinkerton's, Inc.*, 125 Ga.App. 648, 188 S.E.2d 911 (1972). We quote from the Annotation, Right of Privacy—Surveillance, 13 A.L.R.3d 1025, 1027:

> Where the surveillance, shadowing, and trailing is conducted in a reasonable manner, it has been held that owing to the social utility of exposing fraudulent claims and because of the fact that some sort of investigation is necessary to uncover fictitious injuries, an unobtrusive investigation, even though inadvertently made apparent to the person being investigated, does not constitute an actionable invasion of his privacy.

In *Forster v. Manchester, supra*, 189 A.2d at 150, the court stated:

> It is not uncommon for defendants in accident cass [sic] to employ investigators to check on the validity of claims against them. Thus, by making a claim for personal injuries appellant must expect reasonable inquiry and investigation to be made of her claim and to this extent her interest in privacy is circumscribed. * * *

If the surveillance is conducted in a reasonable and unobtrusive manner the defendant will incur no liability for invasion of privacy. *Tucker v. American Employers' Ins. Co., supra*; *Forster v. Manchester, supra*; *Souder v. Pendleton Detectives, Inc., supra*.

On the other hand, if the surveillance is conducted in an unreasonable and obtrusive manner the defendant will be liable for invasion of privacy. *Pinkerton National Detective Agency, Inc. v. Stevens*, 108 Ga.App. 159, 132 S.E.2d 119 (1963); *Souder v. Pendleton Detectives, Inc., supra*; *Schultz v. Frankfort Marine Accident and Plate Glass Insurance Co.*, 151 Wis. 537, 139 N.W. 386 (1913).

In this case we think the court below properly granted a nonsuit for the cause of action for invasion of privacy. In the first place, the surveillance and picture taking were done in such an unobtrusive manner that plaintiff was not aware that he was being watched and filmed. In the second place, plaintiff conceded that his activities which were filmed could have been observed by his neighbors or passersby on the road running in front of his property. Undoubtedly the investigators trespassed on plaintiff's land while watching and taking pictures of him, but it is also clear that the trespass was on the periphery of plaintiff's property and did not constitute an unreasonable surveillance 'highly offensive to a reasonable man.'

Plaintiff does not contend that the surveillance in this case was *per se* actionable. Plaintiff contends only that the surveillance became actionable when the investigators trespassed on plaintiff's property. Plaintiff's brief states the issue as follows:

> 'The issue before this Court is whether trespass upon another's homestead for the purpose of conducting an unauthorized surveillance gives rise to an action for violation of the right of privacy, * * *.'

We think trespass is only one factor to be considered in determining whether the surveillance was unreasonable. Trespass to peer in windows and to annoy or harass the occupant may be unreasonable. Trespass alone cannot automatically change an otherwise reasonable surveillance into an unreasonable one. The one trespass which was observed by plaintiff did not alert him to the fact that he was being watched or that his activities were being filmed. The record is clear that the trespass was confined to a narrow strip along the east boundary of plaintiff's property. All the surveillance in this case was done during daylight hours and when plaintiff was exposed to public view by his neighbors and passersby.

***

The judgment is affirmed.

Exercise 1

1. **What are the elements of invasion of privacy as stated in *McLain*?**

____

____

____

____

____

____

____

____

____

2. Prepare an argument that analogizes your case to the facts and reasoning in *McLain.*

3. Prepare an argument that distinguishes your case from the facts and reasoning in *McLain.*

4. Do you believe Mr. Embry can establish a cause of action for invasion of privacy/ intrusion upon seclusion? Why or why not?

Misrepresentation

13

Fraudulent Misrepresentation: *Varela Furniture & Appliance Store*

1.1 Background

You previously completed work on behalf of Mike Varela, owner of Varela Furniture & Appliance Store (see Part II: Chapter 10). Mr. Varela retained your firm to represent his business after one of his employees illegally parked a Varela delivery van while making an unscheduled delivery. Another driver, Nik Varga, swerved to avoid the truck, collided with a garbage truck, and sustained serious injuries. Mr. Varga sued Varela Furniture under a theory of *respondeat superior*.

While the case was pending, the plaintiff filed a motion for summary judgment, alleging he was entitled to judgment as a matter of law under theories of negligence per se and *respondeat superior*. As instructed by your supervising attorney, you drafted a Response in Opposition to Plaintiff's Motion for Summary Judgment and sent the draft to your supervising attorney. Your attorney indicated that she would review and edit your draft before submitting the Response to the court. The next week, you learned that your supervising attorney failed to file the Response before the deadline.

You know that failing to respond to the plaintiff's motion could cause serious consequences for Mr. Varela. The plaintiff presented strong arguments in his motion for summary judgment, and you are concerned that the court might be persuaded by those arguments. Without hearing from the defendant, the court might not consider evidence that absolves Mr. Varela of liability. Worse, the court might deem the defendant's failure to respond an admission of the plaintiff's arguments. Simply put, the failure to respond creates a significant risk that the court may enter judgment against Mr. Varela without a trial. In that case, the failure to respond also limits Mr. Varela's options on appeal because appellate courts may only consider evidence on the record. If the defendant did not present certain arguments to the trial court, then those arguments may not be raised on appeal.

When you cautiously approach your supervising attorney to discuss the mistake, she is dismissive. She angrily tells you, "I've been practicing law since you were in high school, so I don't appreciate you storming in here like you are Associate of the Year. I will decide how to handle this case, so get back to work."

1.2 Client Interview

Yesterday, your supervising attorney asked you to take notes while she spoke by phone with Mr. Varela. You expected her to discuss the motion for summary judgment and advise Mr. Varela about his options. Instead, she made the following statements:

> After reviewing the plaintiff's arguments and the governing law, I believe Mr. Varga has a very strong case. I am especially concerned that you seemed to authorize, condone, or even encourage your driver's "off the books" delivery. Ultimately, the buck stops with you, and if your drivers are poorly trained, then you are likely liable if they act negligently and disobey traffic laws.
>
> In short, I believe it is risky to pursue this case. Juries are very sympathetic to this kind of plaintiff, especially because your driver clearly violated the posted parking rules. Frankly, juries love gouging big bad companies who seem to have the resources to pay a large judgment.
>
> I think you should strongly consider settling with Mr. Varga before this case goes to trial. I believe you can get a better outcome if you deal directly with him. You may be surprised how far an apology can go in this kind of situation, especially if you back it up with a reasonable "go away" payment.

During the call, Mr. Varela reluctantly agreed to begin settlement discussions. The parties agreed to delay the hearing on the plaintiff's motion for summary judgment pending resolution of settlement discussions.

During negotiations, Mr. Varela agreed to pay Mr. Varga's medical expenses and property damages. He also agreed to pay Mr. Varga $20,000 for costs, fees, and pain and suffering. The parties agreed to dismiss the suit, and the court did not consider the plaintiff's motion for summary judgment.

1.3 Client Call

As you reflected on the advice your supervising attorney offered Mr. Varela, you became increasingly uncomfortable. You suspect your supervising attorney advised Mr. Varela to settle the case to protect the firm and herself from allegations of malpractice. She likely hoped that Mr. Varela would not learn of her mistake because he settled the case before the court ruled on the plaintiff's motion for summary judgment.

After thinking long and hard about this dilemma, you decided to speak with your firm's managing partner to report the incident. The partner was justifiably concerned and asked you to consider whether Mr. Varela might have a claim against the firm based on the conduct of your supervising attorney.

While you were researching the viability of a potential malpractice claim (see Part II, Chapter 10), you received a call from Mr. Varela. He angrily demanded:

Will you please explain why on earth I was asked to pay your firm several thousand dollars for imaginary work?!? I was reviewing my invoices and noticed an invoice billing me for some "Response in Opposition to Plaintiff's Motion for Summary Judgment." As far as I've been told, nothing like that was filed in the case.

As far as I see it, a few things might have happened, none of them good. Best case, this is a massive administrative error, in which case I expect an apology and some compensation for wasting my time. Or possibly, you are trying to pull off a billing scam. If so, then you're trying it with the wrong guy. You can bet I will report this and make sure it gets investigated.

Worst case, someone at your firm prepared a document that never got filed. I'm beginning to suspect that you were so eager for me to settle because someone made a mistake and is trying to cover their tracks. If that's true, then I'll be sure to report that mistake to the court, the licensing board, and anyone else who will listen. I'll also start investigating who can help me sue your firm for messing up my case and then lying to me about it.

1.4 Client Invoice

Mr. Varela emails you a copy of the invoice:

Allen, Burgess and Connor, LLP
Eastvale, Sunport Office

Invoice No. 446-3467

August 24

Bill To: Michael Varela, Varela Furniture & Appliance Store

Invoice Details

Date	Description of Services	Hours	Rate	Total
August 7	Review of motion for summary judgment and supporting exhibits	2.5	$300/hr	$750
August 8	Legal research on case law and precedent	3.0	$300/hr	$900
August 9	Drafting response to motion for summary judgment	4.5	$300/hr	$1,350

Subtotal: $3,000

Expenses: $50

TOTAL DUE: $3,050

Payment due within 30 days of invoice date.

Please make payments via the Payment Portal.

Late payments may be subject to a 5% late fee per month.

Thank you for your business!

1.5 Legal Authority—Misrepresentation

You discuss the case with the firm's managing partner, who asks you to investigate whether the firm might be liable for misrepresentation.

The following excerpts from *Sunport Civil Remedies* outline a cause of action for fraudulent misrepresentation:

> To establish a *prima facie* case of fraudulent misrepresentation, the plaintiff must prove the following elements:
>
> 1) The defendant misrepresented a material fact;
>   a. A fact is "material" if it would influence a reasonable person in the plaintiff's position.
>   b. Generally, a defendant does not have a duty to *disclose* a material fact. Yet if the defendant is in a fiduciary relationship to the plaintiff, then the defendant may be liable for failure to disclose a material fact.
> 2) The defendant knew the information was false;
> 3) The defendant intended to induce the plaintiff's reliance on the statement;
> 4) The misrepresentation induced the plaintiff to act (the plaintiff actually relied on the statement);
> 5) The plaintiff's reliance was foreseeable and justified/reasonable; and
>   a. A plaintiff is not justified in relying on the defendant's *opinion* unless the defendant has superior knowledge to the plaintiff or the defendant owes a fiduciary duty to the plaintiff.
> 6) The plaintiff sustained damages.

Exercise 1

1. **Based on the facts you learned above, can Mr. Varela prove that your supervising attorney made a material misrepresentation of fact? Explain.**

____

____

____

____

____

____

2. **Can Mr. Varela prove your supervising attorney *knowingly* made a material misrepresentation(s) of fact? Explain.**

3. **Can Mr. Varela prove your supervising attorney made the misrepresentation with intent to induce his reliance? Explain.**

4. **Did the misrepresentation induce Mr. Varela to act? Explain.**

5. **Was Mr. Varela's reliance foreseeable and justified? Explain.**

6. What are Mr. Varela's damages? Explain.

____

____

____

____

1.6 Client Email Part 2

While you are conducting your research, you receive another email from Mr. Varela. The email is blank, but the subject line reads, "YOU HAVE TO BE KIDDING ME." The email includes the following attachment:

Allen, Burgess and Connor, LLP
Eastvale, Sunport Office

Invoice No. 446-3468

August 31

Bill To: Michael Varela, Varela Furniture & Appliance Store

Invoice Details

Date	Description of Services	Hours	Rate	Total
August 23	Reviewing and revising draft response to motion for summary judgment	2.25	$750/hr	$1,687.50
August 24	Preparing and filing final response with court	1.25	$750/hr	$937.50
August 30	Client communication and case strategy discussion	0.75	$750/hr	$562.50

Subtotal: $3,187.50

Expenses: $82.00

TOTAL DUE: $3,269.50

Payment due within 30 days of invoice date.

Please make payments via the Payment Portal.

Late payments may be subject to a 5% late fee per month.

Thank you for your business!

Exercise 2

1. **How does this additional invoice change your opinion about the case, if at all? Does it make it more or less likely that Mr. Varela can establish a cause of action for fraudulent misrepresentation?**

____

____

____

____

____

Negligent and Fraudulent Misrepresentation: *Parrill v. Mapleton Realty Corp.*

2.1 Interview Notes

Jillian Parrill requested an office consultation with you to discuss a potential claim she might have as a recent homebuyer. You met with her and learned the following:

MTG. with J. Parrill—Feb. 12 11:30 A.M.

- Jillian Parrill began searching for her first home in Eastvale last year.
- Parrill visited a house listed by Mapleton Realty Corp. (local real estate firm, which markets its agents as specializing in first-time homebuyers).
- Listing agent was Craig Preston with Mapleton.
- Preston told Parill that the house had "all new plumbing and electrical systems" and that the roof had been "fully replaced within the last year."
- Relying on Preston's representations, Parill waived the home inspection contingency so that she could make a strong/competitive offer. Parill was willing to take some risk because she lost out on a couple of previous houses because, she believes, her offers were too low and contained too many contingencies.
- A few months after she moved in, Parill discovered extensive water damage in the walls from leaky pipes and electrical failures that made the home unsafe. She also had a roofing contractor inspect the roof—turns out the roof is well over 10 years old and needs to be replaced.
- Parill discussed all of this with Preston—turns out his statements were based on information provided to him by the sellers, but he never verified the details with any inspection reports or repair invoices. Preston had access to the prior house inspection and appraisal, both of which identified the plumbing and electrical issues Parill is now facing. The roof, in fact, had only been patched and repaired after a storm the year before the sale; it wasn't replaced.
- Parill wants to know if she has any course of action against Mapleton Realty Group for Preston's misrepresentations.
- When asked whether she had any reason to believe Preston knew his representations were untrue, Parill said no. She believes that he relied on the information provided by the sellers. Yet she is angry that he failed to verify before relaying the information to her; she thinks it was incumbent on him to do so.

2.2 Legal Authority—Fraudulent and Negligent Misrepresentation

You review your favorite practice manual, *Sunport Civil Remedies*, and find excerpts outlining the elements of *fraudulent* misrepresentation, which you think might apply vis-á-vis the sellers of the house. You also find an additional section outlining the elements for *negligent* misrepresentation:

To establish a *prima facie* case of fraudulent misrepresentation, the plaintiff must prove the following elements:

1) The defendant misrepresented a material fact;
   a. A fact is "material" if it would influence a reasonable person in the plaintiff's position.
   b. Generally, a defendant does not have a duty to *disclose* a material fact. Yet if the defendant is in a fiduciary relationship to the plaintiff, then the defendant may be liable for failure to disclose a material fact.
2) The defendant knew the information was false;
3) The defendant intended to induce the plaintiff's reliance on the statement;
4) The misrepresentation induced the plaintiff to act (the plaintiff actually relied on the statement);
5) The plaintiff's reliance was foreseeable and justified/reasonable; and
   a. A plaintiff is not justified in relying on the defendant's *opinion* unless the defendant has superior knowledge to the plaintiff or the defendant owes a fiduciary duty to the plaintiff.
6) The plaintiff sustained damages.

To establish a *prima facie* case of negligent misrepresentation, the plaintiff must prove the following elements:

1) The defendant made a false statement of a material fact;
2) The defendant acted with carelessness or negligence in ascertaining the truth of the statement before making it;
3) The defendant intended to induce the plaintiff to act;
4) The plaintiff took action in reliance on the truth of the defendant's statement; and
5) The plaintiff sustained damages as a result of such reliance.

Exercise 1

Evaluate whether Ms. Parill can establish a *prima facie* case for fraudulent or negligent misrepresentation (or both) against the sellers of the house Ms. Parrill purchased and/or against Mapleton Realty Group for the representations made by Craig Preston. Use the facts you learned from your meeting with Jillian Parrill and Sunport's law on fraudulent and negligent misrepresentation.

1. **Can Ms. Parrill establish the elements of a negligent misrepresentation claim against the sellers of the house? Why or why not?**

2. **Can Ms. Parrill establish the elements of a fraudulent misrepresentation claim against the sellers of the house? Why or why not?**

3. **Can Ms. Parrill establish the elements of a negligent misrepresentation claim against the Mapleton Realty Group for the representations by Craig Preston? Why or why not?**

4. Can Ms. Parrill establish the elements of a fraudulent misrepresentation claim against the Mapleton Realty Group for the representations by Craig Preston? Why or why not?

____

____

____

____

____

2.3 Legal Authority—Defenses

Before deciding whether to proceed with a potential complaint against the sellers of the house and/or against Mapleton Realty Group, you want to resolve a couple of issues that have been bothering you about Ms. Parrill's case. In particular, you are bothered by the fact that the sellers did not make their statements directly to Ms. Parrill. The sellers might consequently take the position that they made no representations to Ms. Parrill and cannot be liable to her.

You review *Sunport Civil Remedies* again for information about negligent misrepresentation, and you notice the following commentary . . .

> ***Comment a:*** One who, in the course of his business, profession, or employment, or in any other transaction in which he has a pecuniary interest, negligently or carelessly supplies false information for the use by others in their business transactions, is subject to liability for the financial loss caused to them by their justifiable reliance upon the false information.
>
> However, such liability is limited to financial loss suffered by the person or one of a limited group of persons for whose benefit and guidance he intends to supply the information or knows that the recipient intends to supply it.

. . . and similar commentary to the provision on fraudulent misrepresentation:

> ***Comment c:*** One who makes a fraudulent misrepresentation is subject to liability for the financial loss of another who acts in justifiable reliance upon it if the fraudulent misrepresentation, although not made directly to the other, is made to a third person and the maker intends or has reason to expect that the representation will be repeated to another and that it will influence his conduct in the transaction involved.

Exercise 2

1. **Based on your review of the commentaries in *Sunport Civil Remedies*, are you more or less confident about Ms. Parrill's ability to pursue any misrepresentation claims against the sellers of the house? Explain.**

____

____

____

____

2.4 Legal Authority—Comparative Negligence

You are also concerned that Ms. Parrill waived the home inspection contingency. You wonder whether that decision might somehow bar her claim because the sellers and/or Mapleton Realty Group will assert the defense of comparative negligence. The parties may argue that Ms. Parrill was negligent in failing to have the house inspected before she purchased it, and her damages were caused by her own negligence.

You find the following decision from the Supreme Court of Connecticut, which has laws governing misrepresentations similar to those of Sunport:

Kramer v. Petisi
285 Conn. 674, 940 A.2d 800 (2008)

Opinion

Palmer, J.

The named plaintiff, Myra Kramer, commenced this action against Patricia Abagnale, a real estate agent, and Abagnale's employer, Country Living Associates, Inc., among others, seeking damages for, inter alia, Abagnale's allegedly negligent misrepresentation of the boundary lines of certain property in the town of Fairfield that the plaintiff had purchased from Abagnale's clients, Robert J. Petisi and Carole W. Petisi. In reliance on this court's holding in *Williams Ford, Inc. v. Hartford Courant Co.,* 232 Conn. 559, 586, 657 A.2d 212 (1995), that the doctrine of comparative negligence is applicable to a claim of negligent misrepresentation when only commercial losses are sustained, the trial court permitted the defendants to raise a special defense of comparative negligence. Following a trial, the jury found that, although Abagnale negligently had misrepresented the boundary lines, the plaintiff, by failing to obtain a current survey of the property before purchasing it, was 60 percent contributorily negligent and, therefore, was not entitled to damages. The trial court rendered judgment in favor of the defendants, and the plaintiff appealed to the Appellate Court, claiming, inter alia, that the trial court improperly had permitted the defendants to raise the defense of comparative negligence. See *Kramer v. Petisi,* 91 Conn.App. 26, 27, 879 A.2d 526 (2005). The Appellate Court concluded that the trial court properly had applied the law of comparative negligence to the plaintiff's negligent misrepresentation claim; see id., at 31, 34, 879 A.2d 526; and, accordingly, affirmed the judgment of the trial court. Id., at 39, 879 A.2d 526. We granted the plaintiff's petition for certification to appeal limited to the following issue: "Did the Appellate Court properly apply the law of comparative negligence to the . . . plaintiff's claims of [negligent] misrepresentation against the defendants?" *Kramer v. Petisi,* 276 Conn. 916, 888 A.2d 84 (2005). We answer the certified question in the affirmative and, accordingly, affirm the judgment of the Appellate Court.

The opinion of the Appellate Court sets forth the following facts that the jury reasonably could have found. . . .

***

"In July, 1994, the plaintiff and her husband decided to move from New Mexico to Connecticut. The couple looked at several homes in a ten day period between July 11 and 20. After attending a broker's open house at the Petisis' home, Nancy W. Thorne, the plaintiff's real estate agent, took the plaintiff to look at the house. Although Thorne had spoken with Abagnale, [the defendant's real estate agent,] she did not wait for Abagnale before taking the plaintiff to view the property.

"Shortly thereafter, the plaintiff visited the property with members of her family, Thorne and Abagnale. There were three to five additional visits in the days that followed. At one of the visits, the plaintiff and Thorne walked around the property. The plaintiff asked Thorne about the location of the boundaries. When Thorne replied that she did not know the boundaries of the property, she told the plaintiff that she would go inside and ask Abagnale. Upon her return, Thorne told the plaintiff that the boundary was the western side of the fence, which actually was located on the adjoining parcel, 2250 North Street.

"The plaintiff offered to purchase the property for $1.25 million. After some difficult negotiations, the parties agreed on a sale price of $1.4 million. [. . .] The sales contract also provided that any improvements or appurtenances located on the Petisis' land were entirely within the boundaries of the property to be conveyed. The parties closed on September 26, 1994.

"Prior to the closing, the plaintiff did not obtain a survey of the property. Instead, she relied on a 1982 survey of the property, which indicated the boundaries of the property without the fence. There is some dispute as to whether the plaintiff's attorney [Scott M. Gerard] advised her to get a new survey done or whether it was suggested that the old survey be updated. Regardless, instead of obtaining a new survey, the plaintiff obtained an affidavit in lieu of a survey in which the Petisis stated that they had no knowledge of adverse rights, including easements, rights-of-way or encroachments.

"Despite the affidavit, the seller's disclosure statement indicated that a portion of the land, which was partially fenced in, was not part of the property. The sellers' disclosure form, however, was not given to the plaintiff. Abagnale did not provide this to Thorne or to the plaintiff.

"On April 23, 1996, the plaintiff received notice from [the Scanlons] the owners of 2250 North Street, the adjacent property, that they were asserting their rights to prevent her from adversely possessing a portion of their property. At issue was a .22 acre portion of the property that was fenced in and used by the plaintiff." *Kramer v. Petisi,* supra, 91 Conn.App. at 28-30, 879 A.2d 526.

In 1996, the plaintiff filed an action against the defendants, among others, alleging, inter alia, negligent misrepresentation of the boundary lines of the 2228 North Street property. The defendants filed an answer and affirmatively pleaded comparative negligence as a special defense. In their special defense, the defendants alleged that the plaintiff was contributorily negligent and that any damages that the plaintiff had sustained "were proximately caused by" her failure to obtain "an updated survey of the property." The plaintiff denied that the special defense of comparative negligence was applicable to her claim of negligent misrepresentation.

***

"This court has long recognized liability for negligent misrepresentation. We have held that even an innocent misrepresentation of fact may be actionable if the declarant has the means of knowing, ought to know, or has the duty of knowing the truth . . . The governing principles [of negligent misrepresentation] are set forth in similar terms in § 552 of the Restatement (Second) of Torts (1977): One who, in the course of his business, profession or employment . . . supplies false information for the guidance of others in their business transactions, is subject to liability for pecuniary loss caused to them by their justifiable reliance upon the information, if he fails to exercise reasonable care or competence in obtaining or communicating the information." (Citations omitted; internal quotation marks omitted.) *Williams Ford, Inc. v. Hartford Courant Co.,* [232 Conn. 559, 575, 657 A.2d 212 (1995)].

Furthermore, in *Williams Ford, Inc.,* this court held that the doctrine of comparative negligence is applicable to actions for negligent misrepresentation. *Id.*, at 586, 657 A.2d 212. In that case, we rejected the claim of the defendant, The Hartford Courant Company (Courant), that, in accordance with § 552A of the Restatement (Second) of Torts, "[t]he recipient of a negligent misrepresentation is barred from recovery for pecuniary loss suffered in reliance upon it if he is negligent in so relying." (Internal quotation marks omitted.) *Williams Ford, Inc. v. Hartford Courant Co.,* supra, 232 Conn. at 580, 657 A.2d 212. . . . We therefore held that contributory negligence is not an absolute bar to recovery for plaintiffs seeking damages for such losses resulting from a negligent misrepresentation and that principles of comparative fault are applicable in such cases. Id., at 581, 586, 657 A.2d 212.

The plaintiff nevertheless asserts that the defense of comparative negligence is not available in an action for negligent misrepresentation involving property boundary lines when, as in the present case, the buyer allegedly is negligent in failing to obtain a survey of the property. The plaintiff's claim is based on a line of cases in which this court concluded that contributory negligence is not a defense to an action predicated on a property owner's fraudulent misrepresentation of the property's boundary line. See, e.g., *Warman v. Delaney,* [148 Conn. 469, 473–74, 172 A.2d 188 (1961)]; *Clark v. Haggard,* 141 Conn. 668, 673, 109 A.2d 358 (1954); *Lovejoy v. Isbell,* 73 Conn. 368, 374-75, 47 A. 682 (1900). We agree with the Appellate Court that these cases are inapposite because each of them involved a claim of fraudulent misrepresentation, a separate and distinct tort from the tort of negligent misrepresentation.

Indeed, we long have held that contributory negligence is not a defense to a claim of fraudulent misrepresentation. [Citation omitted] . . . The reasons underlying this rule are persuasive.

Intentional torts are punished not because the actor failed to use reasonable care . . . but because the actor intended the act. The difference between the victim's actions and the defendant's action is not one of degree . . . but of kind, and they are therefore not comparable." *Florenzano v. Olson,* [387 N.W.2d 168, 176 n.7 (Minn.1986); see also 3 Restatement (Second), supra, at § 552, comment (a) ("When there is no intent to deceive but only good faith coupled with negligence, the fault of the maker of the misrepresentation is sufficiently less to justify a narrower responsibility for its consequences. The reason a narrower scope of liability is fixed for negligent misrepresentation than for deceit is to be found in the difference between the obligations of honesty and of care, and in the significance of this difference to the reasonable expectations of the users of information that is supplied in connection with commercial transactions."); 37 Am.Jur.2d 330, Fraud and Deceit § 319 (2001) ("[T]o a charge of . . . [wilful] fraud, the negligence of the party wronged or defrauded may not be interposed as a defense . . . One who has perpetrated a fraud should not be permitted to say to the party defrauded when relief is demanded that he or she ought not to have believed or trusted the perpetrator and was negligent in doing so . . ."). We therefore see no reason to bar the defense of comparative negligence in an action for negligent misrepresentation merely because that defense is not permitted in an action for fraudulent misrepresentation.

***

You also find the following provision from the Sunport Revised Statutes regarding a plaintiff's comparative fault:

Sunport Rev. Stat. § 179. Comparative Negligence as a Bar to Recovery.

Comparative negligence shall not bar recovery in any action by any person or his legal representative to recover damages for negligence resulting in death or in injury to person or property, if such negligence was not as great as the negligence of the person against whom recovery is sought, but any damages allowed shall be diminished in proportion to the amount of negligence attributable to the person for whose injury, damage, or death recovery is made.

Exercise 3

1. **Based on your reading of the holding in *Kramer*, Sunport Rev. Stat. § 179, and the facts you learned from Jillian Parrill, do you believe Ms. Parrill could be found to be comparatively negligent? If so, will that be a defense to both the negligent misrepresentation claim and the fraudulent misrepresentation claim?**

Products Liability

14

In re FreshMart

A potential client recently approached you to discuss an incident that occurred at a local FreshMart grocery shore. Jose Frank was seriously injured when a grocery bag split open, the contents shattered, and Mr. Frank fell in the debris. Mr. Frank believes the store is responsible because "either they have cheap bags or the clerk overfilled them."

Mr. Frank is also angry about an email that he recently received from the store. He wants to know if there is anything that he can do to "get what I deserve."

1.1 Email Correspondence

Re: **Complaint 25-369**

From: **martina.copeland@freshmartcomplaints.com**

To: **Jose.frank.5945@gmail.com**

Date: **November 23**

Dear Mr. Frank,

Thank you for bringing the recent incident at FreshMart Eastvale to our attention. We are truly sorry to hear about your experience on November 2 and hope you are recovering well. At FreshMart, the safety and well-being of our customers are of the utmost importance, and we take all incidents seriously.

After a thorough review of the circumstances surrounding your injury, including witness accounts, security footage, and our safety protocols, we have determined that FreshMart is not liable for the injuries you sustained. The evidence indicates that all employees complied with general recommendations regarding customer care, and there is no evidence the bag was in a defective condition when it left the store. We conclude the breakage of the bag resulted from circumstances beyond our control. Please see attached our internal review of the incident.

Once again, we regret the situation and wish you a speedy recovery. Should you have any further questions or concerns, do not hesitate to contact me directly at martina.copeland @freshmartcomplaints.com.

Sincerely,

Martina Copeland

Customer Complaint Representative

Re: Demand for compensation

From: Jose.frank.5945@gmail.com

To: Info@FreshMart.com

Date: November 2

I am emailing because I was just seriously hurt at one of your stores. One of your employees bagged my groceries into some of your plastic bags, which are apparently too cheap to hold more than four items. One bag had a jar of pickles, a jar of mayonnaise, ice cream, and frozen peas. The bag looked fine when I took it from the store. But while I was putting the bag inside my car, it suddenly broke open. Everything fell on the ground, and all the glass shattered. It was so slippery that I fell, and I sliced my arm open on broken glass. I drove myself to the Urgent Care, where I got several stitches and painkillers for all the bruises on my body.

I wouldn't have been hurt if your store used better bags. Honestly, I don't know why the store was using bags that couldn't handle a few jars. It can't be a surprise to the store that the bags are so flimsy, so the bagger should have at least double-bagged the items if there was a risk the bag would split.

I expect that you will pay my medical costs and also compensate me for my pain. If you can't offer me anything, then I will be forced to find a lawyer. I'm sure I'm not the only one who has been hurt.

Jose Frank

1.2 Internal Report

The following document was attached to the email.

Grocery Bag Durability Assessment

INTERNAL REPORT

Prepared by: Minerva Diggins

Department: Quality Assurance & Product Development

Date: November 21

Report ID: QA-2024-GB-001

1. INTRODUCTION

On November 1, a grocery bag tore while being carried to a customer's car, resulting in product spillage. The customer fell and was injured, but he both refused assistance and declined to offer his name. The customer, Jose Frank, later contacted customer support to file a complaint.

This report aims to assess the durability of the bags, identify potential causes of failure, and recommend corrective actions.

2. BAG MATERIAL AND STRUCTURAL INTEGRITY

- Material Composition: low-density polyethylene (LDPE).
- Manufacturer: Durapak Industries (new supplier as of October 1)
- Recommended Weight: No more than 10 lbs.
- Tensile Strength Test: Lab tests indicate a failure threshold at 17 lbs., which is within industry standards.
- Seal and Handle Durability: Examination of bags shows structural integrity at the seams and handles.
- Supplier Variability: Inspection revealed consistency among supplied items.

3. INCIDENT REVIEW

- Bag inspection: An employee was able to recover Mr. Frank's bags after the incident. An inspection of the bag revealed a split across the side but not the seam. The exact cause of failure is unknown.
- Training: All employees were informed about the new supplier and were instructed to remain within recommended weight limits while loading bags. Employees are offered verbal and written instructions (see Appendix C of the Employee Manual) and confirm receipt in writing.
- Management spot inspection: Floor managers observe employees during three spot inspections each shift. Managers have not reported any incidents related to bag overloading.

4. CONCLUSION

The investigation confirms that the grocery bags currently in use do not have durability weaknesses, and no employee error was identified. No immediate action is required.

1.3 Legal Authority—Products Liability

You begin your research by reviewing Carlin & Dworkin's *Torts and Product Liability in Sunport*:

Products liability doctrines are implicated when a defective product is placed in the stream of commerce and causes injury. Defendants may include manufacturers, assemblers, distributors, suppliers, and retailers.

There are five theories of recovery in products liability cases, some arising in tort and some in contract. Defendants may be liable under several theories, so a careful practitioner will consider each theory as it applies to a client's case. The theories are:

- Strict liability;
- Negligence;
- Intentional torts;
- Breach of *express* warranties and misrepresentations; and
- Breach of *implied* warranties.

***

To establish a cause of action for strict liability, the plaintiff must prove:

1. The defendant is a commercial supplier;
2. The defendant manufactured, supplied, or sold a defective product;
3. The defective product was the actual and proximate cause of the plaintiff's injury; and
4. The plaintiff suffered damages.

To recover damages for injuries caused by a product defect, the plaintiff must first show the product was defective when it left the defendant's control. A product is defective if it is unreasonably dangerous, meaning the defect was something other than what a reasonable consumer would expect in normal use of the product.

- **Manufacturing Defects.** A product has a manufacturing defect if it is not in the condition the manufacturer intended (it did not conform to the manufacturer's own production standards) when the product left the manufacturer's control. For example, if a consumer found rat hair in a can of soup, this might constitute a manufacturing defect unless the rat hair was part of the soup's recipe, which is unlikely. Rather, the rat hair was probably the result of something that occurred during the manufacturing process.
- **Design Defects.** A design defect may exist if: the product includes a condition that would not be contemplated by the ordinary consumer, and that condition is unreasonably dangerous to consumers; or if the risks presented by the product outweigh the benefits of the product.
- **Warning Defects.** A defendant may be liable for harm caused by the defendant's failure to *adequately* warn consumers of dangers presented by the product about which the defendant knows or should have known.

***

A party who causes the product to enter the stream of commerce may be strictly liable for injuries caused by the product's defect. This includes manufacturers, retailers, and distributors. Notably, a plaintiff does not have to prove the defendant's negligence to establish strict liability; the plaintiff need only prove the defendant manufactured, sold, or leased a product with a dangerous defect.

Retailers as well as manufacturers can be liable for injuries caused by manufacturing and design defects, even when retailers are not involved in the manufacturing or design process. In fact, liability may be established even if the retailer could in no way be considered at fault for the product's defective manufacture or design; by serving as a conduit between the manufacturer and the public, a retailer may be strictly liable for any injury caused by distribution of the defective product. In such a case, retailers and manufacturers are jointly and severally liable for injuries caused by defective products. If the retailer is truly "innocent," then the retailer may pursue indemnification against responsible parties.

To establish causation, the plaintiff must show the plaintiff's injuries were caused by a defect that existed when the product left the defendant's control.

A plaintiff does not have a cause of action if the plaintiff misused the product, meaning the plaintiff did not use the product in a normal or foreseeable way.* In addition, a defendant may avoid liability or mitigate damages by showing the plaintiff's conduct contributed to the plaintiff's injuries (comparative negligence).

*While a plaintiff's misuse of a product may negate liability, in some cases, suppliers should anticipate user carelessness or reasonably foreseeable "misuses" of the product. In such cases, a product may be defective if the product's packaging or literature fails to warn consumers of unexpected dangers associated with foreseeable misuses of the product.

1.4 Legal Authority—Strict Liability

You also find the following case, which supports the idea that a retailer may be strictly liable for distributing a defective product:

Vandermark v. Ford Motor Co.
61 Cal.2d 256 (Cal 1964)

TRAYNOR, J.

In October 1958 plaintiff Chester Vandermark bought a new Ford automobile from defendant Lorimer Diesel Engine Company, an authorized Ford dealer doing business as Maywood Bell Ford. About six weeks later, while driving on the San Bernardino Freeway, he lost control of the car. It went off the highway to the right and collided with a light post. He and his sister, plaintiff Mary Tresham, suffered serious injuries. They brought this action for damages against Maywood Bell Ford and the Ford Motor Company, which manufactured and assembled the car. . . .

***

. . . [S]ince it could reasonably be inferred from the description of the braking system in evidence and the offer of proof of all possible causes of defects that the defect was owing to negligence in design, manufacture, assembly, or adjustment, it must be taken as established that the defect was caused by some such negligence.

***

Retailers like manufacturers are engaged in the business of distributing goods to the public. They are an integral part of the overall producing and marketing enterprise that should bear the cost of injuries resulting from defective products. (*See Greenman v. Yuba*

Power Products, Inc., 59 Cal.2d 57, 63 [27 Cal.Rptr. 697, 377 P.2d 897].) In some cases the retailer may be the only member of that enterprise reasonably available to the injured plaintiff. In other cases the retailer himself may play a substantial part in insuring that the product is safe or may be in a position to exert pressure on the manufacturer to that end; the retailer's strict liability thus serves as an added incentive to safety. Strict liability on the manufacturer and retailer alike affords maximum protection to the injured plaintiff and works no injustice to the defendants, for they can adjust the costs of such protection between them in the course of their continuing business relationship. Accordingly, as a retailer engaged in the business of distributing goods to the public, Maywood Bell is strictly liable in tort for personal injuries caused by defects in cars sold by it. [Citation omitted.]

[Plaintiffs] pleaded and introduced substantial evidence of all of the facts necessary to establish strict liability in tort. Accordingly, the trial court erred in directing a verdict for Maywood Bell . . .

[T]he judgment in favor of Maywood Bell Ford is reversed.

Exercise 1

You begin to research potential theories of recovery. You eliminate any theory based on intentional tort or express warranties as there is no evidence to support either claim. Therefore, you first consider whether Mr. Frank has a claim under a theory of strict liability.

You know the first challenge in Mr. Frank's case is proving the bag was defective.

1. **Can Mr. Frank prove the bag was subject to a manufacturing or design defect?**

___

___

___

2. **Is there additional information you would like to know to establish whether the bag had a manufacturing or design defect?**

___

___

___

3. **If Mr. Frank can establish that the bag had a defect, can Mr. Frank show the product defect was the actual and proximate cause of his injury? Why or why not?**

___

___

___

1.5 Legal Authority—Negligence

You next consider whether FreshMart might be liable under a theory of negligence. You find the following case with facts similar to Mr. Frank's case:

Fuller v. Winn-Dixie Montgomery, LLC
Civil Action No. 16-00363 KD M (S.D. Ala. Mar. 29, 2017)

***

This case stems from Plaintiff Kathryn F. Fuller's (Fuller) June 11, 2014 shopping trip to a Winn Dixie ["WD"] grocery store in Mobile, Alabama, where she purchased two cans of soup, a jar of spaghetti sauce and other items. (Doc. 59-3 at (Dep. Fuller at 25)). Fuller purchased her groceries, which were then bagged by WD employee Julia Heath (Heath). Fuller exited the store and as she was leaving, one of the bags she was carrying (containing the soup cans and spaghetti jar) allegedly failed. This resulted in the glass spaghetti jar shattering, severely slicing her left foot. According to Fuller, "I hear[d] the glass shatter on the concrete, and . . . I was bleeding . . ." (Doc. 59-3 (Dep. Fuller at 26)). As alleged, Fuller was injured, underwent surgery, experiences continued problems and suffers from permanent limitations.

On June 7, 2016, Fuller initiated this action against Defendants Winn-Dixie Stores, Inc. and Advanced Polybag, Inc. in the Circuit Court of Mobile County, Alabama (CV 16-901162), and on July 1, 2016 amended the complaint to add Defendant Winn-Dixie Montgomery, LLC. (Doc. 1-1). Fuller's initial claims against Defendants consisted of negligence and wantonness, premises liability and negligent, reckless and wanton hiring/supervision/training. (Doc. 1-1). . . .

***

. . . For [Fuller's] negligence claim to survive summary judgment, Fuller must prove: 1) WD owed her a duty; 2) WD breached that duty; 3) she suffered a loss/injury; and 4) WD's negligence was the actual and proximate cause of her injury. [Citation omitted.] Proximate cause is "an act or omission that in a natural and continuous sequence, unbroken by any new and independent causes, produces the injury and without which the injury would not have occurred." *Crowne Invs., Inc. v. Bryant*, 638 So.2d 873, 877-878 (Ala. 1994). It is "conduct [that] naturally and probably brought about the harm and . . . [that] would not have happened without the conduct." *APJI 33.00 Causation-Definition*.

It is undisputed that Fuller was injured and the court will assume that WD owed a duty to properly bag the groceries. However, Fuller has failed to show the existence of genuine issues of material fact that WD's presumed negligent bagging was the actual and proximate cause of her injury.

At the May 31st hearing Fuller conceded that she does not know what happened—whether the injury was caused by Heath's improper bagging, a defect in the bag, Fuller's jiggling of the items while carrying the bag causing the items to break against one another, or some other reason. The evidence reveals that Fuller testified that she has no idea why the grocery bag broke. (Doc. 59-3 (Dep. Fuller at 30)). Fuller does not have any knowledge as to whether the bag was overfilled or improperly filled, as "I don't think

I paid attention to her actually putting items in the bag[]" and she is "not sure" she knows of anything Heath did incorrectly to cause her injury. (Id. (Dep. Fuller at 31, 33-34, 41-42)). Fuller does not know if there was anything wrong with the bag and/or anything WD could have done to keep the incident from happening. (Id. (Dep. Fuller at 34, 42)). Finally, Heath testified that she did not see any problems from loading the bag with less than five (5) pounds of groceries, which is what she did in this instance. (Doc. 59-7 (Dep. Heath at 64-65)). And other than the video, which fails to support Fuller's contention that improper bagging caused the bag to break resulting in injury to her, Fuller has submitted no evidence to support causation.

To recover for negligence Fuller must show that WD's breach was the proximate and actual cause of her injury. Fuller has presented possibilities to the Court for her injury. Fuller's speculation—and theories in the alternative—as to the cause of her injury is insufficient to survive summary judgment. *See, e.g., Giles*, 574 Fed. Appx. at 984 (finding similarly); *Cordoba v. Dillard's, Inc.*, 419 F.3d 1169, 1181 (11th Cir. 2005) ("unsupported speculation . . . does not meet a party's burden of producing some defense to a summary judgment motion. Speculation does not create a genuine issue of fact; instead, it creates a false issue, the demolition of which is a primary goal of summary judgment[]"); *Brantley v. International Paper Co.*, 2017 WL 2292767, *25 (M.D. Ala. May 24, 2017) ("plaintiffs cannot proceed to trial based on a mere hunch . . . . [Citation omitted]. Fuller has failed to show that Heath's negligence (via improper bagging) was the proximate and actual cause of her injury. Thus, WD's motion is GRANTED as to negligence.

***

Exercise 2

1. **How are the facts of *Fuller* similar to Mr. Frank's case? How are they different?**

____

____

____

____

____

____

____

____

____

____

2. **How does the decision in *Fuller* influence whether Mr. Frank can recover under a theory of negligence?**

3. **Can Mr. Frank rely on the doctrine of *res ipsa loquitur*[1] by showing the defect was of a kind that does not occur in the absence of negligence on the part of the manufacturer?**

1.6 Legal Authority—Warranties

Finally, you consider whether Mr. Frank may have a claim for breach of implied warranties. The Sunport Sales Act defines implied warranties as follows:

> A sale of goods gives rise to an implied warranty that the goods shall be reasonably fit for a particular purpose if:
>
> 1. The buyer, expressly or by implication, makes known to the seller the particular purpose for which the goods are required;
>   - □ The degree of particularity that should be required is dependent on the nature of the good and its general purpose.
> 2. The buyer relies on the seller's skill or judgment.
>   - □ There is seldom direct evidence to show a buyer relied on the seller's skill or judgment because such involves an inquiry into the buyer's state of mind. Instead, courts may consider the buyer's testimony and circumstantial evidence to demonstrate the buyer's reliance.

1. **What is *res ipsa loquitur*?** The doctrine of *res ipsa loquitur* means "the thing speaks for itself." Under the doctrine, a factfinder can infer the existence of a defendant's negligent conduct in the absence of direct evidence. The doctrine of *res ipsa loquitur* applies—and thus an inference of negligence is created—if the plaintiff can prove that: 1) the accident was of the type that ordinarily would not occur in the absence of negligence; 2) the accident was caused by something within the exclusive control of the defendant; and 3) the accident was not due to any action on the part of the plaintiff. See Part II, Chapter 8, *Charlton v. Lemmon*.

- ☐ If the buyer has examined or inspected the goods, then there is no implied warranty with respect to defects that such an examination should have revealed.

A sale of goods gives rise to an implied warranty that goods are of a merchantable quality if the goods are bought from a seller who deals in goods of that kind. A merchant impliedly warrants that the good sold is reasonably fit for the general purpose for which it is manufactured and sold.

Exercise 3

1. **Do you believe Mr. Frank may have a cause of action for breach of implied warranties?**

Strict Liability

15

Calloway v. Pinecrest Golf Club

Your colleague at Hubbs Insurance Company contacts you about a potential referral. Hubbs represents Pinecrest Golf Club, one of Eastvale's most exclusive private clubs. Pinecrest recently received a demand letter from James Calloway, who was injured when he was struck by a golf ball while he was driving past Pinecrest's driving range.

1.1 Police Report

The client file includes the following police report summarizing the incident:

Eastvale Police Department

INCIDENT REPORT

REPORT NUMBER: 015678

DATE & TIME: March 10—2:45 P.M.

LOCATION: Intersection of Oakwood Drive & Fairway Lane, Eastvale, Sunport

REPORTING OFFICER: Officer Daniel Reynolds, Badge #4578

CALL TYPE: Traffic Accident—Hazardous Object (Golf Ball)

1. INCIDENT SUMMARY

At approximately 2:45 P.M., officers responded to a single-vehicle crash at the intersection of Oakwood Drive and Fairway Lane, adjacent to the Pinecrest Golf Club. Upon arrival, officers observed a 2025 BMW Z4 convertible, silver in color (SP Plate: 837-LXT), with front-end damage after striking a guardrail on the right side of the road.

The driver, James Calloway (DOB: 06/14/1985), was found conscious but disoriented and was treated on the scene by EMS for a severe injury to his right eye. EMS transported Mr. Calloway to Eastvale General Hospital.

STATEMENT OF JAMES CALLOWAY, DRIVER

Mr. Calloway was traveling eastbound on Oakwood Drive at approximately 35 MPH when he saw a golf ball suddenly drop from the sky. The top of his convertible was open, and he reported the golf ball struck him in the eye, causing immediate pain and momentary loss of focus. Mr. Calloway veered, overcorrected, and collided with a guardrail. Aside from the injuries sustained when struck with the golf ball, Mr. Calloway did not appear to have other injuries from the crash.

STATEMENT OF VINCENT MERCER, WITNESS AND PEDESTRIAN

Vincent Mercer was traveling westbound on Oakwood Driver and saw the golf ball approaching Mr. Calloway's car. He saw the ball hit Mr. Calloway, and Mr. Calloway swerving before hitting the guardrail.

Mr. Mercer frequently travels this route and noted he has seen multiple stray golf balls land near passing cars. On the day of the crash, Mr. Mercer stated he counted at least five golf balls in the road and in the area near the crash.

STATEMENT OF IMELDA KENSINGTON, PINECREST GOLF CLUB GENERAL MANAGER

Imelda Kensington reported the driving range was only recently completed (February 1). It was moved from the back 50 acres of the course because club guests complained that drainage on the older range made the sod soggy and unsuitable as a driving range.

The tee area for the new range is approximately 250 yards from Oakwood Drive. Ms. Kensington notes the club chose the area because of its ideal terrain and spectacular views. Ms. Kensington asserted the club did not erect safety netting to capture errant balls because most golfers who practice on the range cannot drive the ball farther than 250 yards.

Ms. Kensington indicated that the club has received complaints about balls on Oakwood Drive, and there have been two reported incidents of balls striking cars and causing property damage. Ms. Kensington asserted the club has retained a new safety expert to offer recommendations about ways to minimize errant balls.

INVESTIGATION AND EVIDENCE

Officers located a white Titleist golf ball near the scene, approximately 5 feet from the vehicle's final resting position.

Surveillance cameras from a nearby convenience store partially captured the incident, showing a small object falling toward the vehicle before it swerved.

Physical injury: Mr. Calloway was treated at Eastvale General Hospital. Medical personnel indicate Mr. Calloway sustained a retinal detachment, orbital fractures, and an intraocular hemorrhage/hyphema. Personnel performed emergency surgery to address the retinal detachment, but the injury caused permanent optic nerve damage.

Mr. Calloway's prognosis for vision recovery is poor due to the severity of the trauma, and he will likely experience permanent blindness in his right eye. If his pain persists, then he will likely need surgery to remove the eye.

Damage to private property: Front bumper dented, minor damage to front right tire, scratches along the right side.

Damage to public property: Minor damage to the metal guardrail, no immediate safety hazards identified.

FINDINGS

Based on statements, evidence at the scene, and video footage, it appears the incident was caused by an errant golf ball from Pinecrest Golf Club. While the driver was not speeding or violating any traffic laws, the unexpected impact led to a loss of control, resulting in the crash.

The incident will be reported to the City Safety Commission for review of potential traffic hazards caused by the proximity of the driving range.

No citations issued at this time.

End of Report

1.2 Demand Letter

The demand letter sent to Pinecrest by Mr. Calloway's attorney includes the following assertion:

Pinecrest's gross negligence in operating a driving range so near the road establishes a claim for strict liability. Installing a driving range within reach of the road creates a foreseeable and significant risk of harm to bystanders that cannot be completely eliminated. And while operating a driving range does not by itself constitute an abnormally dangerous activity, operating a range within a few hundred yards of a busy road certainly does. *See Yommer v. McKenzie*, 257 A.2d 138 (Md. 1969).

Your reckless disregard of bystander safety directly and foreseeably caused Mr. Calloway's injuries. Your Club was aware of the risks to bystanders because, in the month the range has been in operation, multiple pedestrians and drivers have reported incidents with golf balls in the street, including incidents when balls have struck passing cars and caused property damage. Mr. Calloway has paid the price for your wantonness and disregard of public safety.

1.3 Legal Authority—Strict Liability

An excerpt from Rosenthal & Vega's *Strict Liability in Sunport* offers the following summary of strict liability jurisprudence in Sunport:

> An actor may be subject to strict liability if the actor engages in an abnormally dangerous activity and causes physical harm. Those who engage in abnormally dangerous activities are, as a general rule, subject to strict liability for the harm caused to the innocent as a result of the activity. The plaintiff is not required to prove that the defendant acted unreasonably, only that the plaintiff sustained an injury from the activity.
>
> Courts consider several factors in determining whether an activity is abnormally dangerous: 1) whether the activity creates a foreseeable and highly significant risk of harm even under the exercise of reasonable care; 2) whether the activity is one of common usage; 3) the appropriateness of the activity to the place where it is carried on; and 4) the extent to which its value to the community is outweighed by its dangerous attributes.

You also find excerpts from the case cited by Mr. Calloway's counsel, which helps inform what constitutes "common usage." In the case, the defendants operated a grocery store and gasoline filling station immediately adjacent to the plaintiffs' home, and the defendants' gasoline tank leaked and contaminated the plaintiffs' well. *Yommer v. McKenzie*, 257 A.2d 138, 138-39 (Md. 1969). The court found the defendants liable for damages under a theory of strict liability. *Id.* at 141:

> Although the operation of a gasoline station does not of itself involve 'a high degree of risk of some harm to the person, land or chattels of others,' the placing of a large underground gasoline tank in close proximity to the appellees' residence and well does involve such a risk, since it is not a matter of common usage . . .
>
> Although there is no evidence of negligence on the part of the [defendants] (indeed such a showing is not required as will be discussed below), it is proper to surmise that this risk cannot, or at least was not, eliminated by the exercise of reasonable care.
>
> ***
>
> . . . No one would deny that gasoline stations as a rule do not present any particular danger to the community. However, when the operation of such activity involves the placing of a large tank adjacent to a well from which a family must draw its water for drinking, bathing and laundry, at least that aspect of the activity is inappropriate to the locale, even when equated to the value of the activity.
>
> ***
>
> We accept the test of appropriateness as the proper one: that the unusual, the excessive, the extravagant, the bizarre are likely to be non-natural uses which lead to strict liability.

This is precisely the distinction drawn by this Court, speaking through Judge Parke in *Toy v. Atlantic Gulf & Pacific Co.*, 176 Md. 197, 4 A.2d 757 (1939) . . .

> . . . 'The basic concept underlying the rule [of strict liability] is that a person who elects to keep or bring upon his land something which exposes the adjacent land or its owner or occupant to an added danger should be obliged to prevent its doing damage . . .' 176 Md. at 212-213, 4 A.2d at 765.

It is apparent to us that the storage of large quantities of gasoline immediately adjacent to a private residence comes within this rule and relieved the McKenzies of the necessity of proving negligence . . .

Yommer, 257 A.2d at 140-141.

Exercise 1

Relying on the legal authority outlined above, can Mr. Calloway establish the elements of strict liability?

1. **Does operating a driving range near a road create a foreseeable and highly significant risk of serious physical harm?**

___

___

___

2. **Could Pinecrest eliminate the risk of harm through the exercise of reasonable care?**

___

___

___

3. **Is operating a driving range a matter of common usage in the area? Is the business appropriate to the place where it is carried on?**

___

___

___

4. Does the value to the community outweigh the dangerous attributes of the activity?

____

____

____

1.4 Consultant Report

While you continue to review the Pinecrest file, you find the following report:

Safe Distance for Golf Driving Range from Road

CONSULTANT REPORT

Prepared for: Pinecrest Golf Club

Prepared by: IronShield Safety Consultants

Date: December 15

1. **Introduction**

   This report provides an assessment and recommendations on the safe placement of a golf driving range in relation to a nearby public road. The objective is to minimize the risk of stray golf balls reaching the road and endangering vehicles, pedestrians, or property.

2. **Industry Standards and Safety Considerations**

   Several factors influence the safe placement of a golf driving range relative to a road, including golfer skill levels, ball trajectory, prevailing wind conditions, and safety barriers. The following guidelines are based on industry best practices:

   - **Minimum Distance Without Netting:** 300 to 400 yards (275 to 365 meters) from tee areas to the road to account for the maximum drive distance of advanced golfers.
   - **Minimum Distance With Safety Netting:** 100 to 150 yards (90 to 137 meters) if high-quality protective netting (minimum height of 40-50 feet) is installed along the road-facing perimeter.
     - *Pinecrest ownership prefers to avoid heightened netting because netting will interfere with aesthetics and scenic views.*
   - **Restricted-Flight Balls:** If the range intends to use reduced-distance balls, a shorter buffer may be acceptable, but adequate testing should be performed.
     - *Pinecrest ownership prefers to avoid insistence on reduced-distance balls, which interfere with the member experience. Pinecrest hosts several prestigious competitions and offers training space for novice, semi-professional, and professional players.*

- **Elevation Considerations:** Driving ranges situated on elevated land should increase setback distances, as elevation can extend ball flight distance.
  - *Pinecrest's proposed location sits at the highest point of the club's property. The elevated location may extend ball flight distance.*

- **Wind Conditions:** Courses in areas with strong prevailing winds should account for potential wind-assisted ball travel.
  - *The proposed range sits in an area that can experience prevailing winds. The area routinely experiences winds above 5 mph and often experiences winds as high as 15-20 mph, even in fair weather.*

3. **Legal Considerations**

Local zoning laws and municipal ordinances should be reviewed to determine any specific requirements regarding the placement of golf driving ranges near public roads.

- *Pinecrest is already zoned for use as a golf range, and moving the range does not interfere with existing approvals. Our consultants were unable to find other restrictions that would interfere with the proposed placement of the new range.*

4. **Conclusion & Recommendations**

Based on the assessment and the client's preferences, the recommended placement of the golf driving range should be at least **350 yards from any road if no netting is installed**. If protective netting is used, a **minimum setback of 100-150 yards is acceptable**. Additional safety measures such as tee placement adjustments and landscaping buffers should be considered to further reduce risks.

It is advised that a **detailed site evaluation** be conducted to determine the best configuration for the range based on environmental conditions and golfer demographics.

1.5 Client Interview

You discuss the report with Ms. Imelda Kensington, Pinecrest Golf Club General Manager. She confirms the information she previously provided to law enforcement and offers additional information about the placement of the range. Specifically:

- Pinecrest declined to install safety netting around the new driving range. "After all, we chose that location because it offers spectacular views of the mountains, and we didn't want to erect ugly netting to interfere with that view. In any case, hardly anyone can shoot the ball farther than the range."
- Pinecrest provides and encourages golfers to use reduced-distance balls. "That said, most players don't want to use the balls, and we don't insist on it. A lot of our players are advanced golfers, and they don't want to handicap their performance. Even our novice players want to see how far they can truly drive the ball."

- Winds do interfere with the trajectory of certain shots. "A lot of golfers, especially those who aren't used to playing on our range, do find their shots go a little haywire when it is windy outside." Ms. Kensington confirmed the wind often blows in the direction of the road adjacent to the range, which contributes to balls landing in that area.
- To minimize errant balls, the Club installed the tee area so golfers hit shots away from the road. "That said, even the best golfers occasionally shank the ball, which is why some balls have still ended up on the road."
- Based on the safety consultation, the Club also installed a berm as a landscaping buffer. "It works most of the time to keep the balls inside the range."

Exercise 2

1. **Does the report and/or information relayed by Ms. Kensington influence your assessment of whether Mr. Calloway can establish a claim for strict liability? Why or why not?**

____

____

____

____

____

____

1.6 Legal Authority—Abnormally Dangerous Activities

As you continue your research about Mr. Calloway's claim, you find the following case:

Ludwikoski v. Kurotsu
840 F.Supp. 826, 826–29 (D. Kan. 1993)

LUNGSTRUM, District Judge.

I. Introduction

This matter comes before the court on the motion of defendant Ryoji Kurotsu to dismiss for failure to state a claim pursuant to Federal Rule of Civil Procedure 12(b)(6) (Doc. # 9). Plaintiff Florence Ludwikoski brings this action after being struck by a golf ball she claims was hit by the defendant. She alleges that the defendant was negligent in the manner in which he hit the ball, and that her injuries are a direct result of defendant's negligence. She also alleges that the defendant was engaging in an abnormally dangerous activity and that he is absolutely liable for her injuries. For the reasons set forth below, the court grants in part defendant's motion to dismiss and denies it in part.

***

In Count II of her complaint, plaintiff alleges that the defendant is strictly liable to plaintiff because golf is an abnormally dangerous activity which creates a high degree of risk of harm. Plaintiff's argument that golfers be held strictly liable to innocent persons who are injured by their golfing activities, is contrary to the law of Kansas as well as that of states across the country. *See Carrigan v. Roussell,* 177 N.J.Super. 272, 278, 426 A.2d 517, 521 (1981). It appears beyond a doubt that the plaintiff can prove no set of facts in support of her theory of strict liability in tort which would entitle her to relief. *Conley v. Gibson,* 355 U.S. 41, 45-46, 78 S.Ct. 99, 102, 2 L.Ed.2d 80 (1957); *Jacobs, Visconsi & Jacobs, Co. v. City of Lawrence,* 927 F.2d 1111, 1115 (10th Cir.1991). Thus, the court finds that plaintiff fails to state a cause of action in Count II of her complaint, and Count II is dismissed.

Kansas has adopted the Restatement (Second) of Torts § 519, which sets forth the general rule regarding strict liability in tort for abnormally dangerous activities as follows:

1) one who carries on an abnormally dangerous activity is subject to liability for harm to the person, land or chattels of another resulting from the activity, although he has exercised the utmost care to prevent the harm.
2) This strict liability is limited to the kind of harm, the possibility of which makes the activity abnormally dangerous.

See Falls v. Scott, 249 Kan. 54, 59-60, 815 P.2d 1104, 1109-1110 (1991); *Williams v. Amoco Production Co.,* 241 Kan. 102, 115, 734 P.2d 1113 (1987). Kansas has also adopted § 520 of the Restatement (Second) of Torts which sets out the following test for determining whether an activity is abnormally dangerous:

> In determining whether an activity is abnormally dangerous, the following factors are to be considered:
>
> (a) existence of a high degree of risk of some harm to the person, land or chattels of others;
> (b) likelihood that the harm that results from it will be great;
> (c) inability to eliminate the risk by the exercise of reasonable care;
> (d) extent to which the activity is not a matter of common usage;
> (e) inappropriateness of the activity to the place where it is carried on;
> (f) extent to which its value to the community is outweighed by its dangerous attributes.

See Falls, 249 Kan. at 59-60, 815 P.2d at 1109-1110; *Williams,* 241 Kan. at 115, 734 P.2d at 1113. Whether the activity is an abnormally dangerous one is to be determined by the court. *Falls,* 249 Kan. at 60, 815 P.2d at 1110.

Plaintiff has not alleged, nor could she allege, facts which would cause the court to conclude that golf is an abnormally dangerous activity under Kansas law as set out above. Golf does not present a high degree of risk of harm, nor is there a strong likelihood that the harm that does result from golf will be great. Clearly the vast majority of golf shots, including those that are hit in a faulty manner, do not cause substantial injury. *See Townsley v. State,* 6 Misc.2d 557, 164 N.Y.S.2d 840, 841 (1957) ("The game of golf, itself, is not inherently dangerous."). An activity is not abnormally dangerous simply because it may possibly produce injury. *See Falls,* 249 Kan. at 60, 815 P.2d at 1110.

Although, as plaintiff contends, the exercise of reasonable care will not eliminate all potential for injury resulting from the game of golf, this court is not persuaded that Kansas courts would find strict liability appropriate. Golf is a very common activity; it is not 'abnormal' in any sense of the word. Its value to the community outweighs its dangerous attributes. Indeed, most, if not all recreational sports involve some degree of risk of injury, yet plaintiff has cited to no Kansas case applying strict liability principles to a recreational sport. Moreover, in this case, the defendant was golfing on a golf course, which is absolutely an appropriate place to be playing the sport.

***

Thus, the court rejects plaintiff's argument that under Kansas law, the defendant's activities in this case should be subject to strict liability, and finds that plaintiff has failed to state a claim in Count II of her complaint.

***

Exercise 3

1. **How does the court's reasoning in *Ludwikoski v. Kurotsu* influence your assessment of Mr. Calloway's case?**

____

____

____

2. **If you conclude that Mr. Calloway will be unsuccessful in bringing a claim for strict liability, what other legal theories could Mr. Calloway use to establish Pinecrest's liability for his injuries?**

____

____

____

Nuisance

16

Wendt v. Silver Creek Farms

One of your associate attorneys recently met with a potential client, Casey Wendt. Ms. Wendt wants to stop certain agricultural practices of her neighbor, Silver Creek Farms. Silver Creek owns and operates a confined-animal feeding facility on its property, and smells from the farm are spreading to Ms. Wendt's property.

1.1 Interview Transcript

You review the transcript of the interview between your associate and the potential client:

Associate	OK, Ms. Wendt, let's get started. With your permission, I'm going to record this part of our conversation to ensure I get everything right. Is that OK?
Casey Wendt	That's fine.
Associate	Great, thanks. Well, I reviewed your intake form, and I see you are here because of the activities of your neighbor, Silver Creek Farms. You said you are concerned about some of their livestock activities, is that correct?
Casey Wendt	I'm more than concerned—I've had it. The smells from their property are absolutely disgusting, and I don't think it's fair that they get to make a profit while we all suffer.
Associate	I understand. Can you tell me more about what they are doing on their property?
Casey Wendt	Sure. They used to run a small operation—Silver Creek Farms. They own 50 acres, and they mostly raised row crops like corn or wheat. They also had a small herd of sheep and a few pigs. Two years ago, they signed a deal with a huge pork distributor. They built a massive building to run an animal feeding operation.

	We weren't thrilled because there wasn't another facility like that near us, but we figured they had a right to do what they wanted with their property. Last autumn, we started noticing a horrible smell from the property. We learned that Silver Creek had been storing animal waste in a huge, concrete lagoon outside the feeding facility. In the fall, they pumped the waste from the lagoon and spread it on their fields as fertilizer. I can't begin to describe how disgusting it was. For weeks, the whole area smelled foul. No matter what we did, our entire house reeked of manure. We started eating out because we couldn't stand the smell while we ate at home. I could barely sleep because it smelled so terrible, even when I tried to seal all the windows and doors. My daughter didn't want to go to school because she was afraid the smell was in her clothes. I work from home, so it's not like I can avoid the smell. I started going into town to work from the library or coffee shops just to get a break.
Associate	Did you file any complaints about the smells?
Casey Wendt	Of course. I filed two complaints with the Westvale health department, and they said they were investigating. I also contacted our zoning board and the Sunport Agriculture Department. The zoning board said they couldn't do anything because Silver Creek's facility doesn't violate our zoning ordinances. The Agriculture Department said they would review the activity. But I can't keep waiting for them to do something. I can't take another autumn with those smells.
Associate	What would you like to see happen?
Casey Wendt	I really just want it to stop. They are making all this money at the expense of their neighbors, and it is ruining our lives. Not only is it impossible to live with the smell, but I am embarrassed to have people over.

Exercise 1

1. **Identify the potential causes of action Ms. Wendt might have against Silver Creek Farms.**

 ____

 ____

 ____

2. Which claim offers likely chance of success, and why?

____

____

____

1.2 Legal Research

As usual, you begin your research by reviewing your favorite practice manual, *Sunport Civil Remedies*. You considered filing claims for trespass and nuisance, but your research suggests Ms. Wendt's strongest claim may be a claim for nuisance. In particular, you decide not to pursue a claim of trespass based on the following excerpt:

> While some jurisdictions have recognized a claim for trespass by airborne particles, courts in Sunport have expressly refused to extend the tort of trespass to invasion by particulate matter because such an invasion does not interfere with a plaintiff's right to exercise exclusive possession of the land.
>
> Instead, Sunport courts note that the proper remedy in such cases is a claim of nuisance. Nuisance affords a plaintiff a remedy when the defendant's conduct, including conduct that results in invasive odors, interferes with the plaintiff's use and enjoyment of the land.

Your research indicates that Sunport defines the tort of nuisance as follows:

> **Chapter VIII: Other Torts**
> SECTION IX: PRIVATE NUISANCE
>
> A defendant is liable for a private nuisance if the defendant's conduct is: 1) intentional and unreasonable; and 2) causes substantial interference with another's interest in the use and enjoyment of their land.
>
> ***
>
> "Unreasonable" conduct includes conduct that is injurious to health, offensive to the senses, or interferes with the comfortable enjoyment of property. Nuisance is often defined by the resultant harm rather than the conduct causing the harm.
>
> ***
>
> The usual remedy for nuisance is damages, but a court may grant injunctive[1] relief if damages are unavailable or inadequate.

1. For a discussion of injunctive relief, see Chapter 4, footnote 2.

Exercise 2

1. **Draft an email to Ms. Wendt explaining why she might have a cause of action for nuisance.**

1.3 Letter from Opposing Counsel

Ms. Wendt agrees with your assessment and is willing to sue Silver Creek Farms for damages. She is also willing to ask the court to enjoin Silver Creek Farms from pumping waste onto their crops.

You send a letter to Silver Creek Farms. You demand that they stop pumping waste on their crops and note that Ms. Wendt intends to file suit if the parties are unable to reach an agreement.

A week later, you receive the following letter:

Westway, LLC

RE: CASEY WENDT MATTER

Counsel for Silver Creek Farms

We represent Silver Creek Farms. We received and reviewed your recent letter demanding that Silver Creek Farms stop pumping animal waste onto its crops. You assert that Ms. Wendt intends to sue for nuisance if Silver Creek Farms continues with its current practices.

While Silver Creek ownership regrets any inconvenience to Ms. Wendt, her potential nuisance claim is barred by Sunport's "Right to Farm" law. Sun. Stat. § 82.674. The Right to Farm Law ensures that agricultural operations cannot be deemed a nuisance if they are conducted in compliance with state and federal laws and employ commonly accepted agricultural practices, expressly including the spreading of manure.

Silver Creek's actions reflect a common agricultural practice in Sunport; most agricultural operations spread animal fertilizer during the autumn to ensure a thriving, robust crop during the subsequent harvest season. Therefore, Silver Creek is shielded from nuisance liability, and Ms. Wendt is unable to pursue a claim for injunctive relief or damages.

Based on the above, we demand that Ms. Wendt retract her threat of litigation.

1.4 Legal Authority—Right to Farm

You are justifiably concerned about the potential implications of the Right to Farm law on Ms. Wendt's claim. You find the statutory provisions referenced in the letter to assess whether Ms. Wendt's claim is truly barred under the law.

Sunport Statute § 82.674

1. No animal feeding operation or its expansion shall be deemed to interfere with another person's comfortable use and enjoyment of the person's property under nuisance or any other cause of action so long as:

   a. The operation complies with all applicable federal and state statutes or regulations;
   b. The operation employs generally accepted management practices; and
   c. The facility or expansion was not a nuisance at the time it began or was constructed.

2. The provisions of this section shall not apply when a nuisance results from the improper or negligent operation of an agricultural operation.

Exercise 3

1. **Do you believe the Right to Farm Act bars Ms. Wendt's claim? Why or why not?**

Appendix
Exercise Sample Answers

PART I—INTENTIONAL TORTS

Chapter 1: Battery and Assault

Battery: *Hainsley v. Patterson*

Exercise 1

1. **Based on the facts you learned during your call with Mr. Patterson and the elements of battery set forth above, do you believe Mr. Patterson may be liable to Ms. Hainsley for battery? (Are both elements satisfied? If not, then which element is lacking?)**

   If you answered "yes," you believe Mr. Patterson may be liable for battery, then it should be because you believe that, based on the facts provided: 1) he acted with the intent to cause a harmful or offensive contact to Ms. Hainsley; and 2) a harmful or offensive contact to Ms. Hainsley resulted because of Mr. Patterson's actions.

   If you answered "no," you do not believe Mr. Patterson may be liable for battery, then it should be because you believe that, based on the facts provided: 1) he did not act with the intent to cause a harmful or offensive contact to Ms. Hainsley; 2) a harmful or offensive contact to Ms. Hainsley did not result because of Doug's Mr. Patterson's actions; or 3) both elements are missing.

2. **Which facts, if any, suggest Mr. Patterson acted with intent to cause a harmful or offensive contact to Ms. Hainsley?**

   Some of the influential facts include:

   - There was a designated smoking area, but Mr. Patterson did not vape there;
   - Mr. Patterson knew Ms. Hainsley frequently walked by the area on her way to the food truck, and she walked directly in front of Mr. Patterson;
   - When Mr. Patterson blew the vapor, Ms. Hainsley coughed, rolled her eyes, and showed disgust;
   - Mr. Patterson laughed in response to Ms. Hainsley's reaction; and
   - Similar incidents occurred over several weeks. Each time, Ms. Hainsley rolled her eyes and stormed off. Mr. Patterson did not move or vape elsewhere.

3. **Which facts, if any, suggest Mr. Patterson's conduct caused a harmful or offensive contact to Ms. Hainsley?**

   Some of the influential facts include:

   - When Ms. Hainsley passed directly in front of Mr. Patterson, he exhaled vapor from his vape pen;
   - Ms. Hainsley coughed, rolled her eyes, and showed disgust; and
   - Ms. Hainsley reacted similarly each time a comparable incident occurred over the next few weeks.

4. Identify any additional information that might be helpful to assess the strength of Ms. Hainsley's claim.

Some of the practical considerations may include:

Intent

- Where was Mr. Patterson standing on the sidewalk? Could pedestrians avoid him?
- Was the weather generally calm, or was it often windy? Did the vapor regularly pass onto the sidewalk?
- How many pedestrians typically travel in the area at that time of day?
- Where did Mr. Patterson blow the smoke? Did he blow the vapor into the air or in the direction of the sidewalk and pedestrians?
- Did Mr. Patterson see Ms. Hainsley as she passed? Did he intend to blow vapor at her?
- Does Mr. Patterson's employer have policies about designated areas for smoking?
- How crowded is the designated smoking area? Is it usually populated with smokers, or do others vape in the area?

Harmful or offensive

- Did the vapor smell? Was there visible vapor?
- Is Ms. Hainsley sensitive to smoke and nicotine vapor? Did she inform Mr. Patterson of that sensitivity?
- Is there any scientific research confirming that exposure to nicotine vapor is physically harmful?
- How does a typical pedestrian feel about the exposure to vaping?
- Are there others in the area who stand on the sidewalk to smoke or vape?
- Are there any ordinances that prevent smoking in the area?

Consent

- Could Ms. Hainsley have taken a different route or walked farther from Mr. Patterson to avoid the vapor?
- Why did Ms. Hainsley regularly pass in the same direction at the same time? Could she take her breaks at different times?
- Did Ms. Hainsley ever ask Mr. Patterson to stop?

Damages/Harm

- What harm has Ms. Hainsley experienced?

Exercise 2

1. How do the facts set forth in Ms. Hainsley's complaint differ from the facts Mr. Patterson relayed to you during your phone call with him on October 15?

Notable differences and additional information include:

- Mr. Patterson explained why he did not smoke in the designated smoking area—Mr. Patterson recently quit smoking and does not like the smell of smoke on his clothing. The complaint suggests Mr. Patterson refused to smoke in the designated smoking area because he was obstinate or intentionally waiting for Ms. Hainsley.

- Ms. Hainsley argued that Mr. Patterson was standing on the sidewalk in a way that forced passersby to walk directly in front of him.
- Mr. Patterson suggested he accidentally blew smoke in Ms. Hainsley's face, but Ms. Hainsley asserted Mr. Patterson did it intentionally.
- Mr. Patterson believed it was a coincidence that Ms. Hainsley passed near him during the first few incidents, and he believed Ms. Hainsley was later timing her breaks to run into him. Ms. Hainsley implied that Mr. Patterson was waiting for her in the area.
- The complaint asserts similar incidents occurred 10-12 times. Ms. Hainsley also asserts that she coughed and verbally objected each time.

2. Which facts from the complaint, if any, suggest Mr. Patterson acted with intent to cause a harmful or offensive contact to Ms. Hainsley?

You might observe the following significant facts from the complaint:

- *para. 6*: Mr. Patterson did not smoke in the designated courtyard; Mr. Patterson vaped on the sidewalk, forcing passersby to walk directly in front of him.
- *para. 7*: As Ms. Hainsley passed Mr. Patterson on the sidewalk, Mr. Patterson "intentionally exhaled, blowing smoke into Plaintiff's path."
- *para. 7-8*: Ms. Hainsley told Mr. Patterson he should vape in the designated area, but he continued to vape on the sidewalk.
- *para. 8*: A similar incident occurred less than two weeks later.
- *para. 9*: A similar incident occurred 10-12 times. Each time, Ms. Hainsley objected, but Mr. Patterson did not change his behavior.

3. Which facts from the complaint, if any, suggest Doug's Mr. Patterson's conduct caused a harmful or offensive contact to Ms. Hainsley?

You might observe the following significant facts from the complaint:

- *para. 7*: Defendant's "smoke" caused Plaintiff to cough.
- *para. 8*: As Plaintiff walked in front of Defendant, he again exhaled, causing smoke to come into contact with Plaintiff and causing her to cough.
- *para. 9*: During each incident, Plaintiff coughed and expressed concern about Defendant's conduct.

4. Do the facts set forth in the complaint influence your conclusion about whether Mr. Patterson may be liable to Ms. Hainsley for battery?

This question calls for an opinion, so there is not necessarily a correct or incorrect response. Your answer should explain whether the new or different facts influence your assessment of the case. Does Ms. Hainsley's characterization of the facts change your opinion of whether the elements are satisfied?

Exercise 3

1. How are the facts in *Leichtman* similar to the facts in Mr. Patterson's case?

Some of the similarities between the two cases include:

- The defendant in *Liechtman* knew the plaintiff was opposed to smoking. Similarly, Ms. Hainsley expressed her discomfort with vaping, and Mr. Patterson knew she objected to his conduct.

- The defendant in *Leichtman* purposefully caused the plaintiff "physical discomfort, humiliation and distress." Comparably, Mr. Patterson found Ms. Hainsley's conduct amusing and consistently blew vapor in her direction, even when she coughed and objected.
- Tobacco smoke "has the physical properties capable of making contact." Vape aerosol is also particulate matter and is capable of making contact.

2. **How are the facts in *Leichtman* dissimilar from the facts in Mr. Patterson's case?**

   Some of the differences between the two cases include:

   - The incident in *Leichtman* occurred indoors in an enclosed space. In contrast, the incident involving Ms. Hainsley occurred outside in a public space.
   - The plaintiff in *Leichtman* was publicly known and had dedicated his career to the cessation of smoking. Yet aside from her comments to, Mr. Patterson did not know Ms. Hainsley or her preferences well.
   - The defendant in *Leichtman* acted in bad faith by inviting Leichtman to the show as part of the Great American Smokeout, ostensibly to discuss the harmful effect of smoking. While there, the defendant blew smoke in the plaintiff's face "for the purpose of causing physical discomfort, humiliation and distress." Contrastingly, Mr. Patterson did not seek out Ms. Hainsley or trick her into passing through the area, where he routinely took breaks. It is unclear whether he intentionally or accidentally blew smoke at her.
   - Vape aerosol does not contain the same level of toxins as cigarette smoke.

3. **How does the court's reasoning in *Leichtman* influence your assessment of whether Mr. Patterson may be liable to Ms. Hainsley for battery?**

   Again, this question calls for an opinion, so there is not necessarily a correct or incorrect response. Your answer should explain whether the court's reasoning influences your assessment of the case. Does the court's interpretation of the law and facts change your opinion of whether the elements are satisfied?

Exercise 4

1. **Review the interview notes, complaint, and legal authority. Applying the facts to the elements, do you believe Ms. Hainsley can establish the elements of battery?**

   The following considerations weigh against Ms. Hainsley's claim:

   - Intent

     Mr. Patterson vapes in a corner off the main sidewalk, where he can avoid most pedestrians. Mr. Patterson avoids the designated smoking area because he dislikes the smell and is trying to quit smoking, not because he wishes to target pedestrians in general or Ms. Hainsley in particular. The route happens to be in the path of the nearby food trucks where Ms. Hainsley gets her morning coffee.

     Mr. Patterson did not intentionally blow vapor toward Ms. Hainsley; any contact was accidental.

   - Harmful or offensive contact

     Second-hand exposure to vape aerosols do not create significant risks of harm, especially when the vapor is discharged outside and far from others.

     Aside from occasionally coughing, Ms. Hainsley never complained of or seemed to experience physical distress from the vapor.

     A reasonable pedestrian would not find the nominal contact offensive or harmful.

The following considerations favor Ms. Hainsley's claim:

- Intent

  Mr. Patterson consistently refuses to vape in the designated smoking area, where pedestrians can avoid smoke and vapor. Instead, he vapes on the sidewalk and is positioned in such a way that those walking by must pass close to him.

  Mr. Patterson continued to vape in the area even after he realized Ms. Hainsley objected to it. Mr. Patterson remained in the spot despite realizing Ms. Hainsley would pass nearly every day for coffee. Mr. Patterson intentionally blew vapor toward her when he realized she was offended and uncomfortable.

- Harmful or offensive contact

  The vapor causes Ms. Hainsley to cough and experience respiratory distress.

  Ms. Hainsley clearly indicated she was offended by Mr. Patterson conduct, but he only mocked her discomfort.

Chapter 1 Battery and Assault

Assault: *George v. The Haunted Inn*

Exercise 1

1. **Scott Pearce acted with the requisite intent to commit a battery.**

   Some of the influential facts include:

   Mr. Pearce "came right up to me—like right into my space." Mr. Pearce was yelling and waving the chainsaw and got "dangerously" close.

   Mr. George told Mr. Pearce to stop, but Pearce would not leave him alone.

   Mr. Pearce chased Mr. George after he became afraid and tried to run away.

2. **Scott Pearce's conduct caused Mr. George to experience reasonable apprehension of an imminent harmful or offensive contact.**

   Some of the influential facts include:

   Once Mr. George arrived at what he thought was outside the exit, Mr. Pearce "started his chainsaw and came right up" to Mr. George. He yelled at him and waved the chainsaw in his face.

   Mr. George ran away to escape Pearce, but Pearce chased Mr. George until Mr. George fell and cut his wrists on the gravel.

Exercise 2

1. **How does the court's reasoning in *Bouton v. Allstate Ins. Co.* influence your assessment of whether Mr. George can establish the elements of a *prima facie* case for assault based on the conduct of Scott Pearce?**

   The following considerations may support a conclusion that Mr. George can establish the elements of assault:

   - Intent

Mr. Pearce approached Mr. George with a chainsaw, yelling and waving it in his face. Mr. George told him to stop, but Mr. Pearce continued to approach him until Mr. George felt fearful for his life. Mr. Pearce even chased Mr. George, knowing Mr. George was scared and was no longer a willing participant in the event.

Mr. Pearce approached Mr. George outside the event, when Mr. George was no longer expecting scares.

- Apprehension

  Mr. George reasonably believed he was about to be harmed. Pearce waved a live chainsaw near Mr. George, and the event occurred outside the area where Mr. George expected actors.

  Mr. George did experience apprehension; Mr. George fled in fear.

The following considerations may support a conclusion that Mr. George can NOT establish the elements of assault:

- Intent

  Mr. Pearce did not intend to harm or truly scare Mr. George. Mr. Pearce was merely playing a character and was likely following his training. Mr. Pearce would not expect guests to truly believe he would harm them and may have had similar interactions with other guests during the event.

- Apprehension

  Even if Mr. George experienced apprehension, it was not reasonable. Pearce never contacted him, and Mr. Pearce's actions were consistent with other characters inside the event. A reasonable person exiting a haunted house could expect additional performances near the event and would not legitimately fear for their safety when approached by another character.

  Pearce never contacted Mr. George or made any other indication that he planned to harm or contact Mr. George.

Exercise 3

1. **Draft an email to Mr. George advising him of the potential implications of the language on the ticket produced by the Haunted Inn. Address the following issues in your email: 1) whether his claim for relief is barred because he *expressly* or *impliedly* consented to interactions like the one experienced with Scott Pearce; and 2) whether Scott Pearce *exceeded the scope of consent* by approaching Mr. George outside the park exit (and therefore Mr. George's claim is not barred).**

   Sample email:

   Mr. George–

   In response to our request for documents, Haunted Inn's lawyer produced the attached, which appears to be a copy of the ticket you received for your entrance into the Haunted Inn. On the back of the ticket appears a Release, Liability Waiver, and Hold Harmless Agreement, with language that the Haunted Inn is likely to argue constitutes your consent to engage in interactions like the one you experienced with Scott Pearce.

   Specifically, Haunted Inn is likely to argue that, because you purchased and used the ticket, you *expressly* consented to be being separated from your party "at any time during the attraction, including in the areas immediately outside the entrances and exits," and that you consented to "physical contact by the actors."

The Haunted Inn may also argue that you gave your implied consent to engage in the interactions with Scott Pearce because you knew what to expect inside the event, and you had similar interactions throughout your visit. Specifically: 1) you acknowledged that you have attended similar events in the past and your decision to attend this one implied your consent to experience risks similar to what you experienced with Scott Pearce; 2) even though you thought the event was "crazy" and included scary settings, you stayed at the attraction, implying that you consented to interactions with actors, including scares involving characters with chainsaws.

However, you might rebut these claims by arguing that you did not give consent to interactions like the one with Mr. Pearce. For one, although you agreed to participate in a scare-based attraction, your consent was limited to conduct occurring within its boundaries or in "areas immediately outside the entrance and exit." Thus, when Scott Pearce chased you beyond the event's boundaries until you fell, he exceeded the scope of your consent. Moreover, you might also argue that you verbally withdrew any consent when you repeatedly told Mr. Pearce to stop. This effectively means that you did not consent to your interactions with the chainsaw-wielding Mr. Pearce.

Please give this some thought and we can discuss further when we meet next week.

Exercise 4

1. **Based on your assessment of Mr. George's claim, would you advise him to accept the Haunted Inn's offer? Why or why not?**

   As you advise the client, consider the following factors:

   - The client's likelihood of success at trial.

     A court is likely to find that Mr. George expressly and/or impliedly consented to scares in the event, including scares immediately outside the exit. Yet Mr. George's case is not without merit; Mr. George has a strong argument that Mr. Pearce exceeded the scope of consent by approaching him outside the event and chasing him even after Mr. George asked him to stop.

     It is unclear whether there is corroborating evidence to support either position. You may wish to speak with Mr. George's friends and/or other guests to confirm whether their impressions match Mr. George's experience.

   - Injuries/damages sustained by the client.
   - The costs of litigation, including some mental and emotional strain. This may include a consideration of each party's tolerance for those costs.
   - The fees already incurred by the client (presumably, you spent considerable time reviewing the case and preparing court filings) and the fact that the settlement offer does not include attorneys' fees.
   - Haunted Inn's interest in avoiding negative publicity.
   - Haunted Inn's resources (the likelihood that they can pay a judgment).
   - The fact that the settlement payment is immediate while a judgment from a court is uncertain and will take considerable time to acquire.
   - Whether Haunted Inn is open to further negotiations.
   - The severity of Mr. George's injuries and whether the proposed settlement adequately compensates him.

Chapter 2: False Imprisonment

Finnegan v. Western Airlines

Exercise 1

1. **List any intentional torts that may have been committed by Western's employees.**

   Among the intentional torts you might consider are:

   - **False imprisonment:** Western employees intended to cause Ms. Finnegan's confinement, she was confined by restraint and by assertion of legal authority, and she was aware of the confinement.
   - **Trespass to chattels/conversion:** Western employees intentionally interfered with and dispossessed Ms. Finnegan of her property.
   - **Battery:** Western employees intended to/knew with substantial certainty that their conduct would cause a harmful and offensive contact with Ms. Finnegan.
   - **Intentional infliction of emotional distress (IIED):** Western employees engaged in extreme and outrageous conduct and intentionally or recklessly caused Ms. Finnegan severe emotional distress.

Exercise 2

1. **What did the court in *Wagner v. Cook County Sheriff's Office* decide about whether an actor can avoid liability for an intentional tort if the actor subjectively believed the action was a "joke" or "prank"?**

   A defendant cannot avoid liability for an intentional tort by claiming their actions were intended as a joke. If the defendant engaged in an intentional act that resulted in harm to the plaintiff, then the defendant may be liable, even if the actor believed the conduct would be welcomed or humorous.

2. **How does the holding in *Wagner v. Cook County Sheriff's Office* and the holding from *Garratt v. Dailey* influence any advice you offer Mr. Finnegan about the findings from Western's internal investigation?**

   Even if Ms. Finnegan's coworkers believed they "acted in a spirit of good-natured camaraderie," Western cannot avoid liability if their actions satisfy the elements of false imprisonment. As stated in *Wagner*, "[o]ne who plays dangerous practical jokes on others takes the risk that his victims may not appreciate the humor of his conduct and may not take it in good part."

3. **Do you believe Mr. Finnegan has a viable claim for false imprisonment against Western for the conduct of its employees? Are all of the elements of a false imprisonment claim satisfied and, if so, by which facts? If not, which element(s) is lacking and why?**

   Below is a possible argument that Western is liable for false imprisonment. If you concluded that Western was not liable, then your answer should explain why an element(s) is not satisfied.

   Western is liable to Ms. Finnegan for false imprisonment based on the conduct of Ms. Finnegan's supervisor and the conduct of Western's security officers.

   A defendant may be liable for false imprisonment if the defendant intends to confine the plaintiff within a confined area, the defendant's conduct causes the plaintiff to be so confined, and the plaintiff is either conscious of the confinement or harmed by it.

Western employees acted with intent to confine Ms. Finnegan. A defendant acts with intent if: 1) the defendant acts with purpose to bring about a certain result; or 2) the defendant acts with knowledge that the result is substantially certain to occur.

Here, Western employees did not act with purpose to confine Ms. Finnegan because they planned the event as a fun-loving prank for a newly promoted employee, and they believed Ms. Finnegan would take it in the same spirit. Yet Western employees acted with knowledge that Ms. Finnegan's confinement was substantially certain to occur. In fact, for the prank to be successful, the employees wanted Ms. Finnegan to believe the officers had authority to detain her. For that reason, they kept her promotion a secret and refused to confirm her questions about whether the incident was a joke. The security officers convinced Ms. Finnegan that they planned to escort her outside to meet law enforcement, they confiscated her credentials and keys, and they forcibly handcuffed her. All employees persisted with the prank even when Ms. Finnegan was visibly distraught and evidently terrified about her confinement. Thus, Western employees knew with substantial certainty that Ms. Finnegan would feel confined.

Moreover, Ms. Finnegan was confined. Confinement can be physical or through threats of force or assertion of legal authority. Here, Ms. Finnegan was physically restrained when she was handcuffed. Ms. Finnegan was also confined through assertion of legal authority because she believed she was being arrested based on an outstanding warrant. Officers seized her badge and keys, and Finnegan believed they had authority to detain her. Ms. Finnegan repeatedly asked whether the situation was a joke, but all parties acted as if their actions were legally authorized. Thus, Ms. Finnegan was confined.

Ms. Finnegan was both aware of and harmed by the confinement. Ms. Finnegan experienced pain when security officers handcuffed her, and she experienced emotional distress during the incident. Ms. Finnegan was "humiliated and embarrassed," especially because the incident occurred in front of a large group of fellow employees and customers. Ms. Finnegan required medication to resolve her distress after the event and reported that she felt embarrassed, degraded, and humiliated. Therefore, Ms. Finnegan was both aware of and harmed by her confinement.

Therefore, Western is liable to Ms. Finnegan for false imprisonment.

Chapter 3: Intentional Infliction of Emotional Distress

Glover v. BIZ Networks, Inc.

Exercise 1

1. **Identify any intentional torts for which BIZ Networks might be liable to Janiece Glover based on the conduct of its reporters and camera crew.**

   Among the intentional torts you might consider are the following:

   - **IIED:** Biz Networks engaged in extreme and outrageous conduct and intentionally or recklessly caused Ms. Glover to experience severe emotional distress.
   - **Assault:** Biz Networks intentionally caused Ms. Glover to experience reasonable apprehension of an imminent harmful or offensive contact.

   *While Ms. Glover may have potential privacy claims, this question only asked about intentional torts.

Exercise 2

1. **Using the language and reasoning from *Zalnis*, identify the elements Ms. Glover will need to prove to establish a *prima facie* case of intentional infliction of emotional distress (IIED).**

   To establish a *prima facie* claim of IIED, Ms. Glover must establish that BIZ Networks:

   1. Engaged in extreme and outrageous conduct;
   2. Acted with intent or recklessness*; and
   3. Caused Ms. Glover to experience severe emotional distress.

   *Unlike other intentional torts, the requisite intent for IIED may be met through reckless conduct.

2. **Applying the facts from the Episode Transcript to each element identified above, discuss whether you believe Ms. Glover can establish a *prima facie* claim of IIED against BIZ Networks.**

   Your discussion might include the following considerations:

   1. Whether BIZ Networks engaged in extreme and outrageous conduct. This is likely the most difficult element to establish because Ms. Glover must show the conduct constituted more than "mere insults" or "indignities." Relevant facts include:

      The reporters peppered Ms. Glover with disturbing questions about her treatment and told her Dr. Hillard used treatments that were not FDA-approved and were known to cause serious adverse reactions. These questions are arguably intended to shock the conscience of Ms. Glover and BIZ Networks' listeners.

      BIZ Networks' camera crew was filming even though they knew Ms. Glover was unaware of the severe swelling to her face and neck. They continued filming as the reporter informed Ms. Glover of the swelling and directed her attention to the mirror. The crew continued to film Ms. Glover as she reacted to her reflection with obvious distress, and they filmed her as she fled from the clinic. This may reflect abuse of the network's position because Ms. Glover did not have a meaningful opportunity to consent.

BIZ Networks concluded the aired segment by referring to Ms. Glover's treatment as "another botched treatment by Dr. Hillard."

2. Whether BIZ Networks acted intentionally or recklessly to cause Ms. Glover severe emotional distress. Ms. Glover should not have difficulty establishing this element. Relevant facts include:

   The reporter stopped Ms. Glover as she exited the treatment room and immediately after she received multiple injections. The crew saw Ms. Glover was experiencing an adverse reaction but did not inform her until after they filmed her for several minutes.

   The reporter asked a series of questions while Ms. Glover continued to have a reaction. The reporter then pointed Ms. Glover to a mirror and filmed her as she reacted. The conduct was deliberately provocative and timed to maximize Ms. Glover's shock.

   The network never secured Ms. Glover's consent before airing the segment and referring to Ms. Glover's "botched" treatment.

3. Whether the conduct of BIZ Networks' reporters and camera crew did cause Ms. Glover severe emotional distress. There is insufficient evidence to establish this element, but relevant facts include:

   Ms. Glover was visibly shocked. She screamed, cried and fled, suggesting severe emotional trauma.

3. Is there any additional information that might help you assess whether Ms. Glover can establish the *prima facie* elements of an IIED claim?

As noted in the answer to the previous question, because the episode synopsis and transcript do not indicate whether Ms. Glover actually suffered any long-term emotional distress, it would be helpful to identify additional information about Ms. Glover's trauma. This might include treatment records, statements from friends and family, etc.

The following information might also inform your theories of the case:

- Did the network have policies about patient privacy and consent?
- Did the clinic allow filming or sign release forms?
- Had Ms. Glover consented to the treatment knowing it was not FDA-approved? Had she ever experienced similar reactions?
- Did the network or the crew discuss how they wanted to approach patients? Was their confrontation with Ms. Glover consistent with that plan?
- Is the full interview available? Can Ms. Glover show the piece was edited for dramatic effect?

Exercise 3

1. Does the Expert Report change your assessment of whether BIZ Networks may be liable for IIED based on the conduct of the BIZ Networks reporters and camera crew?

The Expert Report likely changes your assessment of BIZ Networks' liability because it offers additional facts to support the final element of Ms. Glover's IIED claim—that Ms. Glover did suffer severe emotional distress. In particular, note the following excerpts from the report:

- "Ms. Glover experienced extreme distress when reporters confronted her in the clinic. Ms. Glover expected the clinic to be a private and safe location, and reporters intruded on her privacy without warning."
- "When Ms. Glover did observe her swollen face, she was especially humiliated because she realized she was on camera and had been speaking to reporters in her 'grotesque state.'"
- "Despite her distress, Ms. Glover intended to 'leave well enough alone' until she began experiencing social ostracism."
- "Ms. Glover was humiliated when members of the book club began whispering about her appearance."
- "Ms. Glover asserts that she has since received fewer invitations to social events."
- "Ms. Glover's ongoing distress has affected her appetite and interest in social activities. Ms. Glover asserts that she is often 'unable to leave the house,' and she has stopped engaging in her usual activities."

The Expert Report might also provide additional support for the other elements of IIED. Consider the following excerpts:

- "Ms. Glover expected the clinic to be a private and safe location, and reporters intruded on her privacy without warning. Ms. Glover never gave permission to film her reactions, and she repeatedly asked reporters to leave her alone. Despite that, reporters continued to harass her, likely because they noticed her physical symptoms and wanted to capture the moment of her discovery."
- "During the gathering, the group watched a commercial about the upcoming episode of 'What's Really Happening.' The clip showed an image of Ms. Glover's swollen face with the caption, 'An Injection Too Far: The Price of Vanity.'"

2. **BIZ Networks has asked whether they should settle the claim to avoid any negative publicity. Which factors would you consider in evaluating whether BIZ Networks should try to settle the claim or proceed to trial?**

   You might consider the following factors as you advise the client:

   - The strength of Ms. Glover's case and her likelihood of success.
   - The costs of litigation and any associated negative publicity to BIZ Networks. If the perception is negative, BIZ might also see advertisers or partners withdraw their support.
   - Whether the public's sympathies lie with Ms. Glover or with BIZ Networks' interest in keeping the public informed via investigative reporting. There may also be First Amendment concerns related to freedom of the press.
   - Does BIZ Networks have any concerns about settling these types of claims? Is it worried that settling this claim will invite more IIED claims against it? In contrast, does it believe that winning at trial will affirm the network's right to engage in this kind of reporting?
   - Does BIZ Networks thrive off of "shock" content? Does it want to be known for investigative reporting no matter the consequences?

Chapter 4: Trespass to Land

Wesley v. BlackRidge Energy Production

Exercise 1

1. **Briefly analyze whether Ms. Wesley can establish the elements of trespass to land.**

   The following considerations are relevant to an analysis of whether Ms. Wesley may establish the elements of trespass to land.

   - BEP intentionally pumped proppants into the well near Ms. Wesley's property, and the proppants intruded on Ms. Wesley's property. Even if BEP did not intend to inject proppants onto Ms. Wesley's property, the uncertainty and unpredictability of fracking operations suggests that BEP knew with substantial certainty that fracking operations would cause an intrusion on nearby property.
   - BEP caused proppants to invade Ms. Wesley's property. The proppants caused subsurface fractures and allowed BEP to extract natural gas. The fractures are still open, and BEP continues to extract gas.

Exercise 2

1. **Discuss whether the BEP proppants constitute a continuing trespass to land.**

   The discussion should include the following considerations:

   - BEP began using the well in 2019, when it pumped proppants into the well and opened fractures under Ms. Wesley's property.
   - The proppants keep the subsurface fractures open.
   - BEP continues to extract natural gas from Ms. Wesley's property.
   - It is unclear when the natural gas will be depleted or whether BEP intends to close the well.

Exercise 3

1. **Draft an argument in support of injunctive relief:**

   a. **Identify the "irreparable" injury Ms. Wesley will experience if BEP is permitted to continue operations.**

   Relevant considerations include:

   - □ BEP is removing non-renewable natural gas from Ms. Wesley's property, and the resource cannot be replenished.
   - □ The ongoing operation threatens to damage Ms. Wesley's property.
   - □ By extracting the gas, BEP is depriving Ms. Wesley of any economic benefit from the resource under her property.

   b. **Identify the harm BEP might experience if the injunction is granted.**

   Relevant considerations include:

   - □ BEP expended resources drilling the well, and terminating operations could result in severe economic losses.

- □ Fracking is a complicated and resource-intensive process, and surface owners typically lack the resources to extract natural gas from under their property.

c. Evaluate whether Ms. Wesley's potential injury outweighs the harm to BEP.

Relevant considerations include:

- □ BEP did not secure permission or licenses to extract gas from property adjacent to the well.
- □ The ongoing operation threatens damage to Wesley's property and denies her any economic benefit from the drilling.
- □ These injuries likely outweigh potential harms to BEP.
- □ BEP likely extracted most of the gas from the well, minimizing the harm it will experience if it must halt operations.

d. Identify any public interest in BEP's operations.

Relevant considerations include:

- □ The public has an interest in encouraging energy development. BEP is accessing natural resources that individual owners cannot extract because they do not have the necessary equipment and infrastructure.
- □ The public also has an interest in protecting property rights and punishing trespass.

Chapter 5: Trespass to Chattels

Lupina v. Ross

Exercise 1

1. **Do you believe that, according to the facts set forth in the Memorandum, Mr. Lupina can successfully establish a *prima facie* case for trespass to chattel? (Are all elements satisfied and, if so, by which facts? If not, which element(s) is lacking?)**

   If you answer "yes," then it should be because you believe that, by snatching and running away with Mr. Lupina's coin collection without first paying the $8,200 purchase price in cash, Mr. Ross intentionally dispossessed Mr. Lupina of the coins, used the coins, or intermeddled with the coins. The facts in the Memorandum invite the conclusion that Mr. Ross both dispossessed Mr. Lupina of his coin collection by running away with it and intermeddled with the coin collection by snatching it from Mr. Lupina. There seems to be no question that Mr. Ross acted with intent to take and abscond with Mr. Lupina's property.

2. **Do you believe that, according to the facts set forth in the Memorandum, Mr. Lupina can successfully establish a *prima facie* case for conversion? Why or why not?**

   If you answer "yes," then it should be because you believe that, by snatching and running away with Mr. Lupina's coin collection without first paying the $8,200 purchase price in cash, Mr. Ross intentionally deprived Mr. Lupina of possession of his coin collection or interfered with the coins in a manner so seriously as to exercise dominion or control and deprive Mr. Lupina of the use of his coins. For the reasons outlined above, the facts in the Memorandum invite the conclusion that Mr. Ross did both.

   In order to distinguish whether Mr. Ross committed a trespass to chattel or conversion (or both), the following facts should be considered:

   - Approximately 2 hours (a relatively short period) passed from the time Mr. Ross snatched the coin collection from Mr. Lupina to the time that Mr. Lupina accepted payment from Mr. Ross through the banking app;
   - In Mr. Ross's "moment of uncharacteristic impetuousness," he snatched the coin collection from Mr. Lupina and ran away, which arguably establishes his intent to assert a right inconsistent with Mr. Lupina's right to his coin collection;
   - Mr. Ross ultimately paid the entire purchase price to Mr. Lupina, which helps establish Ross's good faith and intent to compensate Mr. Lupina;
   - Mr. Lupina did experience significant inconvenience when he chased Mr. Ross and fell to the ground. On the other hand, Mr. Lupina received the entire purchase price within a few hours of the incident and did not experience additional financial harm; and
   - The coin collection was not damaged by the events, and Mr. Lupina was ultimately paid the entire purchase price.

Exercise 2

1. **Do you believe Mr. Lupina can prove that his conduct was justified as a "defense of property?" Why or why not?**

   a. **Did Mr. Lupina reasonably believe that force was necessary to terminate Mr. Ross's intrusion?**

   Likely, yes. His $8,200 coin collection was snatched by Mr. Ross, who immediately ran away. He could reasonably believe that force was necessary to stop Mr. Ross.

   b. **Considering the value of the coin collection, were Mr. Lupina's actions reasonably proportionate? In other words, was Mr. Lupina's $8,200 coin collection worth tackling Mr. Ross?**

   This is a matter of degree and there is room for persuasive advocacy, depending on which party you represent. As Mr. Ross's advocate, you must acknowledge that the property was valuable—the coins were worth over $20,000, and Mr. Ross paid $8,200 to "acquire" it. In that light, Mr. Lupina may have been justified to act with considerable force to stop Mr. Ross from absconding with the collection.

   You may need more information to evaluate this factor. It may be helpful to understand the severity of Mr. Ross's injury, including the costs of treatment, the duration of discomfort, etc.

   c. **Did Mr. Lupina reasonably believe that asking Mr. Ross to stop would be useless or that Mr. Ross would cause substantial harm before Mr. Lupina could make a request?**

   Again, this leaves room for persuasive advocacy. On the one hand, there are no facts in the Memorandum to indicate Mr. Lupina said anything to Mr. Ross. On the other hand, such efforts would likely be futile given the fact that Mr. Ross immediately began running away after snatching the coin collection from Mr. Lupina.

Chapter 6: Defenses to Intentional Torts

Self-Defense: Finley v. Merchant

Exercise 1

1. **Based on the legal authority above, what does Mr. Merchant have to establish for his claim of self-defense?**

   Mr. Merchant must show:

   - He reasonably believed Mr. Finley was using or would imminently use unlawful physical force; and
   - He reasonably believed the extent of force was necessary to defend himself.

2. **What additional information would help you assess whether Mr. Merchant can establish that he acted in self-defense?**

   Possible considerations include:

   - What exactly did Mr. Finley do that made Mr. Merchant think he was going to "take a swing"? Did he raise his fists? Lunge? Move toward Mr. Merchant?
   - Which players observed the incident? Can they describe Mr. Finley's conduct immediately before Mr. Merchant hit him?
   - Did Mr. Merchant and Mr. Finley have any prior history?
   - Did Mr. Finley act aggressively toward other players during the game? Did any of them have prior history with Mr. Finley?
   - How hard did Mr. Merchant punch Mr. Finley?
   - Could Mr. Merchant have done something else to avoid the altercation (i.e., step back, push Mr. Finley away, etc.)?
   - What happened between the time Mr. Finley threw the ball and the time Mr. Merchant punched Mr. Finley? How long was that period?
   - Had Mr. Merchant been aggressive during the game?
   - Is there any video coverage of the incident?

Exercise 2

1. **Does the information in the investigation report change your assessment of whether Mr. Merchant acted in self-defense? Identify at least three facts that weaken Mr. Merchant's defense and three facts that strengthen Mr. Merchant's defense.**

   a. **Facts that strengthen Mr. Merchant's defense:**

      - □ Mr. Finley is a strong enough player to join his high school basketball team.
      - □ The pick-up games routinely include amateur and college players, and games are "pretty rough." Mr. Finley decided to participate anyway.
      - □ Mr. Finley joined the game knowing most players were from the college basketball team. Mr. Finley remained in the game even when it was aggressive, and he told his friends he wanted to show he could play against "real" players.

- □ A witness saw Mr. Finley hurl the ball at Mr. Merchant when Mr. Merchant was distracted, and "it seemed like he was aiming for Karl's head." The ball hit Mr. Merchant "pretty hard" in the face.
- □ Mr. Finley's friend confirmed Mr. Finley threw the ball at Mr. Merchant "harder than he should have."

b. Facts that weaken Merchant's defense:

- □ Mr. Merchant is 21 years old, and Mr. Finley is 16 years old.
- □ Mr. Merchant is 6'3" and weighs 205 lbs., while Mr. Finley is 5'10" and weighs 160 lbs.
- □ Mr. Merchant received a scholarship to play college basketball and has played for two seasons. Mr. Merchant also played for his high-school varsity team. In contrast, Mr. Finley recently joined the high school JV team, but he has not played.
- □ Mr. Merchant and his friends knew they were playing with less experienced high-school players.
- □ Mr. Merchant and his friends ignored Mr. Finley's complaints about the aggressiveness of the game.
- □ Mr. Finley's friend alleges that Mr. Finley did not intend to hit Mr. Merchant in the face, and the ball only hit Mr. Merchant because he was distracted.

Exercise 3

1. How are the facts of Merchant's case similar to *Balboa v. Schilling*? How are they dissimilar?

Some of the similarities between the cases include:

- □ **Cause of injury:** In both cases, the defendant punched the plaintiff and caused injury. In *Balboa*, the defendant hit the plaintiff with enough force to cause him to lose consciousness. Mr. Merchant hit Mr. Finley with enough force to break his nose.
- □ **Training/Experience:** In both cases, the defendant had more athletic training than the plaintiff.
- □ **Provocation:** In both cases, the plaintiff seemed to initiate the fight by feinting a punch toward the defendant (*Balboa*) or by throwing a basketball at/confronting the defendant (Mr. Merchant).
- □ **Preceding Circumstances:** Both defendants believed the plaintiff was about to attack them based on the incidents occurring before the assault. The plaintiff in *Balboa* was intoxicated and verbally confronted the defendant. Similarly, Mr. Finley became increasingly aggressive during the game and seemed to provoke a confrontation by throwing the basketball directly at Merchant.

Some of the differences between the cases include:

- □ **Professional background:** In *Balboa*, the defendant was a trained fighter and had training that enabled him to anticipate an attack. In contrast, Mr. Finley is a high school basketball player with significant experience in competitive play.
- □ **Environment:** The incident in *Balboa* occurred in a restaurant, where fights are atypical and unexpected. The incident in Mr. Merchant's case occurred at a basketball game, where physicality is expected.

- **Initiation:** In *Balboa*, the plaintiff feinted a punch. The plaintiff was intoxicated, lending to the defendant's reasonable belief that he was aggressive and threatening. In Mr. Merchant's case, the plaintiff threw a ball that hit the defendant (potentially accidentally and as part of the game), and it is unclear whether Mr. Finley lunged at or started to punch Mr. Merchant.
- **Physical dominance:** In *Balboa*, both the defendant and plaintiff were adults. In Mr. Merchant's case, the defendant was considerably larger and older than the plaintiff.

2. **Based on the article, interview and legal authority, prepare a brief legal argument analyzing whether Mr. Merchant is protected from liability for battery because he acted in self-defense.**

The answer below is intended to be a *sample answer* and suggests one way to analyze the facts and legal issues in the case:

In Sunport, a person may use physical force in self-defense when and to the extent he reasonably believes such to be necessary to defend himself against what he reasonably believes to be the use or imminent use of unlawful physical force.

In *Balboa v. Schilling*, a court held that a professional fighter was privileged to use force against another restaurant patron when the patron appeared to initiate an assault. The defendant, a former professional fighter, was returning from a smoke break outside the restaurant when the plaintiff called out to the defendant and made a feinting gesture as if to hit him. The defendant, who had received training about how to anticipate an attack, punched the plaintiff twice and rendered him unconscious. The court acknowledged that, while physical differences between parties can influence whether a threat is reasonable, the plaintiff's feint, defendant's training, and the context of the incident supported the defendant's belief that a threat of serious harm was imminent. The court concluded the defendant's response was proportionate and limited to neutralizing the threat.

In contrast, Mr. Merchant was not justified in believing he was in imminent danger. While Mr. Finley threw a basketball at Mr. Merchant, it is unclear whether Mr. Finley intentionally or accidentally hit him in the face, and such contact is typical during a physical game of basketball. Mr. Merchant alleges that he thought Mr. Finley was about to attack him but, unlike the plaintiff in *Balboa*, Mr. Finley did not take any overt actions indicative of an imminent attack. Instead, Mr. Merchant's reaction seems retaliatory because he struck Mr. Finley almost immediately after Mr. Finley threw the errant ball. Also, unlike the parties in *Balboa*, Mr. Merchant is significantly larger and more athletic than Mr. Finley, who is a teenager with little basketball experience. The disparity further undermines Mr. Merchant's belief that Mr. Finley presented a physical threat. Therefore, a court is unlikely to find that Mr. Merchant reasonably believed Mr. Finley was using or would imminently use unlawful physical force.

Moreover, Mr. Merchant's force was excessive under the circumstances. Mr. Merchant punched Mr. Finley, a 16-year-old, hard enough to break his nose. Although Mr. Finley's conduct was aggressive, it was not inconsistent with typical contact in a basketball game and did not warrant a response so far beyond the bounds of the game.

Therefore, Mr. Merchant is unlikely to prevail on a claim of self-defense.

Chapter 6: Defenses to Intentional Torts

Consent: *In re Rhys Clarkson*

Exercise 1

1. **Advise Ms. Clarkson about whether she can establish the *prima facie* elements of battery because Ms. Mandel shoved and kicked Ms. Clarkson during the basketball game.**

   Your advice to Ms. Clarkson should consider whether the facts establish that:

   Ms. Mandel acted with the intent to cause a harmful or offensive contact to Ms. Clarkson.

   - The facts establish Ms. Mandel had the requisite intent—she mistakenly thought Ms. Clarkson was going to hit the other Southland player (rather than help her up from the floor), and she therefore shoved Ms. Clarkson, knocking her to the floor, and kicking her.
   - Ms. Mandel clearly intended to contact Ms. Clarkson by shoving and kicking her, and she also intended that such contact be harmful or offensive because she wanted to stop what she saw as an imminent attack on a teammate.

   Ms. Mandel caused a harmful or offensive contact to occur.

   - Ms. Mandel shoved and kicked Ms. Clarkson. Such contact is harmful and likely to cause physical injury, which it did in this case. The contact is also offensive to a reasonable person.

Exercise 2

1. **Prepare an argument in support of the following assertion: Like the conduct at issue in *Hackbart*, Ms. Mandel's actions violated the rules of the game or the "general customs" of competitive basketball.**

   In *Hackbart*, an NFL Bengals player struck a kneeling Bronco player's head and neck with enough force to knock both players to the ground. The court noted, "it is highly questionable whether a professional football player consents or submits to injuries caused by conduct not within the rules. . . ." Applying that reasoning here, it is unlikely that any court will agree that Ms. Clarkson consented to Ms. Mandel's shoving her to the ground and kicking her, neither of which is conduct within the rules. The fact that Ms. Mandel was ejected from the game supports the notion that her conduct was not customary or within the rules of play.

2. **Prepare an argument in support of the following assertion: Like the defendant in *Koffman*, Ms. Mandel exceeded the scope of Ms. Clarkson's consent to contact.**

   In *Koffman*, an assistant football coach, who weighed 260 pounds, slammed a middle school player, who weighed only 144 pounds, to the ground during practice. The player's parents alleged that, while their son consented to physical contact with players of similar age and experience, he did not consent to aggressive contact by adult coaches. The court held that, while football is "inherently dangerous and always potentially violent," reasonable persons could disagree on whether the players gave consent to the kind of contact that caused the plaintiff's injuries.

   Similarly, Ms. Clarkson might argue that Ms. Mandel's conduct exceeded the scope of implied consent. While competitive basketball players impliedly agree to some contact within an inherently physical game, the incident exceeded customary bounds of contact and involved excessive force outside of active play. In both *Koffman* and Ms. Clarkson's case, the defendants did not act in a competitive spirit but with retaliatory intent; the coach in *Koffman* was chiding players after a loss, and Ms. Mandel shoved and kicked Ms. Clarkson in response to what she saw as aggression towards a teammate.

Moreover, Ms. Mandel's attack was especially egregious because basketball does not involve the same level of physicality or aggression as tackle football. While players may have some contact during play, intentional violence is not an ordinary risk of the game. Ms. Mandel, who is significantly larger than Ms. Clarkson, shoved and kicked Ms. Clarkson long after the play ended and after Ms. Clarkson had fallen to the ground.

3. How might Ms. Mandel respond to the arguments above?

Both *Hackbart* and *Koffman* and distinguishable from this case given the relationship between the parties and the nature of the underlying conduct. The defendant in *Koffman* coached a team of middle school players, and the young players did not consent to being tackled by adult coaches. In contrast, while Ms. Clarkson is smaller than the average player at 5'6" and 130 pounds, she should expect to play with larger players at her level of competitiveness, including a player who is 6'7" and 210 pounds. Ms. Clarkson should expect contact and some aggression among other players.

In addition, the coach in *Koffman* assaulted a player during practice, not as part of an active game. In contrast, Ms. Mandel acted during the heat of an emotional, competitive game. Ms. Mandel was not acting with retaliatory or malicious intent; Ms. Mandel acted reflexively and defensively, believing she was preventing an assault on another teammate. Ms. Mandel's conduct was not outside the ordinary customs of the game.

Courts have consistently held that competitive athletes impliedly consent to ordinary and foreseeable contact, force, and even aggression that would be unlawful in other settings. Simililar to football, basketball is played an "an emotional and noisy environment," and players routinely engage in forceful contact while rebounding, screening, and defending. As the court noted in *Hackbart*, the available sanctions are penalties and expulsion, both of which occurred during the game between Ms. Mandel and Ms. Clarkson.

Courts should only impose civil liability for egregious acts that far exceed the customs and norms of the sport. The law should not penalize athletes for reacting to perceived threats during fast-paced and competitive games. Allowing claims like Ms. Clarkson's to proceed could chill participation in the sport.

Exercise 3

1. How would you advise Ms. Clarkson based on those concerns? Identify the factors you might consider.

Some of the possible considerations include:

- **Likelihood of success.** For the reasons analyzed in the previous exercise, you likely have a strong claim for battery. There are several witnesses who can support your allegations that the attack was unjustified. There is also clear precedent supporting your position about the attack. Yet there is a risk that a jury might find the incident was within the scope of risk assumed by competitive athletes.
- **Reputational risk**. A public lawsuit can attract media attention, and some recruiters might find the suit to be a distraction. You could mitigate the concerns with careful PR.
    - There is also a possibility that a suit could be viewed as a willingness to insist upon player safety and fairness in the sport.

- Consider speaking privately with an agent or recruiter to understand the reputational risks.

- **Costs of litigation**. Litigation can be very costly, both financially and emotionally. Litigation can also be time-consuming, which is an important consideration as you begin a rookie year.
- **Counterclaims.** There is always a risk that the defendant could raise claims against you in response to the suit, including defamation claims.

There are alternatives to litigation. Speak with the client about potentially contacting the other player to negotiate about a private settlement. The matter could also be referred internally to the league or tournament officials. The client could also consider whether she wishes to file suit after the draft to avoid her concerns about reputational harm. In that case, she should understand the risks of evidence becoming stale with the passage of time.

Exercise 4

1. **Can Ms. Clarkson establish a *prima facie* case of battery against Dr. Newton?**

   Undoubtedly yes.

   Dr. Newton intentionally cut Ms. Clarkson's leg. The contact was invasive and physically harmful because it involved a laceration. The contact was also objectively offensive because Ms. Clarkson did not give consent. Ms. Clarkson subjectively experienced harm and offense because she complained of discomfort after the treatment, indicated she would not seek further treatment from Dr. Newton, and had to seek further treatment to avoid an infection.

Exercise 5

1. **Briefly summarize the rules articulated in the case above. Specifically, summarize what the court held about the nature of consent in a medical context.**

   There are multiple ways to summarize the dense and complicated language from the case. The primary rules are:

   - As a general rule, a patient must be consulted and consent to medical treatment. While physicians have wide discretion in selecting the best treatments for patients, they do not have "free license" to act without informed consent from the patient.
   - If a patient is unconscious and requires prompt medical attention, then a physician may provide reasonably necessary treatment, and the patient's consent is implied.
   - If a patient does not consent to treatment and no emergency justifies acting without it, then the physician's performance of the procedure is wrongful and constitutes a "technical assault and battery." The physician's conduct is tortious even if the physician acted reasonably (without negligence) and with good intent.
   - While a physician's good faith does not absolve the physician of liability for unauthorized contact, it may be considered when assessing the plaintiff's damages. In addition, if the treatment was beneficial, then the benefit may be considered when assessing "the character and extent of the injury inflicted upon" the plaintiff.

2. **If Ms. Clarkson asserts a claim of battery against Dr. Newton, is Dr. Newton likely to succeed in asserting the defense of consent? Why or why not?**

   Definitely not. Here are some of the relevant considerations:

- **Express consent:** Not only did Ms. Clarkson not consent to the treatment, but Dr. Newton did not even *attempt* to secure consent; Dr. Newton simply lanced the abscess. Ms. Clarkson did not understand what Dr. Newton was doing and was not informed about the nature of the treatment.
- **Implied consent:** Patients who seek medical attention impliedly consent to reasonable, noninvasive physical contact. In this case, Ms. Clarkson sought treatment for her wrist, and she may have impliedly consented to treatment related to that injury. Yet Ms. Clarkson did not ask Dr. Newton to treat the abscess, and Dr. Newton did not have "free license" to provide treatment for that medical condition.
- **Emergency doctrine:** Under the emergency doctrine, a physician may act if the patient is unable to consent and treatment is necessary to prevent serious harm or death. The doctrine is clearly not implicated here. Ms. Clarkson was conscious and communicative during the exam, and the abscess did not present a serious risk of harm or death.
- **Good faith:** Dr. Newton seemed to act in good faith, and her treatment likely benefited Ms. Clarkson. Nevertheless, Dr. Newton acted without Ms. Clarkson's consent, and her conduct was "wrongful." Ms. Clarkson likely has a viable claim for battery.
- **Damages:** Dr. Newton raises a legitimate argument about damages. Based on the facts, Ms. Clarkson sustained nominal damages, and the procedure possibly had a beneficial effect. Therefore, Ms. Clarkson's recovery may be limited.

PART II—NEGLIGENCE

Chapter 7: Duty of Care

Attractive Nuisance Doctrine: *In re Drop or Do Laundromat*

Exercise 1

1. **Assess whether the customer can establish each element of the attractive nuisance doctrine.**

   You might consider the following when assessing whether the customer can establish each element of the attractive nuisance doctrine.

   1. An artificial condition existed on the defendant's property where the defendant knows or has reason to know that children are likely to trespass;

      A Drop or Do employee intentionally left the cart outside the laundromat. The employee left the keys with the cart. All employees knew children frequented the laundromat. In fact, Drop or Do markets itself as a family-friendly business and specifically installed a children's area to make it easier for parents to bring their children while using the machines. It is foreseeable that children may wander around the property, including the area near the employee's entrance, while they are waiting for their parents.

      The characteristics of the cart and its similarity to a go-kart or other recreational cart make it attractive to children. The attractiveness is enhanced by the fact that the keys were either in the ignition or within easy reach, making it easy to operate the cart.

   2. The condition is one of which the defendant knows or has reason to know will involve an unreasonable risk of death or serious injury to such children;

      The cart is a powerful, motorized vehicle large enough to hold an adult driver, so misuse of the vehicle presents a significant risk of injury, especially to children.

   3. The children, because of their youth, do not discover the condition or realize the risk involved;

      Kobe, who drove the cart, was only 8 years old and was unlikely to appreciate the risk of driving the cart. Sam, who was injured, was only 11 years old. In fact, it appears that both boys viewed the activity as a game; Sam dared Kobe to drive the cart and clearly failed to appreciate the inherent risks of driving the motorized cart.

   4. It was reasonably practicable for the owner to either prevent access or render the condition safe without obstructing the purpose of the condition.

      The Drop or Do employee could have easily removed the keys from the cart to prevent unauthorized use. Drop or Do could also adopt policies to ensure that the cart is never left unattended unless it is in a designated area that is not accessible to customers.

   5. The defendant failed to exercise reasonable care to eliminate the danger or otherwise to protect the children.

      See above.

2. **Prepare a list of questions for your next meeting with Mr. Martinelli. What additional information would you like to know to assess whether Drop or Do might be liable for Sam's injuries under the attractive nuisance doctrine?**

   The following information would be helpful in evaluating whether Drop or Do is liable for negligence under the attractive nuisance doctrine. This is not an exhaustive list, so you may have identified other helpful information.

   - What was the nature of the maintenance cart?
     - Did it look like a small vehicle or golf cart?
     - Was it easy to operate?
     - What speeds could it travel?
     - Were there any safety features to prevent unauthorized use?
     - How heavy was it?
     - How many people can fit in the cart?
   - Was it foreseeable that children would find the cart?
     - How often are children outside the laundromat? Is there a play area or other attractive features for children outside?
     - Was the cart in plain view in an area where customers frequently travel?
     - Is it common practice to leave maintenance carts in public areas?
     - Have there been any related incidents?
   - Were the keys easy to access?
     - Where were the keys—in the ignition or in a cubby?
     - If the keys were in a cubby, were they visible? Were they in a closed compartment?
     - Was the cart locked?
     - Were there any policies about where to store the keys?
     - How long had the cart been unattended?

Exercise 2

1. **How are the facts of *Morningstar v. Maynard* similar to the facts of your current case? How are they different?**

   Below are some of the differences and similarities you might have recognized between the two cases:

   Similarities:

   - In both cases, a child was injured while playing on a dangerous instrumentality. In *Morningstar*, the child was injured on a trampoline, which is inherently dangerous, especially with multiple users. In Drop or Do, the child was injured while driving a motorized cart, which also carries inherent risks.
   - Both a trampoline and a cart are recreational, and a child could consider either equivalent to a toy.
   - In both cases, the landowner was not present when the child was injured, but a caregiver was nearby.

Differences:

- In *Morningstar*, the guardian expressly gave the children permission to use the trampoline and watched as they played outside. In Drop or Do, the guardian was inside, it is unclear whether she knew the children were outside, and she was not observing or supervising them. The guardian did not give the children permission to use the cart.
- In *Morningstar*, the trampoline was on private property, and it is unclear whether neighborhood children typically used it. In Drop or Do, the cart was outside a business in public view, and the keys were easily accessible. Moreover, children frequently visit Drop or Do with their parents. In fact, Drop or Do built family areas to make it easier for parents to bring their children to the laundromat.
- While trampolines are associated with injury, injuries are relatively infrequent. Moreover, it is typical for multiple individuals to use the trampoline. In contrast, the risks of a child driving a motorized cart are more foreseeable and arguably more severe.

2. How does the court's reasoning in *Morningstar v. Maynard* influence your assessment of whether Drop or Do might be liable for Sam's injuries under the attractive nuisance doctrine?

Reasonable minds may interpret this question differently. On the one hand, *Morningstar* does set a precedent that may shift culpability to the supervising adult. Because Kobe and Sam were at the laundromat with their mother, one might argue that she was responsible for monitoring their safety. Arguably, like the step-grandmother in *Morningstar*, the boys' mother assumed the responsibility of understanding the dangers involved when she allowed her children to roam the laundromat and potentially encounter hazards.

Yet unlike the supervising adult in *Morningstar*, it is unclear whether the boys' mother was aware of the boys' activity. The court in *Morningstar* reasoned that the adult's understanding of the risks superseded the child's inability to appreciate them. In that case, the supervising adult knew the children were using the trampoline and gave them permission to do so. In contrast, no adult gave Sam and Kobe express permission to use the cart, so no adult assessed the risks of the activity.

In addition, the risks associated with jumping on a trampoline, which is primarily done by children, are different from those associated with driving a maintenance cart, which is primarily done by adults. This influences whether Drop or Do acted negligently by leaving a cart in an area where children might find and operate it, especially because using the cart requires mature skills and reasoning.

3. The parties disagree about whether the keys for the maintenance cart were in the ignition of the cart or in a cubby hole near the ignition. Is your assessment of the claim impacted by where the keys were stored?

Again, this question is subject to interpretation. On the one hand, if the keys were in the ignition, then a child could potentially operate the cart without additional action. If the keys were in a cubby (especially a closed cubby), then a child could only operate the cart after a search, and then the child would still need to understand how to use the key. Put simply, the cart might have been more attractive to children if there were shiny keys dangling from the ignition.

In reality, it probably does not matter. Children are likely drawn to the cart regardless of whether the keys are visible, and if a child is likely to discover the keys while exploring the cart, then there is still a significant risk that they might start and drive the cart.

4. What is the significance of the fact that Drop or Do has an area for kids inside the laundromat?

The presence of the children's area makes it foreseeable that parents will bring children to the establishment and potentially leave them unsupervised while they do laundry. In fact, Drop or Do is essentially inviting parents to do exactly that. It is thus foreseeable that children might wander inside and outside the laundromat while their parents are occupied and distracted.

Consequently, Drop or Do has a heightened duty to anticipate potential hazards and take steps to prevent injury to children who may be unsupervised during their visit.

5. **Does your assessment change if Drop or Do posted signs throughout the laundromat warning parents to watch their children? What if the signs warn parents to keep their children inside at all times?**

   This is influential but not dispositive. It does demonstrate that Drop or Do took some precautions to protect children, but a business cannot avoid its duty of care by simply posting a warning sign, especially if the business breached a duty of care and created a risk of injury to guests. Adults using the facility likely assume that, because Drop or Do invites children to the facility, the business has considered and addressed risks to wandering children.

   In this case, the business created the hazard by leaving a motorized vehicle outside its business, where it was easily accessible to children. A jury is unlikely to find that a posted warning relieves the business of liability for creating an attractive nuisance.

6. **Does your assessment change if children routinely play outside Drop or Do? If Drop or Do installed a play structure immediately outside the laundromat?**

   These facts are extremely influential. If children routinely play outside, then it is foreseeable that children will encounter any objects left outside by the business, including a motorized cart. It also increases the chances that children are unsupervised while their parents are doing laundry inside. This enhances Drop or Do's duty of care to make the outside areas safe for children, and it also undermines the argument that parents are primarily responsible for protecting their children from risks.

   If Drop or Do installed a play structure outside, then Drop or Do invited children to play outside while their parents did laundry inside. Drop or Do then assumed a duty to protect those children from hazards both inside and outside the laundromat, which it likely breached when it left a motorized cart unattended in the area.

7. **Does your assessment change if the maintenance cart had visible notices that the cart was "For Employees Only"? What if the sign included warnings that the cart was dangerous?**

   This is another argument that leaves some room for creativity. Drop or Do may argue that they satisfied their duty to protect customers by offering these warnings.

   Yet a written warning is unlikely to deter a child. The attractive nuisance doctrine recognizes that children are sometimes impulsive or curious, and the warning does not make the attraction less enticing to a child (in fact, the opposite may be true). Moreover, there is also the question of whether a particular child can even read.

Exercise 3

1. **How might Ms. Malone argue that Drop or Do breached a duty of care to her and her sons?**

   This argument likely overlaps with the arguments about the applicability of the attractive nuisance doctrine and may include the following considerations:

   1. Mr. Martinelli owns Drop or Do and controls the premises.

2. Ms. Malone and her children are invitees because they were on the property to do laundry, which is a purpose connected to Mr. Martinelli's business.
3. An unattended motorized vehicle is a dangerous condition. Whether the keys were left in the ignition or a cubby, the cart was apparently accessible to Drop or Do customers and use by untrained individuals presents a risk of injury to others.
4. An employee knowingly left the cart unattended outside the laundromat and knowingly left the keys inside.
5. Drop or Do failed to use ordinary care to maintain the premises in a safe condition. Drop or Do caters to families and knows children are often unattended while their parents are busy inside the laundromat. Despite this, Drop or Do left a motorized cart unattended outside. Drop or Do failed to take reasonable precautions to secure the cart, including by removing the keys, disabling the cart, storing the cart in an area that is inaccessible to customers, posting signs, etc.

2. How would you respond to Ms. Malone's arguments?

Drop or Do will likely concede several of the elements:

- Mr. Martinelli/Drop or Do owned, occupied, and controlled the premises;
- The unsupervised cart that was accessible to customers presented a risk to customers; and
- Drop or Do knew about the dangerous condition.

Depending on additional information revealed during investigation or discovery, some of Drop or Do's arguments against liability might include:

- Drop or Do took reasonable precautions to protect customers because the keys were hidden in a cubby.
- Drop or Do routinely leaves the cart unattended, and this is the first safety incident. The risks of driving the cart are open and obvious and Drop or Do did not have a duty to prevent customers from engaging in an obviously dangerous activity.
- It is not foreseeable that children will start and operate a motorized cart. A reasonable child would know that the cart was not a toy and would avoid it. It was also not foreseeable that children would wander into an area designated for employees, and the children exceeded the scope of their invitation by entering areas not open to the public.
- Ms. Malone failed to adequately supervise her children and should not have let them wander outside. A reasonably attentive adult would caution children against operating a motorized cart. Drop or Do did not assume a duty to babysit or monitor children.

Exercise 4

1. What standard of care applies to determine whether Sam acted negligently under the circumstances?

This is a tricky question. If Sam is negligent, then it is either because he encouraged his brother to engage in unreasonably dangerous conduct or because he did not exercise care in protecting himself once his brother began driving the cart.

At first glance, it might seem that Sam is subject to a heightened duty of care because the activity that caused his injury was driving a motorized vehicle, which is an adult activity. Yet Sam did not *engage* in the adult activity because he did not drive the cart. Sam merely *encouraged* his brother to drive the cart and stood by while his brother began operating it.

Therefore, Sam's conduct will be judged against that of an 11-year-old child of similar intelligence and experience.

2. **If Sam is held to the standard of care of a child of the same age, intelligence, and experience under similar circumstances, did he breach that duty of care?**

   You could probably reach a conclusion either way based on how you interpret the following factors:

   - Would a reasonable 11-year-old understand that it is dangerous for an 8-year-old child to drive a motorized cart? Would a child have enough experience with this kind of cart to properly assess that risk to others?
   - Would a child know to get out of the way to avoid harm?
   - Would a reasonable 11-year-old understand that childish taunts would actually encourage an 8-year-old to operate the cart?

Exercise 5

1. **Prepare a memorandum for Mr. Martinelli. Summarize your legal conclusions and assessments about his potential liability. Make a recommendation based on your findings and the client's goals.**

   The answer below presents one way to analyze the issues in the case. Your answer may differ in format and in the way you interpret the facts.

Memorandum

To: Danny Martinelli

From: Legal Counsel

Re: *Malone Injury*

You asked this firm to analyze whether Drop or Do may be liable for injuries sustained by Sam Malone, who was injured when his brother gained access to and drove a Drop or Do maintenance cart.

Likely yes. Drop or Do left the cart in an area where customers, including children, could access and operate the cart. While Sam Malone's own negligence may limit Drop or Do's exposure, the firm recommends that Drop or Do negotiate a settlement and compensate Sam Malone for his injuries to avoid the negative publicity associated with a public dispute.

ATTRACTIVE NUISANCE

Under the "attractive nuisance" doctrine, a landowner may be liable to a child who is injured on the landowner's property if: a condition existed on the defendant's property that was dangerous and likely to cause injury; the condition was attractive or enticing to young children; the owner knew or should have known of the condition and its attraction for young children; the plaintiff was a young child who was incapable of comprehending the danger involved; the condition was left unattended at a place where young children might be enticed to enter because of youthful curiosity; and it was reasonably practicable for the owner to either prevent access or render the condition safe without obstructing the purpose of the condition.

Here, a Drop or Do employee left a maintenance cart in an area that was accessible to customers. Because the cart is a motorized cart that is relatively large, its misuse presents a risk of injury to the driver and others. The cart is also enticing to young children because it looks like a recreational cart that appears easy to operate, and the keys were potentially visible to any child who approached the cart. Drop or Do knew about the condition because an employee knowingly left the cart, with the keys accessible, in an area where customers might find it. Moreover, Drop or Do caters to families with young children and should have known children might discover the cart. Kobe, who drove the cart, was only 8 years old and was unlikely to appreciate the risk of driving it. Sam, who was injured, was only 11 years old and apparently failed to appreciate the risk of goading his younger brother to drive the cart. The Drop or Do employee could have easily removed the keys from the cart to prevent unauthorized use. Drop or Do could also have implemented policies to ensure the cart was never left unattended unless it was in a designated area that was not accessible to customers.

Drop or Do's position is that it is not liable for the boy's injuries because the boy's mother, Ms. Malone, was responsible for supervising her children and should have prevented them from using the cart. There is some precedent for this position. For example, in *Morningstar v. Maynard*, a 7-year-old boy received permission from his step-grandmother to use a neighbor's trampoline when the neighbors were not home to supervise the activity. The 7-year-old began jumping with three other children, and he was catapulted from the trampoline and fell on the ground. The plaintiff sued the trampoline owners under the doctrine of attractive nuisance, arguing that the owners should have known that children were drawn to the trampoline and were likely to disregard warnings that only one child should use the trampoline at a time. The court found the doctrine of attractive nuisance was inapplicable because the boy was being actively supervised by his step-grandmother, and she assumed the responsibility of understanding the dangers associated with using a trampoline.

Yet the case above is unlikely to alter Drop or Do's liability because Drop or Do invited children to the property and essentially invited parents to leave them unsupervised while parents completed their laundry. The nature of the business and its reputation as a family-friendly business meant Drop or Do knew parents would not actively supervise their children because they relied on Drop or Do to maintain facilities that were safe for children. In fact, Ms. Malone was not supervising her children when they discovered the cart, and she did not give them permission to use it, unlike the step-grandmother in *Morningstar*.

Therefore, a jury might find that Drop or Do is liable for Sam's injuries under the doctrine of attractive nuisance.

DUTY TO INVITEES

Even if a court finds the doctrine of attractive nuisance does not apply, it might nevertheless find that Drop or Do is liable to Sam because Drop or Do failed to satisfy its duty to protect customers.

If a person is on an owner's property for purposes related to the owner's business, then the owner has a heightened duty to inspect the property, discover unreasonably dangerous conditions, and protect customers from them. In this case, because Drop or Do controlled the premises and the Malones were invited guests at the time of the incident, Drop or Do owed them a heightened duty to protect them from unreasonable dangers. Drop or Do failed to satisfy that duty because it left the cart, a motorized vehicle capable of causing harm, in an area that was accessible to guests, including children.

Drop or Do may argue that it did not have a duty to protect patrons in this context because the dangers of using the cart were open and obvious, and a business owner does not have a duty to protect patrons from dangers that a reasonable person would perceive and avoid. Here, using a motorized cart is inherently hazardous, and a reasonable guest would not attempt to operate the cart. Even a child should understand that the cart is clearly used for business purposes and is not available for guest recreation. In fact, a reasonable guest would understand that such use is potentially unlawful. The cart was not in a designated play area, and nothing about its placement suggested it was intended for public use.

Drop or Do may also argue that the children were not invitees because they exceeded the scope of their invitation when they entered an area outside the laundromat. Yet a jury could find that the children were nevertheless invitees because customers and their children routinely wander inside and outside the laundromat while they wait for their laundry to finish. If Drop or Do had notice that customers used the areas around the laundromat, then Drop or Do owes those customers a heightened duty of care.

COMPARATIVE NEGLIGENCE

Sam's recovery may be reduced in proportion to his comparative fault in causing his own injuries. In negligence actions, the court may allocate fault among all parties who contributed to the injured party's harm, including the injured party himself, and the plaintiff's recovery may be reduced in proportion to his or her degree of fault.

To assess whether Sam contributed to his injuries, the court must assess whether Sam acted unreasonably under the circumstances. The conduct of children is not compared to other adults, but to a child of similar age, intelligence, and experience. Thus, the court will expect Sam to exercise the degree of caution that a reasonable 11-year-old of similar intelligence and experience would exercise.

This is a close call. A jury may find that Sam should have appreciated the danger involved in goading his brother to drive the cart, especially because his brother was only 8 years old. Yet a jury might also find that an impulsive 11-year-old might not appreciate the risks involved, especially not the risk that he himself might be injured while standing in the way of the cart.

Even if the jury finds that Sam acted negligently, Drop or Do will still be liable for its contribution to the accident, and the judgment will only be reduced in proportion to Sam's degree of fault.

RECOMMENDATION

The risks of litigation are high for Drop or Do. Drop or Do has gone to great lengths to make the laundromat a family-friendly business, and the negative publicity associated with a public trial could damage that reputation and undermine Drop or Do's goodwill in the community.

Moreover, the costs of litigation are high, especially considering the strength of the customer's claim. It is this firm's recommendation that Drop or Do initiate negotiations for a settlement. Drop or Do might offer to pay Sam's medical expenses and offer Ms. Malone reduced or free services in the laundromat. If appropriate, then Drop or Do might also offer Sam some compensation for his pain and suffering.

Please advise if you would like further analysis regarding the case.

Chapter 7: Duty of Care

Common Carriers and Innkeepers: *Redfearn v. Starr Resorts*

Exercise 1

1. **What are the primary differences between the Plaintiff's account of the incident as set forth in the Complaint, and the employees' account of the incident as set forth in the Incident Report?**

   You might have observed some of the following differences:

   - In the complaint, Ms. Redfearn portrays her conduct as that of a reasonable guest who calmly rode the toboggan ride. In contrast, the Incident Report portrays Ms. Redfearn as intoxicated, belligerent, and non-compliant.
   - The complaint suggests Ms. Redfearn was unaware of the dangers of the toboggan ride. Yet the Incident Report suggests the ride operator warned Ms. Redfearn of the risks and specifically instructed her not to bounce on the ride.
   - Ms. Redfearn alleges the crash was sudden and occurred after the toboggan hit an unexpected bump. The allegation implies that the ride was not well maintained. In contrast, Mr. Dennis alleged that Ms. Redfearn caused the crash because she was bouncing, and he implied that the toboggan crashed because Ms. Redfearn failed to exercise caution around a turn.
   - The complaint asserts Janice Williams brought only "basic first aid supplies," and was inadequately prepared to respond to the emergency. In contrast, the Incident Report suggests Nurse Williams acted promptly and with proper medical attention. The Incident Report further suggests the treatment was appropriate under the circumstances.
   - The complaint does not indicate how Ms. Redfearn was harmed by Nurse Williams's failure to provide an intubation kit. The Incident Report suggests Ms. Redfearn did not sustain any injuries: Ms. Redfearn was properly oxygenated while she waited for treatment, and the EMTs were able to intubate Ms. Redfearn immediately after they arrived.

2. **How will those differences impact Bear Creek Lodge's potential liability?**

   Some of the factors to consider include:

   - Ms. Redfearn's own negligence in both riding while intoxicated and disregarding operator instructions may limit how much she can recover if a court finds that her conduct contributed to her injuries.
   - If Ms. Redfearn appreciated the dangers of riding, then she may be barred from recovering because she consented to some bumps and/or assumed the risks of riding.
   - If the cause of the crash was not Bear Creek's failure to maintain the course but instead Ms. Redfearn's actions in bouncing the toboggan, then, Ms. Redfearn will be unable to establish that Bear Creek's negligence caused her injuries.
   - If Nurse Williams acted reasonably and professionally under the circumstances, then Ms. Redfearn will be unable to establish that Bear Creek Lodge acted negligently in providing medical treatment.

- If Ms. Redfearn did not experience any injuries based on the temporary delay in being intubated, then Ms. Redfearn will be unable to establish damages based on the conduct of the Lodge or its employees.

Exercise 2

1. **Bear Creek Lodge's argument that it did not breach a duty of care:**

The Lodge might make some of the following arguments:

The Lodge did not breach its duty of care to Ms. Redfearn because the Lodge took reasonable steps to warn Ms. Redfearn about the risks associated with the toboggan ride. The ride operator cautioned Ms. Redfearn against riding while intoxicated, and the operator also advised Ms. Redfearn that she should not bounce or shift her weight while riding. Not only did Ms. Redfearn ignore these warnings, but she also verbally assaulted the operator when he cautioned her about the dangers.

There is no evidence that the crash was caused by any defect or malfunction in the ride itself. In fact, the cause of the accident was not any negligence on the part of the Lodge or its employees, but Ms. Redfearn's own conduct. Ms. Redfearn repeatedly bounced while riding, even when the operator cautioned her about an upcoming turn. The resultant crash was caused by her movement, and not any dangers in the ride. The Lodge cannot be held liable for injury resulting from a guest's voluntary decision to disregard clear and reasonable safety warnings.

In addition, the Lodge responded to Ms. Redfearn's medical emergency with prompt and reasonable care. The ride operator called for help immediately after the crash, and Nurse Williams arrived within minutes. Nurse Williams brought appropriate emergency equipment, including an ambu-bag and oxygen. Nurse Williams provided treatment while Dr. Greene continued to perform CPR, and even Dr. Greene acknowledged that Ms. Redfearn was being adequately oxygenated while they waited for EMTs to arrive.

Ms. Redfearn will likely argue that Nurse Williams failed to provide proper medical care because she did not intubate Ms. Redfearn. Yet Nurse Williams refused to perform the procedure because she was not trained, which reflects sound medical judgment. Nurse Williams provided sufficient care while waiting for EMTs to arrive, and EMTs were able to intubate and stabilize Ms. Redfearn quickly after they arrived. Ms. Redfearn was not injured by any delay in intubation, and Dr. Greene later thanked Nurse Williams for her support.

Thus, a jury will not find that the Lodge breached its duty of care to Ms. Redfearn.

2. **Ms. Redfearn's argument that Bear Creek Lodge breached a duty of care:**

Ms. Redfearn might make some of the following arguments:

Bear Creek Lodge breached its duty by failing to operate and maintain the toboggan ride in a way that protected guests from harm. The Lodge suggested the ride was safe for any individual over the age of 10, and Ms. Redfearn relied on that representation when she chose to ride. Despite those promises, Ms. Redfearn was thrown from the toboggan after she hit a large, unexpected bump. Ms. Redfearn was not adequately warned of the risks involved in the ride and could not reasonably anticipate that kind of crash. Bear Creek Lodge breached its duty to guests by failing to make the ride safe or at least warn guests of potential obstructions.

The Lodge might argue that Ms. Redfearn caused the accident because, in part, she rode while intoxicated. In that case, the Lodge should have policies in place to prevent intoxicated individuals from participating, especially because drinks were served as part of the Winter Wonderland attractions.

The Lodge might also argue that Ms. Redfearn caused the accident because she bounced while she was riding. Yet such conduct is likely common among riders, especially young children. The ride should not be so delicately designed that the slightest shift in weight might cause the toboggan to crash. Moreover, the Lodge did not post any warnings about sharp turns along the route, instead relying on shouts from the operator who was some distance away from the riders.

Bear Creek Lodge further breached its duty to Ms. Redfearn by failing to render adequate medical treatment after Ms. Redfearn was injured. The Lodge had a duty to ensure that medical personnel would be trained and qualified to provide proper assistance. Yet Nurse Williams failed to bring the medical equipment necessary to care for Ms. Redfearn. Ms. Redfearn experienced a cardiac arrest and required an intubation kit. Yet while the Lodge has an intubation kit, Nurse Williams refused to bring it. The Lodge apparently foresaw the need for such equipment because the kit was in the tent, and the Lodge cannot fulfill its duty to guests if the tent is stocked with equipment that no staff member is able to use. In the end, Nurse Williams failed to provide any aid that revived Ms. Redfearn; Dr. Green and the EMTs ultimately provided the life saving treatment. Thus, the Lodge did not render meaningful care until others could take over.

Thus, a jury could find that the Lodge failed to satisfy its duty to Ms. Redfearn.

Exercise 3

1. **Do you believe the provisions above minimize the risk of liability for the Lodge? Why or why not?**

   No. Bear Creek Lodge, as an innkeeper, had a heightened duty to protect patrons. Thus, the Lodge is not protected by the statute. Nurse Williams was an employee of the Lodge and was acting within the scope of her duties. Thus, Nurse Wiliams was fulfilling the duty owed by Bear Creek Lodge to render aid for injured guests.

   The Good Samaritan Statute typically applies to bystanders or off-duty responders who are acting without compensation. The public policy goals of the Good Samaritan Statute are not served by absolving a party of liability if they are legally obligated to render care. Applying the principle to a party with a duty to render aid would absolve that party of any obligation to render reasonable and prompt assistance.

Exercise 4

1. **Does the Winter Wonderful waiver comply with the Starr Resorts' principles set forth in the memorandum above? Why or why not?**

   You might identify the following problems with the waiver as drafted:

   1. The waiver fails to identify the primary risks involved in tobogganing. Although the waiver includes safety guidelines, it does not identify the risks inherent in the ride, including falling, colliding with obstacles, sudden jolts, etc. The waiver also fails to include an explicit acknowledgment that the guest understands and voluntarily assumes the risks.
   2. With respect to the release of liability, the waiver does include the exact language required under Starr Resorts' policies. Yet the release is not clear and conspicuous; the language appears in small print at the end of the light-hearted, informal message.

3. The waiver does not include any provisions related to medical treatment. Guests are not required to consent to and pay for medical treatment, and there is no waiver of claims related to provided treatment.
4. Because courts strictly construe waivers, it is probably poor judgment to present the waiver with such informality. The playfulness of the language undermines the seriousness of the legal implications.

2. If you answered "no" to Question 1 above, then how do any of the deficiencies you identified impact the potential enforceability of the waiver in the event of litigation?

You might identify the following risks:

- Because the waiver fails to identify the specific, inherent risks in tobogganing, the court may find guests did not knowingly and voluntarily assume the risks of the activity. Specifically, if Ms. Redfearn was not explicitly warned about the dangers of riding while intoxicated, of bouncing while riding, and of the risks of encountering unexpected obstacles, then a court may find she did not knowingly encounter the risks.
- Because the release of liability is inconspicuous, the court may find it is unenforceable. Exculpatory language must be clear and conspicuous to give the signer fair notice of the terms.
- The omission of language about medical treatment creates a serious risk of legal liability. If Ms. Redfearn successfully argues the treatment provided was negligent, then the Lodge would have no contractual defense. Consequently, even if the Lodge ultimately fulfilled its duty to render aid, Ms. Redfearn might claim damages if the court finds the Lodge failed to render *timely* or *adequate* aid.
- The tone of the waiver may fail to clearly communicate the implications of signing it. It may also cast doubt on whether the signer understood they were signing a binding, legal agreement.
- Ms. Redfearn may further argue that, because she was intoxicated, she did not understand the waiver or the identified risks.

3. If you answered "no" to Question 1 above, then how would you revise the waiver to ensure it complies with Starr Resorts' internal policies and is enforceable?

You might propose the following changes:

- Add headings to identify the sections of the waiver: Acknowledgment of Risk; Release of Liability, Consent to Medical Treatment. This would delineate each section and identify the legal consequences of signing.
- Identify the specific risks involved in tobogganing.
- Make the release of liability clear and conspicuous within the document.
- Add provisions about consent for medical treatment.
- Modify the tone to eliminate jokes and playful language. Alternatively, present the guest with separate documents: one document presenting the rules of the ride; and a separate document that presents the acknowledgement of risk, release of liability, and consent to medical treatment.
- Include language that identifies the document as a legal agreement, and consider including language such as: "PLEASE READ CAREFULLY BEFORE SIGNING."

- Ask the participant to acknowledge they are in a physical condition to participate and agree to comply with posted policies.
- As a practical matter, you might research whether Starr Resorts has any templates or examples to use as a starting draft.

4. **Considering all the evidence in the case, what advice will you offer your client with respect to Ms. Redfearn's claims? Evaluate the strength of Ms. Redfearn's claims and any other considerations that might influence the Lodge's response.**

   As you advise the client, consider the following factors:

   - **Legal Risk**. The material facts are disputed in this case, which means the jury could find either version of the facts plausible. Thus, the jury may find that the Lodge reasonably maintained and operated the ride and provided adequate medical treatment. In contrast, the jury might find the Lodge was negligent in allowing an intoxicated guest to participate in the ride, despite evidence she was moving erratically, and it failed to adequately warn guests of the risks involved in riding. The jury might also find the Lodge failed to properly maintain the course, exposing riders to unreasonably dangerous conditions. Finally, the jury might find the Lodge failed to satisfy its duty to render prompt and adequate aid.

     Given the uncertainty of the legal outcome, there is a significant risk the Lodge may be found liable, especially given its heightened duty of care. The jury might also be sympathetic to Ms. Redfearn's position given her age and the Lodge's promotion of the ride as family-friendly and safe.

     It is extremely unlikely that the waiver will offer any legal protection to the Lodge given the deficiencies noted above. The Lodge's position as an innkeeper may render the waiver inherently unenforceable, and it will certainly subject the waiver to higher scrutiny. The court is unlikely to find that the language properly warned guests of dangers or conspicuously notified them of the legal consequences of participating. In fact, the serious deficiencies of the waiver may contribute to a jury's perception that the Lodge was not serious about guest safety.

     If the Lodge is found liable, then the amount of recovery could be high. While Ms. Redfearn's damages are unclear at this stage of litigation, she could possibly claim damages related to medical expenses, pain and suffering, emotional distress, etc.

     The Lodge may have several possible defenses that mitigate its liability. The Lodge may argue comparative negligence and/or assumption of the risks, which may minimize the Lodge's exposure.

   - **Legal Expenses.** Even if the Lodge is successful at trial, the costs of litigation are high. Defending a personal injury suit through discovery, a robust motion practice, expert consultations, etc. can easily cost tens of thousands of dollars. It is extremely unlikely that Ms. Redfearn's damages will exceed these costs.

   - **Reputational Harm.** Bear Creek Lodge identifies itself as a family-friendly destination, and it draws tourists to the Lodge throughout the year. The Lodge should be eager to avoid the negative publicity associated with a lawsuit involving an elderly guest's heart attack on a children's toboggan ride.

     A confidential settlement could reduce the publicity associated with Ms. Redfearn's claims. Ms. Redfearn could sign a release of all claims as part of the settlement terms.

   - **Insurance Considerations.** Consider reviewing the Lodge's insurance policies to determine the implications of a contested trial. A pre-litigation settlement may be covered by liability insurance.

Exercise 5

1. **Do you believe Starr Resorts should accept the settlement offer? Explain.**

   This is a subjective question based on your assessment of the factors identified above.

   While it is in the Lodge's best interests to settle the case without a trial, the proposed settlement amount is likely higher than the Lodge anticipated, especially without concrete evidence about the extent of Ms. Redfearn's injuries. Depending on the evidence produced during settlement negotiations, the amount may be more than Ms. Redfearn is likely to recover at trial. Yet when considering the potential expenses of litigation, it may nevertheless be more affordable to settle than to proceed to trial. Starr Resorts may also be willing to pay a higher amount given the negative publicity associated with the incident.

   This presents an opportunity to negotiate about the specific settlement amount. Ms. Redfearn is probably willing to settle for less than the amount identified in the letter, so you can approach settlement negotiations with an aim to reduce the final award. A settlement agreement should include no admission of liability, a broad release of claims, and a confidentiality clause.

Chapter 7: Duty of Care

Rescuers/Firefighters Rule: *Gilmore v. J.S. Bar & Grill*

Exercise 1

1. **Based on the three-pronged test outlined in *Garcia*, what must Officer Gilmore show to establish that the Rescuer Doctrine applies to her case?**

   Based on the language from *Garcia*, Officer Gilmore must prove:

   1. Officer Gilmore acted with the intent to aid bar patrons and/or bystanders;
   2. Officer Gilmore reasonably believed bar patrons and/or bystanders were in imminent peril of injury; and
   3. Officer Gilmore's conduct was reasonably calculated to prevent or alleviate the imminent peril.

2. **Do you believe Officer Gilmore can satisfy the three-pronged test outlined in *Garcia*? Why or why not?**

   Probably yes, considering the following:

   1. Officer Gilmore responded to a call for law enforcement involvement, and she intervened with the express purpose of disrupting the violence and protecting the public.
   2. The bar called for law enforcement intervention and reported there was a risk to persons and property. When Officer Gilmore arrived, she encountered a brawl and, based on her training, would have reasonably anticipated that the fight presented a risk of imminent injury to patrons and employees. Officer Gilmore had previously responded to similar incidents, and she warned the owner that someone could be seriously injured.
   3. Officer Gillmore is trained to respond to these kinds of incidents, and she had successfully responded during previous altercations. Officer Gilmore did ultimately succeed in disrupting the fight and arresting the alleged perpetrators.

Exercise 2

1. Does the Firefighter's Rule bar Officer Gilmore's claim for negligence? Why or why not?

You might identify the following challenge presented by the rule:

Sunport's Firefighters Rule (also applicable to police officers) holds that a negligent party is not liable for injuries an officer sustains while responding to the very dangers the officer is professionally obligated to confront. Presumably, this includes injuries an officer sustains while disrupting a brawl started by intoxicated patrons. J.S. Bar & Grill will argue that, even if it acted negligently in overserving patrons who started a fight, Officer Gilmore was hired to train and manage such threats to the public, and she cannot seek damages from the bar for injuries she sustained while fulfilling her public duty.

Yet a creative advocate might argue the bar created risks beyond those inherent in an officer's job responsibilities. The bar created elevated risks because it chose to serve patrons an excessive amount of alcohol outside of normal drinking hours, even after Officer Gilmore warned the bar of the very risks involved in this case.

Exercise 3

1. Can Officer Gilmore establish that J.S. Bar & Grill is liable for her injuries under the provisions above?

Probably. The following are relevant considerations:

1. If an entity serves alcohol to an intoxicated patron who foreseeably causes injury to another, then the entity may be liable for damages under the statute. Notably, the statute also extends liability to injuries sustained by law enforcement officers, *even if the officer sustained injuries while acting in an official capacity*. This essentially overrides the Firefighters Rule. Thus, if Officer Gilmore can prove the statute applies, then she may seek damages.
2. Officer Gilmore can probably show the establishment served alcohol to visibly intoxicated patrons. J.S. Bar & Grill opened early and served patrons throughout the day. The bar had a history of violent incidents caused by intoxicated patrons. Based on this history, Officer Gilmore can likely show that the bar served patrons despite knowing the patrons were intoxicated and violent. There may be physical evidence to further support the claim (*e.g.*, security footage, eyewitness testimony, etc.).
3. Officer Gilmore can probably show the overservice was the proximate cause of her damages. As analyzed above, violent incidents had previously occurred at the bar during the same kinds of events. Officer Gilmore indicates she previously responded to such altercations and warned the owner about the risks created during the soccer events. Thus, it was foreseeable that the overservice would trigger a need for law enforcement involvement and create a risk of injury to responding officers.

Applying the statutory protections in this case advances the public policy goals of the dram shop statute. Dram shop statutes are designed to protect the public and to deter entities from overserving patrons. Those goals are undermined if entities are shielded from liability for injuries to officers, especially if if their actions created the need for law enforcement involvement. Shielding entities from liability under the Firefighters Rule would essentially allow those entities to externalize the costs of their negligent conduct onto public servants.

2. **You would like to identify a resolution that allows the parties to settle the case without costly litigation. Identify possible terms for a settlement with J.S. Bar & Grill.**

In considering terms for settlement, it is essential to consider the parties' goals, resources, and interests. Below are some factors to consider, but you may identify others as you propose settlement terms.

- Because Officer Gilmore is "embarrassed" by the situation, she probably prefers a quiet settlement. Similarly, J.S. Bar & Grill likely wishes to avoid the negative publicity associated with the incident. The bar could suffer serious reputational harm from the perception that it endangered a police officer and promoted public intoxication. This may motivate both parties to reach a private settlement.
- The parties may disagree about whether to include a confidentiality provision in the final agreement. There has already been reporting about the incident, but a confidentiality provision may limit further details from reaching the public. Given Officer Gilmore's embarrassment and J.S. Bar & Grill's reputational concerns, both may be motivated to agree.

  Yet Officer Gilmore may wish to waive confidentiality to call attention to the incident and the risk to public safety. After all, Officer Gilmore wants to deter such conduct in the future and protect other "women in blue."
- Officer Gilmore is primarily motivated by a desire to protect the public. Officer Gilmore is "furious" because she warned the owner that his actions were dangerous and were going to cause serious injury. Officer Gilmore wants to deter similar conduct and protect other law enforcement officers.

  This presents an opportunity for settlement if J.S. Bar & Grill is willing to modify its business practices, including by limiting alcohol service during morning games. The bar might also adopt policies about serving visibly intoxicated patrons, implement employee training, and/or employ private security during high-risk events. The bar might also issue an apology and/or contribute to efforts promoting officer safety and well-being.
- Officer Gilmore already received workers' compensation for her injuries, so she presumably received compensation for missed work and medical expenses. She may nevertheless pursue damages for pain and suffering and emotional distress. The amount should be reasonable as J.S. Bar & Grill is a local establishment and may have limited financial resources.
- Any agreement should include a provision releasing J.S. Bar & Grill from any claims arising from the incident.

Chapter 7: Duty of Care

Primary Assumption of the Risk: *Hamilton v. Everest Heights, Inc.*

Exercise 1

1. **What additional information would you like to know to assess whether the Hamiltons have a viable claim against Everest Heights?**

Some questions may include but are not limited to:

- **How did the injury occur?** What was Zoey doing when she was injured? Did she trip, was she pushed, did she land awkwardly? Was there something on the floor? How many other children were using the apparatus? Did she collide with any of them? Did any of them fall? Were any injured? How close was the apparatus to the unprotected floor?

- **Were the children being supervised?** Were any employees monitoring the activity? If yes, were the employees monitoring the activities per relevant company policies? If not, were there any policies requiring supervision?
- **Was there a problem with the equipment?** Did the floor perform as expected? Were there any defects with installation or maintenance of the floor? Have there been any prior incidents related to the apparatus?
- **Were the children properly instructed?** Was there any instruction about or demonstration of the apparatus? Were guests warned of the risks involved in using the apparatus? Were there any safety rules or signs posted? Did the children comply with those policies?
- **Did the family sign a waiver?** Does the gym have a waiver and release of liability? If yes, did Zoey's parents sign it? What was the language of the document?
- **What were Zoey's injuries?** What treatment did Zoey require? Is she continuing to receive treatment? Has Zoey complained of any emotional trauma? Did Zoey miss school? Did her parents miss work or sustain other damages?
- **What evidence is available?** Are there records related to Zoey's injuries? Who witnessed the event? Does their recollection match Zoey's version of events? Is there any video footage? Have there been any internal investigations?

2. **Are there any legal issues you would like to research to assess whether the Hamiltons have a viable claim against Everest Heights?**

Opposing Counsel asserts that Zoey plans to pursue a claim for negligence. That might raise questions about the following legal issues:

- **Duty and Breach**. What is the standard of care owed by the gym to children using the facility? Presumably, the children were owed a duty as invitees, but was there also a heightened duty because the guests were children? Are there any regulations or safety standards that govern the gym's operation? Was the gym required to provide instruction and/or active supervision to guests?
- **Causation.** Is this kind of injury a foreseeable risk of using the apparatus? Has it been known to cause similar kinds of injuries? Were there measures the gym could have adopted to mitigate such risks?
- **Assumption of the Risk.** Does Sunport recognize express assumption of the risk as a defense for this kind of activity? What legal considerations influence whether waivers and releases are enforceable in Sunport?
- **Comparative Negligence.** Does Zoey's age influence the applicability of a defense of comparative negligence? What standard of care applies to a child using gym equipment also used by adults?
- **Damages**. Are there any limits on damages in this context? May Zoey's parents also claim damages?

Exercise 2

1. **Draft an initial argument supporting the claim that Zoey's potential suit is barred under the doctrine of primary assumption of the risk.**

Under the doctrine of primary assumption of the risk, an individual who voluntarily engages in certain recreational activities is presumed to have assumed the ordinary risks of that activity. The defendant does not owe a duty to protect the plaintiff from those inherent risks. The doctrine applies if 1) the danger is ordinary to the game, 2) it is common knowledge that the danger exists, and 3) the injury occurs as a result of the danger during the course of the game.

Here, the equipment in the gym is designed for jumping, tumbling, and other gymnastic activities. The dangers of using such equipment include falls and resulting injuries. Those risks are obvious to any participants, including children and their parents. Zoey Hamilton fell and broke her arm while she was using the equipment, and she consequently sustained her injury while engaging in exactly the kind of activity the floor was designed for. Thus, because Zoey assumed the risk of injury, the gym did not owe Zoey a duty to protect her from the inherent risks associated with the activity.

Therefore, Zoey's claim is barred under the doctrine of primary assumption of the risk.

2. How do you anticipate the plaintiff will respond to the arguments above?

The plaintiff may concede that using the equipment carries some inherent risks, but that does not absolve the gym from its duty to provide adequate instruction and supervision. Zoey may argue that she did not *knowingly* accept the risks of the activity because the gym failed to properly warn her about using the spring floor.

In addition, because Zoey is only 10 years old, she may argue that she was unable to appreciate the nature and extent of risks and relied on adult supervision. This argument is less likely to influence a court as "[o]nly the conduct of the [recreation provider] is relevant to recovery." *Santho*.

Moreover, Zoey may argue that the floor was improperly maintained, and her injury resulted from a defect in the apparatus itself. In such a case, Zoey may argue the gym breached its duty of care to her as an invitee, including a duty to maintain a safe environment and minimize avoidable risks. Stated differently, the gym's failure to properly maintain equipment "is not a risk inherent in the sport that is assumed by a participant." *Knight*.

Exercise 3

1. You know you may have to produce this report as part of discovery. Draft an email to your client advising them of the implications of the report and the Hamiltons' claim.

Your email should include the following considerations:

- The gym should be commended for its policies regarding waivers and releases of liability. Yet waivers will not shield the gym from liability if the gym was negligent in maintaining equipment or providing supervision.
- The gym should also be commended for posting gym rules near the equipment. It is relevant that Zoey and her friends violated one of the posted rules by jumping with more than five guests; however, a court might find that the gym should have provided sufficient supervision to ensure guests complied with the rules. A court may find that the gym failed to meet this obligation because Ms. Reyes was assisting another guest and was unable to respond when guests violated safety protocols.
- In addition, a court may find that the gym failed to warn guests about risks and protocols. Ms. Patel cannot recall whether she properly instructed the group, which may reveal deficiencies in the gym's policies. It is also unclear whether the signs were visible and conspicuous.
- The gym may be liable if the court finds Zoey's injuries were caused by a defect in the apparatus. In particular, a jury may find that it was unreasonable to position the spring floor in a way that allowed a guest to land onto an unpadded area.
- While Zoey Hamilton may have assumed some of the inherent risks involved in using gym equipment, that may not absolve the gym of liability if the gym failed to provide adequate instruction or warnings or failed to supervise use of the equipment.

Chapter 7: Duty of Care

Negligent Infliction of Emotional Distress: *In re Denise Franklin*

Exercise 1

1. **Can Ms. Franklin establish the *prima facie* elements of a negligence claim against Mr. Graver? Why or why not?**

   Probably not. Consider the following:

   - **Duty:** Mr. Graver owed a duty of care to act as a reasonably prudent driver to minimize risks to other drivers and pedestrians.
   - **Breach:** Mr. Graver breached that duty by traveling 50 mph in a pedestrian zone. Mr. Graver further breached that duty to talking and texting while he was driving, and he was distracted enough to miss surrounding indications that he was entering a pedestrian zone.
   - **Causation:** But for Mr. Graver's conduct, he would not have hit and killed Carolyn Franklin, and the collision was a foreseeable consequence of speeding and driving while distracted.
   - **Damages:** Ms. Franklin will be unable to establish damages because she was not physically injured during the incident. Moreover, Ms. Franklin was not even aware she was in danger of being struck. While Ms. Franklin experienced severe emotional distress, this will not satisfy the element of damages under traditional negligence principles.

Exercise 2

1. **Based on the excerpts from *Redress in the Redlands* and the principles discussed in *Robb*, what must Ms. Franklin prove to establish a cause of action for NIED?**

   Ms. Franklin must prove:

   - Mr. Graver's conduct created an unreasonable risk to Ms. Franklin's physical safety;
   - Ms. Franklin was placed at risk of serious bodily injury or death; and
   - Because Ms. Franklin *knew she was* in the zone of danger, she suffered emotional distress.

2. **Which facts, if any, suggest Mr. Graver's conduct unreasonably endangered Ms. Franklin's physical safety, placing her at risk of serious bodily injury or death?**

   You might identify the following facts:

   - Mr. Graver was driving 50 mph in a pedestrian zone with a speed limit of 20 mph;
   - Mr. Graver was distracted because he was talking and texting;
   - Mr. Graver ignored signs designating the reduced speed limit;
   - Denise Franklin was on the sidewalk facing away from the oncoming vehicle;
   - Mr. Graver struck Carolyn and "barely missed" Denise; and
   - Denise Franklin was in the zone of danger because she was at risk of being struck by the car.

3. Can Ms. Franklin successfully argue that she suffered emotional distress *because* she was in the zone of danger? Does it matter that she was not aware of Mr. Graver's proximity to her and her mother until after the crash?

This is a challenge for Ms. Franklin because, while she experienced severe emotional distress, the distress was caused by witnessing her mother's death, not because she felt apprehension about a near miss.

Ms. Franklin asserted that she was not aware of the oncoming crash until after she heard the screams and the collision. Moreover, the symptoms of distress she describes seem to relate to the anguish she experienced in seeing her mother injured. In this case, Ms. Franklin's distress was not caused by her perception that she herself was in physical danger.

Yet Ms. Franklin might argue that she sensed she was in physical danger because she heard someone yell, "Slow down!" Ms. Franklin also heard the crash and likely experienced apprehension at that moment. Thus, even if she was not fully aware of the impending crash, she may have experienced general apprehension about her safety.

Exercise 3

1. Ms. Franklin's proximity to the accident.

Like the plaintiff in *Dillon*, Ms. Franklin was immediately next to her mother when the crash occurred, and the car "barely missed" her.

This factor makes it significantly more foreseeable that Ms. Franklin will suffer extreme emotional distress because of the crash and the injury to her mother.

2. Whether Ms. Franklin contemporaneously observed the accident or learned of it later.

While Ms. Franklin did not see the car approaching, she heard screams and a crash, and she saw her mother on the ground immediately after the collision. Thus, Ms. Franklin realized the danger and consequences directly after the events.

This factor may make Ms. Franklin's injuries more foreseeable because she was immediately next to her mother when the collision occurred, and she saw her mother unconscious on the ground. Yet Mr. Graver will likely argue that her emotional distress is not foreseeable because she did not directly witness the crash and was not personally afraid for her safety.

3. The nature of the relationship between Ms. Franklin and her mother.

Denise Franklin is Carolyn's biological daughter, and they had an intimate and close relationship.

This factor makes it significantly more foreseeable that Ms. Franklin will suffer extreme emotional distress because of the crash and the injury to her mother.

Exercise 4

1. Which approach to NIED offers Ms. Franklin a better likelihood of success: Sunport's "zone of danger" theory or Solera's "bystander rule"?

Ms. Franklin has a better likelihood of success under Solera's bystander rule. As analyzed above, given the intimate relationship between Ms. Franklin and her mother and Ms. Franklin's proximity to the events, it was foreseeable that Ms. Franklin would suffer extreme emotional distress as a result of Mr. Graver's conduct.

Ms. Franklin may be unable to establish the elements of NIED under the zone of danger rule because, while she was in the zone of danger created by Mr. Graver's reckless conduct, she did not have contemporaneous awareness of the risk. Depending on how rigidly the court interprets the requirement, she may be unable to establish liability.

Chapter 7: Duty of Care

Negligent Infliction of Emotional Distress: *Norland v. Adobe Animal Clinic*

Exercise 1

1. **What are your initial thoughts about Mr. Norland's case? What potential claims might he file, and what barriers do you anticipate?**

   The exercise will further explore Mr. Norland's possible claims, which may include:

   - **Malpractice (professional negligence).** The veterinarian suggested Pickle had terminal cancer based on a cursory physical examination and caused Mr. Norland trauma by suggesting euthanasia. Yet it is unclear whether this comports with professional norms and whether the veterinarian was merely suggesting euthanasia as a possible but not certain outcome. It may require an expert review to assess whether the veterinarian's care was reasonable. It is also unclear whether Mr. Norland's delay in seeking treatment contributed to his emotional distress.
   - **Negligent infliction of emotional distress (NIED).** Courts have previously used the doctrine of NIED to hold physicians liable for misdiagnosing patients. Yet it is unclear whether a court would extend this to veterinary care as courts typically designate pets as personal property.
   - **Negligent misrepresentation.** The veterinarian provided inaccurate information without conducting a thorough exam, and he intended to induce reliance because he suggested treatment options and encouraged Mr. Norland to return for further tests. Mr. Norland foreseeably experienced emotional trauma because of the misdiagnosis.
   - **Intentional infliction of emotional distress (IIED).** This claim is the least likely to succeed, but Mr. Norland might argue that the veterinarian's comments about euthanasia were extreme and outrageous, the veterinarian acted recklessly by providing a diagnosis and suggesting euthanasia after a superficial exam, and Mr. Norland consequently experienced extreme emotional distress.
   - **Other.** Other possible ancillary claims may invoke the veterinarian's fiduciary duties and/or laws related to deceptive trade practice.

Exercise 2

1. **What does the court in *Hedgepeth* identify as the elements of negligent infliction of emotional distress in a medical misdiagnosis case?**

   The court in *Hedgepeth* held that a defendant may owe a plaintiff a duty to avoid causing emotional distress if the defendant has undertaken an obligation to benefit the plaintiff and the undertaking creates a foreseeable/likely risk that the defendant's negligence will cause the plaintiff serious emotional harm.

   To recover damages for negligent infliction of emotional distress, the plaintiff must show: 1) the defendant had a relationship with or undertook an obligation to the plaintiff that implicated the plaintiff's emotional well-being; 2) there was a reasonably foreseeable or likely risk that the defendant's negligence would cause the plaintiff serious emotional distress; and 3) the defendant's breach of that obligation caused the plaintiff to experience serious emotional distress.

2. **Do you believe Mr. Norland can establish the elements identified above? Why or why not?**

   This is a subjective question, and reasonable minds may disagree. Mr. Norland will likely make some of the following arguments:

   - Adobe Animal Clinic undertook an obligation that implicated Mr. Norland's emotional well-being because the Clinic provided care to Mr. Norland's pet. The Clinic knew Mr. Norland relied on Pickle for emotional support, and Mr. Norland repeatedly noted that Pickle was a critical part of his mental well-being. Therefore, it was foreseeable that a breach of the duty to communicate accurately and effectively could cause Mr. Norland severe emotional distress. The veterinarian's recommendations about euthanasia were especially likely to cause emotional harm.
   - The Clinic's breach of its duty was likely to cause Mr. Norland serious emotional distress because the veterinarian knew Mr. Norland was emotionally attached to Pickle, and Mr. Norland explained that Pickle helped him manage mental health concerns. It was also foreseeable that a misdiagnosis of a terminal illness could cause Mr. Norland to relapse and experience more severe trauma than other pet owners.
   - As a direct result of the misdiagnosis, Mr. Norland experienced serious emotional distress, manifested by depression, isolation, alcohol abuse, and a recurrence of PTSD symptoms. Mr. Norland also experienced sleeplessness and missed work.

3. **How will the Clinic likely respond to Mr. Norland's arguments?**

   The Clinic may make some of the following arguments:

   - The Clinic owed a duty to Pickle, not Mr. Norland. The Clinic had a duty to provide reasonable care and advice to the patient, and the Clinic did not have a duty to avoid causing emotional distress to Mr. Norland. In fact, courts rarely allow recovery for emotional distress in veterinary malpractice cases.
   - Mr. Norland's reaction was not foreseeable because the veterinarian merely suggested Pickle had cancer and suggested euthanasia as a treatment option. A typical patient would not experience severe emotional distress in the same circumstances, and the Clinic did not have extensive knowledge about Mr. Norland's mental health concerns.
   - Mr. Norland's reaction was influenced by preexisting mental health conditions, and his reaction was atypical. Moreover, Mr. Norland exacerbated his distress by refusing to secure a second opinion despite the veterinarian's advice, which would have confirmed Pickle was healthy. Pickle was not harmed, and Mr. Norland took no action in reliance on the veterinarian's advice.

Exercise 3

1. **How does the court's analysis in *Rabideau* influence your analysis of whether Mr. Norland has a viable claim for NIED?**

   In *Rabideau*, the court refused to apply the doctrine of NIED to support a plaintiff's claim that she experienced severe emotional distress when the defendant negligently killed her pet. The court found that, while pets provide invaluable companionship, pet relationships do not have the same social value as those of intimate friends and family members. Moreover, pets are legally characterized as property, and courts rarely grant recovery for infliction of emotional distress arising from property loss. The court also found it would be difficult to "cogently identify the class of companion animals because the human capacity to form an emotional bond extends to an enormous array of living creatures." Thus, it is unlikely that Mr. Norland may claim damages under a theory of NIED.

Yet Mr. Norland may argue that *Rabideau* is distinguishable because, the animal in *Rabideau* was killed by a police officer who did not have an existing relationship with the owner or the animal. In contrast, Adobe Animal Clinic undertook a relationship with Mr. Norland that included a duty to communicate effectively. In addition, the veterinarian knew that Mr. Norland relied on Pickle's companionship. In other words, the Clinic undertook a relationship that created a special duty of care to the plaintiff.

Exercise 4

1. **What is the standard of care that applies in this case?**

   Mr. Norland must show Adobe Animal Clinic failed to act as a reasonably prudent veterinarian with similar training and experience under similar circumstances. In this case, the veterinarian was not an oncologist, so his conduct will be compared to that of a reasonable general practitioner.

   This will influence whether the veterinarian acted reasonably when providing a diagnostic evaluation, offering a preliminary diagnosis, and presenting Mr. Norland with information about euthanasia. The reasonableness of the veterinarian's conduct may also be influenced by the veterinarian's awareness that Mr. Norland relied on Pickle for emotional support.

2. **If both experts are qualified and offer plausible interpretations of the same facts, how is a factfinder expected to resolve the dispute?**

   The factfinder must determine which report is more persuasive and/or credible. The factfinder may consider:

   - The experts' relative qualifications and experience;
   - Evidence of bias or lack of objectivity;
   - Whether the expert's interpretation is consistent with undisputed evidence;
   - Whether the expert relied on accepted practices in the field; and
   - The thoroughness of the expert's explanations and conclusions.

3. **Which of the expert reports do you find more influential, and why? How can you undermine the credibility of the other report?**

   This is a subjective question, and there is not a right or wrong answer. The following are the relative strengths and weaknesses of each report:

   Dr. Feldman's report advances Mr. Norland's argument that Adobe Animal Clinic acted negligently. Dr. Feldman determined the veterinarian breached the applicable standard of care because the veterinarian diagnosed a malignancy without confirmatory tests and prematurely introduced euthanasia as a treatment option.

   - Dr. Feldman offered clear support for each conclusion. The report articulated the appropriate standard of care and explained why it was unreasonable to present a "suspicion" as a firm diagnosis. It further identified the close relationship between humans and their companion animals, especially in this case, and it explained why it was reckless to prematurely suggest end-of-life options. The report is compelling and may resonate with jurors, especially pet owners.

- Dr. Feldman relied on authoritative texts and principles to support each assertion.
- On the other hand, Dr. Feldman appears to hold the general practitioner to a high standard, possibly that of an oncologist or cancer expert.
- Moreover, some of Dr. Feldman's conclusions may exceed the scope of her expertise. Dr. Feldman is not a psychologist and did not treat Mr. Norland, yet she included findings about the causal relationship between the misdiagnosis and Mr. Norland's subsequent emotional trauma.
- Finally, the report ignores Mr. Norland's decision to delay treatment. Had Mr. Norland acted quickly to secure another opinion, he may have mitigated his emotional trauma.

Dr. Hawkin's report supports the Clinic's argument that the veterinarian did not act negligently. Dr. Hawkin determined the veterinarian acted reasonably by offering an initial impression, recommending follow-up care, and communicating with compassion about possible treatments.

- Dr. Hawkin offers a more sympathetic perspective about the demands of a general practice. Dr. Hawkin portrays the veterinarian's advice as an initial opinion, subject to further testing. This interpretation may appear more realistic given the limits of what a general practitioner can confirm during a first visit.
- Dr. Hawkin also interprets the interactions as more compassionate and suggests euthanasia was presented as one of various treatment options. Dr. Hawkin suggested it was compassionate to introduce the option early because it would give Mr. Norland time to consider the possibility.
- Dr. Hawkin correctly notes that Pickle was not injured by the veterinarian's conduct.
- Dr. Hawkin suggests that Mr. Norland's delay in seeking further treatment contributed to/caused his severe emotional distress.
- Yet Dr. Hawkin's interpretations are not always consistent with the evidence. For example, a jury may disagree that the veterinarian merely offered an initial opinion when the veterinarian told Mr. Norland the growth was "almost certainly malignant." A jury is more likely to empathize with Mr. Norland and may interpret the veterinarian's advice in a similar way.
- Moreover, Dr. Hawkin's strict defense of the veterinarian may appear to minimize Mr. Norland's trauma and alienate jurors.

Chapter 8: Breach

Res ipsa loquitur: Charlton v. Lemmon

Exercise 1

1. **Identify which facts support each element of a potential cause of action for negligence. Also identify whether there are potential gaps in Ms. Charlton's claim.**

   - **Duty.** The Lemmons owed Ms. Charlton a duty as landowners and employers. The Lemmons also controlled the farm and the dock. Therefore, the Lemmons owed a duty to maintain the property and protect the Charltons from unreasonably dangerous conditions.
   - **Breach.** With respect to breach, there are significant evidentiary gaps because the dock was destroyed. Thus, it is impossible to inspect the dock to determine whether it was reasonably maintained. The parties may attempt to gather witness or photographic evidence of the dock's condition, including evidence of prior falls or injuries, if any.

     There is some circumstantial evidence suggesting the dock was in disrepair. The dock had been built over 30 years ago, suggesting it had likely deteriorated. Ms. Charlton might also suggest that the Lemmons' decision to remove the dock after Ms. Charlton fell was a nefarious attempt to hide the evidence.
   - **Causation.** If Ms. Charlton is unable to prove the condition of the dock was unreasonably dangerous, then she may also have difficulty proving the Lemmons' maintenance caused Ms. Charlton's injury.

     If the dock was not in disrepair, then the Lemmons may argue that Ms. Charlton's fall was caused by factors, including clumsiness, failure to take care while walking, etc.

     If the dock was maintained in an unreasonably dangerous condition, then Ms. Charlton can prove causation. But for the failure to repair the dock, Ms. Charlton would not have fallen. Falling through rotted planks is a foreseeable consequence of failing to maintain the dock.
   - **Damages:** Ms. Charlton sustained damages when she broke her leg.

Exercise 2

1. **Using the court's analysis in *Tinder,* draft an argument about whether the doctrine of *res ipsa loquitur* should apply to create an inference of negligence on the part of the Lemmons.**

   Below is a possible interpretation of the facts:

   The doctrine of *res ipsa loquitur* allows the factfinder to infer breach, even if the plaintiff is unable to provide direct evidence of the defendant's unreasonable conduct. The doctrine applies if: 1) the plaintiff's injury is the type that does not occur but for negligence on the part of the defendant; 2) the injury was caused by an instrumentality within the exclusive control of the defendant; and 3) the plaintiff did not contribute to the injury.

   Here, the collapse of a dock does not ordinarily occur but for negligence on the part of the property owner. The collapse is almost certainly caused by negligent construction or maintenance, which presents a serious risk as docks are designed to support pedestrian use. Unlike an elevator, which might stop for reasons unrelated to negligence, the collapse of the boards signals a structural failure attributable to poor design or upkeep.

As property owners, the Lemmons had exclusive control over the docks. The Lemmons had a non-delegable duty to ensure that artificial conditions on the property did not present an unreasonable risk of injury. There is no evidence that the Charltons or others performed any maintenance on the docks. Thus, the Lemmons had the exclusive responsibility to ensure the dock was safe for use.

There is no evidence suggesting Ms. Charlton contributed to her injury; Ms. Charlton merely walked on the dock when it collapsed. Unlike the plaintiff in *Tinder* who refused to hold the handrails, there is no evidence that Ms. Charlton ignored warnings, had special knowledge about the dock's condition, or otherwise acted negligently.

Exercise 3

1. **How does the email influence your assessment of whether the *res ipsa loquitur* doctrine applies?**

The email primarily informs the final consideration: whether Ms. Charlton contributed to her injury. Arthur Bennet cautioned the Charltons against using the dock because it was "in pretty bad shape." Mr. Bennet noted that he avoided using the dock because it was unstable and beginning to rot. If Ms. Charlton read and ignored the email, then it undermines the argument that Ms. Charlton did not contribute to the harm.

In *Tinder*, the court found that the plaintiff's use of *res ipsa* was undermined because the plaintiff ignored posted warnings while riding the elevator. Similarly, if Ms. Charlton was warned about use of the dock and walked across it anyway, then the court may find that the doctrine should not apply.

Moreover, if Ms. Charlton knowingly encountered the risk, then that suggests her injury was foreseeable and avoidable, not one that does not occur in the absence of negligence on the part of someone in the defendant's position.

*An astute reader might note that this email presents a problem for the Lemmons because it may eliminate the need to rely on the doctrine of *res ipsa loquitur*. The email offers *direct* evidence that the dock was in an unreasonably dangerous condition, which suggests the Lemmons breached a duty of care to Ms. Charlton. The Lemmons knew about the condition, directly or vicariously, because their agent (Arthur Bennet) knew the dock was in disrepair. Thus, the email might offer Ms. Charlton the evidence she needs to prove the Lemmons breached a duty of care to tenants on their property.*

Exercise 4

1. **If Jennifer Charlton files a claim for negligence against the Lemmons and establishes the *prima facie* elements, do you believe the comparative fault doctrine will limit her damages or even preclude her from recovering? Explain.**

Given the email between Mr. Bennet and the Charltons, the doctrine almost certainly applies. This could reduce or even preclude Ms. Charlton from recovering damages.

Ms. Charlton owed a duty to act reasonably and avoid unnecessary dangers to herself and others. Ms. Charlton likely breached that duty by walking on the dock despite explicit warnings that the dock was unstable and rotting. But for her actions in walking across the dock, she would not have fallen and been injured, and falling through the planks was a foreseeable risk of walking across a deteriorating dock. Ms. Charlton sustained damages when she broke her leg.

If the factfinder determines that the doctrine applies, then it should allocate fault among the responsible parties. If Ms. Charlton is less than 50 percent at fault, then the court should reduce Ms. Charlton's damages appropriately. If Ms. Charlton is more than 50 percent at fault, then she will not recover damages.

Chapter 8: Breach

Informed consent: *Battle v. Twist*

Exercise 1

1. **What legal issues do you plan to research before you advise the client?**

   Some of the potential legal issues include the following, non-exhaustive list:

   Negligence

   - What is the applicable standard of care for chiropractors in Sunport?
   - Is there a licensing board or other organization that publishes best practices for chiropractors?
   - Is there a community of experts to offer an evaluation of the provided care?
   - Was the treatment within the scope of the patient's consent for medical treatment?
   - What damages are recoverable in Sunport?
   - What are the requirements to secure informed consent in Sunport? What are the consequences if the provider exceeds the scope of the patient's express or implied consent?
   - What exactly does Sunport Stat. § 114-6 require?

   Battery

   - Under what conditions will medical treatment constitute a battery rather than negligence?
   - Can a provider be liable for negligence *and* battery under Sunport law?

   Other

   - What is the statute of limitations for professional negligence and battery in Sunport?
   - Did the patient impliedly consent to treatment by seeking medical care?

2. **What questions do you plan to ask your client when you speak with him?**

   The following non-exhaustive list of questions might help you better understand the case and the client's legal options:

   - How long have you been a licensed chiropractor in Sunport?
   - Please describe your practice and experience treating these kinds of injuries.
   - Do you secure written consent before treating patients? If yes, do patients sign before each treatment session? What is included in the document?
   - Do you maintain malpractice insurance? If so, with which carrier? Do you know of any limitations on coverage? Have you notified the insurer of the claim?
   - Have you ever been sued or disciplined for professional misconduct?
   - How did the plaintiff become your patient? What were her initial complaints?

- What diagnosis did you reach after your initial evaluation?
- How long have you been treating the patient? What procedures have you performed in the past? What symptoms were you treating on August 30? Why did you elect to perform that specific procedure? Was the procedure standard chiropractic treatment based on the patient's symptoms?
- Do you often perform procedures without describing them to patients?
- Do you maintain treatment records?
- Did the patient decline or object to any procedures in the past?
- Did the patient contact you after August 30 to discuss symptoms or problems? Were you aware of her ongoing treatment with another provider? Is she continuing to receive treatment?
- Is there anything else you would like me to know about the patient?

3. What standard of care applies to Dr. Twist's conduct?

Dr. Twist had a duty to act as a reasonably prudent chiropractor with similar training and experience, acting under similar circumstances and in the same or similar community.

Exercise 2

1. What are your initial impressions of Dr. Twist's Informed Consent form? Do you have any concerns about the enforceability of its provisions?

You might identify the following potential problems with the form:

- The form is vague and generic, and it does not identify a diagnosis or treatment plan. Notably, the form does not identify which procedures will be used over the course of treatment.
- The form identifies some *general* risks associated with chiropractic treatment but fails to identify the *specific* risks associated with Ms. Battle's treatment plan. The form also fails to mention more severe risks, including the injury sustained by Ms. Battle.
- The form mentions "alternative treatment options" but does not identify any.
- The form was signed when Ms. Battle began treatment, and it is unclear whether Ms. Battle was advised about treatment procedures during each visit. If Dr. Twist did not perform a similar manipulation during Ms. Battle's first visit, then he should have informed her about the benefits and risks of the new treatment option during her visit on August 30.

Exercise 3

1. Does the consent obtained by Ms. Battle's signature on Dr. Twist's consent form comply with the consent required by § 114-6? Why or why not?

You might notice the following:

- The form is signed, and patients must expressly consent to receiving treatment. This may shield Dr. Twist from liability for some routine procedures.
- The form does identify the general nature and purpose of the proposed treatment. Yet the form does not disclose the patient's diagnosis or identify specific treatment options.

- The form does identify some potential risks related to treatment, but the terms are generic and do not identify all possible risks associated with individual treatments. Notably, the injury sustained by Ms. Battle is NOT identified as a possible risk.
- The form does not identify reasonable alternatives to the proposed treatment or the likelihood of success.

2. **How would you recommend that Dr. Twist amend the form for future patients?**

The following recommendations might better shield Dr. Twist from liability:

- Tailor disclosures to the patient's diagnosis and specific treatment plan;
- Include material risks specific to each treatment plan;
- Identify reasonable alternatives and their likelihood of success; and
- Document patient questions and responses as part of the clinical record.

Exercise 4

1. **How is your case similar to *Northport Dermatology Clinic*? How is it different?**

The cases are similar in the following ways:

- Both cases involve licensed healthcare professionals, and the plaintiffs pursued similar legal theories (negligence, lack of informed consent, battery).
- Both plaintiffs alleged the medical provider performed a procedure without securing consent and/or disclosing material risks.
- Both plaintiffs sustained serious injuries (sepsis and limb loss, herniated disc, and neck surgery) as a result of the allegedly unauthorized treatment.
- In both cases, the plaintiffs signed disclosure and consent forms, but the forms were deficient.

The cases differ because:

- The provider in *Northport* was a dermatologist, while Dr. Twist is a chiropractor. Chiropractors are generally subject to less regulation.
- The treatment in *Northport* was an invasive surgical procedure, while the treatment in *Battle v. Twist* was an allegedly routine, outpatient procedure.
- While an expert confirmed that the physician in *Northport* misdiagnosed and mistreated the patient, no such evidence is available in this case (yet). Dr. Twist asserts that the procedure was routine and appropriate given the patient's symptoms, and an expert opinion provides initial support for those claims.
- The consent form in *Northport* was deficient only because it lacked specific required statutory disclosures (the risks of treatment), but it otherwise presented the patient relevant information about the procedure. The form in *Battle v. Twist* was wholly deficient and inadequate and did not identify the benefits and risks of any specific procedures.

2. **Do you agree with Opposing Counsel that the precedent from *Northport* makes Ms. Battle's claim a "slam dunk" case? Why or why not?**

This is a subjective question based on how you interpret the evidence. Some of the considerations include:

- **Medical Malpractice.** The court in *Northport* outlined how a violation of the informed consent statute may constitute proof that a medical provider breached a standard of care. Here, Dr. Twist clearly violated the informed consent statute: Dr. Twist did not identify Ms. Battle's diagnosis, her specific treatment plan, risks associated with chosen treatment procedures, treatment alternatives, or the likelihood of success. The violations were more egregious than those in *Northport*, especially given that one of the risks of cervical spine manipulation included a severe injury—a herniated disc. A jury could reasonably believe that Ms. Battle would have refused treatment had she known of the risks involved.

- **Battery.** The court in *Northport* also noted that failure to obtain informed consent may expose a provider to liability for battery. The court held that a patient has not given *informed* consent if the provider has not informed the patient about the risks of and alternatives to treatment. If a provider performs a procedure without consent, then the provider has perpetuated an unlawful contact.

  Here, Dr. Twist did not explain the nature of treatment or the associated risks. Thus, even if Ms. Battle signed a generic consent form and impliedly consented to routine treatment, she did not give *informed* consent to the spinal manipulation, and Dr. Twist may be liable for battery.

Exercise 5

1. **How is this definition of "medical professional" relevant to your defense of Dr. Twist?**

   Notably, the definition of medical professionals does NOT include chiropractors. In most jurisdictions, chiropractors are licensed and regulated under separate statutes because the nature of their services differs in form and scope. As established in *Northport*, the statute is strictly construed and cannot be extended beyond its plain and explicit terms. Thus, Dr. Twist may be exempted from the statute requiring informed consent.

   Yet that does not defeat Ms. Battle's claims. While failure to conform to the statute may have allowed Ms. Battle to prove breach under a theory of negligence per se, Ms. Battle can still pursue claims for negligence/professional malpractice, which could implicate questions of informed consent. Moreover, if Ms. Battle proves that Dr. Twist performed a procedure without authorization/consent, that evidence could still support a claim for battery. The adoption of the informed consent statute suggests that Sunport public policy favors informed consent, and courts likely expect *any* medical provider to disclose the risks and alternatives to treatment. A court may find that, even if a provider is exempted from the statute, a provider must nevertheless secure informed consent to comport with the professional standard of care.

Exercise 6

1. **Prepare a recommendation for your client regarding a proposed settlement.**

   Below is an example of a proposed settlement.

   Confidential Attorney-Client Communication

   RE: Settlement Recommendation—*Battle v. Twist*

   FROM: Attorney for Dr. Twist

   TO: Dr. Steven Twist

   I. OVERVIEW OF CASE

   Sharon Battle has filed a lawsuit against you and your clinic alleging:

   1. **Professional negligence** for performing a cervical spinal manipulation without warning or consent. Ms. Battle asserts this resulted in a herniated disc and subsequent surgery;

2. **Battery** because the neck adjustment was outside the scope of the patient's consent, it converted the procedure to a non-consensual, harmful contact; and
3. **Failure to obtain informed consent** because the material risks of treatment were not disclosed prior to the procedure.

II. LEGAL RISK

The consent form signed by Ms. Battle demonstrates some attempt to obtain consent. Moreover, because chiropractic treatment typically involves spinal manipulation, we might argue that Ms. Battle impliedly consented to a neck adjustment as part of her general treatment. If we move forward, then I plan to consult with experts to confirm your arguments that the treatment provided was routine and appropriate given the patient's symptoms.

Yet courts carefully construe consent forms. Your form was generic and did not identify the specific diagnosis or treatment plan. Moreover, the form failed to identify the risks associated with spinal manipulation, including a herniated disc. Therefore, a court may find that you acted negligently because you did not disclose material risks and consequently did not secure *informed* consent. Juries may be sympathetic to a plaintiff who suffered a serious outcome from a procedure she did not expressly authorize.

If liability is found, then damages could be high, including general damages and medical costs. The plaintiff underwent surgery and alleges lasting harm. The plaintiff might also claim damages for pain and suffering, loss of income, and/or decreased quality of life.

In addition to the risks above, pursuing the case could involve significant litigation costs. The costs to secure expert testimony, depositions, and engage in trial preparation could exceed tens of thousands of dollars. In conclusion, the facts and documentation (particularly the generic consent form) leave you vulnerable to liability. If the court allows the claims to proceed, then a jury verdict in the plaintiff's favor could carry stigma and reputational harm.

III. RECOMMENDATION

Given the considerations above, it is in your interests to reach an early, confidential, and amicable resolution of Ms. Battle's claims. Settling now helps you avoid costs, control the outcome, ensure confidentiality, and protect your professional reputation.

IV. PROPOSED SETTLEMENT TERMS

I believe the offer below is fair and reasonable in light of the potential risks, costs, and uncertainties that further litigation would entail:

In the interest of reaching an early and amicable resolution, we are authorized to extend a settlement offer in the amount of $75,000, subject to the following terms:

1. Plaintiff agrees to a complete and mutual release of all claims, known and unknown, arising out of or relating to the treatment provided by Dr. Twist, including any claims for professional negligence, battery, or failure to obtain informed consent.
2. Dismissal of all present or future claims Ms. Battle may pursue against Dr. Twist or his clinic in connection with this matter.
3. This settlement is offered as a compromise and shall not be construed as an admission of liability or wrongdoing.
4. The terms and existence of this agreement shall remain confidential and may not be disclosed to any third party except as required by law.
5. Both parties shall refrain from making any public or private statements that disparage the other in connection with this matter.

Please let me know if you would like to proceed with settlement discussions, or if you wish to review this in detail during a follow-up meeting.

Chapter 8: Breach

Negligence per se: *Darby v. Ballgamers*

Exercise 1

1. **What are your initial thoughts about the claim? Can Mr. Darby establish the *prima facie* elements of negligence?**

   At this stage, it is somewhat unclear. Consider the following:

   - **Duty:** Ballgamers clearly owes a duty to invitees on the property, including outdoor areas where Ballgamers invited and served guests. This includes protecting guests from unreasonably dangerous conditions.
   - **Breach:** Ballgamers breached that duty by failing to move customers inside. The bar should have monitored the weather and should have known the storm was coming as the TVs were showing weather warnings. Mr. Darby himself indicated he was relying on the establishment to move patrons inside if the conditions became dangerous.

     Ballgamers may also have breached that duty by failing to secure the tent. It is unclear whether Ballgamers properly erected the tent or whether the strength of the storm was unforeseeable (unlikely, given the broadcast warnings to seek shelter). In any case, Ballgamers likely should have removed the tent after learning of the approaching storm.
   - **Causation:** If Ballgamers was negligent in failing to secure the tent and/or in failing to move patrons inside, then that negligence caused Mr. Darby's injuries. But for that conduct, Mr. Darby would not have been hit by the tent and sustained injuries. It was foreseeable that failing to secure the tent could cause the tent to become unmoored and strike patrons. It was also foreseeable that allowing patrons to remain in the tent during a storm could cause injuries if the tent became unmoored.
   - **Damages:** Mr. Darby incurred damages when he sustained physical injuries.

     Ballgamers might argue that Mr. Darby assumed the risk because he saw the warnings but opted to remain outside. Ballgamers will also argue that Mr. Darby was comparatively negligent when he remained in the tent despite warnings to seek shelter.

Exercise 2

1. **Ballgamers violated Eastvale Municipal Code § 415-23.**

   The ordinance applies to Ballgamers because Ballgamers erected a temporary tent in its parking lot near a public right-of-way.

   Expert testimony may be needed, but the evidence suggests Ballgamers failed to ensure the tent was "properly anchored, weighted, or secured . . . to prevent displacement from wind or other environmental factors." It seems unlikely that the tent would become completely unmoored, even under strong winds, if the tent were properly erected.

   Ballgamers may argue that it did not violate the statute because there is no evidence the structure obstructed "pedestrian pathways, bike lanes, or vehicular traffic lanes." Although the tent became unmoored, there is no evidence it moved beyond Ballgamers' property.

2. **Mr. Darby was a member of the class of persons § 415-23 was designed to protect.**

   Mr. Darby will argue the statute was designed to "ensure public safety," which undoubtedly includes protecting patrons and guests using the tent. Mr. Darby was a member of the public and a patron of Ballgamers, and the statute was designed to protect him from injuries caused by the displacement of structures "due to wind, impact, or other environmental factors."

Ballgamers will argue the statute was designed to ensure that outdoor structures did not obstruct "public streets, sidewalks, and rights-of-way." Moreover, the statute emphasizes its purpose in "maintaining accessibility" of those public streets. Thus, Ballgamers will argue that the statute was not designed to protect patrons of a private business but to ensure that outdoor structures do not obstruct public rights-of-way.

Mr. Darby likely has the better argument. Courts construe safety statutes broadly to protect the public, especially when there is clear evidence of harm from exactly the kind of risk the statute describes (wind displacing a tent).

3. **Mr. Darby's injuries were the kind § 415-23 was designed to prevent.**

   Mr. Darby will argue that, because the statute was adopted to protect public safety and he was injured when the unsecured tent became unmoored and struck him, his injury is the kind the statute was designed to prevent.

   Ballgamers will argue the statute was designed to prevent injuries caused by structures falling into or obstructing rights-of-way, and Mr. Darby's injuries are outside the scope of those protections.

4. **The violation of § 415-23 was the proximate cause of Darby's injuries.**

   Actual cause exists because but for the failure to secure the tent, Mr. Darby would not have been struck by the tent and injured. And proximate cause also exists because it was foreseeable that failing to secure the tent could cause the tent to become unmoored and strike patrons. In other words, the tent becoming unmoored and striking patrons was within the scope of the risk created by Ballgamers' failure to secure the tent.

Exercise 3

1. **If the court concludes that the doctrine of negligence per se is inapplicable, then what other legal theories might apply to establish Ballgamers' liability?**

   If the plaintiff proves the elements of negligence per se, then the plaintiff has established a conclusive presumption of duty and breach of duty. This is essentially a shortcut that eases the plaintiff's burden of proof.

   Yet if the doctrine is inapplicable, then the plaintiff may nevertheless prove the elements of negligence. Even if the statute does not apply, Mr. Darby could still argue that Ballgamers acted unreasonably and breached a duty to patrons by failing to secure the tent, by refusing to take the tent down, and/or by failing to move patrons inside during the storm.

Exercise 4

1. **Do you believe the doctrine of implied assumption of the risk will limit or prevent Mr. Darby from recovering damages?**

   Ballgamers might argue that Mr. Darby assumed the risk of injury because Mr. Darby remained under the tent during the storm. Some of the relevant considerations include the following:

   - Mr. Darby knew about the risks of remaining inside because he saw the storm warnings, including the storm warnings advising viewers to seek shelter. Yet Mr. Darby chose to remain outside, conceding that he was waiting for Ballgamers to force patrons inside.

- Mr. Darby voluntarily assumed the risk of injury because he chose to remain outside. The risks of remaining outside during a heavy storm include the risk of the tent being blown over, striking those inside.
- The risks of remaining outside during a storm include the risk of being struck by displaced objects.

Mr. Darby will argue he did not voluntarily assume the risk of injury because he did not appreciate the dangers posed by the poorly erected tent, which was the cause of his injuries.

- Mr. Darby knew about the oncoming storm but had no way of knowing the tent was not secure and might blow away.
- Mr. Darby's decision was not voluntary or informed because he relied on those who erected the structure and monitored its safety to warn him if there was any danger.
- Mr. Darby was injured because Ballgamers failed to properly erect the tent or move guests inside despite storm warnings, not from a natural consequence of the storm.

Chapter 9: Causation

Alternative Causation: *In re Ethan Carter*

Exercise 1

As you assess whether Ethan can establish a *prima facie* case for negligence, you consider the following:

1. **Duty: What standard of care applies to determine whether the boys acted negligently?**

   Because Jake and Miles are minors (on the border between child and adult), one might be inclined to assume they will be held to the standard of care applicable to children. Ordinarily, a minor is held to the standard of care of a reasonable child of the same age, intelligence, and experience.

   Yet when a child engages in an activity that is typically reserved for adults, they are held to an objective standard of care. Using explosives or fireworks is such an activity. Consequently, Jake and Miles owed a duty to act with reasonable care under the circumstances. That includes handling explosives in a way that avoids foreseeable harm to others.

2. **Breach: Did Jake and Miles breach the applicable standard of care? Why or why not?**

   Jake and Miles threw powerful fireworks toward Ethan without warning him, even after Ethan cautioned them to be careful. This conduct was unreasonable under the circumstances because it presented a significant risk of injury to others.

3. **Actual Cause: Is the conduct of Jake or Miles the *actual cause* of Ethan's injury?**

   Ethan will have difficulty establishing that Jake and/or Miles caused Ethan's injuries. Both threw fireworks near him, one of them struck Ethan, and the evidence was destroyed during the explosion. Ethan may be unable to prove which firework hit him and caused his injuries. This explains why your senior partner directed you to *Summers v. Tice* as you may need to rely on theories of alternative causation.

4. **Proximate Cause: Were Ethan's injuries a foreseeable consequence of the boy(s)' negligence?**

   Throwing fireworks without warning presents a foreseeable risk that someone will be burned if the firework strikes or explodes near them. In other words, someone getting burned by a firework that strikes or explodes near them was within the scope of the risk created by the boys' conduct.

Exercise 2

1. **Relying on the reasoning from *Summers v. Tice,* prepare an argument that the negligence of Jake and Miles was the actual cause of Ethan's injuries.**

   Summers v. Tice establishes the doctrine of alternative liability. It applies when more than one person acts negligently, causing injury to the plaintiff, and the plaintiff cannot establish which party's negligence caused the injury. The burden of proof shifts to the defendants to prove "that the other person, or his other act, was the sole cause of the harm." Courts recognize it is unfair to deny the injured party a remedy "simply because he cannot prove how much damage each [tortfeasor] did, when it is certain that between them they did all."

Moreover, as the acting parties, "defendants are in a far better position to offer evidence to determine which one caused the injury."

Here, Ethan cannot prove which firework hit him, but Jack acted unreasonably by throwing an M-80 toward Ethan, and Miles acted unreasonably by throwing a cherry bomb toward Ethan. Both boys admitted their fault and apologized to Ethan. Thus, if Ethan can prove that each boy acted negligently, then the burden of proof will shift to Jack and Miles, and "it should rest with them each to absolve himself if he can." Miles and Jack must distinguish which firework was the actual cause of injury, or both may be liable.

Exercise 3

1. **What arguments might the boys present to avoid or minimize liability?**

   Reasonable Conduct—The boys may argue that their conduct was not negligent because it was typical, adolescent behavior. In fact, Miles's mother dismissed the incident by asserting, "Boys will be boys." The boys may argue that their conduct was not unreasonable under the circumstances.

   Comparative Negligence—The boys will argue Ethan was comparatively negligent because he participated in the activity and failed to move or protect himself, even after he warned the boys that the activity was dangerous. In fact, Miles's mother already asserted that Ethan was "just as much at fault." The boys may argue that Ethan's injuries were caused entirely or in part by his decision to stand near them when they lit powerful fireworks.

   Assumption of the Risk—The boys might also argue that, even if they were negligent, Ethan's claim is barred because Ethan assumed the risk of injury; Ethan also lit fireworks and stood by while Jack and Miles exploded the larger fireworks. Ethan knew the fireworks were dangerous. In fact, Ethan himself warned the boys about the dangers. Ethan nevertheless participated and remained nearby when the boys indicated they would light the larger fireworks. The inherent risks of using fireworks include being burned by them, so the boys may argue Ethan assumed the risk of injury inherent in the activity.

2. **How would you respond to the arguments you identify above?**

   Unreasonable Conduct—While teenagers can be careless, that will not excuse their negligent or reckless conduct, especially if they are engaged in an adult activity. Moreover, this conduct went beyond adolescent mischief: The boys threw explosive fireworks directly at another teenager.

   Comparative Negligence—Notably, unlike Jack and Miles, Ethan will not be held to an adult standard of care. Ethan himself did not engage in an inherently dangerous activity because he did not handle the high-powered fireworks. Ethan only lit smaller, less dangerous fireworks like sparklers and spinners, which are often handled by teenagers or even younger children. When Jack and Miles lit the more powerful fireworks, Ethan was merely a bystander, and simply remaining near someone who is engaging in a dangerous activity does not constitute *participation* in that activity. Thus, Ethan's conduct will be evaluated against a reasonable child of the same age, intelligence, and experience under similar circumstances.

   Ethan's conduct was also more measured and cautious than the other boys. Ethan warned the boys to be careful, and he advised them against using the larger fireworks. Ethan did not have an opportunity to react once he realized the boys threw the fireworks at him, and there is little evidence that he acted unreasonably under the circumstances. Ethan acted in a way most trusting 13-year-olds would act among a group of friends.

Even if a court finds Ethan was negligent in standing by while the boys lit the larger fireworks, his fault is low in comparison to the others boys. Thus, the finding will have a minimal impact on the level of damages.

Assumption of the Risk—Ethan will argue that he did not voluntarily assume a risk that either boy would throw a dangerous firework directly at him. Ethan stood away from the other boys and warned them about using the larger fireworks. Ethan only participated when the boys used smaller fireworks that are often handled by teenagers and younger children. Moreover, his injury was not caused by a risk that is inherent to fireworks; Ethan was injured because both boys recklessly threw fireworks in his direction, and he did not consent to being a target.

Chapter 9: Causation

Proximate Cause: *Baker v. Neon Palms*

Exercise 1

1. **Based on the facts you learned from your office consultation with Ms. Baker, set forth the allegations that you can use to support each element of a negligence claim against the Neon Palms.**

   - **Duty:** Neon Palms clearly owed a duty of care to invitees on the property. Neon Palms owed a duty to protect patrons from unreasonably dangerous conditions on the property and to protect patrons from harm, including by ensuring patrons are not overserved.

     Even if the incident occurred outside the establishment and on public property, Neon Palms may have a duty to protect patrons in the area if patrons routinely use the area to access the bar or to smoke.

   - **Breach:** Neon Palms breached the duty by continuing to serve alcohol to visibly intoxicated patrons, especially after one patron indicated they were overserved.

     Neon Palms also breached a duty to patrons by failing to address dangerous conditions on the property, such as Ms. Morgan's vomit and the icy sidewalk.

   - **Causation:** But for the overservice, Ms. Morgan would not have vomited, Ms. Baker would not have followed her outside, and Ms. Baker would not have slipped.

     Overserving patrons creates a foreseeable risk that they might become sick and, as intoxicated individuals have impaired coordination and impulse control, a risk that they may vomit in inconvenient places. This creates a foreseeable need for "rescue," and it is foreseeable that rescuing friends may be injured, including by falling in their rush to render aid.

   - **Damages:** Ms. Baker sustained damages, including damages associated with a fractured coccyx.

2. **Can you anticipate any arguments Neon Palms might make to avoid or minimize liability?**

   - **Duty:** Neon Palms may argue that it did not have a duty to monitor conditions *outside* the establishment, including the public sidewalk.

   - **Breach:** Neon Palms may argue that it did not overserve patrons. Bartenders have extensive experience monitoring levels of intoxication, and the Neon Palms bartender exercised his professional judgment and continued to serve drinks to Ms. Baker's friends. As none of the guests were driving, there was no risk of the guests causing an accident while intoxicated.

Neon Palms will also argue that it did not breach its duty to address dangerous conditions on the property because it did not have actual or constructive notice of the vomit or the ice. Ms. Morgan vomited moments before Ms. Baker went outside and fell, so the establishment had no opportunity to discover and respond to the danger. Unless patrons routinely vomit in the same area, it was not foreseeable that there would be a hazard in the area.

Neon Palms may also argue that it did not have actual or constructive notice of the icy conditions on the sidewalk outside. It is unclear how long the icy conditions existed on the sidewalk or whether ice routinely accumulated in the area.

- **Causation:** Overserving one patron does not create a foreseeable risk that another patron will follow the intoxicated person outside and slip on an icy sidewalk. Neon Palms may argue that Ms. Baker's decision to hurriedly go outside despite the icy conditions was a superseding act that broke the chain of causation.
- **Comparative Negligence:** Neon Palms might raise other defenses to a negligence claim. Neon Palms may argue that Ms. Baker was comparatively negligent because she knew the sidewalk was icy and could be slippery because Ms. Morgan was vomiting, but she nevertheless rushed to assist Ms. Morgan.
- **Assumption of the Risk:** Neon Palms might argue that Ms. Baker assumed the risk of injury when she voluntarily rushed across the icy sidewalk after she saw her friend vomit on it. That activity carries an inherent risk of slipping and falling.

3. **Are there any other facts you think will provide additional support for the claim? Is there any additional information you would like to know?**

The following information would help assess the strength of Ms. Baker's claim. This is a non-comprehensive list, so you may have other questions:

- Where did the fall occur? Was it in an area controlled by Neon Palms? Did guests often gather in the area to smoke or access the building?
- Is there video footage of the incident? Did any staff members witness the incident? Are any staff members posted outside?
- Was the area well lit? Were there other factors that contributed to a risk of fall?
- Did Neon Palms have policies to inspect the area for ice or other dangerous conditions? What caused the ice to accumulate the night of the accident? Did ice frequently accumulate there? Had there been other incidents involving the fall of a guest?
- Have there been other incidents involving overservice? Have guests ever vomited inside or outside the establishment?
- Does the bar have any policies about overservice or assisting intoxicated guests?
- Was there visible evidence confirming that Ms. Morgan was intoxicated? Did other guests or friends make similar observations?
- Were other guests visibly intoxicated? Did others vomit or have other accidents related to their alcohol consumption?
- Are there receipts or records of how much alcohol Ms. Morgan consumed?
- Was Ms. Baker intoxicated? Could that have contributed to her fall?

Exercise 2

1. **How are the facts from *Crankshaw* similar to the facts of Ms. Baker's case? How are the facts different?**

   Below are some of the similarities and differences between the cases:

   - In both cases, the defendant's negligence arguably caused the third party to vomit. In *Crankshaw*, the plaintiff's friend became ill after eating spoiled food. In Ms. Baker's case, her friend became ill after allegedly consuming too much alcohol.
   - In both cases, the plaintiff was injured while attempting to render aid to the third party. Both plaintiffs slipped and fell in vomit on the floor.
   - In both cases, the plaintiff alleged that the business breached its duty to invitees by failing to clean or warn guests about the slippery floor.
   - Both cases raise the same legal issue of whether the plaintiff's injury was a foreseeable consequence of the business' negligent conduct (serving spoiled food and over-serving alcohol).

   The cases are distinguishable because:

   - The business's conduct in Ms. Baker's case created a more foreseeable risk that a guest would vomit and require rescue. Vomiting is a common risk of over-intoxication, and intoxicated guests foreseeably need assistance given their reduced coordination and impulse control. In addition, falls are a foreseeable risk of drinking.

     In contrast, while serving spoiled food does create a risk that affected guests may vomit, that outcome is less likely to occur contemporaneously at the restaurant. Moreover, such a guest is in less need of assistance as other senses are not impaired.
   - In Ms. Baker's case, Ms. Baker warned the bartender that her friends were consuming too much alcohol, and she asked the bartender to stop serving them. Thus, the business had clear notice of the risk.

     In *Crankshaw*, there is no evidence the business had notice of the vomit on the floor or knew that a patron had become ill.
   - In Ms. Baker's case, her friend vomited immediately outside the bar within view of those inside. The hazard was obvious on inspection, suggesting the business breached a duty by failing to address it.

     In *Crankshaw*, the guest vomited inside the bathroom behind a closed door, and no staff member was aware of the hazard or should have anticipated it.

2. **Does the court's reasoning in *Crankshaw* influence your assessment of Ms. Baker's possible claims? Why or why not?**

   In *Crankshaw*, the court held that a defendant should not be responsible for "the imaginary or possible result of the tortious act" if "other and contingent circumstances preponderate largely in causing the injurious effect." In that case, while the defendant was negligent in serving spoiled food, the court held that the defendant's negligence was not the proximate cause of the plaintiff's injuries because other and contingent circumstances largely caused the plaintiff's injury. In particular, the court found it was not foreseeable that the affected patron would become ill, vomit inside the bathroom, and another guest would fall in the vomit while attempting to render aid.

   At first glance, given the similarities between the two cases, this reasoning seems to defeat Ms. Baker's claim. Yet a court may find the case is inapplicable because Ms. Baker's injuries were a more foreseeable risk of Neon Palms' actions. Unlike serving bad shrimp, overserving alcohol creates a clear risk of vomiting. There is also a foreseeable need for rescue or aid as intoxicated persons often require assistance.

Further, unlike the restaurant in *Crankshaw*, Neon Palms had actual knowledge of Ms. Morgan's condition as Ms. Baker asked the bartender to stop serving drinks to her friends. Yet the bartender continued to serve alcohol. The bar may also have had actual or constructive notice of Ms. Morgan's illness as she was visible from the bar and was sick in an area where guests presumably gather to smoke after drinking, further contributing to circumstances that are likely to lead to vomiting.

Exercise 3

1. **Prepare notes for a call with Ms. Baker advising her of the implications of Neon Palms' assertion that they were unaware of the burst pipe the night Ms. Baker visited the bar.**

   The following are important points to convey to Ms. Baker about the defendant's arguments:

   > In *Byrne v. Wal-Mart*, a customer slipped and fell inside a Wal-Mart store. The court refused to find Wal-Mart liable because the plaintiff failed to conclusively demonstrate what condition caused her to fall, how long it had been present, and whether the store knew or should have known about its presence. The court held that, without evidence of fault, "[p]roof merely of the occurrence of a fall on a floor within business premises is insufficient to show negligence on the part of the proprietor."
   >
   > Neon Palms is relying on this case because it claims the icy conditions outside the bar were caused by a pipe that burst unexpectedly shortly before Ms. Morgan went outside. This is influential because it suggests the bar did not actually know about the ice and did not have sufficient time time to discover and address it. Stated simply, Neon Palms will argue that the mere existence of ice is insufficient to establish that Neon Palms was negligent.
   >
   > While this is influential, there are other factors that suggest Neon Palms was negligent. Ultimately, you did not fall because you slipped on ice; you fell because you slipped in Ms. Morgan's vomit, which was caused by her over-intoxication. We can still argue that the bar knew she had been overserved, creating a foreseeable risk that she would become ill, need support, and someone might be injured while helping her. We might also argue that Neon Palms knew or should have known of the hazard created by Ms. Morgan's vomit because the bartender knew she was intoxicated, and Ms. Morgan was visible from inside the bar.

Chapter 9: Causation

Proximate Cause: Vankirk v. Safe Haven Security Co.

Exercise 1

1. **What are the challenges Vankirk will experience in establishing causation?**

   Below are possible arguments that Safe Haven's actions did not cause Ms. Vankirk's injuries:

   - Safe Haven may argue that, while the security system can alert law enforcement and the homeowner that an intrusion is occurring, the defects in the system did not cause the burglary. Rather, the burglary was caused by the criminal acts of third parties.

Thus, Ms. Vankirk cannot argue that the intrusion would not have occurred but for the negligent wiring.

Ms. Vankirk will likely argue that, had the system functioned property, it would have deterred or interrupted the burglary, and she would not have encountered the perpetrators in her home. Moreover, had the system worked as advertised, then it would have notified law enforcement, who might have disrupted the burglary.

- Safe Haven will argue that the criminal conduct of third parties severed the chain of causation between its allegedly negligent installation and Ms. Vankirk's injuries.

  Ms. Vankirk will argue that the security system was installed to prevent criminal intrusions. Thus, failure to install a proper security system creates a foreseeable risk of criminal acts in the unprotected home.

- Safe Haven may argue that Ms. Vankirk's decision to flee was an intervening act that broke the chain of causation. Ms. Vankirk was injured because she voluntarily moved through the home during an active burglary and collided with one of the perpetrators.

  Ms. Vankirk will argue that failure to install the system creates a foreseeable risk that criminal activity will occur, which may lead to a confrontation with the perpetrators and/or a homeowner's attempt to flee.

Exercise 2

1. **After reviewing your notes above, how do you respond to Mr. Hartgrove's assertion that Safe Haven is not legally liable for injuries caused by "law-breaking hooligans"? What is your opinion about whether Ms. Vankirk can establish that the burglary was a foreseeable intervening cause of her injuries?**

   Given the precedent above, Mr. Hartgrove's assertion is likely incorrect.

   While the criminal acts of third parties are often considered superseding causes that break the chain of causation, a defendant may be liable for injuries caused by the criminal acts of others if the defendant could reasonably foresee that their negligence would increase the risk of harm by a third party's criminal act. For example, in *Central Alarm of Tucson*, the court held that an alarm company could be liable for damages caused by a theft because the theft was a foreseeable consequence of negligently securing the alarm system's key.

   Similarly, the burglary and confrontation in Ms. Vankirk's home was a foreseeable consequence of Safe Haven's failure to properly install the security system. Safe Haven advertised that its system would deter and prevent criminal conduct, and Ms. Vankirk ordered the system with that expectation. Thus, Safe Haven had a duty to use reasonable care in installing the system to prevent the very harm that occurred, a criminal intrusion. Safe Haven's breach of that duty increased the likelihood of criminal activity, and the burglary was a direct and foreseeable consequence of the improper installation.

Exercise 3

1. **What is your recommendation about a settlement with Ms. Vankirk? Explain your answer in light of the client's goals.**

   This is a subjective question that calls for your opinion about the case. Consider the following factors:

   - **Safe Haven wishes to avoid negative publicity.**

     This case has the potential to negatively impact Safe Haven's reputation and goodwill in the community. The public will be extremely sympathetic to Ms. Vankirk, who was the victim of criminal acts in the sanctity of her home because she relied on a system that failed. Ms. Vankirk's descriptions of her fears, injuries, and trauma are likely to elicit strong emotional reactions. Moreover, customers may feel that Safe Haven engaged in deceptive marketing practices.

The impact could cause severe financial losses for Safe Haven if customers lose confidence in Safe Haven products.

If the parties reach a confidential settlement, then Safe Haven may be protected from the reputational harm described above because Safe Haven can exercise some control over the narrative. The agreement should include non-disparagement and no admission of liability clauses.

- **Safe Haven is willing to litigate the case if they are certain to win.**

  While there is a possibility that Ms. Vankirk will be unsuccessful or may receive a reduced award, Safe Haven is not certain to win at trial.

  A jury might find that Ms. Vankirk's confrontation with the intruders was an unforeseeable, superseding cause of her injuries, which would sever the chain of causation and defeat Ms. Vankirk's claim. A jury might also find that Ms. Vankirk was comparatively negligent and/or assumed the risk of injury when she attempted to flee despite the risks. This seems unlikely as Ms. Vankirk fled because she was understandably afraid, and the confrontation with the intruder was accidental.

  Even if the jury does find Ms. Vankirk was comparatively negligent, that will only reduce the final judgment in proportion to her comparative fault. Moreover, the arguments are only relevant to Ms. Vankirk's claims about her personal injuries, not the property damage associated with the burglary.

  Ultimately, Ms. Vankirk has a strong claim for negligence. Safe Haven owed a duty to use reasonable care when installing the system, which included a duty to prevent or deter criminal acts. Initial expert testimony suggests Safe Haven breached that duty by failing to properly install the system. But for the failed installation, the burglary would have been deterred or interrupted. As analyzed above, the burglary was a foreseeable consequence of failing to properly install the system. Ms. Vankirk sustained demonstrable damages as a result of the incident, including physical, property, and emotional harms.

  In addition, there is a risk that, if the jury finds for Ms. Vankirk, the judgment will be high. A jury is likely to empathize with Ms. Vankirk and may wish to punish Safe Haven. A settlement offers a more certain outcome and allows Safe Haven some control over the final payment.

- **Safe Haven wishes to avoid expensive litigation but has significant revenue.**

  This case is likely to involve significant litigation costs. Both parties will likely retain experts to advise about the operation of the system and the installation methods. There may be multiple parties to depose, including Ms. Vankirk, Safe Haven employees, responding police officers, etc. There will be extensive discovery requests, which may lead to disputes. Costs could exceed tens or even hundreds of thousands of dollars, which could easily exceed the costs of paying Ms. Vankirk's demands.

Exercise 4

1. **How does the "shabby millionaire" rule influence your assessment of whether Ms. Vankirk can recover lost income of $30,000?**

The "shabby millionaire" rule is to economic loss what the "eggshell skull" doctrine is to physical damages. It holds that a defendant takes the plaintiff as they find them, even if the plaintiff's income is higher than a typical person. In assessing damages, the factfinder will not award the lost income of a reasonable/typical person, but the lost income of the plaintiff herself. This is true even if the plaintiff is self-employed but can nevertheless document lost opportunities and her customary compensation.

In this case, Ms. Vankirk has an unusually high income, but Safe Haven took her as they found her. If Ms. Vankirk can prove she lost high-paying engagements because she was required to supervise repairs, address her trauma, and replace lost property, then those losses are a direct consequence of Safe Haven's negligence and are recoverable.

Safe Haven may argue that Ms. Vankirk's compensation is speculative and, unless Ms. Vankirk can prove damages by offering prior contracts, documented offers, and tax records, then those damages may be reduced. Moreover, Safe Haven may demand proof that the fallout from the burglary truly forced Ms. Vankirk to give up the engagements. In that case, Ms. Vankirk must prove why the consequences of the burglary required her to take time from work.

Exercise 5

1. **Based on the rules above, evaluate whether Vankirk may recover damages for the injuries Opposing Counsel identified in his original demand letter or during your phone call.**

Claim	Category (Special, General, Other)	Likelihood of Recovery
a. Medical expenses $8,200	Special damages	Medical expenses are directly related to the incident because Ms. Vankirk was injured when she collided with the burglar. Medical expenses are economic losses and are categorized as special damages. Safe Haven may dispute whether it should be liable for cosmetic treatments, which were not covered by insurance because they were elective. Safe Haven may argue the procedures were thus unnecessary, and it should not be liable for "vanity expenses." Yet courts frequently permit plaintiffs to recover costs of reasonable cosmetic procedures that are medically recommended to restore appearance or function, even if the treatments are not covered by insurance. Cosmetic treatments may influence the plaintiff's emotional well-being or social functioning.
b. Stolen property $22,450	Special damages	Property loss is directly related to the incident because the intruders stole several valuable items during the burglary. Property losses are economic and are categorized as special damages. These damages are likely recoverable so long as Ms. Vankirk provides reliable documentation. The award may be reduced if the used property diminished in value. If values are speculative, then Safe Haven may challenge the stated values and demand proof of the actual value or offer competing appraisals.

Claim	Category (Special, General, Other)	Likelihood of Recovery
c. Property repair $6,500	Special damages	Property repairs are directly related to the incident because the intruders damaged property during the burglary. Property repairs are economic losses and are categorized as special damages. These damages are almost certainly recoverable, and Ms. Vankirk has an invoice documenting the costs. Safe Haven may demand a second opinion to evaluate whether the costs were reasonable.
d. Security system replacement $10,500	Special damages	Ms. Vankirk may categorize this as a property repair, which was directly related to the incident because the system was not functioning. Property repairs are economic losses and are categorized as special damages. Ms. Vankirk will argue that she lost trust in the existing system and switched to a different provider. The factfinder may find this cost justified to mitigate further harm or restore protections in Ms. Vankirk's home. Safe Haven will argue that Ms. Vankirk could have simply repaired the existing system and possibly avoided any expense if the system was under warranty. If the new system was more expensive than Safe Haven's system, then Safe Haven could challenge the costs, arguing that it should not be liable to pay for a system upgrade.
e. Lost income $30,000	Special damages	Lost wages are directly related to the incident because Ms. Vankirk lost potential engagements while she was addressing the fallout from the burglary. Lost wages are economic losses and are categorized as special damages. As established above, these losses are likely recoverable if Ms. Vankirk can offer concrete proof of the lost value. Safe Haven may dispute why it was necessary for her to decline the opportunities or whether she could have mitigated damages by outsourcing or delaying repairs.
f. Pain and suffering *Potentially raised at trial	General damages	Pain and suffering are directly related to the incident because Ms. Vankirk was understandably traumatized by the incident. Pain and suffering are noneconomic harms and are categorized as general damages. Ms. Vankirk will likely argue that she experienced physical pain from her bruises, sprain, and facial injuries. She will also likely argue that she sustained emotional trauma from the fear, stress, and disruption to her daily life. General damages are difficult to quantify, and the factfinder will determine the final award. As asserted above, this award could be high if the factfinder is sympathetic to Ms. Vankirk's claims.

Claim	Category (Special, General, Other)	Likelihood of Recovery
g. Punitive damages *Potentially raised at trial	Other	As stated in § 8.8, punitive damages are generally not recoverable in negligence cases. Ms. Vankirk has not alleged that Safe Haven acted with gross negligence, willfulness or malice. However, Ms. Vankirk may ultimately allege that Save Haven's breach—a complete failure to install a functioning security system—constitutes gross negligence. The success of that claim is not clear without additional discovery, but such an allegation might expose Safe Haven to punitive damages.
h. Attorneys' fees *Potentially raised at trial, currently estimated to be $4,000	Other	As stated in § 8.9, litigants must generally pay their own attorneys' fees. You should research whether any statutes permit recovery of fees related to installation of security systems (unlikely). You should also carefully review the installation agreement to determine if there are provisions regarding fees in the event of a dispute. While attorneys' fees may not be court-ordered, Safe Haven could agree to pay fees as part of a settlement agreement. Safe Haven may wish to pay fees to facilitate an out-of-court settlement.

Exercise 6

1. **Will you recommend that Safe Haven accept Ms. Vankirk's demand to pay $74,450? Why or why not?**

As this calls for an opinion, there is no correct or incorrect answer. Your assessment is likely influenced by your analysis in Exercise 5 and your assessment of whether damages are recoverable. Your assessment should balance the following considerations and risks:

- Likelihood of a verdict for Ms. Vankirk: **High**. Ms. Vankirk has strong legal claims and is likely to secure juror sympathies, potentially resulting in a costly judgment.
- Costs of litigation: **High**. The case will involve extensive costs to develop evidence, as assessed above.
- Reputational concerns: **High**. The trial could result in negative publicity, loss of goodwill, and financial harm due to loss of consumer confidence.

If you recommend settlement, then you likely balanced the costs of litigation against the seemingly reasonable demand. Even if some of Ms. Vankirk's damages are speculative or subject to challenge, the benefits of quietly settling may justify some over-compensation.

If you recommend against settlement, then you likely believe the demand is excessive and hope to further negotiate. You may advise the client to challenge some of the demands to lower the final settlement amount. You might also propose a mediated resolution.

Chapter 10: Special Cases

Respondeat superior: *Varela Furniture & Appliance Store*

Exercise 1

1. **Using the legal authority from your research above and the facts you learned from your review of the file, draft an argument to insert into the motion for summary judgment. The heading summarizing your argument is included below.**

The doctrine of *respondeat superior* is inapplicable because Defendant's employee was not acting within the scope of his employment when the incidents described in Plaintiff's complaint occurred.

An employer may be vicariously liable for an employee's negligent conduct under the doctrine of *respondeat superior* if the employee was acting in the course and scope of employment. An employee is acting in the course and scope of employment if the employee's acts are done within the scope of the employee's general authority, in furtherance of the employer's business, and for the accomplishment of the object for which the employee was hired.

If an employee commits a negligent act while temporarily deviating from employment responsibilities, then the employer may nevertheless be liable for the employee's act if the employee's deviation was a mere detour—a minor deviation in time and geographic area. Yet the employer will not be liable if the employee's deviation was a frolic—an unauthorized and substantial deviation.

In *Chorey, Taylor & Feil*, the plaintiff filed a personal injury claim against a law firm under a theory of *respondeat superior* after the firm's employee struck her car and injured her. The firm's employee had been assisting some of the firm's attorneys as they established a new firm, and the employee had agreed to work for the new firm. The employee was driving her personal vehicle to deliver a check for telephone service for the new law firm when she struck and injured another driver. The court held the doctrine of *respondeat superior* was inapplicable because, when the crash occurred, the employee was not acting in furtherance of her employer's business and was not "authorized by her employer to accomplish the purpose in pursuance of which the tort was committed." While the employee's actions may have aided some of the attorneys in the existing firm, the employee's conduct ultimately benefitted a non-existing entity, not her employer.

In contrast, Mr. Sterling was clearly an employee of the Defendant, Varela Furniture, and the alleged tort occurred while he was driving a Varela van. Mr. Sterling was authorized to operate the van to make deliveries, which was the scope of his employment responsibilities.

Mr. Sterling deviated from those responsibilities when he accepted payment to deliver a customer's personal television. Mr. Sterling was not authorized to make the delivery, it was unrelated to any business purpose of Varela, Varela had no control over the job, and it financially benefited Mr. Sterling, not his employer. There is no evidence Mr. Varela authorized the deviation or allowed employees to accept personal jobs from Varela customers. While the deviation was relatively minor in time and scope, even a short deviation can be a frolic if the employee abandons his employment responsibilities to serve personal interests. Thus, Mr. Sterling was engaged in a frolic, a significant deviation from Mr. Sterling's employment responsibilities.

Like the employee in *Chorey*, Mr. Sterling was engaged in personal business, and his employer should not be liable. In fact, Mr. Sterling's delivery was even more disconnected from his employer's business than the employee's actions in *Chorey*. In *Chorey*, the employee was helping lawyers who worked for her current employer as they established a new firm, so her actions were at least tangentially related to her employment responsibilities, and her actions indirectly benefited attorneys in the firm. In this case,

Mr. Sterling accepted payment and made the delivery pursuant to a purely personal transaction.

Therefore, the doctrine of *respondeat superior* is inapplicable because Mr. Sterling was engaged in a frolic and was not acting within the scope of his employment when the incidents described in Plaintiff's complaint occurred.

2. **How might the plaintiff respond to the argument above?**

The plaintiff might make some of the following arguments:

- The deviation was a detour because it was limited in time and scope. Mr. Sterling only had to travel six blocks from his next scheduled delivery to complete the job, and he only spent 30 extra minutes making the delivery.
- Mr. Sterling used a Varela-branded van during the deviation. This supports an inference that the employee was engaged in business for his employer. Mr. Varela gave drivers discretion to determine their route and timing of deliveries, and Mr. Sterling exercised his discretion to make an additional stop. There is no evidence that Varela policies prohibited such activities.
- Mr. Sterling was employed to deliver furniture and heavy items to customers. At the time of the incident, Mr. Sterling was delivering a heavy item, which was within the scope of his employment responsibilities. His conduct was not a radical departure from his job responsibilities and implicated the same skills and equipment.
- Mr. Sterling's actions indirectly benefited Varela because Sterling's action helped maintain goodwill and customer satisfaction. The job was incidental to Varela's business because customers will routinely need assistance removing old items.

Exercise 2

1. **Does this testimony influence your analysis of whether the doctrine of *respondeat superior* is applicable? Why or why not?**

This testimony is extremely influential. Mr. Varela's awareness and tacit approval of Mr. Sterling's actions suggest Mr. Sterling was acting in scope of his employment. If the employer approves of the detour, then the action is no longer unauthorized, and it falls within the scope of the employee's general authority. The employer can no longer argue that the employer did not control the deviation, and the employer should foresee that it might be liable for any negligent acts of the employee during the deviation.

2. **Would it change your opinion if, with Mr. Varela's knowledge, Ian Sterling routinely accepted extra payment to dispose of replaced furniture?**

If the employer permits or acquiesces in an employee's conduct, even if the activity strays from formal job duties, then courts may find that the employee acted within the scope of employment.

Based on the additional facts above, the employer routinely acquiesces to a recurring deviation by an employee, and those deviations are performed during working hours and with company equipment. Thus, the deviation is performed with implied authority and is within the scope of the employee's responsibilities. The activity appears to be a routine part of the business and is tolerated because it presumably benefits (or at least does not harm) the employer.

3. **Would it change your opinion if Ian Sterling customarily gave Mr. Varela a "cut" of his earnings after disposing of used furniture?**

This establishes the clearest argument to hold Mr. Varela liable for Mr. Sterling's actions. If Mr. Varela not only tolerated the recurring deviations but also personally benefited from them, then Mr. Varela can no longer argue that the deviations were unauthorized or performed for the personal benefit of the employee. If Mr. Varela received part of the payment, then Mr. Varela effectively incorporated the practice into his business model, and the employee's actions were performed in furtherance of the business.

Chapter 10: Special Cases

Professional Negligence: *Varela Furniture & Appliance Store*

Exercise 1

1. **Are the elements of a professional negligence claim any different from the elements for a general negligence claim? If so, how?**

   While there are minor differences, the essential elements are the same.

   - As legal professionals, attorneys owe a heightened duty of care to clients. Attorneys must exercise the level of skill, care, and diligence expected of a reasonably competent professional in that field.
   - An attorney breaches that duty if the attorney fails to exercise the requisite level of care. Expert testimony may be required to establish how a reasonable practitioner would have acted and/or how the defendant's conduct failed to comport with the required level of care.
   - The plaintiff must show the attorney's breach was the actual and proximate cause of the plaintiff's injuries. Expert testimony may be required to establish how the breach influenced the client's outcome.
   - Damages may include losses associated with loss of a legal claim, a less favorable legal outcome, etc.

2. **Do you believe Mr. Varela has a viable claim for negligence? Can he plead all of the elements to establish a *prima facie* claim?**

   Mr. Varela will likely make some of the following arguments:

   - The parties had an attorney-client relationship, and the firm owed him a duty to exercise the level of skill, care, and diligence expected of a reasonably competent professional in that field.
   - The firm breached that duty by failing to meet a filing deadline. Despite a reminder from a junior attorney, the supervising attorney failed to properly monitor deadlines and failed to file a response to a motion for summary judgment.

     The firm may also have breached its duty by failing to inform the client of the error. The firm did not discuss the implications of the error or advise the client about his options. Instead, the supervising attorney misled the client by recommending settlement.
   - Mr. Varela may have some difficulty establishing how the breach led to a less favorable outcome. Mr. Varela may argue that, but for the misleading recommendations, he would not have agreed to a settlement.

     Mr. Varela might also argue that, had the attorney filed the response, the court would have denied the motion for summary judgment because there was a material issue in dispute (whether Mr. Sterling was acting in the scope of his employment). This is a clearer argument if the judge grants the motion for summary judgment because the motion was unopposed.
   - Depending on the outcome at trial, Mr. Varela may argue that he sustained the following damages: loss of a valuable defense, increased exposure to liability, attorney's fees, or reputational harm.

PART III—OTHER TORTS

Chapter 11: Defamation

Shakin' Cajun v. Richmond

Exercise 1

1. **Use the limited facts available so far to draft allegations that Mr. Richmond: 1) published; 2) an actionable defamatory statement; 3) of and concerning the Shakin' Cajun; and 4) the statement damaged Shakin' Cajun's reputation.**

   There is flexibility here, but an example of Shakin' Cajun's allegations are below:

   1) By submitting his review to multiple online restaurant review apps, including *Shriek*, which has been ranked the most-used restaurant review app for the last 10 years, Terrence Richmond published his defamatory statements about *Shakin' Cajun*.

   2) Terrence Richmond published at least three defamatory statements: 1) that Shakin' Cajun uses imitation lobster that it passes off as crawfish (it does not); 2) that Shakin' Cajun replaces top shelf vodka with cheaper vodka (it does not); and 3) that Shakin' Cajun has been cited for this activity by the ABC (it has not).

   3) There can be no doubt that Mr. Richmond's review of Shakin' Cajun was "of and concerning" Shakin' Cajun. The review itself mentions "Shakin' Cajun" no less than twice.

   4) Damages* resulting from Mr. Richmond's defamatory statements include damage to *Shakin' Cajun*'s reputation, as evidenced by some of the comments to the review, for example, "*Shakin' Cajun*'s never getting my money again."; "No more *Shakin' Cajun* for me!"; and "I used to love *Shakin' Cajun* but I guess not anymore."

      Additional damages resulting from Mr. Richmond's defamatory statements include the lost profits suffered by *Shakin' Cajun* since Mr. Richmond's publication of his review. Prior to Mr. Richmond's publication of his defamatory statements, *Shakin' Cajun* was operating at full capacity between the hours of 6 P.M. and 10 P.M. on Thursday, Friday, and Saturday nights. In the three months since Mr. Richmond's publication of his defamatory statements, *Shakin' Cajun* has never exceeded 80 percent capacity on any given night between the hours of 6 P.M. and 10 P.M.

      *Note that it may be better to avoid stating an exact "sum" of the plaintiff's damages in an initial complaint; otherwise, you may have to continually amend the complaint with updated estimates about damages.

2. **Are there any additional facts that, if they exist, would strengthen Shakin' Cajun's defamation claim? Are there any that will weaken the claim?**

   Facts that might **strengthen** *Shakin' Cajun*'s claim include facts that leave no doubt as to the falsity of Mr. Richmond's allegedly defamatory statements. For example:

   - Facts proving *Shakin' Cajun* does not use imitation lobster. For example, proof that imitation lobster is more expensive than crawfish, in which case using imitation lobster makes no business sense; proof that Ms. O'Brien has a direct connection to a crawfish source; or restaurant records proving purchase of crawfish.
   - Facts proving *Shakin' Cajun* does not replace top shelf liquor with rail liquor: perhaps a restaurant policy that forbids such conduct, evidence that restaurant workers understand that doing so is a fireable offense.

- Facts showing *Shakin' Cajun* has never been cited by ABC. For example, a full record of ABC's history with *Shakin' Cajun*.
- Facts proving Mr. Richmond was motivated to defame the restaurant. For example, Mr. Richmond had a dispute with the owner, was a disgruntled former employee, or owned a competitor restaurant.
- Facts showing reputational harm. For example, social media metrics showing wide dissemination, negative media coverage, or comments to Mr. Richmond's post that tend to show reliance on his negative review.

Facts that might **weaken** *Shakin' Cajun*'s claim might include:

- Facts that tend to show that *Shakin' Cajun*'s lost profits are or could be attributable to other factors besides Richmond's review, for instance, if the cost of ingredients, liquor, or other restaurant staples has risen due to inflation, tariffs, shortages, or any other reason.
- Facts that might tend to show that any of Mr. Richmond's statements are true or even substantially true.
- The existence of other similarly negative reviews of *Shakin' Cajun*, which will tend to show that Mr. Richmond's negative review (true or not) did not necessarily *cause* the restaurant's damages, if any.

Exercise 2

1. **Assuming you move forward with the lawsuit against Mr. Richmond, what arguments do you anticipate he will make about whether his *Shriek* review is capable of defamatory meaning?**

   Mr. Richmond might make some of the following arguments:

   - Mr. Richmond's statements in the *Shriek* review were just his opinion and thus are not actionable as defamation.

     In *Gross,* the court drew a clear distinction between "expressions of opinion, which are not actionable, and assertions of fact, which may form the basis of a viable [defamation] claim." In this case, a reasonable reader would interpret many of Mr. Richmond's statements to be mere "rhetorical hyperbole," constituting his negative opinion about Shakin' Cajun's atmosphere and ambiance. For example, Mr. Richmond's assertion that the restaurant is an "absolute disaster" and a "culinary criminal," that it smells of "regret," that its wait staff are "bitter," and that the server was a "Space Cadet." These are reasonably interpreted to be the author's subjective opinions and are likely not actionable in defamation.

   - Mr. Richmond may assert that readers understand the exaggerated nature of online reviews and know to read such reviews with skepticism.

     In *James*, the court held that, in determining whether statements have a defamatory meaning, the factfinder must consider the publication as a whole and its effect on the average reader. For example, in *Gross*, the plaintiff alleged that the *New York Times* defamed him after it published a series of articles suggesting that he mishandled investigations and engaged in cover-ups to protect police officers and city officials. The articles appeared in the news section, not as op-eds, and were based on "what purported to be a thorough investigation." The court noted that, while many assertions in the article "would be understood by the reasonable reader as mere hypotheses premised on stated facts," the overall tone of the article "encourag[ed] the reasonable reader to be less skeptical and more willing to conclude that [they] stat[ed] or impl[ied] facts."

Mr. Richmond will argue that the facts are inapposite here. While the articles in *Gross* were published in the news section of a respected paper that follows journalistic standards, Mr. Richmond's review was posted via an opinion app. Mr. Richmond did not imply that he had engaged in any kind of investigation into the business practices of the restaurant. The average reader, reviewing Mr. Richmond's post as a whole, would take the light-hearted and jovial review as an assertion of opinion. Even if Mr. Richmond did suggest that he had inside knowledge about the restaurant, a reasonable reader would interpret his assertions as "mere hypotheses premised on stated facts." Readers will understand the post was a restaurant rant, not an investigative expose and understand' that the review reflects Mr. Richmond's opinions.

- While Mr. Richmond might have had a few details wrong, the statements are, overall, substantially true and therefore not actionable or not capable of defamatory meaning.
- *Shakin' Cajun* cannot establish that Mr. Richmond's negative review caused or will cause those who might have patronized the restaurant to stop visiting the restaurant because of what they read. People leave negative reviews of restaurants all the time and other people still go to those restaurants.

2. How will you respond to those arguments?

You might consider the following arguments:

- Shakin' Cajun will likely argue that several of Mr. Richmond's statements could be interpreted by a reasonable reader to be statements of fact.

In *Gross*, the court outlined various factors to distinguish between statements of opinion and statements of fact. The court considered: (1) whether the specific language in issue has a precise meaning which is readily understood; (2) whether the statements are capable of being proven true or false; and (3) whether readers will understand that the statements are opinion based on "either the full context of the communication in which the statement appears or the broader social context and surrounding circumstances."

The court also noted that statements are more likely to be defamatory if they imply "a basis in facts which are not disclosed to the reader or listener." Such statements suggest that the speaker has information that is unknown to the reader but supports the truth of the statement. For example, in *Gross*, the *New York Times* published a series of articles about the plaintiff that were "calculated to give the impression they were the product of some deliberation." The court found the statements could be interpreted as factual and defamatory assertions.

Mr. Richmond's review includes several statements that suggest he has information that is unknown to the reader and could reasonably be interpreted as factual claims: Mr. Richmond claimed some expertise in identifying crawfish, and he asserted that the restaurant uses imitation meat; Mr. Richmond claimed to witness the bartender replacing expensive alcohol with a cheaper product; and Mr. Richmond alleged that the restaurant had repeatedly been cited by the Alcohol & Beverage Commission (ABC). The statements are specific and precise and are readily understood by a reader. The statements are also capable of being proven true or false: the restaurant can prove which ingredients it purchases and uses in its crawfish dishes; can prove whether it has purchased and used top shelf liquors; and can prove whether it has been cited by the ABC. And while readers will understand that much of the review is hyperbole, a reasonable reader could interpret the specific statements to be factual assertions. In fact, many of the comments responding to Mr. Richmond's posts suggest that readers did exactly that.

While the review does contain colorful language, the statements are part of a narrative that purports to describe factual truths about the restaurant. An average reader could interpret the statements to be a factual report about fraud and regulatory violations.

- The gist of the statements in their entirety leaves no doubt that they are capable of defamatory meaning.

  In *James*, the allegedly defamatory statements appeared in the context of a broader article about the plaintiff's successful business, and the court found the statements were not defamatory in that context. In contrast, the broader context of Mr. Richmond's posts was negative and hostile. The "whole scope" of the article "tends to harm the reputation" of Shakin' Cajun.

- Shakin' Cajun will argue that the allegations are patently false and will attempt to produce evidence of their falsity.

- The average reader will think considerably less of *Shakin' Cajun* and be less willing to patronize the restaurant. This is demonstrated by some of the comments to Mr. Richmond's review. The review damages the restaurant's reputation with consumers and partners.

Chapter 12: Invasion of the Right to Privacy/Intrusion upon Seclusion

Embry v. Harman Woodworks

Exercise 1

1. **What are the elements of invasion of privacy as stated in *McLain*?**

   The court in *McLain* cited the definition from the Second Restatement, and the elements are as follows (the precise wording may vary):

   - The defendant acted with intent to intrude upon the solitude or seclusion of another;
   - The defendant intruded, physically or otherwise, upon the solitude or seclusion of another; and
   - The intrusion would be highly offensive to a reasonable person.

2. **Prepare an argument that analogizes your case to the facts and reasoning in *McLain*.**

   The *McLain* case deals with somewhat similar facts. It also addresses the issue of whether surveillance might be "highly offensive to a reasonable person" and reasons that someone in Mr. Embry's position should expect that his workers' compensation claim would be investigated, impliedly limiting his expectation of privacy.

   Example of an argument analogizing to *McLain*:

   Mr. Embry's claim of intrusion upon seclusion against Harman Woodworks cannot succeed unless he can establish that Harman intentionally intruded upon the seclusion of Mr. Embry's private affairs and that such intrusion was highly offensive to a reasonable person.

   Courts have held that one who claims workers' compensation benefits due to an injury in the workplace "must expect that his claim will be investigated and he waives his right of privacy to the extent of a reasonable investigation." For example, in *McLain v. Boise Cascade Corp.*, 533 P.2d 343 (Or. 1975), the Oregon Supreme Court upheld the trial court's dismissal of an employee's invasion of privacy claim. There, the employer hired investigators to surveil the plaintiff to determine the validity of the plaintiff's claim for workers compensation. The investigators took 18 rolls of movie film of the employee while he was engaged in various activities on his property. Some of the film was shot from a barn behind the plaintiff's house and while the investigators were potentially trespassing on the employee's property. The *McLain* court held that the investigators' surveillance "did not constitute an unreasonable surveillance 'highly offensive to a reasonable [person]'" because the investigators filmed the employee while he was engaged in everyday activities on his own property, and the surveillance was done "in such an unobtrusive manner that plaintiff was not aware that he was being watched and filmed." While the plaintiff was offended by the secrecy of the surveillance, the court noted that the employee knew that he was the subject of an investigation because he was claiming workers' compensation benefits, and he consequently had a limited expectation of privacy.

   The court's reasoning in *McLain* is applicable here. The Harman investigator conducted surveillance "in such an unobtrusive manner" that Mr. Embry did not realize that he was being filmed. Moreover, given that Mr. Embry was collecting workers' compensation benefits, he must expect that his claim would be investigated, and he impliedly waived his right of privacy to the extent of the investigators' reasonable investigation. Given that the investigator did not record any conversations he had with Mr. Embry, but only recorded his movements and visual interaction—all of which are relevant to the investigation—he surveillance cannot be deemed "highly offensive to a reasonable [person]." Therefore, Mr. Embry cannot establish the necessary elements of his claim for intrusion upon his exclusion.

2. **Prepare an argument that distinguishes your case from the facts and reasoning in *McLain*.**

The *McLain* case is distinguishable in that the surveillance at issue in *McLain* was less obtrusive and offensive than the investigation here. Here, the investigator gained access to Mr. Embry's home under the false pretense that he was looking for a missing child, and he had a hidden camera in his fanny pack. That intrusion is significantly more objectionable than an investigator roaming the perimeter of a person's property and making recordings of activities performed outside the privacy of the subject's home.

Example of an argument distinguishing *McLain*:

Defendant relies on *McLain v. Boise Cascade Corp.* to suggest that the covert surveillance of our client was lawful and not actionable as an invasion of privacy. That reliance is misplaced. While both cases involve surveillance in the context of a workers' compensation investigation, the comparative conduct of the investigators distinguishes the cases.

The court in *McLain* held that the surveillance was reasonable because the plaintiff was only filmed outdoors while engaging in publicly visible activities. Moreover, the investigators did not trespass on the plaintiff's property while filming (save for one brief and arguably accidental trespass), and the plaintiff admitted that he was not embarrassed or upset about the content of the recordings.

In contrast, the investigator in this case gained access to and filmed Mr. Embry *in his home*, where Mr. Embry is entitled to the greatest legal protections. Moreover, the investigator gained access to the home by engaging in a series of blatant misrepresentations designed to manipulate Mr. Embry. The investigator reported he was looking for a missing girl, showed a photo of the purported victim, and asked questions about the girl. While inside, the investigator secretly recorded Mr. Embry's movements.

The court in *McLain* recognized that surveillance could be actionable if it were unreasonable, obtrusive, or offensive, which it was in this case. Mr. Embry never consented to the recording, was not aware it was happening, and is embarrassed and upset about the incident. The conduct was objectively offensive as a reasonable person would object to the deceptive intrusion.

Moreover, the public's interest in fact-finding is not implicated in this case as it was in *McLain*. In *McLain*, the validity of the plaintiff's compensation claim was in dispute, and the court found the plaintiff should consequently expect to be the subject of an investigation. The court noted that there is social utility to the investigatory process—"some sort of investigation is necessary to uncover fictitious injuries."

Here, Mr. Embry's claim is in the initial investigatory stage, and there is no accusation of fraud or misrepresentation. While Mr. Embry might expect to be the subject of an investigation, he had no reason to anticipate such aggressive and deceptive investigatory practices. Although investigators have some protections while investigating claims, this conduct far exceeded those protections, and there is no social utility in condoning such practices.

3. Do you believe Mr. Embry can establish a cause of action for invasion of privacy/ intrusion upon seclusion? Why or why not?

This is a subjective question, but the following considerations are relevant:

- To establish a cause of action for invasion of privacy, the plaintiff must show: 1) the defendant acted with intent; 2) to intrude, physically or otherwise, upon the solitude or seclusion of another or his private affairs or concerns; and 3) the intrusion would be highly offensive to a reasonable person.
- Courts have long recognized that the interior of one's home is subject to the strongest privacy protections.

  The defendant may argue that Mr. Embry consented to the entry. Mr. Embry voluntarily interacted with the investigator inside his home, and he consequently waived any claims to privacy. That argument is unlikely to survive scrutiny because the investigator induced Mr. Embry's consent by fraud.
- The investigator acted with intent to intrude. The investigator misrepresented his purpose and claimed to be investigating the disappearance of a young girl. The investigator did so with a purpose to manipulate Mr. Embry's trust and gain access to the home. The entry was not accidental but deliberate and under false pretenses.
- The intrusion was offensive to a reasonable person. The investigator deceptively gained access to Mr. Embry's home and used a hidden recording device to record Mr. Embry's movements.

  The defendant may argue the intrusion was not offensive to a reasonable person because the investigator did not record audio or any intimate, embarrassing or private conduct during the brief interaction.
- The defendant was not protected because he was acting within the scope of the workers' compensation investigation. That privilege does not include a right to engage in fraud to gain access to the subject's home.

  The defendant may argue that he was acting pursuant to his authority to investigate a claim of workplace injury, and courts have recognized that subjects waive some privacy rights when pursuing such claims.

Chapter 13: Misrepresentation

Fraudulent Misrepresentation: *Varela Furniture & Appliance Store*

Exercise 1

1. **Based on the facts you learned above, can Mr. Varela prove that your supervising attorney made a material misrepresentation of fact? Explain.**

   Likely, yes.

   When Mr. Varela received the invoice, he learned that your firm prepared a response that was not filed, and he learned that your supervising attorney failed to disclose that error. While there is not a general duty to disclose a material fact, an attorney-client relationship is a fiduciary relationship. Thus, the supervising attorney (and you, and the firm itself) arguably had a fiduciary duty to Mr. Varela to disclose the fact that the opposition brief was not timely filed. The supervising attorney not only failed to disclose this fact but seemingly attempted to cover it up by urging Mr. Varela to settle and insinuating that his business decisions were driving the need to settle.

   The firm's failure to file the motion is likely a material fact. Had Mr. Varela known of the error, he would have understood that his options were limited, and a settlement was urgent. Thus, disclosing the error would certainly influence Varela's position on whether to settle or not. It should not matter that disclosure of the fact might not have changed his ultimate decision because his decision was not fully informed and was influenced by the attorney's potentially misleading advice. Even if the attorney offered reasonable advice about a settlement, it was compromised by her hidden motivations.

   Moreover, the disclosure would also influence Mr. Varela's decision about whether to seek contribution from the firm because the decision to settle would have been based, at least in part, on the firm's mistake.

   The facts seem to strongly support a claim that the supervising attorney made a material misrepresentation of fact when she failed to disclose the fact that the opposition brief was not timely filed.

2. **Can Mr. Varela prove your supervising attorney *knowingly* made the misrepresentation? Explain.**

   Undoubtedly yes.

   When your supervising attorney spoke with Mr. Varela, she knew that the brief had not been filed, and she actively concealed that error. She also offered misleading advice that was seemingly motivated by her efforts to avoid exposure.

3. **Can Mr. Varela prove your supervising attorney made the misrepresentation with intent to induce his reliance? Explain.**

   Likely, yes.

   While the error made settlement imperative, the supervising attorney insinuated that Mr. Varela's *business practices* exposed him to liability. Thus, the attorney both concealed a critical strategy concern and potentially exaggerated the strength of the plaintiff's claims. Both actions were likely motivated by the attorney's desire to promote a settlement because the settlement obviated the need for the court to rule on the plaintiff's motion for summary judgment and protected the attorney from exposure.

Therefore, Mr. Varela should be able to prove—or at least create the strong inference—that by failing to disclose the error, the supervising attorney intended to induce Mr. Varela's reliance and convince him to settle the case.

4. **Did the misrepresentation induce Mr. Varela to act? Explain.**

   This element may be disputed.

   Mr. Varela will argue that he relied on the advice of your supervising attorney when he agreed to begin settlement negotiations. He may allege that, but for the misleading counsel, he would not have agreed to settle the case. He may also assert that he would have sought independent advice and/or pursued a malpractice claim had he known of the error.

   Yet your supervising attorney may argue that Mr. Varela's decision to settle was motivated by her sound interpretation of the legal claims in the suit, which were unaffected by her failure to file the response to the plaintiff's motion. Your supervising attorney may allege that her advice was accurate and practical, and she was trying to save the client costs association with additional litigation, regardless of whether the response was on the record or not.

5. **Was Mr. Varela's reliance foreseeable and justified? Explain.**

   If a court finds that Mr. Varela's decision was influenced by your supervising attorney's misrepresentations, then a court will almost certainly find that reliance was foreseeable and justified. A client will foreseeably and justifiably rely on the advice of his counsel. That is the objective of an attorney-client relationship and the reason Mr. Varela hired the supervising attorney and the firm in the first place.

   To the extent the supervising attorney might argue that she was just providing Mr. Varela with her "opinion" on the strengths of his case, that is a weak position for the same reason. Mr. Varela was justified in relying on his attorney for her "advice," not just her "opinions" about the recommended course to take in a litigation matter. Presumably, Mr. Varela hired the firm *because* attorneys in the firm have superior knowledge about legal processes, and he reasonably relied on his attorney's expert legal opinions.

6. **What are Mr. Varela's damages? Explain.**

   Mr. Varela's damages arguably include the amounts paid to settle the claim, and perhaps the amounts previously paid to the firm.

   Without a copy of the engagement agreement between the firm and Mr. Varela, we can only assume that the firm agreed to represent Mr. Varela in the Varga litigation, and as attorneys, we are required to represent our clients competently, which unquestionably includes meeting filing deadlines. By missing the opposition filing deadline, the supervising attorney arguably breached the contract between the firm and Mr. Varela, and he is entitled to all damages that comprise the consequence of her breach. Here, that must include some or all of the settlement amount he paid to Mr. Varga.

   There may be some question as to whether that amount should be offset by any amounts he would have paid to the firm had the supervising attorney filed the brief or whether it is fair to require Mr. Varela to somehow prove that the court would have denied the plaintiff's motion for summary judgment. But in any event, he is entitled to all damages that are consequential to the supervising attorney's misrepresentation and breach of the contract.

   There may be additional damages—such as forfeiture or disgorgement—to which Mr. Varela may be entitled as a result of the supervising attorney's breach of her fiduciary duty to Mr. Varela.

   If the supervising attorney is found to have perpetrated fraud (which seems quite likely based on the facts), then Mr. Varela will likely also be entitled to punitive damages.

Exercise 2

1. **How does this additional invoice change your opinion about the case, if at all? Does it make it more or less likely that Mr. Varela can establish a cause of action for fraudulent misrepresentation?**

   The gall of it! It seems unbelievable that the supervising attorney would miss a filing deadline and nevertheless charge the client for her work on the brief that was never filed.

   The second time entry ("preparing and filing response with court") may be deemed *another* fraudulent misrepresentation: By sending an invoice that included a time entry for a task that did not occur: 1) the supervising attorney misrepresented a material fact; 2) that she knew was false; 3) with the intent to influence Mr. Varela's reliance on the statement (i.e., pay the invoice).

   The fourth element could prove problematic because this invoice does not appear to have induced Mr. Varela to act in reliance on the misrepresentation—he sent it to you rather than paying it. By sending to you rather than paying it, we do not have to consider whether his reliance was justified or reasonable (although it would be foreseeable, justified, and reasonable had he paid the invoice because a client should be entitled to presume that the attorney tasks for which he is billed were actually performed by his lawyers, that is, his fiduciaries).

   Mr. Varela has not incurred any additional damages resulting from the second invoice but the fraudulent nature of the invoice and the nature of the fiduciary relationship between an attorney and her client could increase the firm's exposure to liability.

Chapter 13: Misrepresentation

Negligent and Fraudulent Misrepresentation: *Parrill v. Mapleton Realty Corp.*

Exercise 1

1. **Can Ms. Parrill establish the elements of a negligent misrepresentation claim against the sellers of the house? Why or why not?**

   Assuming that the sellers were merely *negligent* in relaying information to Craig Preston about the status of the plumbing, electric, and roof age of the house, then yes. The facts might support a claim for negligent misrepresentation based on the following considerations:

   1. The sellers made false statements with regard to the condition of the plumbing, electric, and roof of the house (which they did);
   2. The sellers acted with carelessness or negligence in ascertaining the truth of those conditions before making their statements (giving them the benefit of all doubt, we can say they were at least careless or negligent when they relayed inaccurate information about the condition of the home);
   3. The sellers intended to induce Ms. Parrill to act (i.e., purchase the house);
   4. Parrill took action in reliance on the truth of the sellers' statements (she purchased the house); and
   5. Parrill sustained damages as a result of such reliance (she unexpectedly had to pay for costly repairs).

2. **Can Ms. Parrill establish the elements of a fraudulent misrepresentation claim against the sellers of the house? Why or why not?**

   It seems more likely that the sellers acted fraudulently in relaying information to Craig Preston about the status of the plumbing, electric, and roof age of the house. It is difficult to imagine how the sellers could innocently (or negligently/carelessly) communicate to Mr. Preston that the house had "all new plumbing and electrical systems" and that the roof had been "fully replaced within the last year" when neither statement was true at the time it was made. The sellers would know that they had not installed new plumbing and electric systems or replaced the roof.

Thus, the facts appear more than sufficient to allege:

1. The sellers misrepresented material facts (facts regarding the status of the plumbing and electrical systems and the new roof are certainly material and would influence a potential homebuyer such as Ms. Parrill);
2. The sellers knew the information was false (this will ultimately have to be proven based on circumstantial evidence or evidence revealed in discovery);
3. The sellers intended to induce Ms. Parrill's reliance on their statements (i.e., induce her to purchase the house);
4. Ms. Parrill's reliance was foreseeable and justified/reasonable because the statements were relayed by an expert—Mr. Preston. While Ms. Parrill may get some latitude as a new homebuyer, this element may be challenging to prove if the sellers convince the court that Ms. Parrill acted unreasonably in waiving contingencies; and
5. Ms. Parrill sustained damages as a result of her reliance on the misrepresentations (she unexpectedly had to pay for costly repairs.

3. **Can Ms. Parrill establish the elements of a negligent misrepresentation claim against the Mapleton Realty Group for the representations by Craig Preston? Why or why not?**

   A claim for negligent misrepresentation against Maple Realty Group for the representations of Craig Preston seems even more straightforward than the claim against the sellers:

   1. Craig Preston made false statements with regard to the condition of the plumbing, electric, and roof of the house;
   2. Mr. Preston acted carelessly or negligently in ascertaining the truth of those conditions before making those statements because he failed to verify the details before making assurances to Parill;
   3. Mr. Preston intended to induce Ms. Parrill to act and purchase the house;
   4. Ms. Parrill took action in reliance on the truth of Mr. Preston's statements (she bought the house, trusting in his expertise); and
   5. Ms. Parrill sustained damage as a result of such reliance (she unexpectedly had to pay for costly repairs).

4. **Can Ms. Parrill establish the elements of a fraudulent misrepresentation claim against the Mapleton Realty Group for the representations by Craig Preston? Why or why not?**

   This seems like the least likely claim to succeed. The facts are not sufficient to allege each element, specifically Mr. Preston's knowledge that the statements were false:

   1. Craig Preston misrepresented material facts (facts regarding the status of the plumbing and electrical systems and the new roof are certainly material and would influence a potential homebuyer such as Ms. Parrill);
   2. Although it is possible that facts learned through discovery establish Mr. Preston's knowledge, it may be difficult to prove that Mr. Preston received truthful information from the sellers and decided to make it untruthful before communicating the information to Parrill;

3. Mr. Preston intended to induce Ms. Parrill's reliance on their statements (i.e., induce her to purchase the house so he could earn any commissions from the sale);
4. Ms. Parrill's reliance was foreseeable and justified/reasonable (it would be because she hired Preston based on his expertise); and
5. Ms. Parrill sustained damages as a result of her reliance on the misrepresentations (she unexpectedly had to pay for costly repairs).

Exercise 2

1. **Based on your review of the commentaries in *Sunport Civil Remedies,* are you more or less confident about Ms. Parrill's ability to pursue any misrepresentation claims against the sellers of the house? Explain.**

   You should probably be more confident about Ms. Parrill's ability to pursue her negligent misrepresentation claim against the sellers of the house. Even though the sellers made their misrepresentations (whether negligent or fraudulent) in the sellers' disclosures that they provided to Craig Preston, not directly to Ms. Parrill, those misrepresentations were made for use by others (i.e., Ms. Parrill). Ms. Parrill is one of the limited group of persons for whose benefit and guidance the sellers knew that Craig Preston intended to supply the information.

   Similarly, with regard to Ms. Parrill's claim of fraudulent misrepresentation, the sellers made fraudulent misrepresentations and are subject to liability for Ms. Parrill's financial loss so long as she acted in justifiable reliance upon the misrepresentations. Again, it does not matter that the misrepresentations were not made directly to her but rather to Craig Preston, because the sellers intended or at least had reason to expect that the representations would be repeated to a potential purchaser of the house (such as Ms. Parrill), and that they would influence the purchaser's conduct.

Exercise 3

1. **Based on your reading of the holding in *Kramer*, Sunport Rev. Stat. § 179, and the facts you learned from Jillian Parrill, do you believe Ms. Parrill could be found to be comparatively negligent? If so, will that be a defense to both the negligent misrepresentation claim and the fraudulent misrepresentation claim?**

   Negligent Misrepresentation

   In *Kramer*, the court held that comparative negligence can be a defense against negligent misrepresentation claims involving the sale of real estate. The court held that buyers should take basic steps to protect their own interests in such costly transactions. While that case specifically involved negligent misrepresentations regarding property boundary lines, it should apply equally here.

   Applying Sunport Rev. Stat. § 179, if Ms. Parrill is found to have been negligent in failing to have the house inspected before she purchased it, such negligence will not bar her recovery against either the sellers or Mapleton Realty Group unless her negligence is found to be greater than the negligence of the defendants. Here, the potential defendants will likely argue that Ms. Parrill was negligent because she waived the home inspection contingency in reliance on representations about the quality of the home. Ms. Parrill waived the protections because she wanted to present an aggressive offer and was willing to absorb more risk.

Moreover, Ms. Parrill did not request documentation to support the allegations about the electric and plumbing systems or the roof. Had she ordered the inspection or documentation, Ms. Parrill would have discovered the misrepresentations and avoided later expenses.

Thus, a court might find Ms. Parrill was comparatively negligent. It seems doubtful, however, that Ms. Parrill's negligence should be greater than that of the defendants because the defendants were duty-bound to communicate accurate information regarding the house. Ms. Parrill's reliance on such information was justified, even if it would have been more prudent to have the home inspected. If Ms. Parrill's negligence is less than that of the defendants, then her claim will not be barred, but any judgment against the defendants will be reduced in proportion to Ms. Parrill's comparative fault.

Fraudulent Misrepresentation

Comparative fault is NOT a defense in a claim involving fraudulent misrepresentation. A plaintiff's negligence cannot be used to reduce or bar recovery if the defendant commits an intentional tort. As the *Kramer* court made clear, "Intentional torts are punished not because the actor failed to use reasonable care . . . but because the actor intended the act. The difference between the victim's actions and the defendant's action is not one of degree . . . but of kind, and they are therefore not comparable."

Chapter 14: Products Liability

In re FreshMart

Exercise 1

1. **Can Mr. Frank prove the bag was subject to a manufacturing or design defect?**

   Additional evidence will clarify these points, but some initial considerations include:

Manufacturing Defect

There is no evidence that the bag deviated from its intended design, and the bag's design was consistent with its specifications. The manufacturer certainly did not intend the bag to be split along the side, but we do not know how that split occurred or the cause of it. An inspection revealed the seams and handles were structurally sound and consistent with design specifications.

As of now, we know that the bag was intended by the manufacturer to hold a "recommended weight" of 10 lbs., and that lab tests showed the bag would fail if holding 17 lbs. or more. We do not know the size of the jar of pickles, jar of mayonnaise, frozen ice cream, and frozen peas, and therefore do not know the weight of those items or the total weight of the bag if all four items were placed inside it.

Mr. Frank may argue that there is evidence the bag was defective. We know that the bag "suddenly broke open" while Mr. Frank was loading groceries into his car, which was a reasonably foreseeable use, and the bag only contained four items, which is not an excessive load for a grocery bag. The break along the side and not the seam may suggest a defect in the materials, possibly a flaw during manufacturing.

Design Defect

Mr. Frank may argue that the bag had a design defect because it was not designed to accommodate common grocery-loading practices. The bags present an unreasonable risk of injury if they cannot withstand the weight of "a few jars."

There may be an argument that the bag could be designed to hold more than 10 lbs., or be designed to ensure it could not split along the side, but we do not have enough information to know the costs associated with designing such a bag and whether those costs outweigh the benefits that an alternative design might have.

Moreover, the bag performed within industry norms, which may suggest it is not unreasonably weak. There are no reports of other bag failures, and spot inspections did not reveal widespread problems. This suggests the bags are performing as designed, and this unusual incident is not emblematic of a systemic design issue.

A consumer would not expect a grocery bag to split along the side or fail to withstand the weight of the four items Mr. Frank had in his bag; however, consumers generally do not expect plastic grocery bags to be all that sturdy—indeed, that is why consumers and grocers alike often double-bag when packing groceries into those bags.

2. **Is there additional information you would like to know to establish whether the bag had a manufacturing or design defect?**

   Additional information may include:

   - How much did the items placed in Mr. Frank's bag weigh—more than 10 lbs. collectively?

- Was the bag of the same specifications as those described in the internal report (the report was prepared by FreshMart so we definitely want to verify its accuracy)?
- The bag was split along the side rather than at the seams. Could it be that an employee used an implement to open a new box of bags and accidentally pierced the bag along its side?
- Did Mr. Frank do anything that could have pierced or split the bag after he left the store?
- Did similar bags fail under similar conditions? Have there been other complaints about the bags splitting on the side?
- Is there photographic or documented evidence about an inspection of the bag? Was it preserved? Is there video footage of the entire incident, from bagging to transport? Does the footage confirm how Mr. Frank handled the bag?
- Does the employee recall the incident and recall why the items were not double bagged? Does the employee remember any defects with the bag?
- Were there any witnesses who observed how the bag was packed and how Mr. Frank handled the bag?
- In addition to information relating to the costs associated with designing a sturdier bag, we might want to know whether other manufacturers have designed bags differently to make sturdier bags.
- We might test other manufacturers' bags with the same four products that were in Mr. Frank's bags.
- We might want to know whether there are other occurrences of this manufacturer's bags or other manufacturers' similar bags splitting along the side rather than at the seams. We might also want to know whether the bags were tested under real-world conditions as well as during lab tests.
- We might wish to research whether these bags routinely fail under normal use, which may suggest an unsafe design. Why did FreshMart switch providers? Were there problems with other bags, or did FreshMart choose less reliable bags to cut costs?

3. **If Mr. Frank can establish that the bag had a defect, can Mr. Frank show the product defect was the actual and proximate cause of his injury? Why or why not?**

   - Assuming Mr. Frank can establish the bag had a defect, Frank can likely establish actual and proximate cause. Mr. Frank will argue that, but for the bag's defect, its contents would not have crashed to the ground and spilled, and he would not have slipped. If FreshMart distributed a defective bag, then it should not be difficult to convince a court that the distribution of the bags was the proximate cause of Mr. Frank's injuries. It is foreseeable that bags will carry heavy and breakable items. Thus, if the bag splits, then there is a foreseeable risk of spills and falls.
   - FreshMart may argue the bag split because it was overloaded or mishandled, and that was the actual cause of injury. FreshMart may also argue that falls resulting in lacerations are not a foreseeable risk of distributing potentially faulty bags. FreshMart may posit that Mr. Frank's slip and fall was a superseding, unforeseeable event that broke the chain of causation. If Mr. Frank lost his balance, panicked, or tried to catch the bag, then those movements may have been the immediate cause of the fall.

Exercise 2

1. How are the facts of *Fuller* similar to Mr. Frank's case? How are they different?

The facts are fairly similar:

- In *Fuller*, products were placed into a plastic bag by a grocery store employee and the bag broke as the plaintiff was carrying it outside, causing its contents to spill and injure the plaintiff. Similarly, in Mr. Frank's case, products were placed into a plastic bag by a grocery store employee and the bag broke when Mr. Frank was loading it into his car, causing its contents to spill and injure him when he fell. In *Fuller*, the plaintiff was injured by shattered glass; here, Mr. Frank was injured because he slipped on the contents that spilled when the glass jars apparently shattered and the frozen products spilled onto the ground.
- In both cases, the bags that split only held a few, relatively typical grocery items.
- In both cases, the plaintiff could not prove the defendant did or did not do something that caused the bag to split and its contents to spill out. In both cases, the store pointed to internal policies that limited the risks of breaks and spills.
- If you decide to move forward with Mr. Frank's case, *Fuller* provides a decent roadmap of the facts you will need to discover and ultimately prove to avoid summary judgment or trial verdict in FreshMart's favor.

Some differences include:

- Mr. Frank offered more legal theories about why the accident occurred. Mr. Frank watched the bagging and offered a coherent narrative about the sequence of events. Moreover, an internal report noted the bag broke along the side.
- In contrast, the plaintiff in *Fuller* did not know why the bag failed and conceded she did not watch the bags being filled. The store noted that the weight of the items was only around 5 lbs, and there was no evidence of mishandling.

2. How does the decision in *Fuller* influence whether Mr. Frank can recover under a theory of negligence?

In *Fuller*, the court clarified that "[s]peculation does not create a genuine issue of fact; instead, it creates a false issue. This emphasizes that Mr. Frank cannot rely solely on the fact that he was injured to establish liability. Instead, Mr. Frank must identify evidence establishing what FreshMart did wrong, and demonstrate how that misconduct caused his injuries. Mr. Frank must also demonstrate how his own conduct was not the cause of injuries.

Mr. Frank has already offered some legal theories to support his claim. If the evidence supports those theories, then he may meet his burden of proof and establish the elements of the prima facie case.

3. Can Mr. Frank rely on the doctrine of *res ipsa loquitur* by showing the defect was of a kind that does not occur in the absence of negligence on the part of the manufacturer?

The doctrine of *res ipsa loquitur* is probably not applicable here—certainly not at this stage as there are too many facts that remain unknown.

First, in order to invoke the doctrine, the break must have been the type of incident that could only happen in the presence of negligence. A bag splitting open is likely the result of negligence on *someone's* part, although we do not know who. Second, it must have been caused by something exclusively in the defendant's control. Here, that means Mr. Frank must prove there is no way the bag could have broken but for something FreshMart and its employees did, and not anything Mr. Frank did. There is not enough evidence to establish that proof at this stage. What if Mr. Frank bumped the bag against something sharp on his way to his car or while he was putting it in the car? What if he knocked it against another bag that had something just sharp enough to pierce the bag? Until more facts are known about exactly what happened, the doctrine of *res ipsa loquitur* will likely not apply.

Exercise 3

1. **Do you believe Mr. Frank may have a cause of action for breach of implied warranties?**

- Mr. Frank's potential claim that FreshMart breached an implied warranty of merchantability is at least plausible. Mr. Frank will have to prove: 1) the existence of an implied warranty; 2) a breach of that warranty; and 3) damages proximately resulting from that breach.

FreshMart is a merchant of plastic grocery bags; they provide them in the ordinary course of business. Bags are expected to carry a reasonable quantity of groceries, including standard items like jars and frozen goods. Mr. Frank used the bag in a foreseeable and ordinary manner: He carried it from the store to his car, where it broke unexpectedly. The bag broke along the side, a location that is not typically expected to fail. Thus, Mr. Frank may have an argument FreshMart impliedly warranted that the bags were safe, FreshMart breached that duty when the bag split (the bag failed when used for its ordinary purpose), and the split was the actual and foreseeable cause of Mr. Frank's injuries.

- Mr. Frank's potential claim that FreshMart breached an implied warranty of fitness is also plausible. Mr. Frank relied on FreshMart employees to select an appropriate bag and safely load his items. The store knew guests would rely on their judgment and also knew the bag would carry heavy, fragile items. The store should also have policies to avoid over-bagging or at least have policies regarding when items should be double-bagged. FreshMart may have breached that duty when it failed to select an appropriate bag or load it correctly.

Mr. Frank's stronger claim is likely a breach of the warranty of merchantability as the warranty of fitness typically applies when the buyer is requesting goods for a non-ordinary or specialized use.

Chapter 15: Strict Liability

Calloway v. Pinecrest Golf Club

Exercise 1

1. **Does operating a driving range near a road create a foreseeable and highly significant risk of serious physical harm?**

   Maybe. The argument can certainly be made based on the language in *Yommer*: No one would deny that a golf club as a rule does not present any particular danger to the community. However, when the operation of the club results in multiple stray golf balls landing on or near passing cars because of the golf club's proximity to a well-traveled road, at least that aspect of the activity may create a foreseeable risk of serious physical harm.

   Indeed, one driving a convertible on that road is certainly not *un*foreseeable, nor is the harm that might result from a stray golf ball landing on a driver or passenger of that convertible.

2. **Could Pinecrest eliminate the risk of harm through the exercise of reasonable care?**

   Many golf clubs—especially those located near roads or walkways that community members use—have large nets installed to ensure that stray golf balls do not fall outside the golf club's property and onto pedestrians or drivers passing by.

   Pinecrest arguably could have eliminated the risk of harm by exercising reasonable care and installing such a net or other protective device to prevent stray golf balls from landing on the well-traveled road.

3. **Is operating a driving range a matter of common usage in the area? Is the business appropriate to the place where it is carried on?**

   Not necessarily. While golf clubs and driving ranges are of common usage in any given community, as the court noted in *Yommer*, "the basic concept underlying the rule [of strict liability] is that a person who elects to keep or bring upon his land something which exposes the adjacent land or its owner or occupant to an added danger should be obliged to prevent its doing damage."

   Here, Pinecrest has elected to operate on its land a driving range that exposes the adjacent land and its occupants (the public in this case) to an added danger, the possibility of being hit by a stray golf ball. Thus, Pinecrest should be obliged to prevent the added danger from doing damage.

4. **Does the value to the community outweigh the dangerous attributes of the activity?**

   Generally, the benefits to the community are likely to outweigh the risks of harm associated with golf. Yet in this case, operating the course near a public road without implementing proper safety measures may shift the balance.

   Golf courses provide users with the benefits of outdoor, physical activity. Golf is also a social sport that promotes participants' mental health and community cohesion. Golf courses and clubs provide myriad employment opportunities. Property values in adjacent areas typically improve with the installation and operation of a well-maintained course.

Yet in this case, there are serious safety concerns related to the proximity of the course to the road. Errant balls may cause property damage and personal injury. Pinecrest should adopt risk mitigation measures to minimize the risks of harm.

Exercise 2

1. **Does the report and/or information relayed by Ms. Kensington influence your assessment of whether Mr. Calloway can establish a claim for strict liability? Why or why not?**

   On the one hand, the report and the information you learned from Ms. Kensington demonstrate that Pinecrest attempted to take several precautions in operating its driving range to make it safe for the community and nearby public roads.

   Yet other facts indicate Pinecrest operations are not in compliance with the report's findings/recommendations. These factors expose Pinecrest to the risk of liability for negligence:

   - Pinecrest opted against the use of protective netting, despite its relatively close proximity to the road.
   - Pinecrest does not insist on reduced-distance balls, but only provides these balls and *encourages* its members to use them.
   - The range location likely extends the flight distance of golf balls given its elevation and the high winds that the location frequently experiences.

   Yet it is difficult to assess whether Pinecrest may be liable under a theory of strict liability because it is unclear whether Pinecrest's operations will be deemed an abnormally dangerous activity. Specifically, it is unclear whether Pinecrest's operation "creates a foreseeable and significant risk of physical harm even under the exercise of reasonable care" because the facts as we know them demonstrate that Pinecrest likely has not exercised reasonable care *at all*. Had Pinecrest complied with the report and minimized the risk of balls passing onto the road, then it is unclear whether the activity would pose a danger to the community.

Exercise 3

1. **How does the court's reasoning in *Ludwikoski v. Kurotsu* influence your assessment of Mr. Calloway's case?**

   The court's reasoning supports the notion that the game of golf is not an inherently dangerous activity, nor is operating a driving range close to a well-traveled public road. The court held that golf is commonplace and has social value, the risk of severe harm is low, and reasonable care can mitigate many risks, even if not all.

   Mr. Calloway may argue the cases are distinguishable because in *Ludwikoski*, the plaintiff was struck after another player negligently hit the ball. In contrast, Mr. Calloway's injury was caused by Pinecrest's poor design that disregarded safety warnings. Yet even if a court finds that placement of the range was arguably reckless or inappropriate, the activity itself is not abnormally dangerous. To establish liability under a theory of strict liability, the plaintiff must establish that the *activity itself* is abnormally dangerous, not that participants or designers created a dangerous course.

2. If you conclude that Mr. Calloway will be unsuccessful in bringing a claim for strict liability, what other legal theories could Mr. Calloway use to establish Pinecrest's liability for his injuries?

Mr. Calloway might well succeed in bringing a claim for negligence to establish Pinecrest's liability for his damages. Pinecrest owed a duty to keep guests and bystanders safe, and they breached that duty by failing to implement recommended safety measures. But for their carelessness, Mr. Calloway would not have been struck and injured, and Pinecrest's conduct created a foreseeable risk that those passing or driving by the range could be struck and injured. Indeed, Pinecrest knew balls were routinely passing to the street and took no measures to prevent injury.

The likelihood of success is significant enough that you may consider recommending to Pinecrest that it make a pre-litigation offer of settlement to Mr. Calloway so it can avoid the costs of litigation and potential negative publicity.

Chapter 16: Nuisance

Wendt vs. Silver Creek Farms

Exercise 1

1. **Identify the potential causes of action Ms. Wendt might have against Silver Creek Farms.**

   Two possibilities might include:

   1. **Trespass:** Silver Creek Farm's operations cause odors and odorous air particles to intrude onto the Wendt's property.
   2. **Nuisance:** Silver Creek Farm's operations substantially and unreasonably interfere with the Wendt's use and enjoyment of their land.

2. **Which claim offers the most likely chance of success, and why?**

   Ms. Wendt is more likely to succeed if she files a private nuisance claim. If she files a trespass claim, then the parties will likely dispute whether odor (or even odorous air particles) actually constitute a trespass on the Wendts' property.

Exercise 2

1. **Draft an email to Ms. Wendt explaining why she might have a cause of action for nuisance.**

   Here is one example of an email communication:

   Ms. Wendt —

   Based on our conversation and my understanding of the facts you conveyed, I did some research into potential claims you may be able to pursue against Silver Creek Farms.

   At this point, the stronger claim appears to be the claim for private nuisance. One is liable to another for a private nuisance if his conduct is 1) intentional and unreasonable; and 2) causes substantial interference with another's interest in the use and enjoyment of their land. Sunport law defines "unreasonable" conduct to include conduct that is injurious to health, offensive to the senses, or interferes with the comfortable enjoyment of property.

   Silver Creek's activity on its land is all of this: It is intentional and causes substantial interference with your family's interest in the use and enjoyment of your land. The injury to you and your family is evidenced by your daughter's embarrassment, your family's inability to enjoy dinner at home, and your inability to work from home because of the smell emanating from Silver Creek's property and operations.

   The usual remedy for nuisance is damages, which will require us to put some value on the harm caused to you. This might include the costs of multiple dinners out, the cost of dry cleaning or replacing clothes if the odor has infiltrated your family's clothes so as to make them unusable, or some sort of protective measures to alleviate the odors and other effects that Silver Creek's activities have on your ability to use and enjoy your home.

   But also relevant—and perhaps more important—a court may grant injunctive relief for a claim of nuisance if monetary damages are unavailable or inadequate. We should seriously consider pursuing this relief because Silver Creek's payment of money to you provides no relief at all, it simply allows you to continue eating out, working outside the home, and replacing your clothes. The injunctive relief we can seek will be to ask a court to *enjoin* Silver Creek from continuing its animal feeding operations—that is, to make them stop those operations altogether.

I look forward to hearing your thoughts when we meet again next week.

Exercise 3

1. **Do you believe the Right to Farm Act bars Ms. Wendt's claim? Why or why not?**

   Probably not, based on your conversation with Ms. Wendt. As she explained, Silver Creek Farms began as a small operation consisting of row crops of corn and wheat, and just a small herd of sheep and a few pigs. It was not until two years ago that Silver Creek entered the agreement with the pork distributor and began conducting its animal feeding operations. This recent practice led to the storing of animal waste in the concrete lagoon and pumping waste from the lagoon to spread on their fields as fertilizer.

   So even if Silver Creek's operations comply with all applicable federal and state statutes or regulations and even if they employ generally accepted management practices, their expansion into the animal feeding (and waste fertilization) operations was a nuisance at the moment it began. Thus, the statute is not applicable to Silver Creek under § 82.674(1)(c).

www.ingramcontent.com/pod-product-compliance
Lightning Source LLC
LaVergne TN
LVHW080016210926
848481LV00011B/3037